ETHNIC GROUPS IN INTERNATIONAL RELATIONS

The European Science Foundation is an association of its 56 member research councils and academies in 20 countries. The ESF brings European scientists together to work on topics of common concern, to co-ordinate the use of expensive facilities, and to discover and define new endeavours that will benefit from a co-operative approach.

The scientific work sponsored by ESF includes basic research in the natural sciences, the medical and biosciences, the humanities and the social sciences.

The ESF links scholarship and research supported by its members and adds value by co-operation across national frontiers. Through its function as co-ordinator, and also by holding workshops and conferences and by enabling researchers to visit and study in laboratories throughout Europe, the ESF works for the advancement of European science.

ETHNIC GROUPS
IN
INTERNATIONAL RELATIONS

COMPARATIVE STUDIES ON GOVERNMENTS AND NON-DOMINANT ETHNIC GROUPS IN EUROPE, 1850–1940

Volume V

JX
1255
.E76
1991
West

Edited by
PAUL SMITH
in collaboration with
KALLIOPI KOUFA and ARNOLD SUPPAN

European Science Foundation
NEW YORK UNIVERSITY PRESS
DARTMOUTH

Published by
Dartmouth Publishing Company Limited
Gower House
Croft Road
Aldershot
Hants GU11 3HR
England

Published in the U.S.A. by
New York University Press
Washington Square
New York, NY 10003

British Library Cataloguing in Publication Data
Ethnic groups in international relations.
1. Europe. International relations. Role of ethnic groups,
   history
I. Smith, Paul   II. European Science Foundation
303.4'82'09

Library of Congress Cataloging-in-Publication Data
Ethnic groups in international relations / edited by P. Smith in
   collaboration with K.K. Koufa and A. Suppan.
     p.   cm. – (Comparative studies on governments and non-
   dominant ethnic groups in Europe, 1850–1940; v. 5)
     "Published for the European Science Foundation."
     Includes bibliographical references.
     ISBN 0–8147–7914–X (cloth)
     1. International relations and culture.   2. Minorities–Legal
   status, laws, etc.   I. Smith, P. (Paul)   II. Koufa, Kalliopi.
   III. Suppan, Arnold.   IV. European Science Foundation.   V. Series.
   JX1255.E76   1990
   341.4'8–dc20   90–41908
                                                                            CIP
ISBN 1 85521 108 4

Printed in Great Britain by
Billing & Sons Ltd, Worcester

Contents

List of Tables

List of Maps

Notes on Contributors

IMMO DOEGE, born 1936 in Falkenburg, Germany; graduated in 1965 from the University of Kiel; educational stays at Braziers Park, Oxon, 1961–65; Senior Master (Studiendirektor) at the *Deutsches Gymnasium für Nordschleswig*, Aabenraa; since 1975 historical research (minority questions and German–Danish relations); since 1983 Director of the *Historische Forschungsstelle der deutschen Volksgruppe*, Aabenraa; his publications are on the German minority in Denmark.

RUDOLF JAWORSKI, born 1944 in Lissa/Leszno, Poland; studied History and German Literature at the Universities of Tübingen and Vienna, 1966–71; Assistant and Professor at the Institute of History and Civilization of Eastern Europe, University of Tübingen, 1975–87; since 1987 Professor of East European History at the University of Kiel; his publications include: *Vorposten oder Minderheit? Der sudetendeutsche Volkstumskampf in den Beziehungen zwischen der Weimarer Republik und der ČSR* (Stuttgart 1977); *Handel und Gewerbe im Nationalitätenkampf. Studien zur Wirtschaftsgesinnung der Polen in der Provinz Posen (1871–1914)* (Göttingen 1986).

PAWEL KORZEC, born 1919 in Lodz, Poland; after the Second World War, studied history in Lodz, graduating in 1948; from 1956 lectured in modern Polish history at the University of Lodz; deprived of his post and went into exile in 1968; from 1969 to 1984 Researcher in the Centre National de la Recherche Scientifique, Paris; received his doctorate from the Sorbonne; now Honorary Director of Research at the CNRS; his publications include: The Revolution of 1905–1907 in the Lodz region (in Polish) (Warsaw 1956); *Ein halbes Jahrhundert revolutionärer Bewegung im Gebiet Bialystok 1864–1914* (Warsaw 1965); *Juifs en Pologne. La question juive pendant l'entre-deux-guerres* (Paris 1980).

BOGDAN KOSZEL, born 1954 in Biały Bór, Poland; graduated in 1977 from the University of Poznań and received his Ph.D. from there in 1980; Chief of the Political Science Unit at the Western Institute, Poznań, 1983; his publications include: *Antagonizmy i współpraca. RFN i jej zachodnioeuropejscy partnerzy 1969–1982* (Antagonisms and

Cooperation. The Fed. Republic of Germany and its West-European Partners, 1969–1982) (Poznań 1985); *Rywalizacja niemiecko-włoska w basenie Dunaju i na Bałkanach 1933–1941* (The German–Italian Rivalry in the Danube Basin and the Balkans 1933–1941) (Poznań 1987).

KALLIOPI K. KOUFA, born 1936 in Thessaloniki, Greece; *Licence ès Sciences politiques – mentation études internationales* – University and Institut des Hautes Etudes Internationales, Geneva, Switzerland; Law – LL.B. at the University of Thessaloniki; received her Post Graduate Diploma in Public Law and Ph.D. in Public International Law at the University of Thessaloniki; Professor of Public International Law and International Organisation, University of Thessaloniki; Head of Department of International Studies of the Law Faculty, University of Thessaloniki; Director of Studies of the Institute of International Law and International Relations of Thessaloniki; Honorary Vice-Consul of Austria in Thessaloniki, Greece; her publications include: *International Conflictual Situations and their Peaceful Adjustment* (Thessaloniki 1988).

ANTONIO MARQUINA BARRIO, born 1945 in Madrid, Spain; Doctor in Political Science; Master of Law; Master of Economics; Rockefeller Fellow in International Relations 1982; Professor of International Relations; his publications include: *La Diplomacia Vaticana y la España de Franco, 1936–1945* (Madrid 1983); *España en la Política de Seguridad Occidental, 1939–1986* (Madrid 1986); *España y los Judíos en el Siglo XX (la Acción Exterior)* (Madrid 1987).

TORE MODEEN, born 1929 in Helsingfors in Finland; Juris Doctor in 1962; Armfelt Professor of Public and International Law, Åbo Akademi, 1968–77; since 1977 Alex Ärt Professor of Local Government, Law and Finance, University of Helsingfors – Helsinki; his publications include: *The International Protection of National Minorities in Europe* (1969); *De folkrättsliga garantierna för bevarandet av Ålandsöarnas nationella Karaktär* (The International Protection of the National Identity of the Åland Islands) (*Scandinavian Studies in Law*, 1973; La Convention de l'Unesco concernant la lutte contre la discrimination dans le domaine de l'enseignement en les îles d'Aland (*Revue des droits de l'homme*, 1977).

LORENZ RERUP, born 1928 in Flensburg, Germany; received his M.A. in 1963 at the University of Copenhagen; 1963–6 head of the research section of the Danish Central Library for South Schleswig, in Flensburg; 1966–72 Lecturer in History at the Institute of History, University of Aarhus; since 1972 Professor (full) of Modern History at the Institute of History and Social Research, Roskilde University; his publications include: *Marcus Rubins brevveksling 1870–1922*, 4 vols (The Letters of the Historian and Statistician Marcus Rubin) (Copenhagen 1963); *Slesvig og Holstens historie efter 1830* (the History of Schleswig and Holstein after 1830) (Copenhagen 1982); *Danmarks historie, tiden 1864–1914* (Denmark's history, the years between 1864 and 1914) (Copenhagen 1989).

STANISŁAW SIERPOWSKI, born 1942 in Leszno, Poland; received his Master's degree in 1965 and his Doctor's degree in 1969; Full Professor and Pro-rector in 1985; 1988 visiting Professor in Rome, Director and holder of chair at the Archivistic Institute of Adam Mickiewicz, University of Poznań; his publications include: *Stosunki polsko-włoskie w latach 1918–1940* (Warsaw 1975); *Narodziny Ligi Narodów* (Poznań 1984); Editor and co-author, *Studia z najnowszej historii Niemiec i stosunków polsko-niemieckich* (Poznań 1986).

PAUL SMITH, born 1937 in Prestwich, England; read Modern History at Balliol College, followed by research at St Antony's College, University of Oxford; received his doctorate in 1965 from Oxford; Assistant Lecturer in History, Queen's University of Belfast; Assistant Lecturer and Lecturer at King's College, University of London; since 1978 Professor of Modern History at the University of Southampton; his publications include: *Disraelian Conservatism and Social Reform* (London 1967); *Lord Salisbury on Politics* (ed.) (Cambridge 1972); *The Historian and Film* (ed.) (Cambridge 1976).

THOMAS STEENSEN, born 1951 in Bredstedt, Germany; studied at the University of Kiel 1973–77 and received his Ph.D. there in 1985; Head of exhibition project 1985–87; received the Conrad-Borchling Prize from the F.V.S. Foundation at Hamburg in 1987; since 1987 Head of the Nordfriisk Instituut, Bräist/Bredstedt; his publications include: *Die friesische Bewegung in Nordfriesland im 19. und 20. Jahrhundert* (Neumünster 1986); *Streifzüge durch die Geschichte Nordfrieslands: Friesische Sprache und friesische Bewegung* (Husum 1987); since 1977 editor of newspaper *Nordfriesland*.

ARNOLD SUPPAN, born 1945 in St. Veit an der Glan, Austria; studied History and German at the University of Vienna 1963–70; Ph. D. and examination on history for mastership 1970; Assistant and Lecturer at the Institute of East and South-East European History of the University of Vienna; Dozent in East-European History 1984; Chairman of the Austrian Institute of East- and South-East European Studies; his publications include: *Innere Front. Militärassistenz, Widerstand und Umsturz in der Donaumonarchie 1918*, 2 vols (together with R.G. Plaschka and H. Haselsteiner) (Wien 1974); *Die österreich-*

ischen Volksgruppen. Tendenzen ihrer gesellschaftlichen Entwicklung im 20. Jahrhundert (Wien 1983); *Geschichte der Deutschen im Bereich des heutigen Slowenien 1848–1941/Zgodovina Nemcev na območju današnje Slovenije 1848–1941* (co-editor with H. Rumpler) (Wien 1988).

DAVID VITAL, born 1927 in London, England; received his M.A., D.Phil., from Oxford University; since 1977 Goldmann Professor of Diplomacy at Tel-Aviv University; since 1988 Klutznick Professor of Jewish Civilization at Northwestern University; among his publications: *The Origins of Zionism* (Oxford 1975); *Zionism: The Formative Years* (Oxford 1982); *Zionism: the Crucial Phase* (Oxford 1987).

Comparative Studies on Governments and Non-dominant Ethnic Groups in Europe, 1850–1940

Titles in the Series

Schooling, Educational Policy and Ethnic Identity
Edited by *J.J. Tomiak* in collaboration with *K.E. Eriksen, A. Kazamias* and *R. Okey*

Religion, State and Ethnic Groups
Edited by *D. Kerr* in collaboration with *M. Breuer, S. Gilley* and *E. Suttner*

Ethnic Groups and Language Rights
Edited by *S. Vilfan* in collaboration with *G. Sandvik* and *L. Wils*

Governments, Ethnic Groups and Political Representation
Edited by *G. Alderman* in collaboration with *J. Leslie* and *K. Pollmann*

Ethnic Groups in International Relations
Edited by *P. Smith* in collaboration with *K.K. Koufa* and *A. Suppan*

The Formation of National Elites
Edited by *A. Kappeler* in collaboration with *F. Adanir* and *A. O'Day*

Roots of Rural Ethnic Mobilisation
Edited by *G. von Pistohlkors* in collaboration with *D. Howell* and *E. Wiegandt*

Ethnic Identity in Urban Europe
Edited by *M. Engman* in collaboration with *F.W. Carter, A.C. Hepburn* and *C.G. Pooley*

Series Preface

This series of eight volumes represents the results of the first major project in historical research to be undertaken by the European Science Foundation. The project's title, adopted also for the series, was carefully constructed to convey with precision the subject matter, and approach, of the enquiry; for the specialist, the lawyer, the diplomat, or the politician there are crucial differences between 'ethnic groups' and 'nationalities' and between 'non-dominant ethnic groups' (which may well be majorities) and 'ethnic minorities'. In plain language, however, and ignoring a multitude of qualifications, this is a study of some of the characteristic historic (as distinct from twentieth-century extra-European immigrant) non-dominant ethnic groups of Europe (usually minorities) and the ways in which their lives, their survival, and their development were affected by governments and the institutions of the state. The aim is strictly historical, to study what has happened in the past and try to understand and explain it. But the existence of ethnic minorities, their aspirations and their problems, is never far below the consciousness of every country in Europe, and they have contributed to many of the most dramatic and significant events in the remaking of the European scene in 1989 and 1990. The strength of deeply-rooted distinctions of religion, language, and culture in determining current political actions has been repeatedly demonstrated; and the apparently unsuspected existence of minorities within minorities, like so many Russian dolls, has continually startled Western press and television reporters. The past definitely does not predict the future: but it does give rise to the present. These volumes are, therefore, essential to the understanding of one of the most fundamental as well as most complex dimensions of contemporary Europe.

The problem addressed in these volumes can be defined as the problem created by imposing the concept of the nation–state on a mosaic of frequently intermingled peoples of differing religion, language, and culture, whose geographical distribution and pattern of settlement simply did not conform to the abstract specifications assumed by the concept. The idea of the nation as a large, supra-local, community of people with certain characteristics and purposes in common, and of the state as the legitimate embodiment of judicial, coercive, and military power, were far from new in the nineteenth century. The fusion of the two ideas, however, owed much to the French Revolution and the Napoleonic Wars; and multiple aspirations for forming new nation–states were the main driving force of the 1848 Revolutions. In spite, and often because, of the reality on the ground, the ideal of one nation, one state commanded increasingly general acceptance, outside some dynastic and aristocratic circles; it was widely believed that no nation could achieve full expression of its distinctive identity unless it was embodied in a state, and that no state could have legitimate authority over its people unless those formed a single nation.

These principles were patently and glaringly contradicted by the great multi-national empires of the nineteenth century, the Habsburg, the Russian, the German, and the Ottoman. It was less noticed that the United Kingdom also belonged to this group, perhaps because it was more liberal, and more unified in language although not in religion, perhaps because the dominance of the English was of such long standing that the existence of the other three nations had become all but invisible to the rest of the world. While most of the other European sovereign states could plausibly claim, for external purposes, to fit the nation–state model, there was scarcely one whose territories did not contain minorities with aspirations for recognition, autonomy, independence, or union with a mother country. France, Spain, Italy, Belgium or Sweden, for example, fit such a description; while the Swiss, uniquely in Europe a nation which was multi-lingual and federal, did not escape minority issues.

The First World War was a power struggle, a struggle for mastery, not a war of nationalities, but as the fighting went on it became increasingly like that as governments sought to sustain popular commitment to the war, or to undermine the unity of their enemies. Its conclusion, for a mixture of practical and idealistic reasons, saw the not too blatantly partisan application of the principle of self-determination to the map of Europe in the treaties of Versailles and Trianon. The multi-national empires, apart from the United Kingdom, fell apart or were dismembered. A new multi-national state, Yugoslavia, was created; and Europe came as close as it has ever been to appearing as a collection of independent sovereign nation–states.

Some of the successor states, such as Poland or Lithuania, were revived after years or centuries of oblivion, while others, such as Czechoslovakia, were new creations. In all of them the previously non-dominant groups gained control, and promptly found themselves faced with minorities within the new borders, consisting chiefly of the former masters. In western and Mediterranean Europe there was no similar *bouleversement*, aside from the withdrawal of southern Ireland from the United Kingdom, and the identity of non-dominant groups remained unchanged throughout the whole study period. Minorities certainly did not cease to exist or to be important in 1940; the Second World War, however, started a markedly different phase in their history, which has lasted for fifty years. During the war several minorities were treated with unsurpassable and previously unthinkable savagery and inhumanity; grievously depleted, they survived. Then, through the years of the Cold War, in some countries minorities were driven underground, marginalised, and virtually deprived of any official, public, existence; minority questions, along with nationalist issues, largely disappeared from the agenda of European international relations; and several western European countries became for the first time countries of large-scale immigration, hosts to new, non-historic, minorities. Europe seemed to have changed irrevocably, to have left history behind, to have jettisoned old minority problems and acquired new ones. Then in 1989 and 1990 the Europe of 1939, or something with a passing resemblance to it, came rushing back to life, and there was more than a hint that elements of the pre–1914 world were re-awakening. All of a sudden it became clear that historians dealing with the events of 1850 to 1940 were, in effect, also throwing light on current affairs.

In the long, and open-ended, continuum of the history of minorities in European countries the period between roughly 1850 and 1940 thus has a distinct unity; the sharp discontinuity of 1914 was, in this perspective, the hinge around which aspirations for national independence were converted into reality. Such was the general context for the proposal by the Norwegian historian John Herstad that the European Science Foundation should mount a major collaborative study of minorities, or more specifically of governments and non-dominant ethnic groups. This proposal was developed into a research programme by a planning committee chaired by Gerald Stourzh, of Vienna, consisting of members from ten different countries, including the late Professor Benjamin Akzin (Jerusalem) and the late Professor Hugh Seton-Watson (London). This programme then ran for the five years 1984-8, with an overall steering committee chaired by myself. The aim of the project was not to produce a narrative or descriptive history of each and every minority or non-dominant ethnic group in Europe, nor to produce an exhaustive, and exhausting, history of the policies and actions of each government towards its minority groups. The aim was at once simpler, more limited, and more demanding: to undertake a number of case studies on a selection of well-defined themes providing different angles of approach to the central topic, and lending themselves to comparative evaluation. From a much larger number of possibilities, eight themes were chosen, and these furnish the eight volumes of the series: Schooling; Religion; Language Rights;

Political Representation; International Relations; Formation of National Elites; Rural Settlements; Urban Settlements.

John Herstad's original idea was that studies in depth of minority groups in particular, sometimes quite small, localities could reveal much about group survival strategies, the most significant and tenacious characteristics of ethnic identities, the most important influences on assimilation, the actual impact and effect of legislation and administrative practices, and many other features which tend to get lost or obscured in the generalisations and rhetoric of national histories. This call to employ local history as a methodology has been followed where the nature of the material permits, especially in the rural and urban volumes. The claim is not that the particular villages and towns chosen for study necessarily merit intense international attention for their own sakes, but that they are microcosms of the larger world in which more general features of ethnicity, culture, custom, and law can be observed in action in the lives of individuals and families. In other chapters and other volumes the emphasis is necessarily on larger regions, and states, whose educational systems, laws and institutions, judiciaries and bureaucracies, ecclesiastical organizations and economic and social structures, set the framework within which direct interaction between non-dominant ethnic groups and the long arm of government took place. In both types of case study the selection of localities, regions, and countries is representative of the variety of different situations, different levels of economic and social development, and different forms of government which were to be found in Europe; but it does not set out to be comprehensive in its coverage, and that is not necessary to the achievement of the objective of writing a thematic, comparative, history.

That objective was pursued by assembling eight teams of experts drawn from 18 countries and a wide range of disciplines: history, law, theology, education, sociology, anthropology, and geography. More than 90 scholars took part in the project, and although all of them had extensive previous research involvement in the field, they developed, deepened, and extended their personal research in order to tackle the specific formulation of issues in the project and in order to put their own material into thematically comparable form. More preparation and research went into this task than can appear in these volumes, whose chapters in many cases are distillations and summaries of larger pieces of work. Several of the individuals who have taken part hope to publish separately longer and more complete versions of their work, especially when it was originally written in a language other than English. The decision to have a single language publication, in English, was made after much discussion and heart-searching. It goes against many long-held traditions of European scholarship in the humanities, but for a science foundation it is clearly the right decision and the one best calculated to make the results of the project most widely accessible. Hence many of the contributions are translations, and while the sense has not been altered the loss of some of the finer points of argument and subtleties of style is regrettably unavoidable.

The working programme of each group was arranged by a co-ordinator, assisted by the collective efforts of his team; and the co-ordinators, assisted by small editorial teams drawn from their colleagues, have been the editors of their individual volumes. Each group has been fully European, multi-national, multi-cultural, and multi-lingual; the co-ordinator–editors have performed difficult feats of academic organization and intellectual discipline with much tact, and with a success which can be judged in these volumes. Each group, and hence each volume, has a different structure, and the significance of the separate contributions and the conclusions to be drawn are excellently handled by the volume editors; it is not the province of this general preface either to anticipate or to summarise them. One general feature of the enterprise, so obvious that it can easily be overlooked, does however deserve emphasis. The humanities work within national cultures and languages in a way that is not true of the natural or experimental sciences. In this project researchers brought up in many very different scholarly traditions have learned each other's ways, and while continuing to speak in many tongues have adopted a common 'language' for identifying the problems for intellectual enquiry and the methods for investigating them. This is the key to successful international cooperation in the humanities, and to have come so far towards achieving it in this project is a major innovation in the methodology of European scholarship. Without sacrificing any of the particularity and indi-viduality of specific circumstances and situations in different places at different times, which are fundamental to the historical method, the varieties of experience of non-dominant ethnic groups have been approached and analysed in a common way which for the first time has made wide-ranging comparative assessment based on firm empirical evidence possible and meaningful.

In an enterprise of this size and complexity many friendships have been formed and many individuals and institutions have given their help. Above all, everyone who has participated in the project would wish to have recorded their appreciation of the incomparable contribution made by Christoph Mühlberg, Secretary of the Humanities Committee of the European Science Foundation throughout the major part of the programme, whose skill in administrative organiz-ation has been matched only by his grasp of the intellectual challenges of the theme and the soundness of his suggestions for meeting them. In addition, unknown to the majority of the authors, Dr Judith Rowbotham has made a vital contribution to the consistency of these volumes in the very demanding work of adding the finishing touches of painstaking sub-editing, which is the more successful the more unobtrusive it seems.

F.M.L. Thompson
Institute of Historical Research,
University of London

1 Introduction

PAUL SMITH

The relationship between governments and non-dominant ethnic groups is keenly affected by the potential which the latter may have for influencing the relations between states and for maintaining trans-state links which have implications for the states of which they form a part or for other states. Within the overall series in which it appears, the purpose of this volume is to look at the significance of non-dominant ethnic groups[1] in relations between states and across state boundaries, their importance (or lack of it) for international politics, and the attempts made to treat their problems in an international frame through the insertion of protective provisions in treaties and other instruments and through the institution of the League of Nations. In the fields both of political science and of history, studies of international relations have, with few exceptions, tended to centre almost exclusively upon the operations of states and have rarely given systematic attention to the groups we are here concerned with.

In the USA, a team of contributors under the editorship of Judy S. Bertelsen has examined the role of 'non-state nations' defined as 'any entity that operates in a manner normally associated with a nation-state but is not a generally recognised nation-state' in international politics.[2] The non-state nation in this use of the term need not be an ethnic group, but the cases studied in Bertelsen's book do all exhibit a history of ethnic cohesion. The focus, however, is on the way that non-state nations perform as 'actors' in international relations rather than on the full range of implications that their existence poses for international society. In practice the studies concentrate on the impact of the activities of those defined as their decision makers in an international context. R. Pearson's attempt at a categorisation of the way in which the national minorities of eastern Europe have figured on the international scene both as actors and – much more – as the focus for outside intervention is broader and more historically based.[3] Indeed Pearson's categories have been useful in constructing the analysis of forms of engagement by groups in the international community which appears below.

In conformity with the approach of the overall project, ethnic groups are here held to be defined by such features as racial, linguistic, and cultural specificity and by long continued common historical experience and societal life, but above all by the conscious- ness and articulation of group identity, by the existence of group organisation, and by the aspiration of the group to some form of autonomous life. A group's 'non-dominance' is defined in relation to the central political authority and institutions of the state which it inhabits, and is not therefore necessarily incompatible with numeri- cal majority or with local or cultural autonomy. In other words, though the groups here studied are usually minorities, the category is not synonymous with minorities, and it is possible to find groups – for example, the Irish in Ireland, or the Finns in Finland before the First World War – which possessed a substantial numerical majority in their own land yet remained in a subordinate position in the state of which that territory formed a part.

Though all contributors to this volume were asked to keep in mind a common set of questions and problems, they were not required to follow any rigid scheme of treatment. Nor have they tackled their theme by attempting to supply in a series of analytical chapters ranging across Europe some sort of typology of the impact of their chosen groups in international relations. Chapters of that kind can easily take too abstract and general a form. It has seemed better to the authors here, specialists as most of them are in the concrete and the particular, to produce case studies within a common frame of reference, placing on the introductory and concluding chapters the responsibility of trying to define the area of the volume's concern and to offer a synthetic overview of its findings.

As in all enterprises of the kind, the selection of case studies has necessarily been influenced by the availability of qualified and willing contributors, and some omissions are to be regretted: especially those of surveys of the international implications of the problems posed by ethnic groups to the governments of the Habsburg, Romanov, and Ottoman empires before the First World War. The topical and geographical coverage produced by 14 scholars from eight European nations and Israel is, all the same, broad enough to illustrate most important varieties of the interaction of governments and groups at international level or under the influence of international consider- ations. The volume begins on a relatively general plane by looking at specifically international and supra-national provision for the treat- ment of groups in the work of the League of Nations and goes on to look at a group that was inherently trans-national, the Jews. There follow ten further studies of groups and their problems and of the attitude of governments towards them, the emphasis falling on the interwar years and on the working of the Versailles and associated treaties and of the League of Nations 'system'. While the authors have had the opportunity of reading and commenting on each other's chapters, the volume as a whole is a collaborative rather than a collective product: responsibility for the content of each contribution rests with the author(s) concerned in association with the editors.

The bias of the volume towards the post–1918 period can be held to reflect the much greater prominence of ethnic groups in the thinking about, and in the conduct of, international affairs in the twentieth century as compared to the nineteenth. The status of groups in international esteem and calculation changed vastly between 1850 and 1940, not exclusively to their advantage. From conservative ideologies, they had relatively little to hope, seeming as they often did to threaten the stability of the European state system by undermining its component parts and multiplying causes of antagonism between them. The national aspirations that some of the groups manifested could be, and were, seen by a statesman like Lord Salisbury in Britain as both contrived and contrary to modern political evolution. As a young man, he wrote in 1859:

> the splitting up of mankind into a multitude of infinitesimal governments, in accordance with their actual differences of dialect or their presumed differences of race, would be to undo the work of civilisation and renounce all the benefits which the slow and painful process of consolidation has procured for mankind. . . . It is the agglomeration and not the comminution of states to which civilisation is constantly tending; it is the fusion and not the isolation of races by which the physical and moral excellence of the species is advanced. There are races, as there are trees, which cannot stand erect by themselves, and which, if their growth is not hindered by artificial constraints, are all the healthier for twining round some robuster stem.[4]

The congress system and the so-called concert of Europe gave the groups a recognition and a role in international affairs largely as the objects of efforts by established states to prevent their claims from disrupting the existing European order.

On the other hand, the stress of liberal ideology on that self-determination of peoples which, by 1870, Fustel de Coulanges, in his debate with Mommsen over Alsace, was claiming to be the authentic modern principle for national organisation,[5] offered groups an increasing prospect of support from international opinion. The attitude of liberalism to the groups was, of course, ambiguous. Its emphasis on freedom, pluralism, and representative institutions offered them considerable rights of self-expression and opportunities to press their claims, but the movement of the liberal state towards rational centralisation and uniformity in administration could sometimes cause the Herderian *Volk* (people) to seem anomalous and unassimilated within the national structure, just as it did to modernising conservative regimes. Toleration might be less a recognition of groups' claims than a technique for their ultimate incorporation. Democracy, if it increased their ability to make themselves heard, exposed them also to the risk of facing a permanent hostile majority in a national assembly exercising unconstrained sovereignty. Liberal nationalism could operate both as a theoretical validation of the aspirations of the self-conscious group and, within the framework of the national state, as a practical obstacle to their realisation. It was hard to draw the line between that acknowledgement of a group's status which might ensure its peaceful integration under a liberal constitution and the encouragement of an unacceptable separatism which might have dangerous consequences not only for national integrity but also for international peace. Nevertheless, within the international forum, the presuppositions and instinctive sympathies of liberalism lent such groups some support. Increasingly it was to that forum and to change in the international scene that some of them had to look for the achievement of their aspirations, or even the survival of their cause, as the growing bureaucratic and police efficiency of states enhanced the power of repression, and the structuring of social and political organisation along class lines cut across (as it was sometimes designed to do) the claims of ethnic allegiance.

International recognition and protection of the rights of members of non-dominant groups – well established in the public international law of Europe since the seventeenth century in regard to the guaranteeing of religious freedom, and even sometimes of laws and customs on transfer of territory between states – was becoming a commonplace by the mid nineteenth century.[6] The transfer of the southern Netherlands to the Dutch kingdom in 1814 and the guarantee of Greek independence by Britain, France and Russia in 1830 both involved stipulations of the civil equality of religious confessions within the states thus formed. In the effort to safeguard the Jewish communities of eastern Europe in particular similar provisions were applied to the declaration on the independence of Moldavia and Wallachia in 1856 and to the Romanian, Serbian, Montenegrin, and Bulgarian states, as well as to the Ottoman empire, at the Congress of Berlin in 1878. The right of option and emigration for subjects wishing to retain their old nationality on the annexation of their territory by a foreign power could also act as a safeguard for members of groups potentially non-dominant in their new states, as applied to the Danes of Schleswig–Holstein in 1864; the Alsatians and Lorrainers in 1871; and the Muslim inhabitants of the areas acquired by Greece from Turkey in 1881. The choice offered by referendums, such as the plebiscites accorded in Nice and Savoy before their annexation by France in 1860 and promised in Schleswig in 1866 was also significant here. Yet such measures involved no more than the protection of the rights of members of groups as individuals. They did not amount to the recognition of groups as such; still less to the assertion on their behalf of any right of collective self-determination.

More significant in the long run was the attempt made at the Congress of Vienna in 1815 for the first time to guarantee the national rights of a group by making provision for the Poles to retain their nationality within such forms of political existence as the respective governments ruling over them might see fit to allow. This was a move which, however nugatory in practice, did provide the base for France in 1831, and Austria and Britain in 1863, to make representations to the Russian government on behalf of the Poles. Austria–Hungary, having unilaterally granted respect for 'national institutions' in annexing Bosnia in 1908, was at the end of the first Balkan War in 1912–13, anxious (for her own political reasons) to secure respect for the nationality of Albanians passing under Serbian and Montenegrin sovereignty.

None of this greatly advanced the political and especially the national aspirations of groups. International law recognised no right on their part to demand separation from the states in which they found themselves. The chances of fulfilling their aims remained generally dependent on the dictates of a state interest usually defined in terms antithetical to them. Perhaps in the early 1900s there was enhanced attention to their claims from statesmen and political scientists concerned about the threat they might pose to the maintenance of European peace. The French historian Charles Seignobos, introducing a collection of studies of *Les Aspirations autonomistes en Europe* in 1913, was anxious that the subjugated 'little nations' should find in France – independent of the monarchies and aristocracies which were their enemies and itself (in his view) happily free of minority problems – the centre of organisation and propaganda which they collectively needed to work upon the 'massive indifference' of the European public. Such intellectual sympathy, however, moved no boundaries and changed no laws.[7]

It would perhaps be too much to say that the groups needed a European cataclysm which would shatter the existing state system and introduce a search for new bases of international order and harmony, but, for example, what else could give real hope to the Poles of Prussia and Russia but the disintegration of the empires which ruled them, and the reconstitution of the central European map on new principles? The First World War forced the Entente powers to moralise their ultimately victorious cause in terms of freedom and self-determination and also brought on to the European stage a USA resoundingly committed to the same principles. The result of this was to oblige all combatants to offer concessions and inducements to ethnic groups in order to ensure their loyalty or to turn them against enemy governments and it revolutionised international recognition of the groups and of their claims to separate existence and to protection. The post-war treaties and the League of Nations 'system' for minority protection institutionalised in a sense the groups on the international scene. The emergence of the European Congress of Nationalities marked the recognition by the groups of themselves as a collective international interest. They now possessed vastly enlarged means of appealing to international opinion and aid, yet this increased prominence brought immense risks with it. It gave them a growing exposure as focal points of international interest, and rendered them more useful as levers and bargaining counters in interstate relations. The danger they might seem to pose to state cohesion and security was thus increased along, consequently, with the degree of repression they might invite. Equally this rendered them more prominent causes of, or more plausible pretexts for, international contention. Their fate in the interwar years, and even more between 1939 and 1945, was to reflect these dangers of their new international status.

The separate studies in this volume are all directed to defining by illustration the ways in which groups function and feature in international relations and the implications which these have both for the groups themselves and for their own and other governments. A particular concern has been to elucidate the major factors which determine the kind and degree of the significance and impact which groups achieve in international affairs. It is obvious that a great deal depends on the nature and situation of the group itself, upon such basic matters as its demographic size and character, geographical distribution, economic and social characteristics and resources, cultural development, organisational means, civil status, rights and disabilities (in regard to such things as language, religion, schooling, voting), and its 'image' in the eyes of the dominant group or groups and of the state authorities. In the space available to them, contributors have been able to do no more than outline these fundamental conditioning factors; but in the case of certain of the groups discussed in this volume, further information may be found in the other volumes of the series.

The most important general distinction in characterising such ethnic groups is sometimes held to be that between 'strong' and 'weak' groups, but its relation to the part they play in international affairs is not necessarily a simple or self-evident one. 'Strong' groups may have greater potential for intruding their claims on international attention, but sometimes less need to do so. Jaworski suggests that the relative strength of the German minority in Czechoslovakia in the 1920s made it possible for that minority to reconcile itself to a position as one of the three ethnic constituents of the Czech state, while the relative weakness of the Germans in Poland made them more inclined to look outward for the support of the external German state. Perhaps more fundamental is the nature of the group's political consciousness and aims, and here the most important question is whether or not they are 'national'. The problem of what constituted 'nationality' was one that exercised the groups themselves, as in the debate on the Frisian case in the European Congress of Nationalities. Some of the groups studied here did not on the whole see themselves as constituting a 'nation' (though they might sometimes use the term) or as aiming at independent national status or union with a national 'mother' state. To that extent they did not directly challenge the integrity of the national state in which they lived or readily lend themselves to manipulation by external states. The Ålanders, Alsatians, and Frisians are cases in point. Other groups did possess a specifically national consciousness and aspiration, which might be related to former membership of an independent national state or be focused on an external 'mother' country, as with the Danish and German groups discussed here, or might have neither a historic statehood nor an external parent state to look to, as with the Ukrainians, but in any case were likely to raise issues of national integrity for the state to which the group belonged and to lend themselves to international complications.

In the manifestation of the group's consciousness and aims on the international stage, much depended on the extent to which it desired or had the means to pursue a 'foreign policy'. A group might seek to establish or exploit external relations in order to advance its claims within its state. It might, as Bertelsen puts it, seek greater resources in allies, 'audibility', etc. and a change in the rules and context of a domestic game that it was consistently losing.[8] On the other hand, or at the same time, it might find itself exploited by external forces seeking to employ it as an instrument or resource for their own purposes. A crude distinction emerges in the group's functioning in international relations between opportunity and instrumentality – its own search for opportunity on the one hand; the instrumentality it possesses for external powers on the other. On the evidence of these studies, some attempt can be made to set out a rough typology of the various ways in which groups and their problems enter into the international sphere, whether in the quest for opportunity or under the pressure of instrumentality, taking first the main forms of external relationship which they contract or are forced into, and second the forms in which their concerns become the object of attempts at international regulation and organisation.

Forms of External Relationship

Groups may form relationships which have an impact on the international scene with:

- an external 'motherland'. This motherland may support the group, both materially and spiritually, without necessarily encouraging it to act against the state which harbours it, especially when that state outweighs the motherland in power terms, or can respond in kind. The Danes, for example, were careful not to incur German hostility by fomenting difficulties in Schleswig. However, that motherland may also exploit the group more or less cynically, for example
    - (i)   as a spearhead for revisionist purposes (in the case especially of *Grenzlandminderheiten* (borderland minorities) like the Germans in interwar Poland), or for the promotion of a foreign policy aimed at the weakening or destruction of other states (National Socialist Germany in its use of the Sudeten Germans) or at the extension of national economic and cultural influence (Spain and the Sephardic Jews of the Balkans);
    - (ii) for the symbolising and stimulation of its internal national feeling (the Alsatians were so used by French and Germans in turn);
    - (iii) as a bargaining counter, which may even be sacrificed in the national interest or at least subordinated to it – as when Greece and Turkey sacrificed the greater part of their respective minorities in each other's countries by the compulsory transfer of populations under the 1923 agreements, thus securing to themselves greater national cohesion as well as improved relations, or when Austria and Yugoslavia in effect collaborated to restrict the concessions they were obliged to make to each other's minorities.
- other outside states. Like the category above, this relationship enters into Pearson's category of 'extra-national patronage'. The interest of the outside state may be humanitarian but is more likely to be instrumental, concerned with exploiting the group's differences with its own state for purposes unconnected with the ends of the group itself, as the German, Czech and Russian governments of the interwar years exploited the situation of the Ukrainians in Poland.
- kindred groups, including *émigrés* from the group itself, in other states. The Jews form the outstanding example of a trans-state group to which there are hardly any parallels (unless gypsies) but

other groups spread across frontiers and still kept up links –
Alsatians, Frisians, Ukrainians.
- the international community at large, through international or
  trans-national organisations and activities (political, cultural,
  sporting, etc.) in which the group figures as an entity.

Forms of International Regulation and Organisation

Especially where the aspirations of the group are seen as a threat to
international stability, or when the claims of groups in general are
seen as conformable to a prevailing ideology of self-determination
and justice and their satisfaction appears as a precondition of peace,
there is likely to be concerted international intervention; and in the
latter case groups themselves may embody their recognition of a
common interest by organising across frontiers. We have thus at least
three forms.

- the possibly forcible intervention of outside states acting in
  concert to regulate by treaty or otherwise the problems of groups
  within their states – this is something like Pearson's category of
  'multi-national partition', the outstanding example in the period
  under review being the attempt of the great powers to resolve the
  situation produced in Europe by the collapse of empires and the
  proliferation of national claims as a result of the First World War.
- regulation of group concerns and protection of groups' interests
  by international agencies and institutions claiming to transcend
  national interest – Pearson's category of 'inter-national protection'. The principal example here is the League of Nations.
- an international organisation in which groups combine to
  develop a collective stance, as in the European Congress of
  Nationalities.[9]

The final aspect of the volume concerns the way in which the
involvement and significance, or potential significance, of groups in
international affairs reacts upon their relations with their own states.
As far as the ethnic group is concerned much depends on how far the
group is encouraged by external influence to take a more adamant
line in pursuit of its claims. The state's response will be governed by
the way in which it and the dominant group within its territory
evaluate the non-dominant group. On the one hand the group can be
seen as a resource in terms of its economic, social, and military
importance (including the strategic value of its territory) and its
potential for acting as a stimulus to and/or focus of national
integration and consciousness and serving as a bargaining counter

vis-à-vis other states. On the other hand it can be seen as a liability in terms of its potential for damaging state interests by corruption or adulteration of national identity, disruption of internal unity, jeopardising of national security, and creation of international complications and conflicts. Governments might sometimes be led into more conciliatory courses through the international dimensions which group problems had assumed, but the reverse was often the case where national integrity, security and pride seemed threatened. The penalty of greater international recognition for groups especially after the First World War, which, if it led to the liberation of some groups resulted also in the creation of others at the peace settlement, was often harsher treatment or even the combination of states to suppress a mutual problem. The post-war settlement and the pursuit of minority protection by the League of Nations sometimes seemed to consist in the imposition by the victors of standards which they did not always apply impartially or to themselves (as when France reabsorbed Alsace–Lorraine without any pause for a plebiscite), and intervention in behalf of minorities was especially resented when it appeared to new states to infringe the sovereignty which they had so hardly won – or perhaps to restrict the freedom of once non-dominant groups to revenge past humiliations on former masters.

International protection could make little headway when considerations of the interest of the states concerned ran against it, and the propensity of 'mother' states to make serious exertions on behalf of their clients depended on the extent of the concessions within their own borders which they might be obliged to yield in return. The treaties had made the position of Germany central in this respect. For the German government in the 1920s, the balance of trade in non-dominant ethnic group transactions was potentially highly favourable and its support for the rights of Germans beyond its borders consequently substantial. However the situation was the reverse for its neighbours with German minorities, and Polish and Danish groups in the *Reich*, for example, were driven to mute their claims in order to protect their mother states against having to engage in highly disadvantageous reciprocal concessions. Hitler's advent to power soon took this category of problem out of the area of conciliatory diplomacy or international regulation. Some non-German groups could perhaps hope to take an exhilarating ride on the German tiger, like the Slovene irredentists in Yugoslavia who were willing to play the National Socialist game in the hope of profiting from a break up of Austria. But all were likely to be swallowed in the end. Work on contemporary ethnic group questions across the world suggests that the dangers of playing a role in international relations may be little less for groups today, when ethnic conflicts are exploited for the purposes of their global strategies by superpowers whose own lack of ethnic homogeneity may give them a direct incentive to pursue the strict subjection of ethnic claims to state interests.[10]

Notes

1. To avoid repetition of this unwieldly term, they will be referred to simply as 'groups' for the remainder of this introduction.
2. Bertelsen, p. 2.
3. Pearson, chapter 5, 'External Intervention'.
4. Cecil, p. 22.
5. See below, pp. 59–60.
6. It is appropriate here to acknowledge the contribution made to the collaborative work of the authors of this volume in the sphere of the international protection of minority rights by Professor Alessandro Pizzorusso of the Institute of Comparative Law of the University of Florence.
7. Seignobos, pp. xvii–xix.
8. Bertelsen, p. 3; p. 250.
9. The authors wish to acknowledge the contribution to work on this volume made by the leading student of the European Congress of Nationalities, Dr Rudolf Michaelsen.
10. See Smith, pp. 148–51. Smith's is one of a number of studies deriving from recent academic recognition of the continuing vitality of ethnicity and ethnic conflict in Europe and elsewhere, but paying relatively little attention to their operation in the sphere of international relations: for example, Esman and Ra'anan.

Select Bibliography

Bertelsen, Judy S. (ed.) (1977), *Nonstate Nations in International Politics: Comparative System Analyses*, New York.

Cecil, Lord Robert (later third Marquis of Salisbury) (1859), 'English Politics and Parties', *Bentley's Quarterly Review*, 1.

Esman, M. J. (ed.) (1977), *Ethnic Conflict in the Western World*, Ithaca.

Michaelsen, R. (1984), *Der Europäische Nationalitäten Kongress 1925–1928. Aufbau, Krise und Konsolidierung*, Frankfurt.

Pearson, R. (1983), *National Minorities in Eastern Europe 1848–1945*, London.

Ra'anan, U. (ed.) (1980), *Ethnic Resurgence in Modern Democratic States: a Multi-disciplinary Approach to Human Resources and Conflict*, New York.

Seignobos, C., *et al.* (1913), *Les Aspirations autonomistes en Europe (Bibliothèque générale des sciences sociales*, xlvi), Paris.

Smith, A. D. (1981), *The Ethnic Revival*, Cambridge.

2 Minorities in the System of the League of Nations
STANISLAW SIERPOWSKI

I

The most important decisions of the Paris Peace Conference are directly relevant to the subject matter of this chapter. First, during a plenary meeting of the Peace Conference on 28 April 1919, the constitution of the League of Nations was accepted, thus becoming an integral part of the peace treaties concluding the war. Despite various plans, the terms setting up the League did not include any provisions dealing with the protection of minorities since these would have had to be observed by all members of the future organisation. For analogous reasons, the treaties did not contain any general provisions concerning the protection of minorities.

Those decisions, and particularly the atmosphere which accompanied their creation, greatly disappointed numerous advocates of the national principle as the foundation for the building of both the new Europe and the new world.[1] The leaders of the victorious countries faced severe criticism coming from various directions. Thus, the idea of including in treaties the imposition of minority obligations on individual states, whether new or considerably enlarged, should be seen as a kind of compensation for the unfulfilled hopes evoked by the idea of national self-determination.

The formal proposal to establish a legally backed international system of minorities' protection was announced by President Woodrow Wilson at the meeting of the Council of Four on 1 May 1919. He referred to the instances of mistreatment of Jewish communities in Poland and Romania. David Lloyd George proposed imposing similar obligations on other new or considerably enlarged states of central and southern Europe. These suggestions were immediately passed on to the members of the Commission on New States and Minorities. The American and British members of the Commission (David Hunter Miller and James Headlam-Morley), who had been working on the issue for a long time, insisted on the necessity of introducing protection for minorities by means of separate treaties. A report on that problem, accepted by the Council of Four on 3 May 1919, enlivened considerably the ongoing disputes.[2]

Great influence was attributed to the memorandum of the Committee of Jewish Delegations at the Peace Conference of 10 May 1919 which had been sent to all the delegates present. This advocated the protection of various groups of religious, racial, and language minorities in Bulgaria, Estonia, Finland, Greece, Lithuania, Poland, Romania, Russia, Czechoslovakia, Ukraine, Yugoslavia, and other territories of eastern and central Europe. The purpose of that initiative, which sought constitutional guarantees and 'potential sanctions on the part of the League of Nations', was to warrant the following:

- civil, religious, and political freedom to individuals;
- the right of organisation and development of national minorities;
- the attainment of equality of status for individuals and for national minorities.

The memorandum also contained an outline of a relevant treaty encompassing nine articles. Its acceptance by the above-mentioned status was to guarantee appropriate conditions for an unconstrained development of all minorities, although the specific interests of the Jewish people were particularly stressed.[3]

The well organised activities of the Jewish representatives had a considerable impact on the shape and nature of minority rights. Those who opposed unnecessarily 'teasing the Germans' were equally influential. The system of minorities' protection, already discussed in Paris, met with an official acceptance in Berlin expressed by the German delegation in their remarks on the peace conditions of 29 May 1919 (paragraph II B). Having pointed to the League of Nations as the most appropriate institution for the regulation of minorities' protection, they demanded definite guarantees for the German inhabitants of the territories to be annexed to other states. The demands concerned, in particular, the right to preserve German schools and churches and to have their own press. Moreover, the need to allow for some cultural autonomy of minorities was stressed. Simultaneously, analogous principles would apply to the minorities inhabiting Germany. These suggestions were among the few to be fully accepted by Lloyd George and Woodrow Wilson and appreciated by Clemenceau.[4]

The process of working out the principles of minorities' protection was strongly resisted by those states directly involved. The main discussion took place at the eighth plenary meeting of the Peace Conference on 31 May 1919. The draft treaty with Austria then considered contained provisions requiring the following states to protect their minorities: Czechoslovakia, Poland, Romania, and the kingdom of the Serbs, Croats and Slovenes. The delegates from these states, particularly the Prime Ministers of Romania (Ion Bratianu) and Poland (Ignacy J. Paderewski) emphasised their acceptance of all solutions, provided that they applied to all the states involved. Bratianu stressed that the founders of the League of Nations 'violated the principle of the equality of states' from the very moment the organisation came into being. In addition, warnings were given against the consequences of introducing division between citizens in domestic relations. The institutionalisation of inequality, both internationally and internally, seemed to the states in question a danger to their harmonious development.

One of the consequences of the combined resistance of the so-called minority states was Clemenceau's letter to Paderewski of 24 June 1919. The President of the Peace Conference extensively justified the aims and goals of the authors of all the treaties dealing with minorities. The mere fact of the existence of the principles was to facilitate – according to Clemenceau – the acceptance of the new situation by the minorities. The aim of entrusting the guarantee of provisions protecting minorities to the League of Nations was to exclude a potential interference with the internal affairs of the countries concerned. Therefore, the provisions concerning the guarantee had been formulated with the 'utmost scrupulousness' so as to deprive of a political character any disputes which might emerge as a result of the application of the provisions concerning minorities.[5]

II

Two particularly important documents were signed at Versailles on 28 June 1919. One of them contained the peace conditions imposed on defeated Germany by the principal Allied and Associated Powers (including Poland). In the other one, the above-mentioned Powers obliged Poland to accept a special treaty concerning the protection of minorities. The significance of that document, also referred to as the Minor Treaty of Versailles, was due to its role as an ideal model. The solutions applied there laid the foundations of the entire system of international minorities' protection.

The Treaty concerned the citizens of a state who differed from the majority as regarded language, race, or religion. They were guaranteed equal rights throughout a given state. Article 12 is here of crucial importance in evaluating the role of the League of Nations in the minority system. Under this article, the treaty was recognised as constituting international obligations which were to be placed under the guarantee of the League of Nations. Any amendments could be introduced only if accepted by the majority of the members of the Council of the League of Nations. Any member of the Council had the right to bring to the attention of the Council any infraction of these provisions. The Council was then free to take any action and apply any means to make its mission effective. Article 12 involved the Permanent Court of International Justice in the minority system. The decisions of the Court were final and without appeal.[6]

While signing the treaty with Austria in Saint Germain on 10 September 1919, Czechoslovakia and Yugoslavia had to accept analogous (though not identical) obligations. The Romanian resistance was equally ineffective, and a treaty was signed in Paris on 9 December 1919. The obligations of Greece derived from the treaty of Sèvres, signed on 10 August 1920.

The other group of the so-called minority states consisted of the defeated countries. Their obligations were enumerated in the following treaties: Austria, that of Saint Germain, 10 September 1919, in articles 62–9; Bulgaria, that of Neuilly, 27 November 1919, in articles 49–57; Hungary, that of Trianon, 4 June 1920 in articles 54–60; Turkey, that of Lausanne, 24 July 1923, in articles 37–45. The minority obligations of countries like Finland, Albania, Lithuania, Latvia, Estonia, and Iraq were submitted to the League of Nations in the form of declarations. The issue of protection of minorities also came up in some bilateral treaties, one of the most famous examples being the so-called Geneva Convention of 15 May 1922, concerning Upper Silesia.[7]

The legal foundations of the system of minorities' protection outlined above aimed at protecting the interests of minorities. They were supposed to function in conditions analogous to those shared by all the other citizens of a given state. Hence, minorities could not possibly demand any special services or more liberal regulations. They were not, generally speaking, entitled to any privileges.

The international system of the protection of minorities was basically formed in the initial years of the interwar period. Later, only Iraq was to join the League of Nations in 1932 and agree to accept the relevant obligations. In that case, reference was made to the resolution adopted during the first Assembly of the League of Nations on 15 December 1920 which made the admittance of some states into the League conditional on their acceptance of the minority obligations.[8] The issue had been subject to controversy ever since it emerged. The original opinion was that the states planning to join the League should not be subject to any additional conditions, apart from those mentioned in the Covenant. This stand was taken, among others, by the President of the political section of the Secretariat General Paul Mantoux.[9] A distinct point of view was represented by the Secretary and Special Delegate of the Joint Foreign Committee, who attempted to attain the maximum increase in the number of states subject to minority obligations.[10] As a consequence, minority obligations were imposed on Albania and Finland during the first assembly of the League of Nations. Other countries, like Lithuania, Latvia, and Estonia demanded to be admitted to the League without any additional conditions. Their resistance was partly successful: for example, after long negotiations, Latvia signed a declaration on 7 October 1923 confirming a voluntary acceptance of minority obligations and agreeing to negotiate with the Council if it decided that the situation of Latvian minorities was not consistent with the rules of the treaties.[11]

III

The main characteristic of the first few years in the functioning of the system was the tendency to widen the interpretation of the minority obligations. This development was advocated by numerous high officials of the Secretariat General, Paul Mantoux being one of them. For example, in March 1920 he pointed to the necessity of appointing a special League representative, entitled to organise 'an inspection system' and given 'the right to insist on sanctions', to Istanbul.[12] Sir Eric Drummond, considered as one of the best organisers of the so-called Geneva institution, consistently aimed at separating the League of Nations from the issues which were beyond the scope of its Covenant. The problems of the protection of minorities concerned him only as far as they constituted a portion of the main function of the League, which was founded to guarantee peace in international relations. A copy of a letter addressed to Fridtjof Nansen (Sir Eric informed Paul Mantoux about it) has the following handwritten remark on it:

> Responsibility for protection of minorities now and till the new order of things ought to be placed where it belongs, namely on the Allies and not on the League. We must be very careful not to involve the League in duties, which it has never assumed and for the performance of which it would certainly lay down very definite conditions.[13]

Establishing the position and the role of the League of Nations in the protection of minorities proved to be a controversial task. Gradually the League came to be seen as having a serviceable function with respect both to its members and to the minorities to be protected. The crux of the matter was expressed by a member of the minority section, who then became its President, Pablo Azcarate, in a conversation with Henry Morgenthau, the President of the *Office*

Autonome pour l'établissement des réfugiés grecs (Office for the settlement of Greek refugees). In November 1923 he said:

> Minorities' questions have been discussed in a very informal way between officials of the Secretariat and officials in the Foreign Offices of the governments concerned. The League has never taken the general position of champion of the minorities as against their own governments: on the contrary, it has been found more satisfactory for the League to work intimately with governments to help them to carry out their own obligations.[14]

This opinion corresponded with the resolutions adopted by the third Assembly of the League of 21 September 1922. It was acknowledged that in normal cases, a semi-official and friendly agreement between the League and the governments of the states which had recognised the minority treaties was the best way of developing good relations between the governments and their minorities. The Secretariat of the League was, at the same time, supposed to help the Council assess whether or not the minorities had been fulfilling their obligations with respect to their respective states.[15]

Particular controversies accompanied the formation of the procedure used by the League of Nations to protect minorities. Treaties and many other agreements of bilateral and multilateral character (except for the convention concerning Upper Silesia) did not make that issue precise enough. Therefore, the creation of the procedure, which received its final shape in 1920–5, was accompanied not only by numerous disputes, but also by detailed analyses, which widened the knowledge of the overall minority problem.

All minority obligations rested under the guarantee of the Council of the League of Nations. The right of calling the Council's attention to any infraction of the clauses of the treaties was originally reserved exclusively to the members of the Council. Soon, however, the right was *de facto* granted to the minorities themselves and to the states which had no representatives in the Council. Such a solution, suggested by the Italian representative Tommaso Tittoni, was approved by the Council on 22 October 1920. It was complemented by the Council resolution of 25 October 1920, which cancelled the individual responsibility of a given member of the Council for calling attention to any violation in the minority protection system of a given state.

A decision was taken as to the appointment of a special internal organ of the Council in the shape of the *Comité du Conseil*, which is referred to in the literature as the Committee of Three. Indeed, it consisted of three members of the Council: its President (that function being subject to regular change) and two other randomly selected members of the Council. With substantial help from the members of the Secretariat they examined all petitions or information sent to Geneva in relation to any cases of infraction or danger of infraction of any of the provisions of the minorities' treaties.[16]

The meetings of the Committee of Three were top secret. The Committee could either transmit the results of its work to the Council for further consideration, or it could close legal proceedings with a document signed by its members. Petitioners were informed neither about the proceedings, nor about their results. The activities of the Committee of Three effectively exempted the members of the Council from the duty of initiating any cases concerning minorities' legislation. This state of affairs changed in June 1929, due to Gustav Stresemann's actions on behalf of the *Volksbund* (People's Union) in Upper Silesia.

Gradually, the Council of the League succeeded in working out procedures for the circulation of petitions between 1921 and 1923. Previously, all the complaints received by the Secretariat had been sent for information to the League. The Council resolution of 27 June 1921 stated that the petitions had to be communicated to the state in question before they were transmitted to the members of the League. The state concerned could inform the Secretary General, within three weeks, whether it desired to make any comments or explanations. In addition, it was granted two months within which to examine the case and to submit its comments.

The above conditions had initially been accepted only by Czechoslovakia and Poland, though later also by Austria and Romania. The remaining states did not agree with the procedure of automatically informing all members of the League about the contents of the petition. Their opinion was most strongly expressed by the politicians from the kingdom of the Serbs, Croats, and Slovenes. Helmer Rosting, a member of the minority section of the Secretariat who chaired the relevant negotiations, anticipated possible complications, since the representative of the kingdom 'was uncompromising'.[17]

Long negotiations on the issue finally satisfied the minority countries. The Council resolution of 5 September 1923 stipulated that both petitions and comments from the governments involved should be communicated only to the members of the Council. To break this rule, either the agreement of a given government or a special resolution of the Council was required.[18]

The above mentioned resolution played an important role in the development of the minorities' procedure in the League, since it outlined the general conditions to be met by the petitions considered by the organs of the League. The resolution stipulated that the petitions:

- must have in view the protection of minorities in accordance with the treaties;
- must not be submitted in the form of a request for the severance of political relations between the minority in question and the state of which it formed a part;
- must not emanate from an anonymous or unauthenticated source;
- must abstain from violent language;
- must contain information or refer to facts which had not recently been the subject of a petition submitted according to the ordinary procedure.

IV

A unique position in this system of minorities' protection between the wars was taken by the Geneva Convention of 15 May 1922, signed after the division of Upper Silesia into Polish and German elements. The bilateral convention concerning half a million Germans in the Polish portion of Upper Silesia and an equal number of Poles in its German portion was the only one of its kind. Since it was valid for 15 years, up to 15 May 1937, Opole Silesia was the only part of Germany where the provisions concerning minorities' protection still held after 1933.

The Geneva Convention devoted about 100 articles to minorities' protection, which involved detailed solutions. The system created was based, on the one hand, on special local institutions and, on the other hand, on the Council of the League of Nations and the Permanent Court of International Justice. The twofold system was reflected in many detailed provisions determining the procedure as regards minorities' protection. The respective articles of the Convention, apart from recapitulating the obligations following from the so-called Minor Treaty of Versailles, specified the rights of minorities as regards civil and political rights, religion, education, etc. Moreover, the Polish and German minorities were granted certain rights not shared by any other minorities.

Article 147 was characteristic of the Geneva Convention. It granted the members of a minority the right to submit a petition directly to the Council. Thus, each petition referring to that article was on the agenda of the forthcoming session of the Council without any preliminary examination. The article was not invoked frequently during the first years of the Convention. However, 41 petitions were submitted to the Council during the three years following mid-1926. This meant, in other words, twice the number of petitions forwarded to the Council on the basis of all other minorities' obligations.[19]

Many petitions from Upper Silesia did not exhaust the local procedure. Thus, on 8 September 1928 the Council established a two-month period for the government in question to convey to the Secretariat any opinions referring to the petitions from Upper Silesia. Further changes were introduced by the so-called Paris Convention of 6 April 1929. Its signing was accompanied by remarkable activity on the part of Mineiteiro Adatci, a spokesman on minorities' issues in the Council, and by the participation of the President of a Mixed Commission (Felix Calonder) as well as the employees of the Secretariat. The Secretary General could, in certain conditions, transfer some petitions from article 147 to a local level. Commenting on the results of the above negotiations, Adatci pointed out 'his willingness to relieve the League of the heavy duty', which was due to the petitioners' often too hasty reference to article 147 of the Geneva Convention.[20]

V

The prominent role of the Council as the main body dealing with minorities' protection in the League should not overshadow the role of the remaining bodies concerned, in particular of the Secretariat. The basic documents outlining the function of the League in the minorities' issue did not touch upon the function of the Secretariat at all. However, the emerging minorities' procedure drew in the regular employees of the League, who showed themselves capable not only of taking responsibility for the work of the Council and the Assembly, but also of suggesting optimal solutions to the issues arising. A Norwegian, Erik Colban, played a crucial role in selecting the staff of the minorities' section, *de facto* the Section of Administrative Commissions and Minorities, before he became its first President. Among his first helpers were: Helmer Rosting of Denmark, a member and G. Lippestad of Norway, a secretary. As the Section grew, the Secretary General demanded a wider range of nationalities. Thus, Pablo Azcarate y Flores of Spain began his work there in 1922; R.N. Kershaw of Australia in 1924; M.A. Cespedes of Colombia and W. O'Sullivan Molony of Ireland in 1925; E.R. de Haller of Switzerland and A.H. Hekimi of Iran in 1926. All of them were members of the Section. The number of administrative staff also increased, with the secretaries coming from the Netherlands, Great Britain, France, and Latvia.[21] The total number of employees of international status oscillated between ten and 11 persons, that is, 1.5 per cent of the total number of employees of the Secretariat, which in 1931 employed as many as 707 people. The cost of the Section took a comparable share of the overall budget of the League.[22]

A characteristic feature of the personnel of the minorities' section was the absence of persons representing the countries with any minorities' obligations or 'interests'. Colban was succeeded in his chair by Spaniards: Manuel Aguire de Carcer (1928–30) and Pablo Azcarate y Flores. At the beginning of 1934, Helmer Rosting was appointed President of the Section to be succeeded by another Dane, Peter Schou in September 1936.[23]

The task of the employees of the Section was to decide whether the complaints, protests, petitions, manifestos, and similar documents sent to Geneva should be considered relevant to the terms of minorities' protection. Each petition was analysed in terms of its form and content. An exhaustive, often several pages long statement was signed by the President of the Section. In an attached conclusion, the petition was either accepted or rejected and further procedure was suggested. About 50 per cent of the petitions received by the Secretariat did not fulfil some (or at least one) of the conditions spelled out by the Council in its resolution of 5 September 1923. Frequent disagreements and controversies arose in connection with the acceptance of petitions. Gradually, however, uniform criteria were worked out and summarized in a paper by M.A. Cespedes.[24] No matter how efficient the members of the Section were in their work, in the consciousness of their responsibility and of the close scrutiny exercised over them, mostly by the petitioners, they still could not escape criticism. The representatives of the defeated countries, notably Germans, stood out in this respect, as they included the minorities' issue (above all, their own minorities) in policies aimed at a revision of the peace treaties – the evidence of their defeat. Other, more differentiated motives were the basis of the criticisms of the Secretariat (*de facto* of the League as a whole) formulated by different influential groups of the International Federation of League of Nations Societies, with its headquarters in Brussels, or by members of the Committee of Jewish Delegations which moved from Paris to Geneva in 1921.[25]

The various approaches to the minorities' issue, and particularly different expectations as to the role of the League, resulted in a paradox. On the one hand, the Secretariat was attacked for allegedly turning down the majority of petitions, and, on the other hand, it was accused of accepting petitions whose form or content contradicted the resolution of 5 September 1923. The bargaining character of that latter criticism was fully revealed in 1929, in connection with the activities which resulted in the so-called Madrid Resolution. The problem of *recevabilité* (admissibility), which was constantly raised, was not then reflected in the suggestions of particular governments submitted at the request of the Committee of Three consisting of Chamberlain, Adatci, and Quiñones de León of Spain.

The employees of the minorities section were responsible for organising various forms of the League's activities as regards minorities. Some meetings of the Council had to analyse ten or more petitions, which might be new or already under consideration. Each was given 30 to 45 minutes, which meant setting aside two to three 'half days' of the regular time devoted to Council meetings; not an easy task, considering the tight schedule of the Council, which was by no means limited to public, private or secret meetings.

The employees of the Section were also the main authors of the reports submitted to the Council. This does not diminish the role of the Council spokesmen, who often contributed considerably to the final solution in a compromise both satisfactory for the petitioner, and acceptable for the states concerned. In appointing these spokesmen, the Council attempted to avoid accusations that the Council was acting as 'a wolf in sheep's clothing'. Hence many reports were given by politicians from outside Europe. Until mid 1926 Brazil's delegate took on the role of spokesman; to be succeeded by Colombia; Japan; and finally with a European base, Ireland and Spain. The last spokesman was appointed by the Council at its ninety-ninth meeting, in September 1937.

The first four years of the Geneva institution must be highlighted in the overall history of the League. Up to the end of 1923 the Council had dealt with the minorities' question and related general issues 42 times in a total of 285 meetings. The League devoted its greatest attention to minorities' issues in 1929, when on 17 occasions its eighteenth meeting tackled both the procedure and general questions on the minorities' problem. A general assessment tending to endorse the existing system of protection was carried out at the meeting in Madrid in June 1929. But discussions continued. In 1933, out of 33 Council meetings, 17 were devoted to minorities; the following year, ten out of 31 meetings of the Council dealt with the issue. In the next few years, the Council would only debate an annual report detailing the results of relevant activities which did not, however, provoke any general discussion.[26]

Minorities' issues were also significant in the activities of the Assembly, which brought together delegates from about 50 states every year, usually in September. Starting with the third Assembly of 1922, an extract from the report on minorities' protection was given by the Secretary General to the sixth (political) committee for further discussion. Despite the protests and efforts of states liable to observe minorities' obligations, the situation did not change radically in the next few years. Advocates of changing the sixth committee of the Assembly from a 'political' to a 'minority' committee would emphasise a special and even central role which it was supposed to play in the overall structure of the League. The opponents of this interpretation suggested that the advocates of minorities' issues at the Assembly forum should give their attention to those 50 per cent of European minorities which were not protected by the Council of the League.

The delegates of Germany, Great Britain, and Hungary turned out to be especially active in the discussions on minorities in the Assembly. Interestingly, Great Britain's leading role lasted until 1924, to be taken over by Albert Apponyi in 1925, when a week long debate on the report setting out the achievements of the Council and the Secretariat did not take up any minorities' issues.[27] In 1926 the problem was not brought up by any delegation; later only an exchange of opinions would take place, without any reference to the sixth committee. Thus, it must be noted that the committee, the centre of all minorities' discussions at the annual Geneva sessions, did not tackle the problem in 1926–9. Instead, the entire, often antagonistic, debate took place in Council. The inadequate results of that procedure, particularly apparent in the so-called Madrid Resolution of 13 June 1929, made the German delegation take the offensive, aimed at the Assembly and its committees. Hence they initiated minorities' discussions in the Assembly for the next four years (1930–3). In 1933 the discussion continued in an atmosphere of scandal evoked by the anti-Jewish action of the Nazis.

The last great debate on minorities took place in the forum of the Assembly in 1934, when delegates from Hungary, Poland, Great Britain, France, and Italy expressed their opinions during five plenary sessions. The proceedings of the sixth committee were especially controversial, concentrating on minorities' issues for seven consecutive sessions, the longest ever period of time. Twenty-five politicians were active in the discussion: Yugoslavia's delegate three times; and representatives from Czechoslovakia, France, Haiti, Poland, Romania, Hungary, and Italy twice.

Germany's departure from the League, and Poland's refusal to cooperate with its organs on minorities' protection issues resulted in effective elimination of minorities' disputes from the Assembly forum and its committees. An attempt to continue discussions on the issue was made by the Hungarian Foreign Minister, General Gabriel Tanczos in 1935, 1936, and 1937.[28] However, his initiatives did not win any verbal reaction on the part of the remaining delegates.

VI

Of all the issues under the heading of minorities' protection, procedural problems stood out as the most time and energy consuming in the proceedings of the League. The disagreements concerning certain aspects, especially legal ones, of the application of minorities' obligations caused not only antagonism but even ruptures between those involved in the emerging system. Instances of a widening interpretation of minorities' obligations found initially in the early resolutions of the Council were subsequently subject to necessary modifications. The governments of Czechoslovakia and Poland were particularly active in this respect. Czechoslovakia became a member of the Council in September 1923 during Edward Benes' intensive attempts to 'interpret and complete' some of these earlier resolutions of the Council.[29]

The initiatives sprang from the conviction that if Germany joined the League, which had been considered desirable, the situation would be highly complicated. Both in Germany and elsewhere, written and spoken advice and warnings could be heard over the fact that becoming a regular member of the Council would entitle Germany to have dealings with the Germans in the territories given away on the basis of the Treaty of Versailles.[30] The efforts of minorities' governments, in particular those of Poland and Czechoslovakia, resulted in the adoption of a Council resolution specifying the composition of the Committee of Three, in order to prevent Germany from participating in that Committee, if the petitioner was a representative of a German minority, or if the petition concerned any of Germany's neighbours.[31]

Soon after Germany joined the League, it became an advocate of the rights of all minorities, especially German ones. Growing controversies on the issue were symbolised by Stresemann's metaphorical and literal 'blow' at the Council meeting in December 1928 at Lugano, continued in the guise of procedural problems at Council sessions in March and June 1929. The ideas formulated at that time were the embodiment of the Stresemann era of minorities' policy, ascribing a crucial role to the League, even though it was practically impossible to fulfil under the terms of the Versailles system. The politicians of the Weimar Republic demanded that the basic principles of the overall minorities' protection system be changed. They aimed at establishing a permanent body, investigatory and supervisory. Moreover, changes in the Council's competence were suggested so that it should deal with the general situation of particular minorities and not only with the analysis of submitted petitions. Finally, it was demanded that the representatives of the states concerned with a given minority should be allowed to participate in the meetings of the Committee of Three.[32]

The results of this German offensive were very limited. A report was worked out by a special Committee of Three (Adatci, Chamberlain, and Quiñones de León) and accepted by the Council at a meeting in Madrid on 13 June 1929 as the so-called Madrid

Resolution. The previous resolutions were combined into one statement, forming a concise and coherent document, which system-atised the procedure used hitherto. The possibility of setting up – on request – a Committee of Five (instead of the Committee of Three) was the new proposal. Such a Committee would assemble to examine petitions not only during the meetings of the Council but also in between them. The Secretary General would be obliged to publish annual statistics in the *Journal Officiel*.[33]

As a consequence of long deliberations in mid 1929, it became clear that cooperation between minority states was consolidated. This was particularly true in the case of Czechoslovakia, Greece, Yugoslavia, Poland, and Romania. The states, often antagonistic in other respects, presented identical stands on basic issues of minorities' protection.

One of the much discussed problems was the plan of setting up, within the League, a minorities' committee, modelled on the mandatory committee. A suggestion to that effect, formulated at the second Assembly by a South African delegate of British origin, Gilbert Murray, had many supporters from the beginning. The strongest support came from leading personalities of the Inter-national Federation of League of Nations Societies. Apart from Murray himself, Robert Cecil and Sir Willoughby Dickinson, the founder of an active minorities' committee within this federation, must be mentioned here. Unanimous support was also given by the participants in the twentieth Interparliamentary Conference, who met in Vienna in August 1922.[34] In addition, annual meetings of the national groups of Europe, also called minority congresses and organised in Geneva from 1925, included among their participants regular advocates of setting up a formal minorities' committee. The idea also enjoyed great popularity among politicians of individual countries, particularly Great Britain, Germany and Hungary, who held official posts in the governments. Finally, the initiative of the Dutch Foreign Minister, Jonkheer Beelaerts van Blokland, presented at the Assembly forum in 1928, stimulated many reactions.[35]

All the proposals faced a negative reaction from the minority states, which stipulated that a real exchange of opinions would depend on the regular committee's taking into account the minorities in all countries. They also demanded the working out of a general convention concerning minority rights, which would be equally binding for all the members of the League. The suggestions emerging in connection with that issue were far from successful. Some, however, like the one presented by Latvia in 1922, were quite influential. Indeed, in a resolution adopted on 21 September 1922, the Assembly stated that, hopefully, the states free from obligation would still apply to their minorities' laws of justice and tolerance analogous to those resulting from minorities' treaties and the practice exercised by the Council of the League.

Those states not liable to minorities' protection treaties considered the above declaration as the end to any concessions in favour of some ambitious egalitarian plan. The struggle on those issues had several aspects worth noting. The first related to the initiative of a Lithuanian delegate Ernest Galvananskas. On 14 September 1925 he suggested to the Assembly the setting up of a special committee to prepare a general convention concerning minorities' protection and including all members of the League. This proposal was withdrawn. Nevertheless, the sixth committee's report noted a difference of opinion among the disputants, some of whom believed that the system of minorities' protection was not compatible with the idea of state equality.[36]

Relevant discussions continued at a Council meeting in December 1925 and resulted in a longer review of the issues by a Brazilian spokesman on minority issues, Afranio de Mello–Franco, in the form of 'some personal observations'. His basic argument consisted of a complete rejection of generalising ideas. They could never include either 19 African countries belonging to the League, or the majority of other non-American countries. A solution to the minorities' problem lay rather in a gradual merger of minority with majority. The founders of the protection system did not want to separate, within certain countries, groups of inhabitants viewing themselves as 'constantly alien'. They had in mind the preparation of conditions indispensable for 'establishing a complete national unity', gradual assimilation in effect even though the word was not used.

The Council, as an organ of the League, never expressed its opinion on Mello–Franco's personal views, which were supported by three other politicians, Benes of Czechoslovakia, Paul Hymans of Belgium, and Austen Chamberlain of Great Britain.[37] The Secretariat also avoided any discussion of the issue, emphasising that the policy of minorities' protection realised under League supervision had a stable character. However, the president of the minorities' section appealed to the Secretary General to make a strong protest against the 'assimilation thesis' during his work on the so-called Madrid report in 1929.[38]

Politicians for whom national minorities provided an instrument in international politics, were among the strongest opponents of assimilation. Professor Ruyssen, a leading personality of the International Federation, also came out against 'the theory of Mello–Franco'. His close collaborator, Sir Willoughby Dickinson, the founder and leader of the 'Minorities Standing Commission', combined his criticism with a suggestion on the introduction of a universal right of minorities to protection. He justified his view by the fact that an organisation such as the League of Nations could not accept that countries should be unequal to one another. The division of countries into two categories, free and under the control of the League, could not endure for long. If no appropriate measures were taken, the disturbances arising might affect the League as a whole.[39]

The generalisation of minority obligations urged by minority countries was initially defined as being defensive in character; a protection against disadvantageous changes in the minority procedure. The stabilisation or, according to others, the stagnation of the minority procedure, determined on by the Madrid report in 1929, began a new stage of the attempts to reach generalisation. At a time of negotiations on equal rights for Germany over armaments, many politicians considered it appropriate and fully justified to come up with an analogous demand over minorities. Hence, in the early 1930s the emerging and strengthening demand for either generalisation or cancelling of the minorities' protection system took on a much more aggressive aspect.

VII

In the course of the polemics the opponents and the supporters of the minorities' protection system formulated hundreds of arguments they regarded as cogent. One of them was referred to with particular eagerness, the idea that although justice would require identical obligations from everyone, in practice some countries, enjoying a higher standard of civilisation, 'had already grown out of' the period of intolerance and thus did not deserve to be under any limitations.

A spectacular denial of this theory came with the racist policies of Nazism, which developed into a state doctrine, and that in a country that had advocated the 'sacred rights of minorities'. Frustration in this respect increased after F. Bernheim's petition from the German part of Upper Silesia, which demonstrated that German legislation had violated the obligations imposed by the Geneva Convention of 15 May 1922. Despite German diplomatic efforts, the petition was placed on the agenda of the eighty-third meeting of the Council (22 May to 6 June 1933). That the German government was indisputably guilty meant that the decision was made in favour of the petitioner and the international idea of fundamental justice.[40]

'The world's conscience', as the Geneva institution was often called, could not possibly ignore the Jewish drama happening in Germany. The actions of the Nazi government were condemned in the Assembly forum by the Foreign Ministers of Sweden and the Netherlands. A delegate of Haiti suggested that concern be concentrated on a general convention, which would secure full protection of life and freedom for every human being, and would guarantee equal rights of all citizens, regardless of their racial, linguistic, and religious differences. Adopting this solution, argued A.F. Frangulis, would render futile any other discussion concerning the generalisation of minority obligations.[41]

The latter proposal, already considered during the previous Assembly, was not accepted by other delegations. The states free from minority obligations resisted changing the system, though they were in favour of work and discussion on changing the procedural process. It was even argued – and quite logically – that a solution giving rise to general criticism could not be adopted. It was further work on refinement of the present system that should constitute a starting point.

An analogous suggestion was formulated by the Secretariat, addressing it particularly to the Polish delegation, which more and more clearly pointed to the necessity of equating the rights and obligations of all members of the League. At the Assembly forum in 1932 Minister A. Zaleski had called the existing conditions of international protection 'contrary to the basic laws of international morality', and contended that the only solution was to set up a general convention on minorities' protection. A formal proposition on these lines was submitted by the Polish delegation a year later, at the Assembly in September 1933, but lively discussions from various viewpoints, particularly during the sixth committee, did not yield any results. The Assembly, having listened to the report on the discussion, decided to reaffirm its resolution of 21 September 1922 (see p. 18).

The discussions on minority issues in the bodies of the League throughout 1933 overlapped with the current state of 'chronic dissatisfaction' with the Geneva institution expressed by German diplomacy.[42] The elements of crisis that had been building up for many years resulted in Berlin's breaking with Geneva. The diplomacy of the 'new *Reich*' at the close of the fourteenth Assembly, had not only failed to achieve any significant success, but also saw a visible decline in the German position in the League, a factor particularly emphasised by Goebbels, who visited Geneva for a few days as a member of the German delegation.

The decision of the German government on 14 October 1933 to denounce the Disarmament Conference and the League had grave consequences for the entire Versailles system. It had frequently been stressed that the League was the foundation of that system, while minority issues played the part of indicators of the changes happening in Europe. If that was the case, it must be noted that the problem of minorities, so greatly exploited in the past, was not reflected in any official statement by the German Chancellor or Foreign Minister between 14 and 16 October 1933.[43]

Germany's denouncement of the League was a great surprise, like the news of the Polish–German non-aggression pact of 26 January 1934. The agreement stopped the press dispute there, so often devoted to minorities' issues. The attenuation of the conflict, so desired and expected in Poland, served to highlight the bilateral negotiations as more fruitful than any multilateral solutions. Taking advantage of the ongoing discussion on accepting the Soviet Union into the League, the Polish government decided to accelerate the resolution of the problem of its minorities' obligations. The campaign was formally started on 10 April 1934 by the putting on the agenda of the forthcoming fifteenth Assembly of a resolution concerning the generalisation of minorities' obligations, while further procedural improvement was advocated in Geneva. On 13 September 1934 Minister Józef Beck announced at the Assembly that the Polish government refused to cooperate with any international organs over control of Polish minorities' protection laws until a uniform system of international protection of minority rights was introduced. Simultaneously, he assured the Assembly that minority interests would stay intact, since they had been and would continue to be protected by the Polish constitution and legislation.[44]

The above declaration, *de facto* denouncing the Minor Treaty of Versailles, brought general criticism from the delegates taking the floor at the Assembly; the sixth committee; the Secretariat; and also in the lobby. While pointing to various aspects of the issue and various points of view, the critics were conscious that the minorities' protection system worked out by the League was being subjected to another attack, with serious consequences.[45]

The stagnation in the minorities' protection system, so obvious after the Madrid report of 1929, gradually turned into a crisis, apparent in the pronouncements of all disputants at the fifteenth Assembly. Similar observations came from other institutions actively engaged in minorities' protection, as when the delegates of the nineteenth Congress of the International Federation adopted a resolution in terms of a general critique of the minorities' protection system as one which satisfied neither the states concerned, nor the minorities. Nor did the current procedural arrangement escape criticism. Despite the Secretariat's 'discreet initiative' that often produced positive results, the minorities-orientated activities of the League, those of the Council in particular, were – according to the Federation – too strongly influenced by the idea that the purpose of the minorities' treaties was, above all, to guarantee internal peace and good international relations.[46] It must be emphasised that the latter objection often constituted a basis for *favourable* opinions about the activities of the League as regarded minorities.

VIII

The procedure for the protection of linguistic, racial, and religious minorities that operated between the wars involved 16 states, including Germany with its obligations in Upper Silesia. That amounted to a third of all the League members, and half of its European members. About 16 000 000 people were subject to protection placed under the guarantee of the League. According to the Secretariat's assessment, that meant half the overall number of people who could, for various reasons, be counted as members of minorities.[47] Some minorities, like the German and the Slovenian ones in Italy, did not have any opportunity to signal their position to the League, although the programme of italianisation imposed by the Italian Fascists caused violent protests. On the other hand, the mechanism of minorities' protection set up because of Polish anti-Semitism did not result in any complaints to the Council from the Jewish community living in Poland.[48] At the same time, the German minority, being in the best position of all the groups living in Poland, sent many petitions, which resulted in long disputes in Geneva. That situation and frequent reference to the Minor Treaty of Versailles, as the model for the whole system, resulted in an interesting phenomenon: out of about 1250 interwar minority cases that the Assembly and the Council were concerned with, over 300 had something to do with Poland, about 200 dealt with Greece and Romania; about 120 with Turkey; about 70 with Albania, Czechoslovakia, and Yugoslavia; 40 with Lithuania, and 20 to 30 with Austria, Bulgaria, Estonia, Hungary, Latvia and Iraq.[49]

Only a small part of the discussions resulted directly from a petition from a given minority, with only 34 interwar cases considered by the Council. An overwhelming majority of the petitions accepted by the Secretariat was handled by the Committee of Three, which thus became the main League body dealing with minorities' protection. In total, the Committee of Three met about 1000 times and considered about 400 petitions, mostly concerned with problems of education, agriculture, citizenship, and various related services. About 500 petitions submitted to the League could not be considered *recevable* (admissible), since they violated the conditions of the Council resolution of 5 September 1923.

These constraints did not relate to the petitions and complaints coming from Upper Silesia, under article 147 of the Geneva Convention. As a result, 100 petitions were submitted to the Council just from that small area, 29 of which concerned its German part, and 71 its Polish part.[50] Special offices were even set up in Katowice and Opole to consider the complaints related to the minorities' problem. In 1922–37 they dealt with almost 13 000 cases, a small part of which (five per cent) came from Poles, and only one per cent from Jews, exclusively in the German part of Upper Silesia. Those dissatisfied with the decisions could appeal to the Mixed Committee, with Felix Calonder as President. During his term of office (1922–37) he received 2283 complaints, including 1613 from the German minority, 522 from the Polish minority and 148 from the Jewish minority. Calonder issued final decisions in the form of 'giving an opinion' in 127 instances; 1929 cases were solved by mutual agreement, and 227 were left unresolved.[51]

The experiences of the interwar period demonstrated that the motto of protection rights for minorities appropriate at that time, was mainly taken up by the enemies of the Versailles system. Some minorities, the German one in particular, which was the strongest and best organised minority in Europe, became subject to irredentist actions, which could be tolerated neither by the governments concerned, nor by the League. The League, even though 'of nations', was an organisation of autonomous states. Therefore, the organs of the League, particularly the Council and the Secretariat, considered the minorities' problem mainly from the viewpoint of its members, and not the minorities themselves. The lack of understanding of that basic issue often resulted in disagreements. Such were most fully expressed in criticisms of the League as an organisation that avoided any effective actions relating to the minorities' position. Expectations raised by the constitution etc. envisaged the organs of the League as ideally actively engaged against any given state considered 'guilty' of violating certain minority obligations.[52]

In practice the organs of the League implemented action over the position of minorities as specified in the treaties in many different ways. In simple terms, one might say that the Secretariat supervised the contents of the minorities' protection treaties; the Council concentrated on political issues and took relevant decisions; whereas the Assembly (particularly its plenary meetings), as well as the committees, dealt with the cases of a generally humanitarian character.

Simultaneously, the minorities' cases played a crucial role in the overall activities of the League. A more prominent position in the hierarchy of the issues considered by the Geneva institution was occupied by such problems as security (arbitration and conciliation), mediation in conflicts and disagreements between states, and disarmament. Less important in the hierarchy were the problems of mandates, the cases of Gdańsk and the Saar, economic and financial issues, transportation and transit, intellectual cooperation, and social and humanitarian activities. Independently, a very high position in the structure of the League was taken by labour issues which were concentrated in the International Labour Organisation; and disputes of a legal character, which were given special status by the Permanent Court of International Justice. Neither of those organisations, functioning in the structure of the League as autonomous bodies, contributed in any significant way to the minorities' issue. Particularly striking was the minimal contribution of the Court of Justice's jurisdiction to the shaping of minorities' protection procedure. The observation emphasises the *political*, and not – as is generally believed – the *legal–international* character of the minorities' system. The legal aspect of the system was in fact limited to the procedure, whereas its content, its very nucleus, was determined by political elements. Thus, the solution to the accumulating problems was not sought on legal grounds. Instead, methods used in international politics were applied. At the heart was always, and still is, the search for compromise solutions. However, each compromise in terms of minorities' problems brought only moderate support from its makers and violent attacks from the dissatisfied, who complained of defeat, treason, and infamy.

The number of subjective interpretations concerning both detailed cases and the system as a whole was increasing along with the nationalistic evolution of Europe and the world. The fact that some states or nations claimed the right to be right in this respect inevitably led to a deterioration in the League's main role as *mediator of compromise* and *coordinator of understanding*. Spectacular evidence of that process, which went through various stages between the wars, was the denunciation of cooperation by two regular members of the Council – Japan and Germany. The accompanying movement of the axis of international relations towards confrontation worked to the detriment of many issues, and that held true for the problem of national minorities. The positive evolution of that issue lies in the application of the idea of democracy to both internal and international relations. The interwar period, particularly the second decade, revealed an opposite tendency. It is those circumstances that were responsible for the League's lack of success, which was bound eventually to affect the area of minorities' protection.

Notes

1. Lebiediev; Levin, jr.
2. Viefhaus, pp. 61 ff; Sharp pp. 177 ff; Tillman, pp. 154–5.
3. The memorandum was issued as a booklet in French and English. A copy is available at the Archives de la Société des Nations (hereafter ASDN) in Geneva: 41/9956/9956; R:1655. The English text is published by Viefhaus, pp. 228–31.
4. Herbert, pp. 42–3; Zaleski, pp. 29 ff.
5. Feinberg, pp. 96 ff. The characteristic documents of the emerging system, particularly useful from the point of view of interpretation, were published in

an official edition of the League of Nations, see Société des Nations, *Journal Officiel* (hereafter *JO*). Supplément Spécial, 73 (1929).

6. The English version is quoted in, for example, Modeen (1969), pp. 157–60.
7. *Annuaire de la SdN 1920–27*, pp. 435–6; Korowicz (1924), pp. 13–16.
8. *JO I Assemblée, Séances Plénières*, p. 569.
9. ASDN: 41/8861/7727; R: 1647 Mantoux's opinion, 29 November 1920.
10. ASDN: 41/8861/ 7727: R: 1647. Lucien Wolf to Mantoux, Geneva, 5 December 1920.
11. Sierpowski (1984b), pp. 154 ff.
12. ASDN, Fonds: Paul Mantoux, P: 31, note of 17 March 1920.
13. ASDN, Fonds: Paul Mantoux, P: 31, Sir Eric Drummond's note on a copy of a letter to F. Nansen, Geneva, 12 October 1922.
14. ASDN: 2/32279/31152 P. Azcarate's note of a conversation with H. Morgenthau, 8 November 1923.
15. *JO III Assembleé, Séances Plénières* pp. 185–6.
16. *JO* 1920, annex 115, pp. 142–4; *Protection des minorités de langue*, pp. 13–15. An extensive discussion on the issues is excellently illustrated by the archival materials of ASDN: R: 1647.
17. ASDN: 41/15713/1316; R: 1644, H. Rosting to Sir Eric Drummond, 19 October 1921.
18. *JO* 1923, pp. 1291 ff.
19. *Die Völkerbund Petitionen*, p. 9, Kimmich, p. 139.
20. *Protection des minorités de langue*, p. 233, Korowicz (1938), pp. 140 ff.
21. Ranshofen–Wertheimer, pp. 95–104, 241, 286, 356 ff.
22. Gütermann, pp. 348–9.
23. Mouton, pp. 95–104.
24. ASDN: S: 338 P. Azcarate to Sir Eric Drummond, 31 March 1930.
25. ASDN: 41/10702/9829: R: 1648 L. Motzkin to Sir Eric Drummond, Paris, 26 January 1921. For the sake of brevity, the activities of many international organisations have been omitted here, even though they influenced the work of the League of Nations as regards minorities' issues. However, the problem is worth noting here, in particular in connection with the fact that the exponents of those organisations often expressed the same opinions or wishes in various bodies of the League as the official representatives of Great Britain, South Africa, or Hungary, for example Sir Willoughby Dickinson, Gilbert Murray, Robert Cecil, Arthur Brown, Albert Apponyi. According to the minorities' section of the Secretariat, at the end of 1926 the following organisations dealt with the minorities' issue from a protective point of view: *Union Interparlementaire*, International Law Association, Women's International League for Peace and Freedom, *Conseil International des Femmes*, Royal (British) Institute of International Affairs, *Union Catholique d'Etudes Internationales*, *Union Pan-Européenne*, *Union Universelle des Etudiants Juifs*, *Alliance Israélite Universelle*, Joint Foreign Committee of the Jewish Board of Deputies. ASDN; S: 338 (*Second Rapport sur les activités des organisations privées dans le domaine des questions relatives aux minorités*, p. 44).
26. ASDN: S: 399 (*Liste des documents du Conseil et de l'Assemblée*).
27. *JO VII Assemblée, Séances Plénières*, p. 71.
28. ASDN: S: 399 (*Liste des documents du Conseil et de l'Assemblée*).
29. *JO* 1923, pp. 717–18.
30. Kimmich, pp. 77 ff; Sierpowski (1986), pp. 17 ff, 75 ff.
31. *JO* 1925, pp. 878–9.
32. *JO* 1929, pp. 516–19.
33. *JO Sup. Spéc.* 73/1929, pp. 43–86.

34. ASDN: 41/23094/7727; R:1648 Th. Adelswärd to Sir Eric Drummond, Vienna, 22 August 1922.
35. *JO IX Assemblée, Séances Plénières*, pp. 68 ff.
36. *JO VI Assemblée, Séances Plénières*, pp. 77, 105–6, 396.
37. *JO* 1926, pp. 139–44.
38. ASDN: S: 338, Azcarate to Sir Eric Drummond, 26 April 1929.
39. ASDN: 41/50210/7333: R: 1670.
40. *JO* 1933, pp. 930 ff; Fink, pp. 350–7.
41. *JO XIX Assemblée, Séances Plénières*, pp. 46, 51.
42. Walters, p. 440.
43. *Völkerbund* 75, 20 October 1933, pp. 7 ff; Sierpowski (1983a), pp. 33–6.
44. *JO XV Assemblée, Séances Plénières* pp. 42–3; Michowicz, pp. 71 ff.
45. Veatch, p. 380.
46. ASDN: 13/10634/3243; R: 5177.
47. ASDN: 41/35552/6590; R: 1647 (H. Rosting's note).
48. Zarnowski, p. 228.
49. ASDN: S: 399 (*Liste des documents du Conseil et de l'Assemblée*).
50. Gütermann, p. 346.
51. Korowicz, pp. 169 ff; extensive materials: ASDN: 4/27684/922 and 4/39943/922.
52. Sierpowski (1984a), pp. 193–7; 207–10.

Select Bibliography

Bibliographical Note

The latest bibliographical handbook concerning the League of Nations, compiled by Ghebali, lists the studies on racial, religious and linguistic minorities. It amounts to 500 titles of books as well as articles in some leading periodicals. A detailed analysis of this work demonstrates, above all, a great interest in national minorities' issues between the wars. However, the author of the bibliography was not so successful in seeking out the more recent works on the involvement of the League of Nations in minorities' issues. In order to illustrate the vastness of this phenomenon, one can take the example of contemporary Polish historiography, scarcely mentioned in the bibliography in question. Yet a Polish bibliography on minorities in the period between the wars would probably include about 1000 items.

An analogous technique applied to the majority of national historiographies, especially of the so-called minority states, would result in comparable conclusions. At the same time, the national historiographies (not to mention journalism, so abundant in that respect), have frequently been compiled under the pressure of self-interested arguments and of past experiences generally bad. Taking into account the above-mentioned factors, one has to go back to the original sources which, most exhaustively and most adequately, reflect the activity of the League of Nations as regards minorities' protection.

Archival investigations at the Archives de la Société des Nations in Geneva were largely facilitated and partly directed by earlier explorations, particularly thorough in the case of Marie–Renée Mouton and Christoph Gütermann. The author has analysed, in particular, the materials of the Bureau (au cabinet) du Secrétaire général and of the sections of Administrative Committees and Minorities, as well as of the Information Section, Political Section, the personnel office, and the so-called 'Fonds privés', including the documents of Drummond, Avenol, and Mantoux, as well as the archives of the International Federation of League of Nations Societies.

Annuaire de la Société des Nations (1927–1938), Geneva.

Barros, J. (1968), *The Aland Islands Question: its Settlement by the League of Nations*, New Haven and London.

Barros, J. (1979), *Office without Power: Secretary-General Sir Eric Drummond 1919–1933*, Oxford.

Birn, D.S. (1981), *The League of Nations Union 1918–1945*, Oxford.

Feinberg, N. (1929), *La question des minorités à la Conférence de la paix de 1919–20 et l'action juive en faveur de la protection internationale des minorités*, Paris.

Fink, C. (1972), Defender of Minorities: Germany in the League of Nations, *Central European History*, vol. 4.

Ghebali, V.Y. (1980), *Bibliographical handbook on the League of Nations*, 3 vols, Geneva.

Gütermann, Ch. (1979), *Das Minderheitenschutzverfahren des Völkerbundes*, Berlin.

Herbert, K. (1927), *Das Recht der Minderheiten*, Berlin.

Iljuchina, R.M. (1982), *Liga Nacij, 1919–1934*, Moscow.

Jonca, K. (1984), 'Trzecia Rzesza wobec problemu ochrony mniejszości narodowych 1933–1941', in Czubiński, A. (ed.), *Rola mniejszości niemieckiej w rozwoju stosunków politycznych w Europie w latach 1918–1945*, Poznań, pp. 407–18.

Kimmich, Ch.M. (1976), *Germany and the League of Nations*, Chicago.

Korowicz, M.St. (1938), *Górnoślaska ochrona mniejszości 1922-1937*, Katowice.

Korowicz, M.St. (1924), *The League of Nations and Minorities*, Geneva.

Lebiediev, N.I. (1978), *Wielikij Oktjabr i pierestrojka miezdunarodnych otnoszenij*, Moscow.

Lee, M.M. (1974), Failure in Geneva. The German Foreign Ministry and the League of Nations 1926–1933, PhD., University of Wisconsin.

Levin, N.G. (jr) (1968), *Woodrow Wilson and World Politics. America's Response to War and Revolution*, New York.

Michowicz, W. (1963), *Walka dyplomacji polskiej przeciwko traktatowi mniejszościowemu w Lidze Narodów w 1934 r*, Łódź.

Modeen, T. (1969), *The International Protection of National Minorities in Europe*, Åbo.

Modeen, T. (1970), 'The Situation of the Finland–Swedish Population in the Light of International, Constitutional and Administrative Law', *McGill Law Journal*, vol. 16.

Most, E. (1981), *Grossbritannien und der Völkerbund. Studien zur Politik der Friedenssicherung 1925 bis 1934*, Frankfurt.

Mouton, M.R. (1969), La Société des Nations et la protection des minorités. Exemple de la Transylvanie, 1920–1928, unpublished thesis, University of Grenoble.

La protection des minorités de langue, de race et de religion par la Société des Nations (1931), Geneva.

Ranshofen–Wertheimer, E.F. (1945), *The International Secretariat. A Great Experiment in International Administration*, Washington.

Sharp, A. (1978), 'Britain and the Protection of Minorities at the Paris Peace Conference 1919', in Hepburn, A.C. (ed.), *Minorities in History*.

Sierpowski, S. (1984a), 'Les dilemmes à la Société des Nations au sujet des minorités', *Polish Western Affairs*, 2.

Sierpowski, S. (1983a), 'Germany's Withdrawal from the League of Nations', *Polish Western Affairs*, 1.

Sierpowski, S. (1986), *Mniejszości narodowe jako instrument polityki miedzynarodowej 1919–1939*, Poznań.

Sierpowski, S. (1983b), 'Le mouvement de soutien à la Société des Nations', *Acta Poloniae Historica*, 48.

Sierpowski, S. (1984b), *Narodziny Ligi Narodów. Powstanie, organizacja i zasady działania*, Poznań.

Spenz, J. (1966), *Die diplomatische Vorgeschichte des Beitritts Deutschlands zum Völkerbund 1924–1926*, Göttingen.

Tillman, S.P. (1961), *Anglo–American Relations at the Paris Peace Conference of 1919*, Princeton, New Jersey.

Veatch, R. (1983), 'Minorities and the League of Nations', in *The League of Nations in retrospect*, Berlin.

Viefhaus, E. (1960), *Die Minderheitenfrage und die Entstehung der Minderheitenschutzverträge auf der Pariser Friedenskonferenz 1919*, Würzburg.

Die Völkerbundpetitionen der Minderheiten und ihre Behandlung. Eine Zusammenstellung (1929), Berlin.

Walters, F.P. (1965), *A History of the League of Nations*, Oxford.

Zaleski, W. (1932), *Miedzynarodowa ochrona mniejszości*, Warsaw.

Zarnowski, J. (1986), 'Polska a miedzynarodowy system ochrony mniejszości 1919–1934', in Sierpowski, S. (ed.), *Studia z najnowszej historii Niemiec i stosunków polsko-niemieckich*, Poznań.

3 European Jewry 1860–1919: Political Organisation and Trans-state Political Action

DAVID VITAL

I

The present topic is one of particular complexity. In certain major respects the history and structure of European Jewry were (and remain) unique, amenable to analysis in the categories commonly applied to the history and structure of other European nations only with difficulty, if at all. On the central question of whether national political organisation and action were either feasible or desirable there has been no consensus even within Jewry itself; nor has there been any way in which what was once termed a 'national decision' on such a question could be taken. Yet the slow, uncertain, often unpopular rise of a modern Jewish national and political tendency across the borders of existing states that marks the history of the Jewish people in the period in question and the further history and consequence of that tendency have manifestly been among the chief forces for change in Jewry down to our own times.

Accordingly, the topic which it is proposed to explore may perhaps be most usefully defined as that of the interplay between the rise of this modern national tendency in Jewry and the evolution of the forms of political (or near political) organisation and action that were available to European Jews and actually adopted. It is characteristic of this interplay that it comprised an element of choice. In general, it may be said in this connection, that even a cursory examination of the nation as a social and political structure and of nationalism as a social and political dynamic suggests that these are rarely, if at all, entirely natural and spontaneous – as opposed to invented and artificial – phenomena. In an important sense and to an important degree they tend to be manmade: at least partly products of design such that, if they are to occur, and of necessity if they are to succeed, there must be more or less deliberate encouragement and nurturing of them by interested parties. The rise and fall of nations and the waxing and waning of nationalist tendencies, moods and movements, far from being part of some primordial human order on a par with the family or clan or tribe, are likely to be at least part-products of special and explicit thought, purposeful social action, and organised, institution-alised arrangements.

In this respect, at least, it is thus well in accord with the general pattern that the distinctive – and in many ways crucial – component of modern Jewish nationalism has been the political. Insignificant, virtually invisible, in the early period of the modern era (say, the first decades of the nineteenth century), it took on ever more formidable proportions as the modern national tendency gathered force. Indeed, so much so was this the case that it is not too much to argue that modern Jewish nationalism, at its most powerful, most characteristic, and most important as regards its role in Jewish society and its cumulative impact on the history of the Jews, is political before all else. Equally, it is by the assimilation of political categories into its thinking and the adoption of political modes in its action – and all for the attainment of explicitly political purposes – that modern Jewish nationalism has been rendered unmistakably modern and a fresh stage in Jewish history for which no precedents or analogue can be discerned, at any rate since the onset of the Exile was ushered in. However, where the modern national tendency in Jewry and specifically Jewish political action have differed markedly from such tendencies and activities in and on behalf of other non-dominant ethnic groups in nineteenth and twentieth century Europe has been in the fact that it is action in the trans-state context that has chiefly characterised it and best provided for its articulation.

The terms 'political' and 'national' are, of course, notoriously loose. But it is plain that in the present context, namely that of Jewish public life, they point to a distinction that may properly be drawn between, on the one hand, the intercessionary activity of self-appointed notables on behalf of their own communities or on behalf of its individual members; and, on the other hand, action by supra-communal groups on behalf of particular communities or of some publicly proclaimed, supra-communal, and therefore, by still clearer implication, national (but in terms of formal status and citizenship trans-national), interest. In the former case, the interest or cause would tend to be specific and limited in scope and relevance. In the latter case, the scope and relevance would necessarily be wider by reason of the mode of action adopted, but still more by reason of the supra-communal function assumed by the activists concerned.

Such a function would entail the understanding that action by Jews for Jews was legitimate regardless of the formal, legally defined nationality of those involved, notwithstanding certain matters of principle that would unfailingly arise. In what way, for example, if any at all, should such trans-state or cross-national action be limited? Were there causes that might not properly be adopted and promoted, or circumstances (as in wartime) in which otherwise legitimate causes might not, in practice, be pursued? What means, methods and resources might properly and usefully be mobilised in such supra-communal interests? What levers of influence and pressure might be wielded? What ought or ought not to be done in a particular cause if due regard was to be paid to the safety and well being of Jewish individuals and communities not directly concerned with it? Who might properly represent Jewry in any such supra-communal causes; who not? How ought such causes to be defined? To what degree and in what circumstances, if any, did individual Jews, let alone communal leaders and functionaries, owe a form of allegiance or loyalty, to say nothing of obedience, to such representatives?

All these general issues, together with questions and dilemmas specific to time and place, arose ineluctably with the shift from mere private intercession (by local Jewish notables before the authorities on behalf of their brethren: *shtadlanut*) to public, representative political action. The sharper the shift, the sharper the issues. The rise of an overtly national, politically orientated movement in Jewry necessarily posed them with special force for it confronted the Jews (in ways that they had not known for centuries) with the twin issues of authority and power. Who was to speak for the Jews? What was such a spokesman to say? How far could he bind them as he treated with other forces in the political arena? These were questions to which an invertebrate Jewry was incapable of providing clear answers, nor was it really required to do so. Only the attempt to graft a political, necessarily trans-state structure on the body of Jewry rendered them urgent, the establishment of such a structure being both the *conditio sine qua non* (fundamental requirement) of Jewish national political life and the initial tactical aim to which all who sought political authority and power in Jewry had necessarily to strive.

II

It is in this light that the early forms of 'Jewish diplomacy' are most usefully seen. 'Jewish diplomacy' is a tricky and in some ways misleading term: it may be taken to suggest organisation and system where in fact there were none. But it has been favoured by many students of the subject and has the advantage of drawing attention to what it chiefly and correctly denotes, namely action by groups and individuals whose base is in one country, directed at the authorities in another. To this there must be added two provisos. One is that the subject of the action be one of genuine public, not private, importance and that it concern the status, welfare, or safety of Jews defined as such; that it deal, in effect, with some aspect of what was commonly known in the nineteenth century and the first half of the twentieth as the 'Jewish problem'. The second is that those undertaking the action be able and willing to bring some form of pressure or influence to bear on the foreign government in question and that it is this pressure which is at the base of whatever change of policy or conduct ensues. It is thus that the action is rendered *political* even where the spirit and intention behind it are benevolent and philanthropic. Of course, in practice, the line distinguishing such political or 'diplomatic' action from the ancient forms of philanthropic intercession was rarely clearcut. In some cases it may be seen to have dissolved. In others, on the other hand, the will and ability to exert pressure – to induce one government to act against another, to mobilise economic resources for use as either carrot or stick, to rouse public opinion – were unprecedented in their frank and overt character and the confidence displayed by those who sought to bring such classic instruments of public policy to bear. Moreover, increasingly, the purpose of the campaign tended to be broader than a remedy for the specific case of persecution or injustice which (as commonly happened) had been its precipitant. As often as not, there was a larger purpose, namely to induce fundamental and lasting change in the condition of the Jewish community or communities on behalf of which the activists sought to act.

Like the old forms of private, local, intercession the new political or diplomatic action was action by the fortunate in the interests of the unfortunate. Unlike those forms, it was founded less on intracommunal inequality of condition than on intercommunal inequality, namely on the ever more striking differences between the condition and status of Jews in some countries as opposed to those obtaining in others. The phenomenon in itself was a remarkable product of the civil emancipation, the economic achievements, the rapid casting off of old habits of thought and conduct and, more generally, the vast growth in self-confidence which marked the upper and middle levels of Jewish society in central and western Europe and north America at this time.

The contrast with their fellows in other parts of the world, notably in eastern Europe and the Islamic lands, was in fact plain to see. The spectacle of endemic squalor and persecution barely mitigated by slow and unwilling reform and scattered islands of well being was painful to all but the entirely insensitive and unthinking. It was thus

not unnatural that it was from the ranks of those who, in their social
and economic achievements and their concomitant rise in status in
both the public at large and the Jewish communities to which they (if
only nominally) belonged, had gone furthest (and so, in their persons
and careers best epitomised the transformation of western Jewry)
that the leading activists tended to come. Political action in this form
was therefore typically action by the *notables* of Jewry: the very
wealthy and the very grand, the statesmen and the politicians in the
lands of their residence and adoption, the leaders of the new,
essentially secular Jewish institutions which were taking shape in all
the countries in question, and finally, if more rarely, the men of
letters (in the language of their country) and the established
academics.

These notables were to all intents and purposes self-selected. At
best, they were representatives of self-selected, self-perpetuating
oligarchies. The crucial sources of their authority within Jewry and
their capacity to lead and speak for it lay in their position and function
in the larger non-Jewish world. Some had been formally elected to
leading positions in such quasi-representative institutions as the
Board of Deputies in London and the *Consistoire Central* (Central
Council) in Paris. Such election commonly, however, hinged on their
attainments in the economy, or in politics, or in the professions, or in
the press – generally, in society at large. Moreover, by a paradox such
notables seem rarely to have been aware of, their ability to act in a
Jewish interest turned on their status in the non-Jewish world in the
further respect that a great deal depended on the willingness of what
might be termed the target government to treat with them; and that
too was usually a function of their status in the non-Jewish world.
Scope for action and room for maneouvre were therefore always
limited. Sights were necessarily kept low. Prudence, discretion, and
incrementalism were the watchwords by which the enterprise was
invariably governed. Accordingly, the more specific the case, the less
typical or the more unusual the injustice, the more easily (relatively
speaking) was it remedied and the fewer eggs needed breaking in the
process. For then the resistance of governments to such action was
more easily softened and, above all, the limits of such power as the
notables of western Jewry did possess need never be reached and
tested and the true poverty of the political resources at their disposal
never exposed.

It is thus that the Damascus Affair of 1840 (action by a group of
socially and politically prominent French and English Jews on behalf
of members of a small community in the Levant falsely charged with
ritual murder) was for many years the textbook case of successful
action on behalf of unfortunates caught up in a tangle of what was
ultimately hardly more than localised intrigue. Rightly, it was

accounted an important precedent for 'cross-national' cooperation by Jewish notables from a variety of countries. It led, in time to the first modern, trans-national Jewish organisation, the *Alliance Israélite Universelle* (Universal Israelite Alliance). But it also exemplified the limits of what such cooperating notables might usefully aim at. Thus minor alleviation of the pre-First World War condition of Romanian Jews was possible from time to time by pressure through London by the Conjoint Foreign Committee (of the two most important institutions of Anglo–Jewry, the Board of Deputies and the Anglo–Jewish Association), but not lasting reform of their status.

As for the distress of Russo–Polish Jewry, it was too deep, too extensive and too bound up with the underlying ethos and structure of Russia's government and society in what was, after all, one of the world's great powers, for such modes of action to hold out real hope of change in the condition and status of the Jews in question as a direct consequence of such Jewish political action. The western Jewish notables, even when they had the ear of the Russian statesmen, even when they threatened, or actually exerted, economic pressure, were confronted with a task that was entirely beyond their power to deal with and to which their techniques, in the final analysis, were irrelevant. Indeed, it could be (and, in the event, was) argued that caution, discretion, incrementalism, seeking to operate behind the scenes and wherever possible through the official channels available to other governments, only compounded the failure. Even, it could be that such prudential modes inhibited the employment of resources and techniques that could have been more effective; and that they could not but ultimately undermine the authority of the notables within Jewry itself, thereby gradually clearing the way for more radical tendencies and bolder spirits to move to the fore.

On the other hand, it may, in retrospect, be seen that even failure had its uses in that it left a mark on all concerned. The refusal by the New York financier Jacob Schiff to join his non-Jewish colleague Morgan in the launching of the great Anglo–French loan during the First World War unless Russia, wartime ally of the British and the French, softened its anti-Jewish policy – or, alternatively, itself derived no benefit from the loan – led nowhere directly. The condition Schiff had set was not one the Entente powers could comply with. But it tended to confirm in the minds of the western governments the importance of Jewish opinion and the need to take account of it – which is what they did in the last years of the war and in its immediate aftermath.

Be that as it may, the western notables of Jewry themselves were caught in a fundamental contradiction. It stemmed from the fact, already alluded to, that both the basis of their authority within Jewry, such as it was, and the basis of their power, such as it was, to act in the Jewish interest, were in all decisive respects external to Jewry itself. If this was so in real terms; so too was it nominally – which is to say, that it was crucial to their position and central to their own private perception of it, that they were not only Jews but equally English-men, Frenchmen, Germans, Americans and so forth. The interests of their own governments had therefore certainly to be respected and that respect had to be demonstrated. Cooperation with parallel Jewish bodies in countries with which their own happened to be in conflict was necessarily inhibited.

The fate of the *Alliance Israélite Universelle* as a comprehensive trans-state Jewish institution, rather than *de facto* as not only Paris based, but of distinctly French orientation, was sealed by the Franco–Prussian War and the long aftermath of Franco–German hostility. The range of contact and coordination with the Jewish communities and communal leaders in the target countries, none of them free and open societies, could not but be restricted and dealings with local leaders treated as a matter of great delicacy. The reper-cussions that action taken in a target country might have in their own had always to be taken into account as well. Accordingly, the arguments for non-interference and inaction were always strong, so strong, indeed, that it is, if anything, the determination of these public spirited notables – hardly typical of their own class as such in their high conception of where their duty lay – that needs explaining. Many seem to have been burdened by the fear that the failure of Jews in one part of the world to make progress in civil society put the success of those who had achieved formal equality with non-Jews elsewhere at risk. Evidently, some were moved by an exceptionally strong sense of *noblesse oblige*. But it remains a factor that the very elements of their situation which made 'diplomatic' action on their part possible, and on some occasions very effective, ruled them out as candidates for the true national, political leadership of Jewry, and as managers of thoroughgoing political action on behalf of the Jewish people as such. But of course, they did not seek such a role. It would have had to be founded on full identification with the Jewish people defined in explicitly national terms and upon the view that it was their collective interests that were paramount. That would have been thoroughly inconsistent with the position, status and interests to which they cleaved.

III

The failure of the philanthropically minded notables of western Jewry to come to grips with the 'Jewish problem' in its acute, eastern

European form and context was therefore twofold. Its daunting scale rendered them incapable of coping with the problem in its material aspects; and the ambiguities of their own situation, along with their reluctance to put their own, and their fathers', achievements in the west itself at risk, rendered them incapable of fully grasping it intellectually. The Jewish problem seen as a national problem was not one they could cope with, or for that matter, could wish to recognise. Nor was the segment of Jewry chiefly in question, in practice the Jews of eastern Europe, a group or class which, at least on the face of things, they were suited to lead. They were too remote, culturally no less than geographically. Least of all did they desire to assume the leadership and its responsibility. The field was therefore open to very different and – having regard to the forms of public action that had been customary in Jewry until very modern times – entirely novel types of claimants to leadership, influence, authority, responsibility. These emerged on the basis, broadly, of two distinct and mutually exclusive platforms or approaches.

One approach conceded that ascriptive national characteristics as commonly understood (historical, cultural, linguistic, etc.) were indeed of the greatest importance, virtually indelible, and in certain carefully defined respects benign; but held that they were none the less subordinate both in weight and value to class characteristics and class differences. It was the latter that were cardinal. It was in socio-economic terms, before all else, that the problem of the Jews must be understood and tackled. The Jews of eastern Europe, in the mass, were seen as sharing the common lot of the other peoples, in the mass. They were therefore bound both by condition and, so to speak, duty to make common cause with them. Such a duty entailed joining in the effort to establish a new political and social order everywhere, but first and foremost at the centre of Jewish demographic gravity, in Russia. In effect, it was their duty to help promote revolution.

A call such as this, unreservedly to inject the Jews into the bodies politic of the countries of their domicile was, of course, totally at variance with the ancient, accepted norms of Jewish practice in the Exile. Equally, it ran counter to all that Jewish notables, both within Russia and outside it, had consistently stood for, whether as a matter of political principle or out of regard for their respective private interests. Still, the Russian Jewish revolutionaries had at least this in common with the notables, that, if not fully loyal and obedient children of the Emancipation, they were at least believers in its central message. There is a sense in which they were no less faithful than their more fortunate brethren in the west to the propositions that, subject to certain reforms, the Jews could and should stay put. The idea was that despite everything they were, and could probably remain, legitimate and acceptable constituents of the states and societies to which they currently belonged. Finally the feeling was that the operation to be performed on the bodies politic of imperial Russia, Romania, and Austria–Hungary respectively should be, so far as they, the Jews, were concerned, therapeutic and rehabilitatory in character, not surgical. Amputation was not necessary; the thinking of those who prescribed it was perverse.

The second approach was in some respects more radical, in others more conservative. Its conservatism lay in its acceptance of national distinctions and divisions in general and the national distinctiveness of the Jews in particular as being primary. In this respect it accorded easily with traditional Jewish notions, self-images, and social practice. It was radical in that it both dismissed as illusory the prospect of incremental improvement for all Jews which the western Emancipation had been held to offer and, at the same time, regarded their contemporary condition as, if not intolerable in practice, then certainly insufferable in principle. The Jews might have to remain in their Exile a while longer. Disgracefully, some might – some evidently would – prefer it. Certainly, the extraction of the Jews in great numbers from that Exile would be an immense undertaking and their resettlement elsewhere, under an entirely fresh, purpose designed social and political regime, would absorb vast resources of energy, money and time. Yet it was in that direction and to such purposes that the Jews should aim. All other plans and ideas were doomed to collapse and failure.

It may be said of this latter approach that no other was founded on so scrupulous and hard headed a reading of the map of Jewish history and on so comprehensive a view of the Jewish condition. Nor did any other approach seek to take so fully into account as this one did the nature and inner logic of the hatred the surrounding people bore for the Jews, the ease with which it could be manipulated politically, and its eternally erupting consequences. Neither did any other approach present as one of its chief claims to acceptance the offer to gain for the Jews a restored dignity – or even regard their individual and collective dignities as matters of high concern. Nor, finally, did any other seek, however hesitantly at first, to provide the basis for a wholly fresh relationship with other nations, in its view, the only one worth having, namely one of equality: equality of status and equality of esteem. Here, then, was an approach to the matter of the Jews that was in all important and accepted senses of the term *national* – but, seen against the background of the existing state system, trans-national or trans-state.

Both tendencies held that a change of direction was vital, a fact that stood them in good stead in the continuing fight for the hearts and minds of the impoverished, set-upon Jews of eastern Europe, ever more sceptical of the old verities and the old style communal leadership. The class oriented, socialist, revolutionary creed and parties – notably in the explicitly Marxist form and as embodied in the *Bund* (the 'General Jewish Workers' Union in Lithuania, Poland and Russia', closely connected, at times allied in these years with the Russian Social Democratic Workers' Party) – had the edge for many years. Seemingly, its business was more obviously and convincingly with the here and now of Jewish life. In contrast, the out-and-out nationalists could be made to appear as mere visionaries: over ambitious, over pessimistic, over demanding, and over critical in turn. But it was evident at the time, and is clearly so in retrospect, that it was they, that is, the Zionists, who alone of all tendencies in Jewry embodied the national principle in what can properly be termed its modern form – shorn, or virtually so, of all religious content, without overt qualification, with little or no mental reservation. It is accordingly they alone who were disposed to turn their minds seriously to a reforming of Jewry on the basis of authentic national institutions and through uninhibited, unashamed national (and therefore implicitly trans-state) political action.

IV

Hibbat Zion, the early form of Zionism – proto-Zionism, as it can be termed – contained many of the germs of Zionism proper. Central to the proto-Zionist outlook, as later to that of Zionism proper, was the conviction that the Jews must save themselves, by their own efforts, and that their needs and interests differed in important respects from those of other peoples. This did not mean that the interests and needs of Jews and non-Jews could not be rendered compatible and a *modus vivendi* between them devised. It did mean that there had first to be a thoroughgoing change in the condition and status of the Jews, a change that the Jews themselves must plan and execute themselves. Only then would there occur a change of heart on all sides and a more serene chapter in the history of tormented Jewry be ushered in.

The nub of the matter was the isolation and homelessness of the Jews, a hopelessly invertebrate body of people scattered in pockets great and small, incapable of defending themselves against the continual attack on their security and dignity to which they were subject – and to which, in the very nature of things, they would continue to be subject so long as they differed so markedly from all other nations, notably those among whom they resided in particularly large numbers. If both dignity and safety were to be restored they must have their own country. This last was an absolute condition. Its attainment was conditional, in turn, on organisation. There must be a means of mobilising the by no means negligible human and material resources of the Jews. There must be national leadership. There must be constructed the instruments whereby decisions and action could be taken in the common national cause and to the common end. More generally, the salvation of the Jews would not follow automatically upon the salvation of other peoples and other social classes if that was ever brought about; and it was an error to pin one's faith on the steady march of liberal ideas from west and north to east and south. The problem of the Jews was a particular and peculiar one. It required a particular and peculiar solution. None but the Jews themselves could or would seek it. The principle to which everything boiled down was self-help. From its adoption all good things would flow: material improvement, a cultural renaissance, dignity, equality, safety.

Taken together, these views and principles of conduct formed the basis for a national policy; and there was implied within them a programme that was political in goal and method. But the founders and leaders of *Hibbat Zion* never moved very far along the lines of thought and action which they had begun to sketch and on which they seemed, at first flush, to have embarked. At its most characteristic, namely as conceived and led by Leon Pinsker and his associates in southern Russia in the 1880s and early 1890s, *Hibbat Zion* had little by way of institutional cement or resources to keep it together and on a firm and purposeful path of any kind. Throughout the some 15 years in which it occupied the modernist–nationalist stage virtually unchallenged it remained a loosely bound, imperfectly articulated association of (autonomous) associations. The ideological lead was vague. The concrete targets in view were severely limited: encouragement, on a very small scale and in a low key, of the return of Jews to *Erez–Israel* (Palestine) and, with rather more verve and determination, their resettlement there in farming villages.

However the scale was so extremely modest, the resources available so disproportionate (even with the munificent help of Edmond de Rothschild) to the crushing material distress and concomitant social ills and afflictions of the Jewish communities chiefly in question, that the latter could scarcely be affected by anything *Hibbat Zion* might accomplish in real terms and on the ground. Morever, the venture, small as it was, was at continual risk because of the declared and generally active hostility of the Turkish authorities. Fear of a Turkish decision to act decisively against them was therefore a continual inducement to the *Hovevei Zion* both in Europe and in *Erez–Israel* to walk very softly and to be less than frank – and indeed less than clear even in their own minds – about their ultimate aims. Another was the objection maintained by the Russian autocracy as a matter of governmental principle to organised supracommunal action of any kind by Jews in Russia, even though action by Jews in respect of the resettlement of their people in *Erez–Israel* (as the Russian bureaucracy itself eventually realised) was in no sense subversive of the regime. The external brakes on thought and action were thus severe. Hope of providing an alternative to stagnation and impending disaster could never be better than dim.

On the other hand, the argument for political action was becoming ever more solid in both its possible modes and arenas: firstly, in the 'diplomatic' form directed at the two governments, the Russian and the Ottoman, with a view to inducing them to alter policy. Secondly, the argument existed in the common form of politics, that is to say within Jewry itself, with a view to the indoctrination and mobilisation of the Jewish community in eastern Europe. The two modes and arenas of action would of course always be connected functionally. Failure to gain the Russian government's support for, or at the very least its acquiescence in, the Jewish national cause so defined made it virtually impossible to mobilise recruits to it in large numbers. Failure to gain the favour of the government in Turkey left this particular school of national–political action without a credible target to aim at. Failure to mobilise a sufficiently large number of recruits for the national cause entailed, in turn, a double loss. This was the failure to achieve the status of a public authority and power within Jewry and a concomitant failure to establish the movement as one with which the governments in question might finally judge they had good reason to treat.

Yet this, the case for political action, was never put with force and *Hibbat Zion* did no better than seek to break out of the vicious circle in the old manner, namely by enlisting the notables of western Jewry. It would be in the hands of the latter that the effective political leadership of the movement, if there was ever to be such, would be placed. It would then be their responsibility to judge what could and could not be done; and it would be on their assets and resources, not on those of the mass of Jewry whose future was at issue and at stake, that success would depend. Indeed, had the invitation (embodied in Pinsker's original manifesto and repeated from time to time) been taken up in earnest, conceivably some small progress in very specific and immediate matters might have been made within the Ottoman domain. There might have been the easing of restrictions here, the turning of a blind eye there. But it was not taken up and, as the experience with Edmond de Rothschild demonstrated, even generous support on the ground, in *Erez–Israel* itself, for the settlements directly, tended to be granted at the cost of a certain circumscription of the movement's outlook and a narrowing of its ambition.

As for matters within Russia, overtly nationalist political activity there by and for a non-Russian people was, of course, impossible except underground; and action in clear defiance of the police was, for the solid citizens who made up the leading circles of *Hibbat Zion*, literally unthinkable. In any event, it would have been strongly opposed (and probably denounced) by the traditional religious and secular leadership of Russian Jewry had it been attempted. But perhaps of greater weight in accounting for the failure of the *Hovevei Zion* to strike out in the new direction with the determination and clarity of view that were characteristic of the very first stages of the movement was the inability of all concerned to shake themselves quite free of habits of thought which for centuries, by and large, can be found to have coloured the deeds and affirmations of all those who sought to lead their fellow Jews in matters pertaining to the public domain. These may be marked down as prudence (not to say timidity), a preference for the private and the discreet as opposed to the public and the inflammatory, and a sense of the fragility of one's position so deep as to verge at times on the incapacitating. More generally there was a certain dour, sceptical, even pessimistic, assuredly not unwise outlook which seemed always to have been lurking, as it were, in the recesses of the leaders' minds, but emerging as a swift corrective to anything that smacked of the bold, the sanguine, the radical. Thus in the abstract there was much in *Hibbat Zion* that was new. In practice, however, the clarity of their vision tended rapidly to be clouded over with many of the reservations and inhibitions that were characteristic of those who, unlike themselves, specifically and explicitly represented and fostered immobilism, supreme caution and none but incremental change. *Hibbat Zion*, in sum, verged on the political without ever assuming, even covertly or unwittingly, a true political character. Neither its declared purposes, not its methods, nor again its institutions, were political in spirit, let alone in substance. At best, this occurred only indirectly and in embryo. The reliance, at times explicit, at other times implicit, on the notables of western Europe was nothing if not retrogressive. None the less, *Hibbat Zion*'s role in the preparation of the ground for the rise of a national political movement in the full sense of the term was crucial.

The sources of this apparent paradox lie in the realm of ideology and its propagation. For it is certain that the effect of the rise of *Hibbat Zion* on the general climate of ideas in Jewish public life, while never decisive or dramatic, was a marked one. The local associations were weak, but such associations were formed, or coalesced, more or less spontaneously, in almost all the major Jewish centres, especially in the lands of Jewry's greatest distress. The fact that the movement was preponderantly middle class and moderately secularist (and there-fore, by the same token, composed of men and women who tended to have achieved a modest degree of integration into society at large) undoubtedly militated against radical action on their part. On the other hand this social composition helped enormously to propagate the idea of *Hibbat Zion* – above all the fundamental idea that there could be a clear, yet non-assimilatory alternative approach to the Jewish question – throughout the Jewish world, and with great rapidity. These were members of the reading and writing public *par excellence*, the Jewish intelligentsia, who, whatever may have been their shortcomings as men of action, were nothing if not able in the examination and manipulation of ideas. Thus by the time Zionism proper, under its foremost leader and virtual inventor, Theodor Herzl, burst on the scene in 1896–7, there was in being a class of people who were already attuned to many of its central tenets and willing to listen, at the very least, to arguments for a vastly more ambitious plan of campaign.

V

Herzl's programme was unique in that it was explicitly political. In its original form it argued for the establishment of a state; and even after a certain amount of watering down of this stated goal had occurred in the early stages of his movement it was still clear to all that political autonomy, that is to say Jewish self-government in some form, was an absolute requirement. The environment in which the Jewish national movement had necessarily to operate was seen by Herzl and the Herzlians as primarily political in character. The key forces populating it – the great powers – had necessarily to be engaged and treated within a political mode. The Jewish people, the Jewish 'masses', had to be mustered and led. An open, elected, representative assembly (the Zionist Congress, the first meeting of which was in 1897) in which the major issues before Jewry might be thrashed out and the broad outlines of national policy determined and an executive (the Actions Committee) elected by the Congress to function as a sort of provisional Jewish government were central to his plan. There was to be a bank as the movement's financial arm; and in due course newspapers, a publishing house, regular lines of communication between the movement's centre and its periphery, a central office to help implement policy and outlying missions to represent it.

Taken together, these were – in form, if not always in efficacy – the classic instruments of government and policy. There were no armed or police forces or other instruments of external or internal coercion. But otherwise the chief institutions, along with many of the common practices and routines of government, were planned and acquired within the first decade or so of the Zionist Organisation's history. There followed the major elements and forms of political life (in its parliamentary democratic mode) itself – albeit, once again, with the important exception of those hingeing, ultimately, on force and coercion. Parties evolved. Leadership was fought for. Office was sought and contested. Policy was debated. Votes were canvassed. Allies were courted. All these were in evidence well before the territory to which they were intended ultimately to be applicable was available even in theory and long before the independent state which they would, in some sense, embody was even on the horizon.

The importance of this rapid establishment of political structures, along with their successful articulation, was twofold. In the first place, an arena was established upon which the attention of all who subscribed to a modern form of Jewish nationalism was naturally concentrated. The effect of this was to encourage enormously sympathisers in all degrees and in all countries (though still preponderantly in eastern Europe). Secondly, by virtue of its Congress, its elections, and its other quasi-governmental (but trans-state) institutions and procedures, the Zionist movement gained for itself kinds of legitimacy and authority which no other Jewish institution or body could claim or could equal. As such, Zionism in its practice, no less than Zionism in its purposes, began to be seen as being better attuned to the needs and standards of the times than other, more traditional, if equally indigenous Jewish tendencies and movements. It was much more clearly part of the modern, forward looking world in which the 'nation' was rapidly replacing the 'church' (or God himself) as the source of final authority. It was a movement and a programme which foreign statesmen could readily understand and contemplate dealing with. In brief, it equipped the Jews with an instrument by means of which, if they so wished, their collective needs might be articulated and policy on their behalf laid down. Indeed, it is crucial to an understanding both of the opposition to Zionism within Jewry and of the immense change in the Jewish scene which Zionism was to precipitate, that it was at least as much the idea that such collective needs might be defined at all, and that general, *national* remedies might be pursued, that struck the contemporary mind – and struck it with enormous force – as the particular definitions and specific remedies the Zionists actually proposed.

In the final analysis, the success of the Zionist enterprise in these initial stages depended, before all else, on recognition by Jews and by others, the more so as the two varieties, or sources, of recognition were interdependent. The Zionists could not gain access to the arena of established international politics in which the decisive responses to their demands would be made, if they were to be made at all, by mere imposition. The forces regularly inhabiting that arena had first to recognise them as in some sense, if only for certain purposes, representative and effective spokesmen for the Jewish interest. The prior condition on which they depended for this was a degree, a fairly high degree, of acceptance within and by Jewry itself. At the same time their acceptance in and by Jewry as legitimate and suitable spokesman depended in turn, certainly in part, on the degree to which the governments and ruling circles inhabiting the larger world outside Jewry were prepared to treat with them. The Zionists, in brief, had somehow to pull themselves up by their own bootstraps. Their position – their capacity for action, in effect – hinged on a delicate structure of influence. This they were able to erect, sustain, and develop only because they alone among the public bodies active in the pre–1914 Jewish world were prepared to make the large, if not, on the face of it, pretentious claim to speak across frontiers for the Jewish people as a whole, having established at least a semblance of national authority and having sought actively to treat with several governments of the day on an explicitly political basis.

True, after the first ambitious spurt of energy and action there occurred a series of tactical retreats in matters of detail and a certain narrowing and reduction of aims and options. So it was under Herzl, so it was, and much more plainly, after Herzl's death in 1904. There then ensued a particularly long interval of weak leadership and uncertain tactics, second thoughts even on matters of principle, and a marked tendency to seek relief from the ever present prospect of failure in the undoubtedly absorbing, but always small scale settlement activities in *Erez–Israel*. By the eve of the First World War the thrust of the original Herzlian Zionism had so weakened that it may fairly be said that the movement was tending strongly towards the patterns of thought and action that had been characteristic of *Hibbat Zion* a generation earlier, which Herzl and his following had begun by rejecting. Even that famous disparagement of European liberalism and legal emancipation as putative sources of salvation for the Jews which had been common and fundamental to *Hibbat Zion* and political Zionism alike was failing to gain automatic assent as Zionist activists found themselves drawn into the internal politics of the lands of their domicile, notably in Russia and Austria. That the origins of these trends may be traced in part to lack of progress towards the goals of Zionism proper in *Erez–Israel* itself and in the international political arena where its fate – and perhaps that of the Jews generally – seemed likely to be played out served only to underline the seriousness of the decline. Yet despite the winds of disbelief that blew upon the new Jewish national flag in the years immediately subsequent to his death, it was never quite hauled down.

It may well be asked why this is so. What, after all, at the end of his day, had Herzl accomplished? His negotiations with the Ottoman government had been long and tortuous, but had led nowhere.

Ottoman hostility to the Zionist enterprise remained firm. If anything, it was clearer and stronger than before. His negotiations, and those of his successor David Wolffsohn, with the Russian government had provided some short-term relief for the Zionists in their pursuit of small scale, low key activities within the empire free of police persecution. However the promise of major political assistance and cooperation in Istanbul held out by the powerful Minister of the Interior Plehve in 1903 dissolved rapidly in the face of the ill will displayed in other sectors of the Russian administration and vanished altogether in the wake of Plehve's death by assassination in the following year.

The decidedly greater breakthrough achieved by Herzl in his negotiations with the British government – greater in that the promise was explicitly of a semi-autonomous region for the Jews, albeit in east Africa – led nowhere. Ferocious opposition within the Zionist movement itself had stopped it as condoning a decoupling of the principle that the solution to the problem of the Jews and to their distress must be territorial from its twin – namely, that the only territory the Zionists could legitimately consider was *Erez–Israel*. Lastly, while the hostility of some of the notables of western Jewry towards Zionism in general, and to Herzl and his most loyal followers in particular, had softened somewhat (the head of the house of Rothschild in England was an important case in point), it remained that hardly anything had come of Herzl's old plan of mobilising Jewish capital on behalf of the most urgent Jewish needs and in the collective Jewish interest.

Yet what remained of his legacy was cardinal. The Zionist institutions continued to function and were in being and in reasonably good working order when new men in new circumstances arose during the First World War and especially in its aftermath to make good use of them. The ideas of political Zionism remained alive and, what is more, lost much of their seeming improbability in the new circumstances consequent upon the upheavals of the war. In the crucial years 1915–19, they reemerged as ideas whose time had finally come – in the sense that they were beginning to be judged as they had never been judged before. In the sense also that arguably they made good social and political sense after all; that demonstrably they pointed to lines of policy and action in the near east that certain powers in the land (Great Britain in the first place, but to some extent the other Entente powers as well) were prepared to consider for their own national benefit; and that the Zionists were, for certain if admittedly limited purposes, useful partners.

In the new climate of opinion in which the collapse of old empires and time-worn political systems on the one hand, and the rise of renascent nations and new states on the other, were the rage it was the public and political (as opposed to the private and intercession-ary) approach to the dilemmas, predicaments and afflictions of the Jews that tended to win the ears of those who mattered most. That Zionism argued for a profound reform of Jewry both internally and in its external relations; and that it offered, or more precisely claimed to offer, a real and dramatic alternative to all that had gone and been attempted before – now stood it in good stead.

Zionism had from the first been a programme and a creed that was particularly and enormously attractive to those Jews who were hardest pressed and who, at the same time, in their social attributes and in their own minds were most clearly members of a Jewish nation – untroubled (or unaided), that is to say, by any separate, parallel national identity, or aspirations thereto, speaking a national language, living in fairly compact groups and in reasonably well defined areas. These were, or course, the Jews of eastern Europe. It was to them that these ideas had always had a natural appeal. And of all the categories and classes of Jews, it was they who were most prepared to countenance a radical cure to their predicament – much as it had been they, all along, as private individuals, who had been readiest to take the no less bold, near irreversible step of migrating overseas. It was now they who tended most strongly to recognise the Zionist organisation as their representative national movement. There were still serious competitors at hand, especially in the socialist camp, but also in that of religious orthodoxy. But none was now markedly stronger than they and none now appeared better qualified or more legitimate – least of all in the eyes of the Zionists themselves whose powerfully boosted self-confidence communicated itself to the great powers as never before and to great effect. The meaning of the incorporation of the Balfour Declaration in the League of Nations Mandate for Palestine was that it had been accepted in just such terms.

Select Bibliography

The bibliography that follows has been limited to published items that are fairly easily available and are, for the most part, in the English language. Specialist research, of which there is still a great need, requires the study of sources (secondary as well as primary) that are often obscure and in a variety of languages, of which Hebrew and Yiddish are probably the most important.

Borochov, Ber (1972), *Nationalism and the Class Struggle*, reprinted Westport, Conn.
Chouraqui, André (1965), *Cent ans d'histoire. L'Alliance Israélite Universelle et la renaissance juive contemporaine, 1860–1960*, Paris.
Dubnow, Simon (1970), *Nationalism and History: Essays on Old and New Judaism*, New York.
Ettinger, Shmuel (1976), 'The Modern Period', in Ben–Sasson H.H. (ed.), *A History of the Jewish People*, Cambridge, Mass.

Gelber, N.M. (1964), 'La question juive en Bulgarie et en Serbie devant le Congrès de Berlin de 1878', *Revue des Études juives*, CXXIII.

Hagen, William W. (1980), *Germans, Poles, and Jews; The Nationality Conflict in the Prussian East 1772–1914*, Chicago.

Iancu, Carol (1974), 'Adolphe Crémieux, l'Alliance Israélite Universelle et les Juifs de Roumanie', *Revue des Études juives*, CXXXIII.

Janowsky, Oscar I. (1933), *The Jews and Minority Rights*, New York.

Katz, Jacob (1973), *Out of the Ghetto; The Social Background of Jewish Emancipation 1770–1870*, Cambridge, Mass.

Katz, Jacob (1970), 'The Jewish National Movement; A Sociological Analysis', *Confrontation*, Jerusalem.

Lehman-Wilzig, Sam N. (1978), 'The House of Rothschild: Prototype of the transnational organization', *Jewish Social Studies*, XL.

Mallison, W.T. (1964), 'The Zionist–Israel juridical claims to constitute "The Jewish People" nationality entity and to confer membership in it: an appraisal in public international law', *George Washington Law Review*, XXXII, 5.

Poliakov, Leon (1985), *The History of Anti-Semitism, iv, Suicidal Europe 1870–1933*, Oxford.

Seton-Watson, Hugh (1977), *Nations and States*, London.

Stillschweig, Kurt (1944), 'Nationalism and Autonomy among eastern European Jewry: origin and historical development up to 1939', *Historia Judaica*, VI.

Szajkowski, Zosa (1942), 'The Alliance Israélite Universelle and east-European Jewry in the '60s', *Jewish Social Studies*, IV.

Szajkowski, Zosa (1957), 'Conflicts in the Alliance Israélite Universelle and the founding of the Anglo–Jewish Association, the Vienna Allianz and the Hilfsverein', *Jewish Social Studies*, XIX.

Szajkowski, Zosa (1960), 'Jewish diplomacy; notes on the occasion of the centenary of the Alliance Israélite Universelle', *Jewish Social Studies*, XXII.

Szajkowski, Zosa (1967), 'Paul Nathan, Lucien Wolf, Jacob H. Schiff and the Jewish revolutionary movements in eastern Europe 1903–1917', *Jewish Social Studies*, XXIX.

4   The Alsatians and the Alsace–Lorraine Question in European Politics, c. 1900–1925

PAUL SMITH

'All the same it's for Alsace–Lorraine that our soldiers are getting themselves killed. The Alsace–Lorrainers are the cause of the war.' The author and journalist Emile Hinzelin, who recorded these sentiments in Savoy in the middle of 1918,[1] was not the only agent of the French propaganda services reporting back from the provinces in the second half of the First World War that many Frenchmen and Frenchwomen saw the prolongation of the struggle, as well as its origin, as the fault of populations which they regarded as only dubiously French, or even – the Alsatians especially – as decidedly German. The question of Alsace–Lorraine, and more particularly of Alsace, whose 'Germanness' could be asserted with greater plausibility than was possible for much of Lorraine, revealed the ambiguities of the concept of nationality and the force of regionalist and particularist sentiment, and provided not only a point of conflict between France and Germany but also a stimulant, and perhaps an irritant, to their national consciousness. Moreover, as well as an obstacle to European peace, it supplied a test case for the European debate about self-determination and the rights of non-dominant ethnic groups within states.

When victory in the Franco–Prussian war enabled the new German empire, by the Treaty of Frankfurt in 1871, to annex Alsace and a large part of Lorraine its act was justified by Bismarck mainly on strategic grounds, to which could be added the importance of Lorraine's iron ore deposits, but it was felt necessary also to justify the transfer of populations by reference to their true national identity. The Franco–German controversy over that identity opposed two quite different ideas of nationality, exemplified in the famous debate between the historians Mommsen and Fustel de Coulanges, which preceded the

59

annexation. Much of the argument centred on Alsace, taken by France from the Holy Roman empire as late as 1648, and still largely Germanic in its language and culture, despite the efforts at gallicisation made since the 1830s, mainly through the educational system and notably under the Second Empire. Already by the late 1860s, German patriots had been taking up the theme of the Germanic identity of Alsace on the basis of ethnographic, linguistic, cultural, and historical arguments. To their Herderian and deterministic view of nationality, French apologists responded with the idea of the nation as a community of will and aspirations and of nationality as a matter of free political choice. The long participation of Alsace in the destinies of the French nation was held to have effected an assimilation which overrode differences of origin, language and culture. As the Alsatian journalist Boersch put it, in May 1867:

> Time, ways of life, age-old habits, the mutual experience of successes and of setbacks, common fortunes shared over years and centuries establish an affinity, laws of sympathy and fellow feeling, an identity of inclinations and interests which can no longer be overcome by lifeless memories and arguments taken from ethnographic science.[2]

Fustel de Coulanges, who had just left the chair of history at Strasbourg, flatly denied in 1870, in opposition to Mommsen, that nationality was created by race or language.

> Men feel in their hearts that they are a single people when they have a community of ideas, interests, feelings, memories, and aspirations. That is what makes the mother country. . . . We have in the nineteenth century a principle of public law which is infinitely clearer and more incontrovertible than your so-called principle of nationality. Our principle is that a population can be governed only by the institutions that it freely accepts, and that it consequently ought not to form part of a state except by its will and free consent. That is the modern principle. It is today the sole foundation of order, and everyone who is both a friend of peace and on the side of the progress of humanity should rally to it. . . . If Alsace is and remains French, it is solely because she wishes to be so.[3]

In asserting the principle of self-determination as the foundation of European peace, order, and progress, Fustel de Coulanges was able to appeal to a wide body of European opinion for which the transfer of populations like cattle, without regard to their opinion, was contrary to its notions of modern civilised practice as recently exemplified in the plebiscites which had preceded the annexation of Nice and Savoy.

The British Prime Minister, Gladstone, belonged to this school. He told the Cabinet that the proposed transfer was 'repulsive to the sense of modern civilisation', and would have addressed a remonstrance to the German government at the end of September 1870, had he been able to carry his colleagues with him. He thought it 'by no means impossible that these little provinces may be the central hinge on which for years to come the history of Europe may virtually depend', and that hence the question was not just one between the belligerents but one of legitimate interest to all the European powers. He would have liked to call on France and Prussia to allow free elections in Alsace–Lorraine to test the popular will, and he did his best to intrude his views upon the German government through the Oxford Professor of Philology, Max Müller, who was a friend of Bismarck's close collaborator in foreign affairs, the Prussian civil servant Abeken. It was in this latter endeavour that he discovered how difficult it was likely to be to secure the settlement of the Alsace–Lorraine problem along lines that conformed with his sense of liberal principle and of the public international law of Europe. Müller turned out to sympathise strongly with the demands of German nationalist feeling for compensation for France's 'attack': 'those who are guilty of the war', he told Gladstone, 'ought to be thankful that there is a province which is but half French, which was originally all German, and which they may restore to Germany with a good grace'. Abeken took an even stronger line in brushing aside the idea of self-determination:

> The French sentiments of the people of Alsace and Lorraine prove to me all the more strongly that we are duty bound to bring back the German race to the German empire. We have to cure them of a fearful disease, that future generations, though blushing at the disgrace of their forefathers, may grow up to a healthy life.[4]

From the first, therefore, the annexation of Alsace–Lorraine symbolised a collision not only of national interests but of the idea of self-determination with the right of conquest and the *völkisch* (folk) variety of nationalism. Nothing could prevent the new German state from having its way, however, and in the immediate aftermath of the treaty of Frankfurt there was no prospect of a speedy revision of the question. The sole concession in the treaty to individual and group sentiment in the ceded provinces was to allow their inhabitants to opt for French nationality on condition of moving to France before 1 October 1872. About 128 000 people left (some 8.5 per cent of the population); as much, probably, for reasons of employment and to evade German military service as for patriotic motives.[5] To the extent that it removed some of the more francophile elements, the emigration made a contribution to germanisation, which was reinforced by an influx of military, civil servants, and others from

Germany amounting by 1910 to about 400 000 (131 000 in Alsace) out of a population of 1 870 000.

Alsace and Lorraine were incorporated into the *Reich* as a *Reichsland* (imperial territory), not a part of the new German federation on a level with the states that comprised it, but its common possession, and hence a symbol of its unity which was of considerable importance to German nationalist feeling. From 1879, the government of the provinces was headed by an imperial *Statthalter* (Governor), assisted by a Secretary of State and a Ministry located in Strasbourg. An indirectly elected provincial parliament, the *Landesausschuss*, exercised legislative and budgetary powers in conjunction with the *Bundesrat* (Federal Council) and subject to the ultimate authority of the *Reichstag* (imperial parliament), the preliminary consideration of laws being entrusted to a 12 member Council of State nominated by the emperor. Fifteen deputies, 11 for Alsace, represented the provinces in the *Reichstag*. Apart from the imposition of German law and administration and the substantial presence of German immigrants and soldiers, the principal agency of germanisation was the remodelled educational system, staffed at secondary level by German teachers, and headed by the imperial university in Strasbourg, set up in 1872 specifically to act as a mission for German scholarship and culture.

'Innovations disturb these people, they are great lovers of their old customs, good or bad', noted Louis XIV's Intendant in Alsace, La Houssaye, in 1701,[6] and upon a population as strongly imbued with a sense of special identity as was the Alsatian, externally imposed political, legal, administrative, and educational institutions would take time to make their mark. Alsace might, from the point of view of German nationalists, be a German land, but as the German immigrant bourgeoisie of the official and professional classes measured the strength of their Alsatian counterparts' resistance to displacement and domination it was obvious that its assimilation to the *Reich* would not be simple or immediate. Yet Alsatians, if particularists, were also for the most part realists, and by the 1890s, as a new generation came to the fore, there were signs that the practical incorporation of the province into the mainstream of German life was progressing fast, in the absence of any strong likelihood that the European situation would bring about a reversal of the verdict of 1871. 'Protestation', the outright opposition to the new order, which was powerful in the early 1870s and stimulated in 1884–7 by the Franco–German tensions inflamed by Boulangism in France, was ceasing in the 1890s to represent a real alternative in Alsatian politics to the search for some kind of permanent *modus vivendi* within the empire.

The rapidly advancing integration of the Alsatian into the German economy was a major cause of change. One effect of economic development and of the consequent modernisation of economic and social structures was the emergence of a significant working class and socialist movement which from the first, through the agency of the *Sozialdemokratische Partei Deutschlands* (Social Democratic party), operated in a national German, rather than a merely Alsatian, context, and helped to persuade the Alsatian bourgeoisie that it could no longer maintain its grip on the masses by mobilising them in support of the politics of protestation, but must come to an arrangement with the immigrant German bourgeoisie to contain the socialist challenge in the framework of the class system and politics of the *Reich* as a whole.[7] Like the local Social Democratic party, the Alsatian Catholic party which came into being in the mid 1890s tended to link up regional with national politics, even if the question of its adhesion to the German *Zentrum* (Centre party) was controversial.

There had always been exponents of 'autonomy' in Alsatian politics, willing to trade acceptance of the annexation for some form of regional self-government. Bismarck had, in 1878, squashed the idea that Alsace–Lorraine might become a grand duchy; a federal state, governed perhaps by the crown prince of Prussia. By the 1890s, however, there was a second wave of autonomism. It was part of the expansion of political and intellectual activity and debate encouraged in the *Reichsland* by a gradual liberalisation of the regime which led to the freeing of the press in 1898; the removal of the remains of the passport system in 1900; and the abolition of the exceptional dictatorial powers of the *Statthalter* in 1902.

The new movement was accompanied by a reawakening of Alsatian consciousness and an earnest search for the essence, and for the affirmation, of *alsacienité* (Alsatian feeling) in language, literature, art and history. This was animated in large part by the group responsible for the *Revue Alsacienne Illustrée* (Illustrated Alsace Review), and supplied to some extent the means of transcending class divisions in the name of a traditional Alsatian identity, embodied above all in the Alsatian dialect. There was of course a tension between cultural particularism and German national allegiance, and this was reflected in the political sphere. From 1904, the *Landesausschuss* was pressing for Alsace–Lorraine to be accorded the status of a confederated state within the *Reich*. The *Statthalter*, Wedel, was drawn to ask the emperor in February 1908 to rescue the Alsatians from the feeling of being 'second class Germans'.[8] It remained, however, a problem for the imperial government how far concessions to autonomist sentiment could be made without weakening the attachment of the *Reichsland* to the empire, and alarming German nationalist opinion.

'Is Alsace still a German territory?' ran the heading of a press cutting, apparently from the *Hamburger Nachrichten* of 19 November 1908, which complained that the *Journal d'Alsace–Lorraine* (Alsace–Lorraine Journal), had put its newsboys into *Zouave* uniforms and that a Mulhouse shopkeeper had been displaying pictures which looked forward to the reclamation of Alsace–Lorraine by France.[9] The Ministry in Strasbourg in whose files it appears hardly needed the reminder that anything which cast doubt on the successful germanisation of the annexed provinces would expose it to bitter criticism from the large body of nationalist opinion, which saw in Alsace and Lorraine the battle prize won during the very foundation struggles of the *Reich* and so the outstanding symbol of German unity. German nationalists were both vehemently insistent that Alsace was innately German, and deeply suspicious of the loyalty of its inhabitants. They knew that some Alsatians retained substantial French sympathies and connections, and they viewed the survival of French language and culture and the notion that Alsace might properly constitute a meeting ground between French and German civilisations as a serious political danger. Not all members of the PanGerman League were as obsessive as Herr Fick, 'who vacationed in Alsace in order to check the progress of germanisation by counting French and German headstones in local cemeteries'. Nevertheless one of its leaders in 1907 placed among its 'national' concerns the *Entwelschung*, or 'delatinisation' of Alsace–Lorraine, and one of its publicists attacked the idea of bilingualism in the two provinces as calculated to breed 'national hermaphrodites'.[10]

Such views were not unusual, especially on the language question, which was seen as the ultimate determinant of national identity by Germans outside as well as inside the *Reich*. Another of the Strasbourg Ministry's newspaper testimonials was from the *Egerer Zeitung* of 25 May 1912, alleging that there was a failure of assimilation in the *Reichsland*:

> The language is the people . . . We see to what bilingualism leads! Bilingualism leads to mongrel language, to characterlessness. The people is lost the moment it becomes bilingual. You can feel and think and have a national being only in one language!

Pressure of this kind tended both to make a conciliatory policy in Alsace and Lorraine difficult for the governments either in Berlin or in Strasbourg to follow, and to alienate rather than subdue Alsatians and Lorrainers. The PanGerman League's policy of making the provinces part of Prussia in order to secure tight central control from Berlin did not appeal much even to immigrant German officials, let alone to the indigenous population; and the League had no local branches in the *Reichsland*, where the Colonial Society equally failed to take root.

German nationalists had some genuine grounds for their fears, for even in the early 1900s strong French influences and connections remained in the *Reichsland*, as well as some sentimental attachment to the *mère patrie* (motherland). Language was their vehicle. Much of the Alsatian bourgeoisie continued to use French, in business as well as in private life, as did many of the clergy, and it was taught in secondary schools, though the bulk of the population, passing through the primary schools, learned only German. Personal, family, business and cultural contacts with France continued, though attenuated by time and sometimes by official hostility. There were some deliberate efforts to sustain a French orientation and allegiance in Alsace, for example through such associations as the *Souvenir Français* and (after that had been forbidden) the *Souvenir Alsacien–Lorrain*. In the hands of some of its adherents, the Alsatian 'nationalism' of the years preceding the First World War became almost a facet, at least in a cultural sense, of French nationalism. Wetterlé and his Colmar group provide an example. They took up the cause of bilingualism, and their paper, the *Nouvelliste*, declared in April, 1909: 'Never let us forget that the French language forms part of our nationality'.[11]

Yet it seems that little of this signified a desire for the return of Alsace to France, certainly not at the expense of a renewed Franco–German conflict in which Alsace would be a battleground and Alsatians faced with painful and divisive choices. Bi-culturalism was more a defence against the destruction of an Alsatian identity by remorseless germanisation and the basis for the assertion of a special mediating role for Alsace between the civilisations of France and Germany than it was a refusal of German, or an assertion of French, political allegiance. Even ritual gestures like attendance at the annual Bastille day celebrations on French soil, at Belfort or Nancy, were acts of sentimental renewal rather than of political protest. The government of the *Reichsland* did not feel obliged to take much notice of them except at times when Franco–German tension imparted an unusual significance to them. Even when Boulangism stimulated a rise in acts of pro-French bravado, the penalties hardly suggested that the authorities felt themselves to be facing high treason or dangerous subversion. Wearing a hat in the French national colours publicly got the gardner Schnebelin, from Mulhouse, three months and a fine of 80 marks or ten days in August 1887, roughly an average sentence for that sort of offence.[12]

As generations grew to maturity that had no memory of belonging to France and had been formed by a German educational system and service in the German army, so the prospect of the fading away of French sentiment in Alsace came closer. But something depended on the ability and willingness of the *Reich* to show that autonomist aspirations could be satisfied in the German context, and on the avoidance of a renewal of Franco–German conflict which would open up a real possibility of a reversal of the verdict of 1871. The constitutional reform finally accorded to Alsace–Lorraine in 1911 replaced the *Landesausschuss* by a *Landtag* with deputies elected by manhood suffrage and a partly nominated upper house, and also gave the *Reichsland* representation in the *Bundesrat*. However it fell short of granting equality with the states of the German confederation. The imperial *Statthalter* designated the *Bundesrat* representatives and shared power with the parliament, to which the Ministry in Strasbourg was not responsible.

The autonomists were obliged to continue their campaign for a fuller recognition of Alsatian individuality within the *Reich*. Confidence that their objects could be attained, however, was severely shaken by the Zabern incident in 1913, when insults offered to Alsatian conscripts by a junior German officer resulted in a clash between the local population and the German military. The sequel demonstrated the reluctance of the German government either to nurse Alsatian susceptibilities or to subject the power of the army which had founded the German state to civilian and constitutional control. By this time, the deterioration of the European situation since the first Moroccan crisis of 1905–6 and the increase of nationalist excitement in Germany and France had made the possibility of war and thus the reopening of the question of Alsace–Lorraine more real than it had been for a generation.

This in turn had caused the authorities to irritate Alsatian opinion by clamping down on displays of sympathy towards France which might have been overlooked as trivial in calmer days, including those for which the meetings of sporting societies, sometimes involving the participation of French clubs, supplied a convenient occasion. The response from the Ministry in Strasbourg to Wetterlé's provocative pamphlet, *Le sentiment populaire en Alsace–Lorraine* (popular feeling in Alsace–Lorraine) was to wonder, in February 1913, whether it should not try to seal the *Reichsland* off from France as had been attempted in the late 1880s.

> If Herr Wetterlé, however, says (p.31), 'They (the Alsace–Lorrainers) find it unacceptable that a crime should be made out of their sympathies for France, where they number so many relatives and friends in the army and the administration', then he demonstrates that it was a mistake on the part of the German government to refrain from cutting off these links between the territory and France as it used to do and to allow the French extensive rights as visitors. Wetterlé's pamphlet is the best vindication of Bismarck's passport regulations.[13]

Undersecretary of State Mandel's comment emphasises how little confidence German officials were able to muster that Alsace, after 40 years of German rule, had been securely assimilated. It also embodies the tendency towards a harder line which, a year later, caused the Ministry in which he served to be replaced by one headed by a Prussian civil servant, under a new *Statthalter*, the former Prussian Minister of the Interior, Dallwitz. Yet for all the Alsatians' dissatisfactions few of them in 1913 and 1914 were looking for rescue by French arms, and despite the excitement of nationalist feeling in France it was doubtful how many Frenchmen burned to cross the Vosges to their aid.

The role of the Alsace–Lorraine problem in determining France's attitude toward Germany was very limited, despite the substantial *émigré* presence in France and the symbolic importance of the lost provinces for French nationalism. The Alsatians who had settled in France did not form a powerful political pressure group. By 1872, the difficulties of absorbing the influx of Alsatians had demonstrated that for a good many French people they were an alien breed, often regarded as more German than French whatever their choice of nationality. The first task of the emigrant Alsatians was to secure acceptance and employment. The societies which they formed – at least 60 of them in different parts of metropolitan France and north Africa by the First World War – tended to be for mutual assistance and sociability rather than for the upkeep of political grievances or the exertion of political influence. This is emphasised by their titles: *Société de Protection des Alsaciens–Lorrains Demeurés Français* (Society for the Protection of Alsace–Lorrainers remaining French) the largest and richest founded in 1872; *La Lyre Alsacien–Lorraine de Paris* (Alsace–Lorraine Choral Society of Paris); *Société Amicale des Alsaciens–Lorrains de Bourges* (Friendly Society of Alsace–Lorrainers in Bourges), etc. An Alsatian school was established in Paris in 1873, and journals devoted to the lost provinces followed – *La Revue Alsacienne* (Alsatian Review) (1877–90) and the weekly *L'Alsacien–Lorrain* (The Alsace–Lorrainer) from 1880. The first avoided politics; the second, however, looked toward the reunion of the provinces with France. Yet even *L'Alsacien–Lorrain* found Déroulède and the *Ligue des Patriotes* (Patriotic League) too venturesome when they began to attack the opportunist republic, and it did not give wholehearted support to Boulanger. Some Alsatians occupied important positions in French life, or achieved prominence in other ways. The best known scion of an Alsatian family in late nineteenth century France was Captain Alfred Dreyfus, whose case brought out the ambiguity with which Alsatians were viewed in France. As a whole, however, they exerted no special influence as a group on the policy and outlook of the republic. As in Germany, so in France, the role of the Alsatians and the conception of them entertained by public opinion depended less on themselves and their real characteristics than on their relevance, fluctuating with time and mood, to the emotional and polemical needs of nationalism.

The Alsace–Lorraine question was bound to figure prominently in the attempt to reinvigorate French patriotism in a way that would assuage the humiliation of 1871 and consolidate the unity of the republic that had emerged from the defeat. The idea of *revanche* (revenge) provided an emotional salve and a common national goal. As propagated through the lay school system, where patriotism was cultivated virtually as a civic religion, it relied heavily for its appeal and its imagery on the emotive symbol of the two lost provinces. They were mute and suffering reminders of the moral wrong inflicted on France, on Europe even, by the Treaty of Frankfurt, whose rescue formed a worthy object for the call to collective effort and self-sacrifice. The *General Manual* designed for the training of his teachers by Ferdinand Buisson, director of primary education, recommended them to place a flag draped in black on the map of France where Alsace and annexed Lorraine should have been. At a more adult level, Déroulède's *Ligue des Patriotes*, founded in 1882, included in its aims the revision of the Treaty of Frankfurt and the restitution of Alsace–Lorraine to France.

The propaganda of *revanche* required the reiteration of a particular image of Alsace–Lorraine combining the lachrymose and the picturesque in equal proportions. Daudet's famous story, *La Dernière Classe* (The Last Class), wringing the last drop of sentiment out of the final lesson in French in an Alsatian school, typified the tendency to depict the annexation as an act of brutality directed against the innocent and the weak. It was all summed up in the endlessly repeated representation of the lost provinces as two sisters in folk costume penned behind the new frontier by Prussian military might. Yet *revanche* was an inspirational myth, in the Sorelian sense, rather than a practical programme. The notion of Alsace–Lorraine which underpinned it was also a myth, and one increasingly hard to sustain after the 1880s, as *protestation* died away and autonomism signalled the channelling of the aspirations of Alsatians and Lorrainers into the framework of the German empire. Successive French governments, recognising with Gambetta the folly of exposing the infant Third Republic to a renewed contest with Germany so long as it remained diplomatically isolated, carefully refrained from provoking their neighbour over Alsace–Lorraine.

Alliance with Russia in the early 1890s did little to modify this cautious attitude, for if it greatly improved France's capacity to stand up to Germany, it provided no springboard for *revanche*. The Russians were not interested in fighting for the rectification of France's eastern frontier. Moreover, the jaunty jacobin nationalism of the republicans was giving way to a new nationalism of the right, inwardly rather than outwardly directed, defensive rather than bellicose, looking less to the revision of the national frontiers than to the protection of the national identity by the elimination of elements and influences not truly French. This brand of nationalism had less need of the Alsace–Lorraine question as a stimulant. Insofar as its view of the constituents of national identity stressed language, culture and history, the soil and the ancestors, bringing it very close to the Herderian, *völkisch* nationalism of Germany, its attitude to Alsace in particular could prove ambivalent. It is true that Barrès, with Maurras its main literary expositor, was a Lorrainer who assimilated the cultural particularism of the two provinces to the French tradition. Yet it was he who, in *Leurs Figures* (*Their faces*), seemed to place Alsace in an ambiguous light, when he referred to 'the spirit of the old Nancy, indigenous Nancy, not mingled with Alsatians, Protestants or Jews', and declared: 'It was the constant destiny of our Lorraine to sacrifice itself so that germanism, already filtered by our Alsatian neighbours, should not deprive Latin civilisation of its character'.[14]

Barrès, Bazin with *Les Oberlé* (1901), and 'Jean Heimweh' (Fernand de Dartein) in a string of works in the 1890s, all helped to keep the lost provinces in the public eye. But there was much wishful thinking in Heimweh's assertion in 1892 that

> This inexorable question of Alsace–Lorraine divides Europe into two opposing camps. . . . With us, on the French side, along with the whole of this nation, are all those who, in other countries, aspire to a better condition, those disinherited by fortune, suffering classes kept in tutelage or in servitude, captive and oppressed races, the unfortu- nate of all sorts and conditions, all supporters of the French Revolution, and of the rights of man and of peoples.[15]

In fact, at the end of the century, Alsace and Lorraine were hardly universally studied symbols of human rights or even of French national pride.

The evolution of opinion on the matter of self-determination might one day allow a revision of their status; meanwhile, few Frenchmen thought of risking the security of the nation by starting a war for them, and some found their cult mawkish and unreal. 'It seems to me to have endured long enough, this farce of the two enslaved little sisters, kneeling in their mourning dress, at the foot of a frontier post, weeping like heifers' wrote Rémy de Gourmont in *Le Joujou patriotique* (The Patriotic Toy) (1891).[16] The 140 or so replies collected by the *Mercure de France* in 1897 on 'Alsace–Lorraine and the present state of opinion' were not unanimous for the return of the provinces to France. Some looked to advance the cause of peace by neutralisation under European auspices; some thought the question worn out or found the annexation justified by the laws of war or by the Germanic culture of the Alsatians.[17]

What revived the importance of Alsace and Lorraine for French nationalism was the worsening of Franco–German relations from 1905 onwards. As apprehension over German power and ambition grew and the possibility of having to fight a war of national defence became more real, so the two provinces supplied once again a convenient symbol of German brutality and a useful stimulant of national feeling. Raymond Poincaré was a member of the committee. *Vers l'Alsace* (Towards Alsace) founded in 1907; a *Ligue des Jeunes Amis d'Alsace–Lorraine* (Young Friends of Alsace–Lorraine League) was established by right wing Catholics in 1912. Literary works multiplied, and Ducrocq's review *Les Marches de l'Est* (The Eastern Borderlands), founded in 1909, associated the situation of Alsace and Lorraine with that of all groups – Polish, Danish, Czech – suffering the oppression of pangermanism. 'Long live Alsace–Lorraine! Down with Germany!' was heard from excited youth in the demonstrations which followed the great military review of 12 March 1912 at Vincennes. The British Ambassador in Paris reported in February 1913:

> Public attention is now constantly called to the two lost provinces, and cries of 'Vive l'Alsace–Lorraine!' are frequently raised when regiments appear in the streets. Theatrical managers are utilising this tendency of public opinion and producing plays of an ultra-patriotic character. A play at the Theatre Réjane called 'Alsace', which deals entirely with the question of 'La Revanche', is at present one of the most popular pieces in Paris, and the tirades in it against Germany are received with rapturous applause by the audience.[18]

Patriots seized avidly on every incident in Alsace–Lorraine which could be taken to demonstrate the French sympathies of the inhabitants: the inauguration in October 1909 of the monument to the French dead at Wissembourg in Alsace and the clash of the Alsatian population with the German military at Zabern in 1913 were the outstanding examples which were used to validate the assumption that Alsatians and Lorrainers continued, as they had done ever since 1871, to await the hour of liberation. The Alsatian–Lorrainer community in Paris made considerable efforts in the early 1900s to establish links between French politicians and journalists and those exponen ; of Alsatian 'nationalism' who placed Alsatian particularity in a French framework. Through Henri Albert, editor of the *Messager d'Alsace–Lorraine* which started up in 1904, Barrès made contact with Pierre Bucher of the *Revue Alsacienne Illustrée*, and there were also links with Wetterlé and his paper, the *Nouvelliste d'Alsace–Lorraine*. Two brilliant Alsatian illustrators and caricaturists. Zislin and Hansi, who were mordant satirists of German rule, were acclaimed in Paris in 1911. It was perhaps Hansi's albums, the first of which were published in Paris in the following year, that did more than anything else to fix in the popular mind a literally highly coloured image of an Alsace peopled by stage figures in picturesque costume, conducting their lives as a continual series of gestures of cheeky defiance towards German rulers too stupid to understand them, and of ritual fidelity to their French past.

If, as the threat of European war became more acute, the question of Alsace–Lorraine served to stoke the ardour of nationalists in both France and Germany, it attracted also the attention of peace lovers who saw it as a major potential cause of conflict and a test of the ability of the European powers to settle their disputes by conciliation. The French and German pacifist movements had, indeed, long mulled over the problem as the essential obstacle to the Franco–German *rapprochement* which they regarded as a precondition of European peace. They made little progress, for the French, and others, saw the annexation of 1871 as an offence against international morality which must be repaired, while the Germans shied from the damage which any recognition of French claims would inflict on their appeal at home and argued that the construction of a more equitable European order must proceed from the acceptance of the *status quo*. The issue had to be excluded from the agenda at Universal Peace Congresses, and led to some sharp exchanges in the early 1900s. Alphonse Jouet published in the leading French pacifist journal a call in 1903 for the restitution of the two provinces in return for a French colony. In April 1904 the French peace societies demanded a plebiscite and passed resolutions to the effect that the Treaty of Frankfurt was a violation of justice. These claims were unacceptable to the German pacifists. However a compromise patched up at the Lucerne Congress of 1905, which postponed a solution until the establishment of a system of international justice, palliated the dispute and enabled all pacifists to support full autonomy for Alsace–Lorraine within the empire as an interim measure. Significantly, however, Quidde, the President of the *Deutsche Friedensgesellschaft* (German Peace Society), told the national congress of the French peace society, the *Association de la paix par le droit* (Association for Peace through Justice), at Lyon in May 1914, that Frenchmen should not think that the improvement of conditions in Alsace–Lorraine could be a precursor of Franco–German conciliation – 'this improvement will rather be one of the most certain results of conciliation'.[19]

The idea of exchanging a French colony for Alsace–Lorraine had been aired at the turn of 1898–9 by the Alsatians Lalance and Keller in the context of a possible *rapprochement* between Germany and a

France incensed against England by the Fashoda incident. Alsatians and Lorrainers had, of course, more interest than anyone in promoting a reconciliation which would relieve their homeland from the prospect of becoming once again a battleground. Some of them fiercely disliked the role assigned to them by nationalist polemic in France and Germany. Lalance was an early apostle of the notion of Alsace as a mediator between the two nations. Alsatian politicians steadily supported various international associations aimed at the maintenance of peace. Members of the Alsace–Lorraine Centre party were frequenters of the meetings of the Interparliamentary Union, whose Geneva congress of 1912 resolved that full autonomy for Alsace–Lorraine among the confederated German states would be a decisive step towards Franco–German *rapprochement*.

In 1913–14 the campaigns conducted mainly by French and German socialists against the bill for three years' military service in France and the bill for the increase of military and naval strength in Germany attracted considerable support in Alsace–Lorraine. In May 1913 the second chamber of the *Landtag* pronounced in favour of Franco–German understanding and against the arms race in Europe. It was a motion approved by the socialist organised Franco–German parliamentary conference which met in Berne in the same month, with the participation of socialists and centrists from Alsace–Lorraine. These latter were thanked by their colleagues for having facilitated the coming together of their two countries, and two months later voted against the German military law in the *Reichstag*. The Alsatian socialists contended that solidarity between the working classes of the two nations must pave the way for Franco–German understanding. Whether such understanding would lead to a change in the status of Alsace–Lorraine was another question. Heimweh had hoped that the triumph of socialism in Germany would bring a willingness to relinquish the two provinces to France on the ground of self-determination, and Jaurès had seen the achievement of a democratic Europe, free from militarism, as providing the conditions in which Alsace–Lorraine could secure its rights. But by 1913–14 many on the left were opposed to raising the nationality issue. The French socialist leader, Sembat, saw lasting peace with Germany as depending on French recognition that the territorial settlement of the Frankfurt treaty was final, and *L'Humanité* concluded from a series of interviews with Alsatian politicians that the autonomy of Alsace–Lorraine within the *Reich* was compatible with a Franco–German entente.

The focus on Alsace–Lorraine as a source of conflict was natural but misplaced. The French governments of the early 1900s were no more prepared than Gambetta and the opportunists to risk a war for the sake of the lost provinces, and the recovery of Alsace–Lorraine was not a practical object of French diplomacy. It is true that no French government could formally relinquish the aim of seeing the injustice of 1871 righted. Delcassé, as Foreign Minister, was disturbed by the prospect that the Hague Peace Conference of 1899 might guarantee the European *status quo* and thus block the French claim to Alsace–Lorraine. The provinces remained a stumbling block to a full Franco–German accommodation of the kind pursued by Caillaux in 1911. Yet they had virtually no relevance to the outbreak of war in 1914, a war imposed on France by the impossibility of abandoning the Russian alliance in face of German menaces if she were to retain her position as a great power. It was the war that made the question of Alsace–Lorraine a significant Franco–German, indeed European, political issue once again, and not the Alsace–Lorraine question that made the war, and this was true as much for the bulk of French public opinion as for Viviani's Cabinet of 1914. Looking back, Marc Bloch (himself of Alsatian parentage) wrote of his contemporaries of 1914:

> As for Alsace–Lorraine, if it is true that, with the first battles of August 1914, the image of the martyred provinces emerged suddenly from the discreet obscurity in which it had still been wrapped a few days earlier, that was simply under the impact of necessities already accepted. Since it had been necessary to take up arms, it was scarcely any longer supposed that it was possible to lay them down again without having first of all liberated our lost brothers. While peace lasted, the fine eyes of the Alsatian girls in the lithographs would never have exerted enough influence over a public opinion concerned above all for the safety of the domestic hearth to persuade it that the country should be propelled cheerfully into the most terrible danger solely in order to dry their tears.[20]

War, when it has to be justified to the populations mobilised to fight it, demands the production of war aims. It was natural for the Viviani government to select at the outset the recovery of Alsace–Lorraine as the major French objective in the conflict, an objective which was broadly agreeable to public opinion once hostilities were under way and offered a considerable addition to national power, especially if the frontier of Alsace could be extended to the 1790 or 1814 limits to take in more of the Saar coalfield. But having become a principal war aim, Alsace–Lorraine became also, more and more obviously as the war dragged on, a principal obstacle to the ending of the slaughter by a negotiated peace. Its inhabitants were caught between two irreconcilable nationalisms, neither of which understood or trusted them, with their loyalties divided and their homeland in the zone of battle.

French propagandists alleged, with a good deal of circumstantial evidence, that some German troops moving into Alsace in 1914 were told by their officers to consider themselves in enemy territory.[21] War brought out all the German nationalist misgivings as to whether Alsace and Lorraine had been truly assimilated to the *Reich*, misgivings perhaps unconsciously made concrete in a phrase used in a Foreign Ministry communication to the *Statthalter* in May 1917 which attracted a marginal exclamation mark in Strasbourg: 'the relations between Germany and Alsace–Lorraine'.[22] Though not very many of them appear to have deserted to the French, the loyalty of Alsace–Lorraine conscripts was thought sufficiently doubtful for most of them to be sent to the eastern front from 1916. Being in an operational zone, the civilian inhabitants of Alsace and Lorraine were inevitably subjected to the full rigours of military government, and this, with the losses and privations of the war, produced a shift of opinion which caused the *Statthalter* to inform the Foreign Ministry in September 1917, in commenting on arrangements for German propaganda on the subject of Alsace–Lorraine:

> The answer to the question whether the overwhelming majority of Alsace–Lorrainers do not want to become French is, since the war actually broke out, in contrast to the state of mind of the majority of the population *before the war*, at the very least disputable. Hence it is necessary to be careful about emphasising the will of the Alsace–Lorrainers to remain German, so as to avoid weak points arising which could easily be exploited by enemy propaganda.[23]

Two months later, the reply to a Foreign Ministry request to arrange, for the benefit of neutral opinion, demonstrations of solidarity with Germany was that to convene bodies like town councils and chambers of commerce would only produce expressions of support for autonomy, seen as an inevitable measure of justice for which no reciprocal service or thanks was required.[24] The German government was deeply unwilling to relax its grip upon Alsace–Lorraine: on the contrary it sought to tighten it. Not only were French claims flatly ruled out as elements of a peace negotiation, but schemes of incorporation into Prussia or Bavaria or partition between them were discussed. The *Heimatdienst* and the *Elsässer Bund* acted as vehicles of national propaganda, and the *Landgesellschaft Westmark* planned the expropriation of French property in Alsace–Lorraine to provide land for 'military colonies'. It was only in October 1918, when military defeat was an inescapable fact, that the autonomy demanded by most local opinion was granted, and by that time it served only to set off a debate which carried the problem of the provinces' future beyond the framework of the crumbling German empire. The *Reichstag* deputy Ricklin declared that the Alsace–Lorraine question had become an international one. Haegy called for the application of the right of self-determination. A plebiscite, reunion with France, and the establishment of a neutral republic were all ideas being canvassed when, in November, the German revolution had its pale echo in Strasbourg and the Alsace–Lorraine *Landtag* sought to establish an independent position for the provinces by turning itself into a *Nationalrat* (National Council). None of this greatly interested the government of the French republic, whose troops entered Strasbourg a few days later.

One of the leading advocates of Alsatian 'nationhood' before the war, Anselme Laugel, had returned from lecturing in Lyon in 1909 deeply discouraged by French incomprehension of the political aspirations of Alsace–Lorraine. His audience's exclusive interest in evidence of Alsatian attachment to France mirrored all too well the blinkered character of German reactions on the other side.[25] From the outset the war involved a painful collision between French preconceptions of Alsace–Lorraine and its inhabitants and the reality thereof. The French units which stormed into Alsace in 1914 found themselves 'liberating' not the figures of folklore and patriotic imagery but a largely germanised population, mostly unable to speak French and often loyal to the *Reich*. The evacuees and refugees flooding into France in the early days of the war, the Alsatians especially, often found themselves regarded and treated as a species of *boches* (Germans) in a way which suggested that the official image of the lost provinces had either failed to penetrate the popular mind or was too farfetched to stand an empirical test. In the 1915 version of Captain Danrit's (Lieutenant Colonel Driant's) war novel, *La Guerre souterraine* (The Underground War), the villainous German spy poses as an Alsatian, and many French people found it difficult to distinguish between the two breeds – or did not bother. Yet doubts either about the provinces' devotion to France or about France's dedication to their cause could not be allowed to surface by a government irrevocably committed to continue the war until their recovery.

French officialdom had two tasks during the war, to prepare for the eventual reintegration of Alsace and Lorraine into the French state, and to persuade both Allied and neutral opinion on the one hand, and domestic opinion on the other, that French claims to the provinces were justified and worth the sacrifices required to vindicate them. The first undertaking was in many ways the easier and involved less distortion of realities, but it was far from straightforward. Before the war, France had had no policy towards Alsace–Lorraine, because the return of the provinces was not a practicable object. Now the French state had to begin to define its attitude to a culturally distinct population having not only a strong social and political self-consciousness but also a significant experience of devolved administration and regional political life which was bound to make its assimilation to the highly centralised Third Republic a difficult one.

As the war progressed, the French government gradually acquired some acquaintance with the complexities of the Alsace–Lorraine situation and at least some of the bases of a policy for the provinces. This partly came about through the practical necessities of dealing with a large number of Alsace–Lorraine immigrants, refugees, evacuees, volunteers, deserters from the German army, and prisoners of war, and with the population of those districts of southern Alsace which were held by French troops from 1914 and administered according to their existing laws under the Hague conventions. In addition it resulted partly from the need to study the technical problems of the assimilation of Alsace–Lorraine into the French economy and into French law and administrative practice after a gap of 40 years. Of the string of military and governmental bodies which arose to deal with Alsace–Lorraine matters, the most important in trying to envisage the shape of the future were the *Conférence d'Alsace–Lorraine*, set up in 1915 under Louis Barthou's chairmanship, with a strong representation of Alsatian exiles such as Helmer, Laugel, Weill, and Wetterlé, and the *Sections d'études* (study groups) (dealing with legislation, administrative organisation, finance, education, economic questions) established under the auspices of the *Service d'Alsace–Lorraine* from 1917. The work of both was supplemented by two influential unofficial bodies, the *Groupe Lorrain* and, more important, the *Comité Siegfried*, concerned with economic matters, whose membership included Barthou, Jules Cambon, Méline, and de Wendel. These organs realistically accepted that there could be only a gradual adjustment in Alsace–Lorraine to French law and practices and did much to work out the technical bases of reintegration. It is, however, questionable whether, in the *Conférence d'Alsace–Lorraine* in particular, the influence of *émigré* personalities always assisted a dispassionate assessment of the provinces' problems and needs, and the government continued to lack a sophisticated comprehension of the political difficulties likely to arise.

The external and internal propaganda campaign to convince allied, neutral and domestic opinion that the restitution of Alsace–Lorraine to France was a precondition of a tolerable peace became of vital importance in 1917. The failure of the Nivelle offensive in April, the collapse of Russia, the entry into the war of the USA, the spread of war weariness among military and civilians alike, and the expectation of peace negotiations curtailed both France's ability to enforce her terms and the willingness of her population to fight for them. The British and American governments were unenthusiastic about Alsace–Lorraine: the Lloyd George ministry favoured subjecting

France's claims to a plebiscite. A plebiscite also seemed to be implied by the reference to taking the aspirations of populations into account in the settlement of disputes such as those between France and Germany in Pope Benedict xv's August 1917 attempt at mediation. The longstanding support for a plebiscite among French socialists was emphasised when the national council of the Socialist party opted for it in June.

Insofar as the French case against the annexation of 1871 rested on an assertion of the right of self-determination, it was obviously vulnerable to the response that self-determination was what should decide the fate of Alsace–Lorraine in a future peace settlement, but the Cambon brothers were not the only ones in French government circles who doubted the outcome of a plebiscite, and every possible argument was deployed against it. When the subject was debated in December 1917, the socialist Albert Thomas was able to persuade Wetterlé and several more of his fellow members of the *Conférence d'Alsace–Lorraine* that a consultation of the population *after* reunion with France would enable the self-determination dear to allied and neutral opinion to be safely combined with the redress of the great moral wrong of 1871, which no plebiscite could be allowed to hinder.[26] The official view, however, was against a plebiscite at any stage. Alsace and Lorraine were simply held to have remained French through 40 years of heroic endurance, making their return to France at the first opportunity the natural reparation of the violence committed against them by the Treaty of Frankfurt (which the German declaration of war in 1914 was sometimes regarded as having abrogated). The question, contended the Foreign Minister, Pichon, on 17 December 1917, was one not of French territorial claims but rather of international morality, the test of the justice of any peace settlement. It was on these lines that the *Bureau d'Etudes d'Alsace–Lorraine*, set up in July 1917 under the War Ministry, conducted its extensive propaganda effort in the USA, Britain, and elsewhere, while at the same time it sought with a barrage of largely pictorial propaganda and a network of lecturers and cinema outlets to instil into a reluctant French population a favourable image of Alsatians and Lorrainers and a determination to go on fighting for them.

That the French government was not going to pause over self-determination or autonomy in Alsace and Lorraine was evident as soon as the Armistice terms allowed it to occupy the provinces. Local political aspirations were brushed aside with the *Nationalrat*; the welcome given to the French troops was taken as supplying any necessary plebiscite; and, from Paris, Undersecretary of State Jeanneney established a system of control through *commissaires de la République* in Strasbourg, Metz, and Colmar that was designed to prepare the way for the absorption of the provinces into the standard

French departmental framework. The immediate problem rested on the divergence between jacobin centralisation and the wish of Alsatians especially to see substantial powers of regional government devolved to Strasbourg. Friction was inevitable from the first, not least because of the precipitancy of the French and the difficulty which the French state experienced in matching the standards of administrative efficiency which its new subjects had come to take for granted under its predecessor. Some of the problems of the early days of French rule were common to all the regions just recovered from German occupation – supply, communications, reconstruction, and resumption of economic life. Others, of an acute nature, were specific to Alsace–Lorraine and to the encounter of a triumphant but insensitive nationalism with populations whose real characteristics were hidden from it by the myth which had justified their conquest, and proved exasperating when revealed.

The first task for the French, facilitated when the treaty of Versailles gave them the two provinces with far fewer safeguards for the German minority than obtained in other former German territories, was to eliminate pro-German elements, especially German immigrants, from the administrative and judicial cadres, and to screen Alsatians and Lorrainers suspect from a national point of view by means of the *commissions de triage* (screening committees). Then came the phased implantation of French law and administrative practice, involving the introduction of French civil servants and bureaucratic formulas. This was bitterly resented by natives who were kept out of higher civil service posts by the expectations of the first and the unfamiliarity of the latter, as well as, in the case especially of Alsatians, by ignorance of the French language. The reorientation of the economy towards France and the conversion of assets held in German marks were complex problems. The effort to replace German by French as the primary language led to great transitional difficulties, particularly in education, and not least because of its bearing on the intractable religious issue. German was the language of religious and moral instruction for the great mass of the Alsatian population. Its threatened displacement added to the alarm, felt especially by the Catholic church, at the prospect that the rule of the lay republic would mean an anti-religious policy and in particular the abrogation of the Concordat (which had remained more or less in force in Alsace–Lorraine) and the separation of church and state. The declaration of the new Herriot ministry in June 1924 that it intended to introduce into Alsace and Lorraine the full range of republican legislation, which meant of course the lay laws, touched off a wave of opposition.

Even in the first months of French rule, these questions, aggravated by resentment at what was felt to be the dilatory action of a

distant authority and at the absence of elected regional representation, created the so-called *malaise alsacien*, which in March 1919
induced the French government to establish a *Commissariat Général*
for Alsace–Lorraine with considerable powers of regional decision,
headed in its first ten months by a front rank politician, Alexandre
Millerand. This was a transitional regional government which did
much to conciliate local opinion, but it was constantly under pressure
from the centralists in Paris, where control of many of its administrative functions had been transferred by the time of its suppression in
October 1925, when it was superseded by a *Direction Générale* in Paris
under the immediate authority of the Prime Minister. By then, the
ground had been prepared for a revival in the later 1920s of
autonomism in Alsatian politics. Before 1914, autonomism had been
in part (as its adherents were anxious to stress immediately after the
war) a means of sustaining a French as well as an Alsatian identity
against the pressure of German cultural and political nationalism, but
it was now to lead some of its adherents to look towards a renewal of
the German connection, with the encouragement of irredentist
elements in Germany itself.

The principal international objection to the French claim to
Alsace–Lorraine had been the likelihood that its realisation would
form a new source of permanent bitterness with Germany. In the
immediate aftermath of Versailles this apprehension seemed unjustified. German public opinion, while it regretted, on the whole
accepted the loss of Alsace–Lorraine – a less emotive matter than the
loss of territory in the east – and at governmental level the Weimar
Republic had other things to think about. The 'Executive Committee
of the Free Republic of Alsace–Lorraine' run by Ley, Muth, and Rapp,
first in Munich and then in Baden–Baden, making appeals to both
international and Alsatian opinion with the idea of securing League
of Nations intervention in the future of the provinces, probably
received some German government money until Rapp's exposure as
a fraud in 1920. In general, however, the German Foreign Ministry
was convinced that the allegiance of most Alsatians and Lorrainers to
France was not in doubt. The appearance, in 1922, of the Alsatian
party founded by Klaus Zorn de Bulach, whose family had figured
prominently under the German regime, simply caused it to reflect
that, despite grievances against French administration, there was no
real minority problem in Alsace and Lorraine.

Only when the Herriot government's initiative in 1924 aroused
serious discontent in the two provinces was the German government
tempted to take a hand in the cultivation of autonomism through
such tools as Robert Ernst. He was an Alsatian whose *Verein Alt
Elsass–Lothringer* ('Society of Old Alsace–Lorrainers'), with its
publication, *Elsass–Lothringen Heimatstimmen* ('Voices from the

Alsace–Lorraine Homeland'), had helped to keep together the Alsatians and Lorrainers who had chosen Germany, or been driven there, after the war. Ernst's was one of the more irredentist of the organisations representing those inhabitants of Alsace–Lorraine, perhaps 150 000 or 200 000 in number, in the main German immigrants and their Alsatian or Lorraine consorts and children, who had willingly or unwillingly left the two provinces for the *Reich*. The *Hilfsbund der Vertriebenen Elsass–Lothringer im Reich* ('Friendly Society of Expelled Alsace–Lorrainers in the *Reich*'), publishing the *Elsass–Lothringische Mitteilungen* ('Alsace–Lorraine Bulletin'), was concerned mainly with mutual assistance and the satisfaction of personal claims against the French authorities. The *Wissenschaftliches Institut der Elsässer und Lothringer im Reich* (Scientific Institute of Alsatians and Lorrainers in Germany) at the University of Frankfurt, which was founded in 1920 by German university teachers expelled from Strasbourg, was devoted to the history and culture of the lost provinces.

These bodies were of some interest to organisations concerned with the protection and promotion of germanism beyond the *Reich*. These included the *Verein für das Deutschtum im Ausland* ('League for German Culture Abroad'), the *Deutsches Ausland-Institut* ('German Institute for Foreign Countries') in Stuttgart, and the *Deutscher Schutzbund* ('German Protection League'), which, though established to aid the German cause in the territories subjected to plebiscite by the treaty of Versailles, set up a press office for Alsace–Lorraine of which Ernst became director in 1921. When, therefore, in May 1925, the *Zukunft* ('Future') began publication in Strasbourg, summoning Alsatians and Lorrainers to defend their national rights, including the use of German in the schools, administration and courts, the slow current of autonomist feeling which it stimulated could hope for nourishment from sources both private and official across the Rhine. In October 1925, at Locarno, the Franco–German frontier of Versailles was recognised by Germany and guaranteed by Britain and Italy. Behind the scenes, however, the German Chancellor, Stresemann, under heavy pressure from nationalist opinion, was making it clear that there had been no 'moral' renunciation of Alsace–Lorraine, that the protection of ten or 12 million Germans living under a foreign yoke remained a leading object of German policy, and that cultural links with the *Deutschtum* of Alsace–Lorraine must be kept up.[27]

Stressemann was glad to abandon any demand for self-determination by plebiscite in Alsace–Lorraine, believing in the likelihood of an overwhelming majority for France, at least while the French were in possession. His position reproduced that of the French government at the close of the war. The inhabitants of Alsace and Lorraine must be assumed to be what the nationalist imperatives of the great states that were their neighbours required them to be; consultation of their opinion only risked obscuring their true identity. Nationality – on this point the French had come close to embracing the German arguments which they had refuted in 1871 – was independent of and superior to the transient exercise of political will. It was a bleak outlook for the right of non-dominant groups to decide their future. Yet Alsatians and Lorrainers had shown and would continue to show the ability of a tenacious particularism to resist all the pressures which the nation–state could bring to bear and to retain and even reinforce an identity in which different national cultures could find, if not a synthesis, then at least a point of dialogue.

Notes

1. Archives Nationales (hereafter AN), AJ30/112, undated report (receipt stamped 6 July 1918) by Hinzelin to the *Bureau d'études d'Alsace–Lorraine* on his lecture tour in Savoy.
2. C. Boersch, in *Courrier du Bas-Rhin*, 19 May 1867, quoted in L'Huillier (1970a), p. 424.
3. Fustel de Coulanges (1870) replying to Theodor Mommsen's three letters to an Italian newspaper collected as *Agli Italiani*.
4. Schreuder.
5. Wahl, pp. 190–2.
6. Quoted in Livet, p. 315.
7. See Igersheim, c.iii.
8. Quoted in L'Huillier (1970b), p. 451.
9. Cutting in Archives départementales du Bas–Rhin (hereafter ADBR), AL27/I/7ª/5, with consequent report by the Mulhouse chief of police, 5 December 1908.
10. Chickering (1984), pp. 79, 93, 122.
11. Quoted in Igersheim, p. 136.
12. See ADBR, AL87/5612, table B, sentences for carrying or offering for sale forbidden emblems, 1871–1912.
13. ADBR, AL27/I/7ª/1, memorandum by Undersecretary of State Mandel, 12 February 1913 (copy).
14. The *Livre de poche* edition, Paris, 1967, p. 287.
15. *Triple Alliance et Alsace–Lorraine*, quoted in Girardet, pp. 239–40.
16. Quoted in Poidevin and Bariéty, p. 153; but Becker, p. 31, n. 82, warns against attaching too much significance to de Gourmont's article.
17. Poidevin and Bariéty, pp. 153–4.
18. Gooch and Temperley, X(2), 461, Sir F. Bertie to Sir E. Grey, 19 February 1913.
19. Chickering (1975), pp. 290–305, 'Alsace–Lorraine and Rapprochement with France'.
20. Bloch, p. 155. Compare the conclusion of the German Ambassador in Paris, von Schoen, in a note of 5 February 1914 (Lepsius, Mendelssohn– Bartholdy, and Timme, XXXIX, 15667) that Frenchmen were not going to risk their lives for Alsace–Lorraine. These views of contemporaries seem confirmed by the work of Becker, pp. 53–62, 330–2.
21. AN, AJ30/111, folder 'Bardet', contains an undated (September 1918) cutting

from the *Journal du Lot* with details of an enquiry among German prisoners on this point.

22.   ADBR, AL22/81(l), Foreign Ministry to *Statthalter*, 11 May 1917.
23.   *Ibid.*, *Statthalter* to Foreign Ministry (draft), 10 September 1917.
24.   *Ibid.*, *Statthalter* to Imperial Chancellor, 20 November 1917.
25.   Igersheim, p. 119.
26.   *Procès-verbaux*, II, 29th session, 24 December 1917.
27.   For German links with and policy towards Alsace–Lorraine, 1918–25, see Bariéty, pp. 5–22, and Dreyfus, pp. 90–3.

Select Bibliography

Bibliographical Note

The sources for the role of the Alsace–Lorraine question in European politics after 1871 lie partly in the considerable contemporary literature on the subject, the best guide to which is perhaps the subject indexes of the Bibliothèque Nationale, Paris, and see also Wehler and extracts in Girardet, partly in the archives of foreign offices, politicians, pacifists, etc. Much diplomatic material is available in print, notably in *Die grosse Politik* and *Documents Diplomatiques Français*.

Almost all modern writing on the theme looks at it less as a European than as a Franco–German issue. Chickering places it in the context of the peace movement in *Imperial Germany and a World Without War*; otherwise see the works of Poidevin and Bariéty on Franco–German relations and of Becker on French opinion in 1914, together with Seager, Sieburg and Ziebura.

The very large literature on Alsace since 1871 necessarily makes some reference to international aspects. The section 'Recherches–débats' in the most suggestive short survey of Alsatian history, 1871–1914, F. Igersheim's *L'Alsace des notables* is a valuable guide to issues and sources. Very extensive bibliographical information is supplied in two important pieces by Wehler. Important recent monographs with extensive information on sources and bibliography include Baechler and Hiery. For the complexities of Alsatian domestic politics, there are some further useful works by Dreyfus, Mayeur and Rothenberger. On many matters of detail, reference must still be made to two massive repositories of information produced (partly for partisan purposes) between the wars: Rossé, et al., *Das Elsass* and Wolfram. Scholars have still far from completely mined the huge corpus of source material for the history of Alsace after 1871 which exists in the Archives départementales du Bas-Rhin, Strasbourg (including the records of the administration of the *Reichsland*, 1871–1918), the Archives départementales du Haut–Rhin (Colmar), and the Archives Nationales (Paris)

Baechler, C. (1982), *Le Parti Catholique Alsacien 1890–1939*, Paris.
Bariéty, J. (1977), *Les relations Franco–Allemandes après la première guerre mondiale: 10 Novembre 1918 – 10 Janvier 1925, de l'exécution à la négociation*, Paris.
Becker, J. -J. (1977), *1914: Comment Les Français sont entrés dans la guerre*, Paris.
Bloch, M. (1946), *L'Etrange défaite*, Paris.
Chickering, R. (1975), *Imperial Germany and a world without war: the peace movement and German society, 1892–1914*, Princeton, USA.
Chickering, R. (1984), *We men who feel most German: a cultural study of the Pan-German League 1886–1914*, London.
Dollinger, P. (ed.) (1970), *Histoire de l'Alsace*, Toulouse.
Dreyfus, F. (1969), *La vie politique en Alsace, 1919–36*, Paris.

Fustel de Coulanges, N.D. (1870), *L'Alsace, est-elle Allemande ou Française. Réponse à M. Mommsen*, Paris.

Girardet, R. (1966), *Le nationalisme français 1871–1914*, Paris.

Gooch, G.P., and Temperley, H. (eds) (1926–38), *British documents on the origins of the war 1898–1914*, 11 vols, London.

Hiery, H. (1986), *Reichstagswahlen im Reichsland. Ein Beitrag zur Landesgeschichte von Elsass-Lothringen und zur Wahlgeschichte des Deutschen Reiches 1871–1918*, Düsseldorf.

Igersheim, F. (1981), *L'Alsace des notables (1870–1914): la bourgeoisie et le peuple alsacien*, Strasbourg.

Lepsius, J., Mendelssohn–Bartholdy, A., and Thimme, F. (eds), (1922–7), *Die grosse Politik der europäischen Kabinette 1871–1914: Sammlung der diplomatischen Akten des Auswärtigen Amtes*, 40 vols, Berlin.

L'Huillier, F. (1970a), 'L'Evolution dans la paix (1814–70)', in Dollinger, P. (ed.), *Histoire de l'Alsace*, Toulouse.

L'Huillier, F. (1970b), 'L'Alsace dans le Reichsland (1871–1918)', in Dollinger, P. (ed.) *Histoire de l'Alsace*, Toulouse.

Livet, G. (1970), 'Le XVIII siècle et l'esprit des lumières', in Dollinger, P. (ed.), *Histoire de l'Alsace*, Toulouse.

Mayeur, J.M. (1970), *Autonomie et politique en Alsace. La constitution de 1911*, Paris.

Mommsen, Theodor (1870), *Agli Italiani*, Berlin.

Poidevin, R., and Bariéty, J. (1977), *Les relations Franco–Allemandes 1815–1975*, Paris.

Procès-verbaux de la Conférence d'Alsace–Lorraine, (1917–19), 2 vols, Paris.

Rossé, J., Sturmel, M., Bleicher, A., Deiber, F., and Keppi, J. (eds) (1936–8), *Das Elsass von 1870–1932*, 4 vols, Colmar.

Rothenberger, K.H. (1975), *Die elsass–lothringische Heimat- und Autonomiebewegung zwischen den beiden Weltkriegen*, Frankfurt.

Seager, F.H. (1969), 'The Alsace–Lorraine Question in France, 1871–1914', in Warner, C.K. (ed.), *From the Ancien Regime to the Popular Front*, New York.

Schreuder, D. (1977–8), 'Gladstone as "Troublemaker": Liberal foreign policy and the German annexation of Alsace–Lorraine, 1870–1871', *Journal of British Studies*, XVII.

Sieburg, H.O. (1969–70), 'Die Elsass–Lothringen–Frage in der Deutsch–französischen Diskussion, 1871–1914', *Zeitschrift für die Geschichte der Saargegend*, 17–18.

Wahl, A. (1974), *L'Option et l'émigration des Alsaciens–Lorrains (1871–1872)*, Paris.

Warner, C.K. (ed.) (1969), *From the Ancien Regime to the Popular Front*, New York.

Wehler, H.U. (1961), 'Elsass-Lothringen von 1870 bis 1918. Das 'Reichsland' als politisch-staatsrechtliches Problem des zweiten deutschen Kaiserreichs', *Zeitschrift für die Geschichte des Oberrheins*, 109.

Wehler, H.U. (1979), *Krisenherde des Kaiserreichs 1871–1918. Studien zur deutschen Sozial- und Verfassungsgeschichte*, pp. 23–69, 430–49, Göttingen, 2nd edn.

Wolfram, G. (ed.), (1931–6), *Das Reichsland Elsass–Lothringen 1871–1918*, 3 vols, Frankfurt.

Ziebura, G. (1955), *Die deutsche Frage in der öffentlichen Meinung Frankreichs von 1911 bis 1914*. Berlin.

5   The Schleswig–Holstein Question to 1933

LORENZ RERUP AND IMMO DOEGE

I The Danes in Schleswig–*Lorenz Rerup*

The Reconstruction and Dissolution of the 'Helstat' 1851–66

Like the duchies of Holstein and Lauenburg, the duchy of Schleswig (in Danish called 'southern Jutland' or 'Slesvig') was until 1864 a part of the binational Danish *helstat*[1] which was governed in a particular manner, but it did not – like Holstein and Lauenburg – belong to the Germanic Confederation. Only in the duchy of Schleswig did a part of the population speak Danish: the other two duchies were simply German speaking. With the exception of Flensburg, Schleswig was mainly an agricultural area until the Second World War. It covered an area of 9100 sq km and had a population of 396 000 in 1855, of whom approximately 170 000 had Danish as a mother tongue; 153 000 German; 27 000 Frisian; and 45 000 a mixed mother tongue.[2] Often but not always the language was nationally decisive; there were German speaking Danes as well as Danish speaking Germans. At this point a large proportion of the lower classes had not yet formed their attitudes towards the new national problem.

The tension between the nationalities, which had built up in the 1840s, came to a climax with the 1848–50 civil war. The Prussians and the Confederation intervened, but their intervention failed due to the general European interest in the balance of power in this area. Neither side achieved its war aims: the Schleswig–Holstein movement did not succeed in separating the duchies from Denmark, nor the Danish National Liberals in uniting Schleswig as closely as possible with the kingdom. In 1851–2 a conservative Danish government promised Austria and Prussia not to incorporate Schleswig and not to bind it closer than Holstein to the kingdom. In addition a constitution for the joint affairs of the reconstructed *helstat* was promised, to be approved by each part of the realm before it became valid. These joint affairs consisted mainly of finance and military and foreign policy. In the London Protocol (8 May 1852) the integrity of the *helstat* was confirmed by the great powers, Sweden and Denmark. The succession to the Danish throne was settled, but the Protocol also emphasised the title of the Germanic Confederation in Holstein and Lauenburg.[3]

In the royal ordinance of 28 January 1852 Schleswig was also promised provisions that were to offer and ensure 'exactly the same justice and vigorous protection to the Danish as to the German nationality in this duchy'.[4] In the reconstructed *helstat* loyal parts of the population were indeed treated equally but after a three year civil war there was of course more opposition on the side of Schleswig–Holstein than on the Danish side. The attempt to agree on a constitution for the joint affairs of the realm did not succeed. The inhabitants of Holstein could not accept the dominance of Denmark in such a constitution, whereas for the Danes it was impossible to place the much smaller duchies on an equal basis with the kingdom. As the constitutional issue had been blocked, the previous absolutist government, which had been restored after the war, had to be continued in the duchies. This form of government was, however, slightly restricted by assemblies of the estates of the duchies. The government liked neither Danish nor German opposition movements or individual initiatives. Absolutist decisions on the joint affairs of the realm had also to be continued.

A pre-national minority problem arose in middle Schleswig as a new Language Act was introduced as early as 1851.[5] Around 1800 Danish had been the common language of the area. The Language act, drawn up by conservative officials, aimed at regaining for the Danish language those districts in middle Schleswig where Danish was still the mother tongue of many people. South of the present border between Denmark and the Federal Republic of Germany, in an area that (with the exception of the Frisian west coast) stretched from the Schlei estuary and north of the shore of this inlet to just before Husum, Danish was introduced as the teaching language in primary schools. Only four hours in German were to remain. The act also provided for alternative services in Danish in the churches of this area, where about 85 000 people lived. In Flensburg, however, and in the Frisian and southern parts of Schleswig, the language spoken in schools and churches continued to be German. In the northern half of Schleswig Danish was spoken as previously, but in the towns of this part of the country use of Danish and German alternated from then on in schools and in church services. The success of this policy, the inventors believed, could perhaps result in Schleswig being secured as a part of Denmark if the *helstat* disintegrated in the future. The Language act was restricted to an area which did not have any natural boundaries and did not contain the more southern, obviously German speaking, parts of the realm, which were still binational.

The Language act, however, met a strong passive resistance from the population, especially in the eastern and southern parts of middle Schleswig, and greatly accelerated the transition to Low German as the colloquially spoken language. Outside the monarchy, this language policy and the unsolved constitutional problems produced an indignant reaction from the German press. The duke of Augustenburg, who was sent into exile after the civil war, and the German National Association skilfully stirred up this indignation. In 1861 the language provisions were slightly slackened after remonstrances, made by the British government.[6]

After the war of 1864 Denmark was forced to hand over the three duchies to Prussia and Austria through the Treaty of Vienna (30 October 1864). The division of Schleswig was discussed unsuccessfully during the Conference of London (April to June 1864), which took place during a truce. The peace treaty included an option (article XIX) allowing the inhabitants of the duchies until 1871 to decide whether to remain Danish subjects or not. After the 1866 war between Austria and Prussia the peace treaty of Prague (23 August 1866) was arranged by the French emperor. The transference article (article V) of this treaty contained a clause initiated by Napoleon III. The article handed over to Prussia all newly acquired Austrian rights to the duchies 'on the condition that the inhabitants of the northern districts of Schleswig are to be united with Denmark if they express the wish to become part of Denmark through unrestricted voting'. This option, as well as this North Schleswig clause, had far reaching consequences for the Danish population in Schleswig.[7] Those who elected to retain Danish nationality in terms of this option will be hereafter referred to in this article as optants.

The Danes of North Schleswig in Prussia 1867–1914

In 1867, after the Treaty of Prague, the duchies were annexed by Prussia as the province of Schleswig–Holstein. Most of the people who lived in the Northern part of this province were Danish minded, including the people of Flensburg, but not those of Tønder and Højer. Both elections to the North German Federation in 1867 showed a Danish majority in this area. Even after the formation of the German Empire the inhabitants of north Schleswig who lived in the first constituency were always able to send a Danish representative to the German *Reichstag*. In Flensburg, however, the Danish minded people lost their majority, when the Social Democratic party became a major force in the early 1880s. Emigration and immigration, as well as the question of the option, were responsible not only for the loss of the majorities in Haderslev, Aabenraa and Sønderborg in the following decades, but also for a reduction in the total number of Danish votes.

From 1887 the number of votes climbed again, due to a comprehensive organisation of the Danes. The social base of the Danes in north Schleswig consisted chiefly of the rural population. Their organisational and politically active group was composed mainly of owners of medium sized farms. In north Schleswig around 1900–3, 79 per cent of all farmers who owned at least two horses were Danish; 16.1 per cent German; and 4.9 per cent nationally indifferent.[8] As the Danish movement was established within a highly developed agricultural system it was able to resist tenaciously the germanisation policy of the authorities and also to develop and maintain an amazing organisational network. After the turn of the century this network contained more than 200 associations of all kinds,[5] among them the *Vælgerforeningen for Nordslesvig* (North Schleswig Voters Union). In 1912 during the last election for the German *Reichstag* 41.5 per cent of the Danish voters were members of this union.[10] The organisational network covered only the area that became united with Denmark in 1920.

Despite their local dominance the Danes could not influence local government very much. Even though the suffrage for the *Reichstag* was relatively unrestricted for that time – every man over 25 who had full civil rights was entitled to the vote – Prussian electoral laws distinguished between voters according to their tax payments. This distinction could be manipulated locally. Besides, a large part of the administration was carried out by Prussian officials. The Danes, however, lived in a community founded on a system of law where appeals against some actions by the authorities could be taken all the way to the German Supreme Court in Leipzig, if necessary. Danish associations and Danish newspapers were greatly hindered but the Danes often fought against these obstacles successfully. Around 1890, for instance, it was almost impossible to hold a Danish meeting in a public house as the innkeeper would be in fear of losing his licence. In the course of the next 20 years, however, the population established 48 private village halls.

Prussian school policy had a particular impact. After 1864 German was restored as the teaching language in schools in middle Schleswig and in the towns of north Schleswig but for a while Danish remained the language spoken in schools in the countryside of north Schleswig. In 1871 a certain number of German lessons were introduced in these schools. In 1878 the language spoken in schools changed and now had to be half German and half Danish. Also the continuation of private schools was made impossible. In 1888, apart from some lessons in religious education, German became the only language spoken in schools. The response of the population was to send their children to agricultural colleges, schools of further education and folk high schools in Denmark after they had finished their compulsory period of elementary education. A special school association, which had been founded in 1892, supported and arranged the schooling of 6182 young people up to the First World War.[11]

Up to the end of the 1870s the Danes in north Schleswig continued the so-called policy of protest through which, by putting stress on the North Schleswig clause in article V of the Treaty of Prague, every opportunity was used to protest against the connection with Prussia and to underline the special position of north Schleswig. The elected representatives of the Prussian parliament refused, for example, to take the compulsory oath of loyalty to the Prussian constitution and young men became optants or emigrants to avoid Prussian military service. The abolition of the clause in 1878 and the Prussian germanisation policy made a new response necessary, and this was slowly developed. The new policy, the so-called negotiation policy, worked on a long term basis and within it a tightly knit Danish organisation network was built up. On the surface the policy was concerned with active participation in Prussian and German political life in order to ensure the north Schleswig Danes the best cultural and economic conditions possible, where convenient in cooperation with suitable German parties.

Especially in the years between 1897 and 1901 the Danes had a hard time under the High President of the province, E.M. von Köller. The harassments that resulted from the 'Köller policy' were directed particularly against optants and caused an outcry in Germany and abroad.[12] This policy was directly related to German foreign policy against Denmark at that time. It managed only temporarily to dam up the Danish movement.[13]

The unequal balance of power between the great power, Prussia/Germany, on the one hand and the small state, Denmark, on the other hand made it difficult for the kingdom to support the Danes in north Schleswig. They were, however, obviously regarded as a part of the Danish people that lived unjustly under foreign rule. This attitude influenced the strong anti-German atmosphere among the population. The Danish public observed the destiny of the people in Schleswig with intense sympathy. An early sign of this sympathy was displayed in September 1865, when 2200 people from Schleswig visited Copenhagen. They arrived on six steamers, were given private accommodation and were fêted at large banquets. Such journeys were often repeated. Several associations supported the Danish organisations in Schleswig with, for instance, books and contributions to Danish private schools, which were tolerated until 1878. Partially free places at schools in Denmark for young people from north Schleswig made school attendance easier. These places were often made available by the schools and meant an indirect public subvention. In 1882 the big brewer J.C. Jacobsen financed a book written especially for the Danes in north Schleswig containing a history of Denmark in the form of 40 narratives.[14] Ten thousand copies were distributed so that parents could counteract the germanisation resulting from school lessons. A society, founded in 1884, which disseminated information about conditions in north Schleswig arranged 26 evening lectures in Copenhagen up to 1889. Between 500 and 600 people attended these lectures regularly.

In 1887 opposition academics also formed an active group which worked for Schleswig. The condemnation of the 'Köller policy' united the Danish parties, including the social democrats, who had up to that point considered nationalism a bourgeois affair. There existed, however, different opinions of how to solve the north Schleswig question. Most conservative circles predicted the occurrence of war between the great powers of Europe, with even Danish participation, or they imagined that the powerful marital ties of the monarchy to Russia and England could help somehow. The parties to the left of the conservatives preferred to believe in the idea of national self-determination which would eventually be generally accepted. They were also convinced that a new democratic Germany would voluntarily return the Danish part of the country. The Danish social democrats shared this opinion. They believed that in the socialist societies of the future inhabitants of border areas could decide themselves where the border should be.[15]

From the end of the 1880s the Danish relief actions for Schleswig were coordinated by the head of the Danish Record Office, A.D. Jørgensen (1840–97), who was born in north Schleswig.[16] He was the author of the above-mentioned history. This coordinating work gained a farreaching importance owing to the teamwork of Jørgensen and H.P. Hanssen (1862–1936), a young man from north Schleswig. In 1888 Hanssen initiated the North Schleswig Voters Union and he eventually became the leading Danish politician in north Schleswig. Among other ideas he accepted Jørgensen's idea that in the event of a new border the line should be legitimated neither by constitutional law nor by history but should correspond to the ethnic boundaries of the Danish people.

Corresponding to the Danish policy of neutrality the official politics of the Danish government were characterised by extreme caution. There were, however, exceptions. In April 1866 a hint from the French Foreign Minister led Denmark to offer Bismarck a defensive military alliance for the forthcoming war against Austria (which had occupied Holstein). In return for the alliance Denmark asked for Schleswig, if possible down to the Schlei inlet. Bismarck did not find this offer worthwhile.[17] In 1867–8 Prussia started to negotiate for the fulfilment of the North Schleswig clause in article V. These negotiations were related to a momentary tension between Prussia and France, the Luxemburg question. They failed because of excessive Prussian demands upon the position of the small German minority, which would be left behind in the returned area. After Denmark's experiences of 1852–64 with the German powers and the Germanic Confederation it was impossible for Denmark to accept international guarantees which would have allowed bigger states to intervene in its affairs.[18]

In 1870, at the outbreak of the Franco–German war, Denmark nearly participated on the side of the French. Public feeling in Copenhagen was very much in favour of this. French naval units as well as a special French envoy had already arrived. Only a few cool headed people around the government managed to delay the decision. The temptation vanished after the first German victories in eastern France.[19] After the French defeat it was almost impossible to count on a fulfilment of the North Schleswig clause. Another reason for this was that Russia had a fairly good relationship with the new Germany. In 1877 the north Schleswig member of the German *Reichstag*, who was supported by Poles, Alsatians and members belonging to the Catholic Centre party, brought the question up in vain, although the Danish government had tried to quieten him down.

In April 1878 the North Schleswig clause was abolished by a secret Austro–German deal. This was an Austrian service in return for German support during the Congress of Berlin. The genuine date was only revealed in 1920. In February 1879 contemporaries were told that the abolition had taken place in October 1878. This misinformation was to cover up the real reason and also to give the impression that the abolition had been a reaction to the engagement and later marriage of the Danish princess Thyra to the Duke of Cumberland, the pretender to the kingdom of Hanover. His country had, in 1866, been annexed by Prussia. At the same time the Danish royal house was attacked by German newspapers. The Danish government had to accept the abolition but at the same time it expressed the hope that the abolition might open the way for new negotiations. The German answer was so unfriendly and menacing that it was only 40 years later, at the end of the First World War, that the government officially brought up a solution to the north Schleswig problem.[20]

During non-official occasions the question repeatedly turned up. In 1890 the Danish Ambassador in London had the idea of blocking the exchange of Zanzibar for Helgoland in order to link the return of north Schleswig with this deal.[21] The Danish Virgin Islands were also several times thought of as possible elements for exchange.[22] During secret talks in 1906 the idea of a military alliance with Germany was aired if north Schleswig should be returned.[23] The Danes in north

Schleswig did not abandon the idea that they had acquired a indelible 'third party right' through the clause, and they also refused to give up the idea of national self-determination which was the basic idea of the clause.

A particular link between the north Schleswig problem and foreign politics lay in the possibility of influencing the Danish government by giving the Danes special treatment. This happened chiefly after 1890 when Russia and France entered into collaboration. The strategic significance of Denmark in the western part of the Baltic sea also increased immensely due to the opening of the Kiel canal (1895) as well as the build up of the German navy (from 1898). In addition the German emperor greatly mistrusted the Danish royal family. Tsar Alexander III and Edward VII were married to daughters of Christian IX. The 'Köller policy' of the turn of the century, which Wilhelm II had personally agreed to, was to make Denmark obedient. The reason for its abolition in 1902–3 is to be seen in the emperor's attempts to come closer to Russia.[24] After Russia had been weakened by the war of 1904–5 against Japan, it tried to come to an agreement with England, which made Denmark's position even more interesting. For several years a Danish officer talked secretly with the head of the German general staff on behalf of the Danish prime minister. He tried to convince him that Denmark would fiercely defend its neutrality against, for example, an English landing at Esbjerg or on Zealand. In this connection the Opants' Children Convention of 11 January 1907 played an important role. It was the only tangible result of these negotiations.

The option provisions were not clearly defined in article XIX of the Treaty of Vienna (1864). People exercised their option by moving to Denmark but the treaty emphasised that they could keep their property in their country of birth. Also a *'droit d'indigénat'* (right of indigenous status), which could never be lost, was mentioned. Everybody born in the *helstat* before the ratification of the treaty had this right within its borders. The option possibility expired six years after ratification. During the period of protest several waves of emigration took place when older men were also called up for military exercises. When the Franco–Prussian war broke out many emigrated to Denmark without going through the requisite formalities. The 1872 Convention of Aabenraa brought the ambiguity of article XIX to an end. The optants were allowed to return but as they were Danish citizens they could be expelled if they caused 'trouble'. That meant that they did not possess a vote and also that they had to act passively in the struggle between nationalities. There were numerous people in this category. In 1874 there were 2482 optants in the first constituency in contrast to 11 931 Danish and 1970 German voters. In the course of time their number decreased; after 1870 young people who did not want to do their military service had now to emigrate and were not allowed to return. Between 1889 and 1894 approximately 1500 of the optants were naturalised.

In 1901 and 1902 their number increased again because at the end of the 'Köller policy' the authorities turned 1200 people, who had often been outstanding local leaders, into optants in order to remove their political rights. Until 1898 the children of Danish optants who lived in north Schleswig were stateless. In this year Danish citizenship law was modified so that these children obtained automatic Danish citizenship. The difficult situation of the stateless people born before 1898 was only solved by the Optants' Children Convention in 1907, resulting from German interest in a suitable Danish neutrality policy. On request these stateless children now could become Prussian citizens. This affected 4000 to 5000 people.[25] In the preamble to this convention the Danish government had to recognise indirectly the abolition of the North Schleswig clause in article V once more. It was also obliged to promise indirectly to prevent its officials from supporting the activities of the Danes in north Schleswig.[26]

Prussian and German policy concerning the Danes in north Schleswig was to turn them into loyal, German speaking citizens. Except for this primary aim, state policy cannot be described very easily. Apart from the harsh actions of the military authorities in the early years, Prussia generally behaved in a restrained way and adopted a policy of wait and see during almost the entire period of Bismarck's government. Prussia was in many ways a progressive state, and Bismarck relied on its notorious integrating powers.[27] A clear exception to this was the germanisation of the school system in 1878 and 1888, as well as the later attempts to persuade Germans to settle and to buy Danish farms in north Schleswig. This policy with a little delay and some mitigation plainly followed the example of the Prussian policy in the eastern provinces. The administration in Berlin in the later years was, if the impulsive emperor did not enforce his ideas, generally characterised by moderation and a predominance of foreign policy considerations. Under no circumstances was the north Schleswig question either at home or in foreign policy a big problem for Prussia/Germany.

After the first High President Carl von Scheel–Plessen had left office in 1879 the local administration, as well as the political climate, were increasingly permeated by national ideas. Nationalists often used governmental powers ruthlessly to force through their aims. The harsh local policy was eagerly assisted by the German Association for Northern Schleswig, which was founded in 1890. By 1909 it had opened 60 local branches throughout north Schleswig. In this association, which became the voice of an intolerant panGerman nationalism, local civil servants played an outstanding role.[28] Critics put their opinions forward in the weekly newspaper *Christliche Welt*, edited by the theologian Martin Rade in Marburg. In this weekly Johs. Tiedje from north Schleswig published in 1909 a comprehensive critical view of the situation in north Schleswig.[29] This line of thought led to the foundation of an Association for German Peace Work in the Nordmark. Johs. Schmidt–Vodder who later represented the German minority in the Danish parliament, led this association. Its effect, however, remained small.[30]

The First World War and the Plebiscites, 1914–20

The First World War paralysed the activities of the Danish associations and the newspapers in north Schleswig were censored. The Danish member of the German *Reichstag*, H.P. Hanssen, could, however, continue his work. Approximately 30 000 north Schleswig men were called up and had to fight on various battlefields. A good 5000 never returned.

In the spring of 1915 the German Ambassador in Copenhagen repeatedly hinted at a possible solution to the north Schleswig problem when the war was over. The Danish Foreign Minister did not follow this up so as not to compromise the neutrality of the country.[31] From August 1916 the Foreign Office in London was also occupied with the question of what should happen to north Schleswig when the Germans were defeated. Although conservative Danish circles tried several times to influence the Foreign Office into pushing forward farreaching demands it maintained the stance that Denmark should be given the Danish part of Schleswig after the war.[32]

In October 1915 the head of the Danish social democrats, Th. Stauning, discussed among other problems the north Schleswig question with the leaders of the German Social Democratic party. They agreed that people should have the right of self-determination, which the German party intended, when in power, to carry through. In 1917 the question turned up again via the Stockholm Manifesto of the neutral Social Democratic parties. This manifesto advocated: 'An amicable solution to the north Schleswig problem through an understanding between the participating states on the basis of a correction to the borders, after consulting the inhabitants.' On 7 October 1918 the head of the Swedish Social Democratic party, Hjalmar Branting, published an article in which he demanded a just solution to the north Schleswig question, although it had not been mentioned in President Wilson's 14 points. Later articles and his correspondence with Stauning prove that Branting did not, in contrast to the Danish social democrats, think of a solution through a

German–Danish agreement but rather through a general peace conference. It was just this course of action that Stauning sought to avoid by his letter of 17 October to the German Social Democratic leader Friedrich Ebert. In Stauning's eyes a solution through the Allied powers would be 'very unpleasant for Denmark', and therefore he suggested a German initiative, for example through a statement in the *Reichstag*. No great discrepancy on this question seems to have existed between the two parties. The attitude of the social democrats in Schleswig–Holstein was more ambiguous. They tried to keep north Schleswig as a part of Germany through several autonomy proposals, but they also ended up with a fundamental recognition of the right of self-determination.[33]

At the beginning of October 1918 the German government asked for armistice negotiations, based on the 14 points which President Wilson had outlined in his speech to the US Congress on 8 January 1918. In this outline the north Schleswig problem was not actually mentioned, but the 14 points rested on the right of self-determination for all nations, and therefore the German Foreign Office took it for granted, that the north Schleswig problem would be put forward.[34] On 23 October in the *Reichstag*, H.P. Hanssen called for the implementation of the right of self-determination in north Schleswig. He also referred to article V of the Treaty of Prague. Every claim based on this article was refused by the Germans, but Hanssen (and the Danish ambassador) was told unofficially that Wilson's principles would also be valid for north Schleswig. This answer was available officially and in a written form on 14 November. It did not indicate who should present the claim. The German Foreign Office would have preferred direct Danish–German negotiations but H.P. Hanssen knew through his links with Denmark that the Allied powers insisted on solving the question at the forthcoming peace conference.[35] Considering the future relationship between Denmark and Germany, the Danish government would probably have also preferred a German–Danish agreement but the very rumours about this possibility had induced Allied diplomats on 12 and 14 October to warn the government. On 23 October, which was by chance the same day on which H.P. Hanssen made his speech in the *Reichstag*, the two houses of the Danish parliament decided that only a change of sovereignty, which corresponded with the principle of nationality, would fulfil the wish, the feeling and the interest of the Danish people. They also agreed that the implementation of the right of self-determination, which had been recognised by both belligerent camps, must be prevented from causing damage to either side in order to secure the coming reunification.

On 16 and 17 November the council of the Danish Voters Union in north Schleswig made its decision on the future border. H.P.

Hanssen got his way: first voting should take place *en bloc* in north Schleswig and second north Schleswig was defined as the area situated north of today's frontier (that is without Flensburg). Other resolutions dealt with the voting procedure, as well as the concession made to south Schleswig circles that adjacent districts in middle Schleswig could ask for a separate vote. Two members registered reservations even though the decision was unanimous. The result together with the German letter of 14 November was presented to the Danish Ambassador in Berlin.[36]

This concord on the future frontier did not last. Among nationalistic conservative circles the *Dannevirke* movement arose. It relied on the wishful thinking of circles in south Schleswig and intrigued against the social–liberal government in Denmark with the help of foreign diplomats in Copenhagen, especially the French. Public opinion was also stirred up. This extra-parliamentary drive was not interested in plebiscites but took it for granted that an internationalisation of the Kiel canal, which might be established by the Allies, must have a northern frontier which might be the Schlei–Dannevirke line. Thus Denmark could annex most of Schleswig without future risks. The Flensburg movement had a much wider foundation. It was built on the right of self-determination but modified it by emphasising that the Prussians should not automatically benefit by the changes in people's attitudes since 1867. The election results of 1867 could be, if necessary, the basis for a new borderline. In fact this line on self-determination had been used for Alsace–Lorraine in December 1918. After the plebiscites in 1920 this movement called for an internationalisation of middle Schleswig in order to give the population enough time for undisturbed national reflection. In Schleswig these movements, and in particular the Flensburg movement, led to a lot of tension inside the Danish organisations. In December 1919 H.P. Hanssen received only 35 out of 66 votes in a vote of confidence, held by the council of the Voters' Union. In Denmark too bitter antagonism replaced the concord of 1918. Public opinion as well as political life were split into two almost equally sized camps. Finally these tensions, which were sharpened by social and other political questions, led to the downfall of the social–liberal government and to a serious crisis in Danish political life.[37]

The reaction of the German population was complicated by the collapse of the German Empire. The revolutionary workmen's and soldiers' councils had only a temporary local influence in the border area. It was more important that the social democrats were soon able to become the governing party, and the party which supported the new republic. At the beginning of February 1919 delegates of Social Democratic parties met for a conference in Berne. Here, German and Danish social democrats agreed on a solution to the border question, which corresponded to the decisions made by the Voters' Union on 17 November 1918. In Flensburg, however, a vote was to take place only if asked for by 25 per cent of all people entitled to vote.[38] At first this composed attitude of the leading German social democrats did not meet with sympathy from local party branches. The middle class parties expressed their opinions, especially in the German Committee for the Duchy of Schleswig, which started its public work on 31 October 1918. Originally it intended to stay outside party politics. During some politically inflamed months the Committee distanced itself from the allegedly Danish orientated policy of the German government. Only in April 1919 did it accept Wilson's 14 points, but even then it had reservations. At the end of April 1919 the Prussian government appointed Adolf Köster, who later became a German Foreign Minister, to be a special State Commissioner in Schleswig–Holstein. He was given extensive authority and a lot of financial resources in order to coordinate the German preparations for the plebiscites. These preparations took place among a population which did not comprehend the military situation of Germany and was, therefore, outraged at the conditions of the Treaty of Versailles.

The peace conference had met the official Danish wish for separate votes in two zones, that is in north Schleswig *en bloc* and in middle Schleswig by commune. German military and higher officials had to leave these zones before the plebiscites, and the zones were then placed under an international commission. The Dannevirke movement had pushed through plans for a plebiscite in a third zone, and it was only after a protest by the Danish government that it was dropped by the peace conference. But an error in the voting rules was discovered too late. It was not only people who were born in north Schleswig and had been expelled who were given the right to vote in accordance with Danish wishes, but also people who were born in north Schleswig and later moved. This error gave the German side considerably better voting results.[39]

On 10 January 1920 the Treaty of Versailles came into force and two weeks later the designated international commission – *Commission International de Surveillance du Plebiscite Slesvig (International Surveillance Commission for the Schleswig Plebiscite)* – took over the voting area from 25 January until 16 June. The commission consisted of four members: an Englishman, a Frenchman, a Norwegian and a Swede. It worked effectively and in spite of national excitement, which was particularly characteristic of the voting in the second zone, it achieved fair play.[40] The commission was supported by French and English military forces, by the local administration and by a special police force. Köster became the official delegate of the German government to the commission. All costs of this arrangement, including the feeding of the population, were shared by Germany and Denmark.

The vote in north Schleswig – the first zone – took place on 10 February 1920; 101 652 votes were cast, in other words a turnout of 91.5 per cent. Of these votes 75 431 (74.9 per cent) were for Denmark and 25 329 (25.1 per cent) for Germany. The vote in the second zone – in Flensburg and parts of middle Schleswig – was held on 14 March. There was a turnout of 91.1 per cent of which 51 724 (80.2 per cent) voted for Germany and 12 800 (19.8 per cent) for Denmark. In Flensburg the share of votes cast for Denmark (25 per cent) was slightly higher.[41]

In both cases the people entitled to vote who were not residents but who were born in the voting area played an important role. In the second zone they numbered 18 711; 9.2 per cent of them voted for Denmark and 79.5 per cent for Germany. In the first zone also the proportion of the 24 047 people in this same category who voted for Denmark was considerably smaller (63.2 per cent) than among the local residents (78.4 per cent). Voters in this category influenced the results especially in the towns of north Schleswig and in the southern areas of the first zone. Apart from Haderslev the towns showed a German majority, but only in Tønder and the small town of Højer did these German majorities have any strength without the votes of the non-residents. In the countryside only the parishes of Tinglev, Udbjerg and the rural areas of Højer had, with or without non-resident voters, a German majority. Other parishes in the southern areas of the first zone had a small Danish majority, which increased without the inclusion of non-resident voters.

Despite the clear description of the voting provisions in the peace treaty[42] and despite the clear result of the votes cast the southern borderline of the first zone was questioned as the final border. Both the Dannevirke and Flensburg movements on the Danish side tried to achieve an internationalisation of Flensburg. The French and the Norwegian members of the International Surveillance Commission recommended putting the new frontier south of four middle Schleswig parishes in the second zone. The German attempt to ask for a more northerly border, the Tiedje line, after the man who made the proposal, caused a greater sensation. It went from north of Højer, Tønder, Ravsted and Tinglev to Rinkenæs. In this area – called the Tiedje belt – in total 5557 Danish and 6794 German votes were cast; of these 4775 were for Denmark and 4825 for Germany, if non-resident voters were subtracted. The slight predominance of German votes in the Tiedje belt was, however, achieved only through massive German majorities in Tønder and Højer in the western part of the area.[43] This use of the *en bloc* principle in favour of Germany aimed at trying to produce equal sized minorities on both sides of the new frontier. Tiedje's proposal did not influence the Commission's decision. In the following decades, however, it repeatedly produced insecurity about the durability of the frontier. On 15 June 1920 the Conference of Ambassadors informed Denmark officially of the new borderline and north Schleswig was transferred to Denmark.

The Danes in South Schleswig, 1920–33

South of the new border the two plebiscites of 1920 left a Danish minority which was centred on Flensburg and its immediate vicinity. Smaller groups were scattered all over south Schleswig, including regions south of the second zone. Nowhere did this minority have a local majority or a dominating position.

Danish was mainly used as the language of communication within the organisations and the institutions of the minority, but not all its members were Danish speaking. South of the new border some communes existed in which old style Danish had survived as the everyday language, but it did not have a national significance. There were no other objective characteristics which distinguished the inhabitants who were in favour of Denmark from those in favour of Germany. National consciousness, expressed in various ways, was conclusive. A person from Schleswig who was a member of *Den slesvigske Forening* (the Schleswig Association) and sent his children to a Danish school was undoubtedly Danish minded. But there were many other criteria, including those that consisted of things the doing of which was, for some, simply unthinkable, for example being a member of German national associations or participating in special German events. Other forms of behaviour, for example family parties, activity in trade unions or an interest in chamber music, did not have a national significance.

Not all people from Schleswig who were in favour of Denmark fulfilled all these criteria or even had the opportunity to do so, either because there were no Danish schools in the neighbourhood or because the economic and social pressure of their environment was overpowering. This minority consisted mainly of people with modest means, in other words low paid urban workers and in the country-side smallholders and agricultural workers. Most of the chairmen and honorary agents of the Schleswig Association's local branches belonged to the same social groups. South Schleswig was a remote corner of Germany, only industrialised in the Flensburg area. Therefore the critical years after the First World War and again the great depression in 1929 severely affected the province and especially this minority. During the winter of 1932–3, two-fifths of the parents whose children went to schools in Flensburg were unemployed in contrast to four-fifths of the parents whose children attended the Danish primary school in that town.[44] These people, however, elected mainly self employed traders, professionals and some farmers to become the general leaders of the minority. In this – politically middle class minded – group they found people who had sufficient resources to deal with the tasks of leadership, who could master both languages and who corresponded socially and ideologically to the private groups in Denmark, which committed themselves to national work in the border area.

The minority organisations – like official Danish policy – did not have any irredentist aims.[45] They simply wanted to get together, strengthen and protect the Danes in south Schleswig. Some people, especially in the leading group and some of their supporters in the kingdom, did hope secretly that the old Danish land and its germanised population would one day find its way back to Denmark. This was by no means, not even for these people, a hope which could be expressed in political practice. In 1921 the main organisation had approximately 6000 members and in 1932 circa 4300. In 1923 the numbers peaked at almost 8900. Several times during elections roughly 4700 votes were cast for Danish candidates who had a chance of being elected only locally. The Flensburg group of the Schleswig Association did not participate in the last general elections after 1930 because the Danish minded workers in Flensburg wanted to vote politically rather than cast their vote as a national demonstration. Until 1933 the Danish minority seems to have been nearly half the size of the German minority in north Schleswig. For the Danes in south Schleswig the year 1920 meant a radical upheaval. The conservative, Flensborg Avis, which had been to date the largest newspaper in north Schleswig, was separated from most of its readers by the border. The new frontier turned the southern outposts of a strong Danish movement into a small leftover group which had to build up its own ideological and organisational basis in a variety of ways. This occurred under the after-effects of emotions which had been stirred up by the voting period and during the first uneasy years of the young German republic which wanted principally to offer its minorities a democratic frame.

A main problem of the south Schleswig Danes was access to Danish schools.[46] The Weimar constitution of 1919 promised in article 113 that 'foreign speaking parts of Germany' must not 'be restricted in their free traditional development, especially not in the usage of their mother tongue during schooling'. Provisions for carrying out this article were, however, missing and the reality in Prussia was for many years different to theory. Only in Flensburg did the municipality establish a local Danish primary school (1920) but the children enrolled were selected by language tests. In 1920 only 240 of more than 900 children were admitted. A Danish private school for further education could be opened but it was only allowed to admit pupils older than ten. The language tests were not abandoned till 1926, when a special Prussian edict permitted the establishment of public and private junior schools but still only within the second zone, and at least one of the parents of each child had to originate either from the second zone or from Denmark. Finally the Prussian decree of 31 December 1928 abandoned the second zone restriction and recognised simply the principle of national consciousness: 'The acknowledgment of membership of a minority must be neither checked nor challenged'. Up to 1933 the number of Danish schools increased to nine: two in Flensburg (1920), six in the environs of the town (1926–9) and one in the town of Schleswig (1930). Apart from the one in Flensburg all schools were private because the parents shared the opinion that the influence of the parents' council was too small at public schools.

Because of the social structure of the minority these private schools depended on support from Denmark. South Schleswig parents founded the *Dansk Skoleforening* (Danish School Union) in 1920 in order to deal with school matters. This minority group consistently felt that local German groups tried to prevent the opening of new schools by influencing parents.[47] They would have preferred it if school matters had been the responsibility of Germany and not locally of Prussia, and if they had been regulated by legislation and not by administrative measures. Ultimately, however, official school policy changed to a course which was not unsatisfactory.

Apart from some emigrants, who had settled in north and south America, no Danish minority existed in other countries with which people in south Schleswig could share experiences. They worked, however, closely together with Frisians in west Schleswig who, in 1923, had founded the Frisian–Schleswig Association[48] (see Thomas Steensen's chapter). This association brought together the 'national' Frisians who strove to develop their own tradition in connection with nordic culture. For that reason they had voted for Denmark in the 1920 vote. They regarded themselves as a national minority in contrast to the overwhelming majority of Frisians who were members of the North Frisian Association and considered themselves as Germans with a special feeling for their native country. The teamwork between Danes in Schleswig and the Frisians was mainly political. Danes supported the chairman of the Schleswig–Frisians during county council elections. Also, the two groups united their German newspapers in 1925 and in March 1924 they participated in the foundation of the *Verband der nationalen Minderheiten in Deutschland* (Association of National Minorities in Germany). This association was based on a Polish initiative and consisted of, apart from Poles, Frisians and Danes, Sorbs and later also Lithuanians living in east Prussia. The aim of this association was to exchange experiences and to cooperate in the organisation of elections because a mandate directly achieved at regional level at elections to the *Reichstag* and the *Landtag* would help towards securing additional seats on the national list, which might be gained with smaller quotas of votes. In Upper Silesia the number of Poles was still high enough to gain a direct mandate –but only for the Prussian *Landtag*. Occasionally they could benefit from votes of the other minorities. This electoral teamwork continued until 1933 but after a few years it was already without any practical importance because the Polish direct mandate had been lost. The Danish workers in Flensburg did not favour cooperation with the Poles, and neither the groups in the kingdom nor the Danish Foreign Ministry agreed with the idea of linking the situation on the German–Polish frontier with the problems in Schleswig. The minorities maintained a residual cooperation, and only after Hitler's takeover in 1933 did the activity of the association die down.

The cooperation especially took the form of joint action at the annual *Europäischer Nationalitätenkongress* (European Congress of Nationalities), which in October 1925 met in Geneva for the first time.[49] Polish as well as Danish minorities and – according to Danish wishes – Sorbs but not Frisians from Schleswig were invited to this congress. Among others the Germans from north Schleswig were against the admission of the Frisians. For the German minority in Denmark, as well as for German nationalist groups in Schleswig–Holstein, the Frisians were a Danish organisation in disguise and a disturbing factor in their border policy. Despite Polish and Danish demands the Frisians were not invited to following congresses. In 1927, principally at Polish instigation, this resistance occasioned the withdrawal of the Association of National Minorities in Germany from the Nationalities Congress. In this connection the idea of cultural autonomy, supported both by the German minorities and by the German government, was of importance for the Poles as well as for the Danes. This idea had been a precondition for the summoning of the Congress, but both the Danes and the Poles had been very reluctant to support an autonomy of this kind. The implementation of it would have given the advantage to those minorities with a social structure powerful enough to support a cultural autonomy. This was often the case with the German minorities in east Europe but not with the Poles or the Danes. Also a farreaching cultural autonomy, for which the mother country was to pay, could give a more powerful country the possibility of an unwanted influence inside a weaker country. Finally the idea of national registration appeared alarming. All members of a minority would have to be entered in a national register in order to share in the cultural autonomy. This procedure would be dangerous for minorities which had large socially insecure groups among their members. After the break of 1927 the Danish minority kept a passive connection with the Congress through an observer, though it was now dominated by German minorities from outside Germany. This connection ultimately ended in 1933.[50] In 1928 the Danish minority arranged a meeting in Flensburg at which some congress leaders participated. However, the connections of the Danish minority with the Association and the Congress did not have any larger practical importance.[51]

Although the Danes in south Schleswig had only sparse contacts with minorities other than the Frisians, they had numerous and various connections with their mother country and with organisations in Denmark. During the reunion celebration at Dybbøl in 1920 the Danish Prime Minister promised the people of south Schleswig that they would not be forgotten. Succeeding Danish governments kept this promise and supported financially the cultural activities of the minority. Officially for Denmark and for the political parties, however, the question of the border, controversial in 1919–20, was now definitely decided. This consensus was joined by another one in Danish foreign policy: a bilateral agreement between Germany and Denmark about the treatment of the minorities of both sides was unwanted. This well known Danish attitude, also expressed at the peace conference in 1919, rested on Denmark's experiences in the years before 1864. A stronger power could always find an excuse to meddle in the internal affairs of a smaller country but the weaker country did not share this ability.

The Danish minority had to come to terms with these fundamental decisions even though it meant many years of insecurity for it. In October 1921 the German government suggested a bilateral agreement to Denmark in order to regulate the situation of the minorities. The Danish government rejected this suggestion by pointing out that the treatment of the minority had to be a consequence of the fundamental laws, as well as of liberal legislation in both countries and should not be the result of a bi-lateral agreement.[52] This attitude did not exclude negotiations. In 1923 the Danish Social Democratic party asked for a conference about the problems of the border area, which took place in Flensburg in November.[53] Among others, the leaders and representatives of the German and Danish Social Democratic parties participated. The conference distanced itself from 'chauvinistic agitation' on both sides, and demanded a stricter control of public funds paid out for the cultural support of the minorities by both mother countries. The conference also recognised the border of 1920 as the 'legally valid border'. This recognition, which the Weimar Republic never offered, led to fierce attacks by the more right wing German parties on the Stauning–Wels agreement of 1923.

Shortly before the formation of the first Social Democratic government in Denmark, in April 1924, Danish minority policy north of the border was criticised by the German group of the *Union internationale des associations pour la société des nations* (International Federation of League of Nations Societies). The Danish side, however, defended its minority policy so successfully that the German attack was not continued.[54] At the invitation of the Danish Foreign Ministry a German and a Danish delegation of officials and school experts discussed schooling problems on both sides of the borderline in Copenhagen in October 1924. They only wanted to achieve a clarification, not a solution of the problems. In the long run the negotiations and the obvious difference between conditions north and south of the border were important for later minority regulations in south Schleswig. In 1924 28 public and 12 private schools for German minded people existed in north Schleswig. In all 2791 children attended them. For the Danish minded in south Schleswig one public school and one private secondary school existed – both in Flensburg – with a total attendance of 614 children.[55]

For the Danish government it was not as easy to influence the minority in south Schleswig as might have been expected in view of the financial dependence of the minority. The decentralised structure of the minority organisations was already a hindrance to be surmounted by personal talks with a number of minority leaders, as for example when the Danish consul had to disseminate advice from the Foreign Ministry.[56] On top of that the minority offered at the beginning a possible domestic problem in Denmark. For many years the bitter controversy of 1919–20 led to continuing stress in the relationship between parliamentarians and those groups in Denmark which had been prepared to go to the utmost constitutional limits before and during the Easter crisis in 1920. Within the *Grænseforeningen* (Danish Border Union)[57] these groups were originally numerous, especially in Copenhagen. This Union had been founded as a central organisation for many older associations which had worked for the support of the Danes in north Schleswig before the First World War. Some of them had a close personal relationship with the leaders of the Danes in Flensburg, especially with the editor-in-chief of the *Flensborg Avis*, who had also played an important role when the Border Union was founded. Half heartedly, it is true, the editor-in-chief, like the Border Union, faced reality, ie the border of 1920. The parliamentarians, however, were careful and distrustful. They did not want either the national excitement during the Easter crisis to be repeated or the Danish relationship to the Weimar Republic to be compromised by the irresponsible behaviour of private circles.

Public subsidies to a minority in another country were something new. During the Prussian period before the First World War they had been unthinkable. The funds then furnished to the Danes in north Schleswig were donated by private circles. This unfamiliarity, the parliamentarians' mistrust and also the wish to exclude these subsidies from the arguments between parties led to a special arrangement. In 1921 the public funds were handed over to an Allocation Committee in which the major parties in parliament, ranging from the *Konservative Folkeparti* (Conservative People's party) to the Social Democratic party, each had one member. In the same year the government, the parties and representatives of the minority in south Schleswig agreed that public money was to be used only for cultural purposes,[58] such as schools, libraries, certain associations and clubs, as well as schooling and apprenticeships in Denmark for young people and similar tasks. The salary of the Danish vicar in Flensburg was given to the general organisation of the Danish Church Abroad, which usually maintained seamen's churches. The money was not to be spent for any political activity, for agitation or even for newspapers or leaflets published in German. Geographically the subsidies were limited to the second zone. This is why the school in Schleswig, which was founded in 1930, and also the Danish General Secretariat in Flensburg from 1924, had to be supported by the Border Union.[59] Like other private schools in Prussia, the Danish schools also received a small grant from the Prussian state.

Other funds were given to the Danish minority from the widespread network of associations in Denmark, which had roots in the pre-war period. When these associations gathered under the Border Union umbrella they passed on some of their subscriptions to the Union, but the larger ones would support for example a school or an association in Schleswig directly. They held local meetings in which people from south Schleswig either made a speech or participated as guests. Their resources also came from donations and an annual collection of money, which was held on 18 April, the anniversary of the storming of the Dybbøl fortifications. The Border Union also edited the monthly magazine *Grænsevagten* (Frontier Guard), which regularly observed the situation in the border area and published important declarations and documents. In 1927 cooperation between the Border Union, the Language Association and the North Schleswig Schools Union was established by a joint committee. This cooperation indicated that the wounds of 1919–20 were beginning to heal. In 1932 the Border Union finally freed itself of its last bitter feelings about the 1920 decision.[60] The small League Denmark–Danevirke–Danebrog, which worked in the most southerly areas of Schleswig and also paid for leaflets in German,[61] stood outside this widespread national cooperation, which became still more elaborate after 1933. When the Danish newspaper in Flensburg got into difficulties at the end of the 1920s it was taken over by a limited company in 1930. A considerable part of the necessary capital came from Denmark, particularly from a large Copenhagen ship owner.[62] The grants from the kingdom were indispensable because the smallness of the minority and its social structure precluded sufficient self support. However, it was also necessary to secure the permanent payment of funds. This consideration led finally to widespread cooperation on public subsidies and later also to cooperation on private grants. It helped to reduce the after-effects of the 1919–20 border quarrels and at the same time to isolate those groups that were still in favour of a chauvinistic policy.

Until the middle of the 1920s the situation of the Danish minority in its host state was unclarified and often difficult. On the one hand this was a consequence of the critical years of the young Weimar Republic, for instance the inflation of 1922–3 and the internal uprisings. The last of these also concerned the minorities, when the German language Danish press was forbidden for a few months in 1923–4 because of alleged separatist tendencies.[63] On the other hand the uncertain state of the minority was – especially in Schleswig–Holstein – an after-effect of the bitter 1920 voting campaign. The minority position was also complicated by various German authorities, which all pursued different aims. On the one hand there were the largely irreconcilable local groups previously mentioned, which strove for a revision of the frontier and co-operated closely with the Germans in north Schleswig. On the other hand there was the Prussian state and Germany as a whole. For Prussia the problems in Schleswig were small in contrast to its problems on the eastern border, which were much bigger and more complicated. The problems in Schleswig, however, were repeatedly related to those in the eastern areas. The German Republic had to carry out its general foreign policy with consideration for the German minorities, especially those in eastern Europe. This combination is exactly what seems to have made German participation in the education negotiations of 1924 in Copenhagen easier.[64]

Prussia reacted hesitantly when in 1925, the German Foreign Minister suggested giving cultural autonomy to the minorities in Germany. The reason for Prussia's reluctance was that it preferred a schooling system which was controlled by the state, whereas the *Reich* preferred private schools, for strategic reasons and also because it did not want to be responsible for a proper minority schooling system.[65] The minorities concerned were also a problem. Only after long negotiations was the school system in Schleswig regulated by the Prussian edict of 9 February 1926, which contradicted the idea of autonomy.[66] It caused problems within the local German group and the *Schleswig–Holsteiner–Bund* (Schleswig–Holstein Union) installed a new leadership which coincided with the new ideas of the Foreign

Ministry in asking for a more generous border policy.[67] In the meantime the idea of general German legislation for minority affairs had been dropped, because minorities only lived in Prussia and Saxony (the Sorbs). Therefore, the idea of autonomy was also dropped because it required general legislation.[68]

Finally, after two years work, the Prussian edict of 31 December 1928 was formulated by a commission from the Ministry of Education. This edict was to regulate the Polish minority schooling system, which the east Prussian authorities especially had opposed. The background for this opposition was the sharp antagonism between the social Democratic/Liberal government and the leading groups in east Prussia, which were mostly of a nationalist conservative point of view. This edict, which was also extended to Schleswig, included the final provision about people's free choice according to their national awareness, and it made it possible for the minority to establish schools outside the second zone. In that way a satisfying framework for the life of the Danish minority was finally built up. However, they were to be hard hit by the economic crisis, and a few years later, in 1933, the promising first signs of a new, more conciliatory development were – even at local level – completely destroyed.

II The Germans in Denmark – *Immo Doege*

The German Minority In Denmark, 1920–33

In the Schleswig plebiscite of 10 February 1920, zone I voted against remaining in the German *Reich* by a majority of 75 431 (74.9 per cent) to 25 329 (25.1 per cent). In accordance with the *en bloc* policy agreed upon by the Allied powers for this zone, the northern region (3980 sq km or 45 per cent) of the former duchy of Schleswig, with some 160 000 inhabitants, was thus ceded to Denmark.

Only in 41 communes of zone I had there been a majority vote for Germany. Sizeable German majorities were, however, obtained in Tønder (Tondern) (76 per cent) and Højer (Hoyer) (73 per cent), with slight majorities in Sønderborg (Sonderburg) (55 per cent) and in Aabenraa (Apenrade) (54 per cent). This meant that a belt of territory close to zone II had voted mainly in favour of Germany (76 communes with 6735 German and 5658 Danish votes). Most of these communes were situated in an area known by the Germans as the *Schiefes Viereck* (crooked rectangle) and by the Danes as *den truede firkant* (the threatened rectangle) between Tønder, Løgumkloster (Lügumkloster), the Aabenraa fjord and Graasten (Gravenstein). This region is usually termed *Tiedje-Gürtel* (Tiedje belt) and the line marking its northern boundary the *Tiedje-Linie* (Tiedje line) after the German frontier expert Johannes Tiedje, who suggested that the frontier be drawn north of the *Schiefes Viereck* (see maps 1 and 2). This proposal, which would have meant approximately equal minorities on either side of the new border, was submitted to the International Commission for Schleswig by the German government on 17 March 1920. Although rejected by the Commission, it continued to feature in subsequent German deliberations regarding possible border revision.[1] The southern boundary of zone I thus became the final frontier between the kingdom of Denmark and the German *Reich*.

As a result of the frontier revision, the Germans in north Schleswig were separated from the *Staatsvolk* (main body of the German people) and henceforth formed the German minority in the Danish kingdom. In February 1920 they numbered approximately 38 000, but almost immediately after the plebiscite German officials and public service. employees began to move back to the *Reich*. Some of the German social democrats converted to Danish social democracy, which meant that the number of those who were German minded in north Schleswig declined in the years which followed. For the period following the plebiscite, the Germans in the whole region of north Schleswig (south Jutland) (the area is known as *Nordschleswig* in German and *Sønderjylland* in Danish) may be assumed to have numbered approximately 32 000.[2] As mentioned above, the Germans were concentrated in the *Schiefes Viereck* south of the Højer–Tønder–Tinglev (Tingleff–Graasten) line, particularly in the towns of Sønderborg, Aabenraa and Haderslev on the east coast of north Schleswig. The remainder of the German minority, living north of the Tiedje line and the old German–Danish border along the Kongeaa (Königsau) river, was scattered (and these people thus known as *Streudeutsche*).

Any attempt to describe the German minority in the usual terms applied to define a 'national minority' proves difficult. O. Kimminich, specialist in international law, realising the problems which arise in describing some minorities, offers the simplified definition that

> a minority in the sense of international law has the same defining characteristics as a people: common language, common culture, common historical fate. The minority thus appears in principle to be the same as a people or a nation, though without a state.[3]

Kimminich moreover links smallness of number to his concept of a national minority. In 1931 Viktor Guttmann called for 'racial, cultural and economic singularity' to justify a *Volksgruppe* (national group) as a minority as well as 'common significant experience, shared fate' and the 'presence of a cultivated, powerful will to exist'.[4]

According to the League of Nations' definition, the German minority in north Schleswig cannot be regarded as a 'genuine' minority, because its area of settlement is not in the midst of a foreign state but on the border of one whose people are of the same ethnic origin.[5] In the same vein H. Eibl commented in 1933 that 'if a part of a people inhabits an area adjacent to the territory occupied by the main mass of the same people there is a case for maintaining not that the group is a minority in another state but that the border has been wrongly drawn'.[6] The currently valid United Nations' definition requires, along with other criteria for the existence of a minority, that 'the group must be loyal to the state whose citizenship its members possess'.[7]

For the German minority in the period following 1920, therefore, the following criteria would apply fully: 'conscious cultivation of their common linguistic and cultural heritage'; the 'common historical fate' of defeat in the plebiscite, where their 25 per cent against the Danish majority meant that they were 'relatively small in number' and 'a powerful will to exist'. However, 'racial and economic singularity' cannot be ascribed to the German minority in Denmark. Nor can they be differentiated in terms of religion, as they shared a profession of the Lutheran Protestant faith with the Danes. In terms of the United Nations' definition given above, on the other hand, the German minority was, until 1945, basically disloyal to the host state to which it had opposed belonging. Frequently, the decision to be counted as part of the German minority was purely subjective. Also a certain percentage of the north Schleswig population could not be definitively assigned to one political camp, although exact figures for those who were *blakkede* or indifferent to the national question cannot be gauged.

There have so far been few demographic studies of the structure of the German minority 1920–45.[8] From the material we have been able to consult, the following picture emerges of the occupational structure in urban and rural areas:

Table 5.1: Urban areas

1	Workers	34	8.6%
2	Farmers	85	21.5%
3	Craftsmen/Traders	182	46.0%
4	Seamen/Fishermen	21	5.3%
5	Professionals/Officials	34	8.6%
6	Widows	7	1.8%
7	Other	32	8.2%
		395	100%

Table 5.2: Rural areas

1	Workers	504	34.7%
2	Farmers	558	38.4%
3	Craftsmen/Traders	251	17.3%
4	Seamen/Fishermen	19	1.3%
5	Professionals/Officials	24	1.7%
6	Widows	37	2.5%
7	Other	61	4.1%
		1 454	100%

These figures show that three occupational groups were dominant after 1920: farmers and farm owners (around 35 per cent), manual workers (29 per cent) and the skilled and commercial trades in town and country areas (around 23 per cent). Conspicuous as a minority are professionals and officials, comprising only approximately three per cent, a phenomenon which will require closer examination below.

A rather different picture emerges from the composition of the committees of the group's political organisation, the *Schleswigscher Wählerverein* (Schleswig Voters' Union), canvassing in all elections as the *Slesvigsk Parti*, or *Schleswigsche Partei* (Schleswig party). In this respect, farm owners are in the majority, with 53 per cent of the positions, followed by the skilled and commercial classes with around 23 per cent and an almost equal group of graduate professionals, editors and teachers with 22 per cent. The complete absence of workers stands out.

An examination of linguistic behaviour is important in the case of a minority in a border region. According to the available data, which concern the homes of 1854 pupils at the German private schools on 1 December 1934, 57 per cent of families spoke *Sønderjysk* or *Plattdänisch* (the south Jutland variation of Danish) and 30 per cent High German, while German and Danish were considered languages of equal use in 13 per cent of homes. In examining the high profile of the Danish dialect, it is worth mentioning that from a German point of view almost all Danish studies report that practically two thirds of the native German population were Danish speaking or had Danish as their mother tongue (first language). In accordance with these findings, German is often described as the language of newcomers rather than the native German minority. This approach applies criteria which were frequently used from the mid nineteenth century onwards to draw conclusions about the national affiliation from language use. From today's perspective it would perhaps be more correct to point out that the vast majority of the minority group were *bilingual* and that their use of language was not necessarily indicative of national orientation. It is quite probable that many people in north Schleswig were what some sociologists call *zweiströmig* (two stream), which means they lived in and felt part of both German and Danish culture and lifestyles.

Immediately after the plebiscite, the Germans in north Schleswig began to organise themselves politically. The leading figure was soon Johannes C. Schmidt, formerly pastor in Vodder (Wodder).[9] After a period of preliminary deliberation in August 1919, he took the initiative and founded the *Schleswigscher Wählerverein* (see above) in July 1920. The party published its political aims in the German newspapers of north Schleswig on 18 August 1920. Besides emphasising the 'historic ties with Schleswig', the party demanded a revision of the new German–Danish frontier on the basis of a 'purely and justly implemented law of self-determination'. Further it called for complete cultural autonomy, in other words the right of Germans to enjoy self government in all matters relating to education, religion, social and philanthropic institutions. It pledged itself to a *kräftige, gesunde Mittelstandspolitik* (strongly middle class orientated policy) and to 'just, liberal and social legislation'. At this stage in the development of its aims, the party finally separated politically from the German minded social democrats between July and August 1920. The social democrats had been expressly mentioned in the party's provisional programme of 20 July, with reference to their cooperation in the run up to the plebiscite. Apparently it had then still been hoped that the social democrats would work together with them in 'matters concerning school and church'.[10]

Symptomatic of this development in relations with the German minded working classes is the composition of *Schleswigscher Wählerverein* committees in comparison with, say, the class structure in private, which meant German, schools. As mentioned above, around 35 per cent of pupils at private schools in rural areas, and around nine per cent in towns, were the children of workers, yet not one worker sat on such a committee.

The *Schleswigscher Wählerverein* was eventually divided into four *Kreisvereine* (regional associations) with a large number of *Ortsvereine* (local groups). It did not manage to attract a large membership from among the German minority, as the membership figures for the four *Kreisvereine* in the mid 1920s show:[11]

Tønder	2002	members
Sønderborg	251	
Aabenraa	718	
Haderslev	789	
	3760	members

Nevertheless, the party's political programme does appear to have had widespread support within the German minority. This is demonstrated by the polling results of the *Slesvigsk Parti* in the elections to the *Folketing* (the lower house of the *Rigsdag*, the Danish parliament).[12] The German minority was enfranchised from the start and the *Slesvigsk Parti* was exempted from the ruling that any new party formed in Denmark required 10000 signatures before being allowed to register.

Table 5.3: General election results

1920	1924	1926	1929	1932	1935	1939
7505	7715	10 422	9787	9868	12 617	15 016

Three factors explain the initial drop in the number of votes in comparison with the 1920 plebiscite results when votes for Germany were 25329 or 25.1 per cent. Not all Germans entitled to vote in the plebiscite lived in north Schleswig (there had been a number of so-called non-resident voters); German officials had been forced to move to areas within Germany after losing their posts in north Schleswig; and the German working classes who supported social democracy tended not to associate with the German minority, at least in party political terms (see above). Although the figures show a progression in the absolute number of German votes, particularly from 1926 onwards, the increase in percentage terms was inconsiderable (in 1920 there was 14.3 per cent; and in 1939 there was 15.9 per cent). One reason for this was the continuing influx of Danes from other regions of the country, a process no doubt partly encouraged by the Danish government. Between 1920 and 1939, therefore, the German minority had only one member in the *Folketing*: first pastor Johannes Schmidt and from 1939, Dr Jens Möller, a veterinary surgeon from Graasten. The German minority obtained no seats in the *Landsting* (the upper house of the *Rigsdag*) with its indirect electoral procedure via electoral colleges. However, it was represented in most of the nine communes in north Schleswig for which statistics are available and in three of the four *Amtsraad* (district councils).[13]

Table 5.4: Seats in the communes

1922	1925	1929	1933	1937	
34	38	37	33	30	seats

Table 5.5: Seats in the *Amtsraad* (1935)

Tønder	3 seats (out of 13)
Sønderborg	1 seat (out of 11)
Aabenraa	2 seats (out of 11)
Haderslev	no seats (out of 13)

Until the spread of National Socialism among the German minority after 1933, the *Schleswigscher Wählerverein*'s political activity was chiefly shaped by its 1920 guidelines. Their political interests centred around three main issues:

- The call for frontier revision, for *die neue Entscheidung* (a new decision).
- The wish for complete cultural autonomy.
- The question of the proportion of German ownership of farmland in north Schleswig or the *Bodenkampf* in German, the *Jordkampen* in Danish, the 'fight for the soil'.

The Danes kept a critical eye on these German demands, which were a constant source of potential conflict and led to many fierce controversies at local and national level.

The German call for frontier revision was, perhaps deliberately, never precisely defined. It is unlikely that anyone apart from a small radical group calling itself *Königsaubund* seriously considered a return to the 1918–20 border along the Kongeaa river. If anything it was the Tiedje belt which was proposed, possibly with sections of the Aabenraa district.[14] The *Schleswigscher Wählerverein* strongly opposed the Stauning–Wels agreement of 1923 and expressed regret at the stance taken by the German social democrats, claiming it showed 'a lack of national dignity' to allow such an agreement to be made.[15]

The desire for complete cultural autonomy in matters concerning schools and the church will be discussed in more detail below. The question of keeping as much land as possible under German ownership was accorded particular importance by the *Schleswigscher Wählerverein*. Johannes Schmidt considered the indigenous German farmer a guarantee against the fading of *Deutschtum* (the German presence) in north Schleswig. German efforts in this sphere were, however, hindered by the general agricultural crisis in north Schleswig in the 1920s. After 1926, when the *Kreditanstalt Vogelgesang* (a mortgage bank) (see below) was established, the national division in the struggle for farmland ownership hardened. By 1945, despite increasing financial support from the *Reich*, only some 3000 hectares (83 farms) were able to remain in German hands. By comparison, *circa*

34 000 hectares changed from German to Danish ownership between 1920 and 1939.

The basic political line of the *Schleswigscher Wählerverein* between 1920 and 1933 can only be described as heterogeneous. Statements made by Schmidt and other leading party representatives reveal chiefly *völkisch* and conservative, German nationalist and national–liberal traits, with a complete rejection of the Treaty of Versailles. Racist, revolutionary and socialist thought does not appear to have been of any significance within the minority. The first of these listed traits does, however, indicate a certain predisposition towards National Socialism and almost certainly contributed to the rapid spread of this ideology in the German minority around 1933.

The German minority's major cultural organisation was the *Deutscher Schulverein für Nordschleswig* (German School Union for North Schleswig), founded on 4 May 1920, again by Johannes Schmidt.[16] The organisation undertook primarily to assist the establishment and running of German private schools, as there was little opportunity to influence the state run elementary communal schools. After the plebiscite, the Danish government had passed a number of education acts designed to take account of the particular situation in north Schleswig and of the existence of the German minority.[17]

The laws of 30 June 1920 and the law of 1 May 1923 made the following provisions for the *folkeskole*, the nine grade elementary school in Denmark. In towns, the schools were to be divided into two sections, one with Danish and one with German as the language of instruction. From grade three onwards the children in each section would receive four to six periods of instruction in the other language. The parents were free to choose which section of the school their children attended. Elected School Commissions and the *Skolekonsulenter* or *Schulkonsulenten* (School Inspectors) were charged with the supervision of schools, and the communes had the responsibility of funding. In the rural communes the law required that a special course with German as the language of instruction must be established if demanded by ten per cent of the voters, representing at least ten children under 14 years of age. Also, unless there was such a course given sufficiently near, it had to be established if those voting for it, while less than 10 per cent of the voters, represented 24 children of school age.

This, in effect very liberal, arrangement for state run elementary schools was, however, regarded with increasing scepticism by the German minority.[18] Administrative practice at local level was subjected to particular criticism: it was felt that the school authorities exploited the scope the law gave to them to the disadvantage of Germans, motivated by a nationalist desire for rapid assimilation of the minority. There were complaints about frequent rejection of applications for German school sections on formal grounds or the dilatory handling of such applications, which in some cases led to a delay in the establishment of German school sections. This in return resulted in loss of pupils to the Danish speaking sections.

The most serious problem for the Germans lay in the appointment and person of the teachers in state run German school sections and in the stipulation of curriculums by school commissions, in which Germans were usually in a minority. There was a steady decline in the number of available teachers trained at German seminars in north Schleswig prior to 1920, and since the amendment to the education laws on 1 May 1923 allowed only Danish citizens to teach at state run schools, it was no longer possible to recruit teachers from across the border in Germany. This gradually led to a situation where the schools still offered instruction in German as provided by law, but through teachers of Danish persuasion. In the opinion of the German minority, therefore, the state run school system in north Schleswig provided 'Danish schools with German as the language of instruction'.

The German minority felt itself to be at a particular disadvantage in secondary education. Following the law of 30 June 1920, state run *Gymnasien* (classical secondary schools) were established in four towns in north Schleswig, with Danish as the language of instruction. German was taught only as a second language. There was also a lack of German *Realklassen*, an optional tenth grade qualifying, for example, for entry to the lower grades of the Danish civil service. Demands from the minority that German sections should be created at the state run *Gymnasien*, terminating with the general university entrance examinations, were rejected by the Danish Education Ministry, making Germans fear that they would be deprived of a younger generation of graduates with a German language educational background.[19]

This dissatisfaction with public sector education resulted in a growing desire for German private schools. These were permitted by Danish school law and specifically by the education provisions for north Schleswig, provided that instruction be 'on a par' with that in state run schools. The Education Ministry was empowered to subsidise private schools if the latter 'fulfilled the general conditions for the receipt of such subsidies and if the situation was favourable'.[20] A minimum of ten pupils was required to set up a school, and the local school commission had the right to inspect the school's management of its budget.

From the mid 1920s onwards, the number of German private schools rose steadily, a development particularly helped by generous financial support from Germany for this purpose. The figures for

German speaking private schools in the period 1920–35 are as follows:

Table 5.6: German speaking private schools

	Municipal Schools (German Sections)		German Private Schools	
	Schools	Pupils	Schools	Pupils
1921	23	2830	6	311
1923	27	2800	7	234
1931	27	2209	27	1114
1935	34	2361	53	1954

The private schools received financial support and assistance in the recruitment of teachers from the *Nebenstelle Nord* (Northern Branch) of the *Deutsche Stiftung* (German Foundation) in Schleswig. A direct influence of the *Nebenstelle* on curriculums before 1933 cannot be ascertained. The director of the *Nebenstelle Nord* saw German private schools purely as *Volkstumsschulen* (which roughly translates as 'schools for the preservation of German culture'), a view shared by the *Wohlfahrts- und Schulverein für Nordschleswig* (a welfare and school association for north Schleswig, see pp. 121–2 below), which was a further pillar of the German schools. Together with the *Schleswig–Holsteiner–Bund*, a patriotic association (see below) it organised *Patenschaften* (sponsorships) from Schleswig–Holstein and throughout Germany. Its main task, however, was the running and extension of a network of German libraries in north Schleswig and the organisation of cultural events for the minority.

In the late 1930s, after prolonged and difficult negotiations with the Danish Education Ministry, the *Schulverein* succeeded in carrying most of its demands for greater independence of the German school system in north Schleswig. Private and state run German schools were henceforth to be supervised by a German *Schulamt* (Schools Department) and the German *Skolekonsulent*. German school commissions were set up for German schools, and the use of most textbooks in service in Germany was also authorised for the German sections of the state run schools.

A solution was also found to the question of secondary education. From 1933 onwards, the *Studentereksamen* (higher school leaving certificate) could be obtained in German at the *Deutsches Gymnasium* in Aabenraa. In its letter of authorisation, however, the Danish

Education Ministry made it quite clear that the examination in German, although serving like its Danish counterpart as the general university entrance qualification, 'would not be valid for entry into the Danish civil service'.[21] The establishment of *Realklassen* at four German private schools was also authorised, though with the same restrictions for the civil service as applied to the higher school leaving certificate.

Besides the *Schleswigscher Wählerverein* and the *Schulverein*, which the German minority regarded as being of crucial importance for its existence in Denmark, the Germans had a number of other organis-ations and associations, all with the aim of reinforcing their position as an independent group within the host state of Denmark. Many of the organisations followed the pattern of Danish associations and organisations in north Schleswig before 1920, which had been created to counter Prussian efforts at germanisation.

The youth organisation, *Deutscher Jugendverband für Nordschleswig* (German Youth Group for North Schleswig), also founded by Johannes Schmidt, had a large membership in its capacity as a federation of all German *Jugendbünde* (youth unions). In 1934 there were four district associations with a total of 36 clubs and 1600 members. Between 1921 and 1923, Schmidt amalgamated the *Schleswigscher Wählerverein*, the *Schulverein* and the *Jugendverband* within a single umbrella organisation, the *Gesamtverband*.[22] In the area of social service, the *Frauenbünde* (German women's unions) were amalgamated to form the *Wohlfahrtsdienst Nordschleswig* (North Schleswig Welfare Service) from 24 January 1929. Social services and financial aid were also offered by the *Deutsche Selbsthilfe* (German Self-Help Organisation). German farmers were organised in the *Landwirtschaftlicher Hauptverein für Nordschleswig*, the main agri-cultural association. At local level there were many sport and gymnastic clubs which were in turn members of the *Turnverband Nordschleswig*. Frequently contact with Germany was sought: the largest organisation in this sphere was the *Bund für deutsche Kultur* (Union for German Culture) which had about 10 000 members in 35 local branches in 1936.

In church affairs, the pattern was similar to that in education. In the four towns of north Schleswig there was provision for both Danish and German speaking clergy. The law of 31 October 1920 permitted two pastors to be appointed per parish, each with pastoral responsi-bility for either German or Danish parishioners. The *Menighedsraad* or *Gemeindekirchenräte* (Parish Councils) were to have Danish and German members. In rural areas, Germans were under the pastoral care of the *Deutsche Freigemeinden* (German independent churches) provided for under general Danish law. These independent German parishes, collectively the *Nordschleswigsche Gemeinde* (North

Schleswig Churches) (consisting in 1935 of six parishes), were in organisational terms part of the Lutheran church of Schleswig–Holstein. Buildings belonging to the Danish Lutheran church were also at the disposal of the independent German parishes.

From 1920 to 1929 the German minority was served by four German language newspapers published in Aabenraa, Tønder, Haderslev and Sønderborg respectively. In 1929, however, the papers were amalgamated for financial reasons, and on 1 February 1929 the first issue of the *Nordschleswigsche Zeitung* was printed in Aabenraa. It was to remain the mouthpiece and vehicle of communication of the German minority until the end of the Second World War.[23] Publishers in Germany who supplied funds for the *Nordschleswigsche Zeitung* (*Concordia* and later *Vera Verlagsanstalt* in Berlin) exercised a considerable influence on the paper's political line, particularly after 1933. From 1931, the chairman of the supervisory board was Ernst Schröder, director of the *Grenzmittelstelle Nord* (cf. p. 123 below), who was in close contact with government departments in Berlin.

The German minority also maintained links with trans-state German and supranational minority organisations. Knowledge of this is derived mainly from the contacts cultivated by Johannes Schmidt. This leading minority politician not only kept in close touch with the German Foreign Ministry in Berlin and the German embassy in Copenhagen; he also represented the interests of his compatriots in the *Verein für das Deutschtum im Ausland* (see p. 121 below) as well as in the *Deutscher Schutzbund* (German Protection League, see p. 123 below), which in his opinion offered German minorities the prospect of a realignment of the questions concerning them in a European perspective.[24] Of particular significance for him was the activity of the *Verband der deutschen Volksgruppen in Europa* (Association of German National Groups in Europe) and its work for German minorities through the medium of its legal adviser C.G. Bruns. The Association's goals with respect to cultural self-administration and linguistic and ecclesiastical freedom, as well as its demand for economic equality, were largely identical with the aims of Schmidt's *Schleswigscher Wählerverein*.

Collaboration with the Association of German National Groups in Europe led Schmidt to cooperation with the *Nationalitätenkongress* (European Congress of Nationalities) a body he saw as a 'federation' of the minorities in Europe and a vehicle for concerted action.[25] At the Congress' annual conferences, Schmidt made an impression as a wise and careful man and was widely respected. Here, too, he aired his opinions on cultural autonomy and the right of minorities to obtain cultural ties with their 'mother country', as well as calling for an appropriate proportion of land ownership to secure the minority's existence. Schmidt also published his views in *Nation und Staat*, a German periodical dealing with the European minorities' question of which he had been cofounder in 1927.

The German minority maintained no links with the Interparliamentary Union, the International Federation of League of Nations Societies, or the International Law Association. Schmidt attended only two interparliamentary conferences, in Copenhagen and Berlin. These international associations were, in his view, 'an outpouring of the spirit of Geneva, of the League of Nations, that instrument conceived to consolidate and perpetuate the conditions of Versailles'.[26]

The Policy of Germany's Authorities, Organisations and Parties Towards the German Minority in Denmark (c. 1918–1933)

Generally speaking it has to be said that the whole question of north Schleswig was accorded considerably less importance by Berlin authorities in the years between 1918 and 1933 than, for example, that of the German minorities along the eastern border of the German *Reich*.

The border of the *Reich* with Denmark from 1920 was never officially recognised by the German government. Upon the signing of the final protocol and the frontier map, the German frontier commissioner was induced to point out in an annotation that in the view of the German government 'the frontier established between Denmark and Germany does not take account of the national right to self determination solemnly declared by the Allied great powers'.[27] The German *Reich* also refused to sign a tripartite treaty with the Allies and Denmark which would guarantee recognition of the new frontier by the signatories.

To the German government, to sign would have meant sanctioning an unjust frontier arrangement and a restriction of the choice of citizenship as well as a refusal of protection for the minority. German efforts to achieve a bilateral agreement securing this protection for the minority had been rebuffed on 7 May 1920 by the Danish Foreign Minister H. Scavenius in the presence of Germany's Ambassador, von Neurath.

In spite of this, a revision of the German–Danish border did not appear to be a demand of any topical significance during the Weimar Republic, as the Weimar government was apparently at pains to behave as correctly as possible towards its northern neighbour. Nevertheless, a latent concern for frontier revision can be discerned. In the Stresemann era north Schleswig also began to be increasingly included in the general desire for a strengthening of the *Auslandsdeutschtum* through direct material aid. After the German currency reform in November 1923 and the subsequent stabilisation of the German economy, more funds from the *Reich* were channelled into education and cultural work in north Schleswig.[28] The resulting increase in German activity, for example, the establishment of new private schools (in 1921, six private schools with 311 pupils; in 1931, 27 private schools with 1114 pupils) and libraries (in 1927, 13 libraries with 852 users; in 1930, 36 libraries with 4886 users), was regarded with growing mistrust by the Danes.[29]

In a Cabinet decision of 31 March 1926 the German government had voted 30 million *Reichsmark* for the promotion of German economic interests in *grenz- und minderheitendeutschen Gebieten*, regions close to the *Reich*'s borders or having a German minority, 'particularly in those areas lost as a result of the Treaty of Versailles'. With the cooperation of, and under the supervision of, a parliamentary committee, part of this sum found its way to north Schleswig via a number of private commercial firms (such as *Ossa Vermittlungs- und Handelsgesellschaft*, *Verifikon* and others), and also through Swiss and Dutch banks and with the assistance of private individuals.[30] The German Foreign Ministry, however, retained the right to intervene in the distribution of funds. In 1930, on the initiative of the German Foreign Minister, the sum was substantially increased to 60 million *Reichsmark*, 15 million being set aside for specifically cultural and political work in the border regions.

The funds were administered by Department VI in the Foreign Ministry and by the *Deutsche Stiftung* (German Foundation). The latter's *Nebenstelle Nord* (see above, p. 116) soon achieved a particularly significant role in this process under the directorship of E. Edert, an official from the Schleswig–Holstein provincial school authorities in Schleswig. The *Nebenstelle Nord* allocated funds for the building and maintenance of, for example, schools and libraries, and for the payment of teachers' salaries at German private schools in north Schleswig.[31] Other funds were channelled into cultural organisations such as the *Volkshochschulverein* (a union of adult education institutions) and the *Jugendbünde*.

After 1926, financial support from German government sources intended to secure land ownership by Germans in north Schleswig gained particular political significance. The Germans in Denmark felt themselves to be at a disadvantage, both as a result of the Danish government's settlement policy in north Schleswig and in the granting of loans for land purchase by Danish credit institutions. For this reason G. Vogelgesang, a German lawyer in Haderslev, founded the *Kreditanstalt Vogelgesang* in 1926. The aim of the bank was to keep as much land as possible under German ownership and to keep German farmers in north Schleswig, not least in view of possible frontier revision at some date. Around 90 per cent of the share capital of 495 000 Danish *Kroner* was put up by *Ossa*, which ensured, however, that payments were made through the medium of a Schleswig–Holstein bank consortium, in order to avoid political complications.

On *Ossa's* recommendation Vogelgesang extended his activities in late 1928 by establishing the *Höfeverwaltungsgesellschaft A/S*, a society which took into receivership German farms in danger of bankruptcy with loans from the *Kreditanstalt*. By 1932 some 70 farms had been taken into possession.[32] From 1930, funds for the bank's work were supplied by the German government through a Swiss investment and credit company, *Aktiengesellschaft für kontinentale Beteiligungen und Kredite*, based in Zurich. Besides his financial activities, Vogelgesang was also a source of information on *volkstumspolitische Fragen* (questions of nationalist policy) for German authorities. His reports were sent to the German embassy in Copenhagen, as well as to the *'Kult. B'* department of the Foreign Ministry in Berlin.

Vogelgesang's activities aroused suspicion among the Danes in North Schleswig, who generally regarded the *Bodenkampf* (the German struggle to retain land ownership) as a provocation. It did not take long for a Danish counterorganisation to emerge. On 24 January 1927, the *Landeværnet* (Land Protection) Association was founded, a credit institution with the aim of supporting Danish farmers and enabling them to retain their land. *Landeværnet* was set up on private initiative. In the same year the Danish government established its own fund for land purchase loans in the region, the *Sønderjysk Hypoteklaanefond*.[33] The Germans in north Schleswig did not just benefit from state aid from Germany: another important source of aid was the *Verein für das Deutschtum im Ausland*, an organisation for the promotion of German culture and influence outside Germany, which administered a substantial portion of private funds. This organisation expressly stated that its help was not to be an encroachment upon the rights of foreign states towards their citizens. *Volksdeutsche Gruppen* (German national groups) were, however, to be given full opportunity to participate as loyal citizens in the economic and political life of the states in which they lived. For its work in North Schleswig, the *Verein für das Deutschtum im Ausland* could draw on its regional association in Schleswig–Holstein and on a large number of local branches.

During the Weimar period there was a number of organisations in the German frontier province of Schleswig – Holstein which assumed a degree of importance in German frontier policy. The *Wohlfahrts- und Schulverein für Nordschleswig*, the welfare and education association, had already been founded in 1919 during the run up to the plebiscite. It was based first in Sønderborg and from 1920 in Flensburg.

Officially a private association, it nevertheless received material assistance from the German government as well as from the provincial authorities in Schleswig–Holstein. Its activities were centred on private schools and libraries, and also on the welfare sphere, in collaboration here with the *Wohlfahrtsdienst Nordschleswig*. The Association also provided grants for the training of young Germans from north Schleswig and supplied funds for election campaigns if the elections were *nationalpolitisch wichtige Wahlen* (of major political importance for the minority).

The most important of the nationalist and frontier organisations in Schleswig–Holstein was the *Schleswig–Holsteiner–Bund* (Schleswig–Holsteiners Union), founded by conservative members of the *Deutscher Ausschuss für das Herzogtum Schleswig* (German Committee for the Duchy of Schleswig) on 6 July 1919. Like the *Verein für das Deutschtum im Ausland*, the *Schleswig–Holsteiner–Bund* had numerous local branches in Schleswig–Holstein, besides many linked organisations throughout Germany, the so-called *Butenschleswigholsteiner* (expatriate Schleswig–Holstein groups). In Flensburg alone the *Schleswig–Holsteiner–Bund* had some 6000 members in 1919. Apart from a set of goals relating to cultural policy, it also aimed to form and maintain a German irredentism in southern Denmark with an ultimate view to 'revision of the frontier in Schleswig', which it held to be 'politically and economically intolerable'. It called for a 'just interpretation of the law of national self determination'.[34] In the mid to late 1920s, a slight relaxation in attitude towards Denmark could be observed on the part of the *Schleswig–Holsteiner–Bund*, although in the final years of the Weimar Republic it returned to a more hardline attitude towards the border question.

In almost irreconcilable opposition to the *Schleswig–Holsteiner–Bund* was the *Grenzbund für deutsch–dänische Verständigung*, an organisation for the promotion of German–Danish relations, founded in 1919 by a group of social democratic members of the German Committee for Schleswig. The *Grenzbund* worked towards general *rapproachment* between Germans and Scandinavians, using Schleswig–Holstein as a bridge for cooperation between German and Danish social democrats. With its realistic attitude towards the 1920 border decision it could also contribute to the preparation of the Stauning–Wels agreement of 25 November 1923, in which representatives of both countries urged their people to 'do their utmost to thwart the nationalist incitations of chavinists' and to 'work for a recognition of the border between Denmark and Germany agreed upon in 1920 following the plebiscites provided for in the peace treaty'.[35] In comparison with the influence of the *Schleswig–Holsteiner–Bund* on the situation in the border region, however, the *Grenzbund* was of only limited significance.

All in all, a rather confused picture emerges of the involvement of German *Reich* authorities and organisations in Schleswig–Holstein in matters affecting the frontier region during the plebiscite period and the early years of the Weimar Republic. There was no clear coordination of tasks between the Foreign Ministry and other *Reich* departments and the Prussian authorities and the authorities in the province of Schleswig–Holstein. Nor could the respective fields of activity of several semi-official and private organisations be properly delineated. The *Deutscher Schutzbund* (German Protection League) of 1919 was the only attempt to coordinate and centralise all relevant German activities. In 1922 a clear division of activities between the *Schutzbund* and the *Schleswig–Holsteiner–Bund* enabled a common and therefore stronger stand to be made on border policy.

From 1922 onwards, the *Grenzmittelstelle Nord* assumed an important coordinating role. Its task, before and also after 1933, was to serve 'as a link between institutions within the *Reich* concerned with frontier policy on the one hand and the German minority on the other'.[36] Its Director Ernst Schröder, born in Haderslev, was a confidential agent of certain Berlin authorities. A native of north Schleswig, he pursued one aim only: that of maintaining the German minority and strengthening it by any means available. Schröder's sphere of activity also included German *Volkstumsarbeit* (national awareness efforts) in the northern areas of the province of Schleswig–Holstein, which were regarded by Denmark, and particularly by the Danish minority in the areas concerned, as provocation and agitation against Danish interests.

In retrospect, the official policy of Germany in the period from the plebiscite to the end of the Weimar Republic appeared to aim at minimising tension between Germany and its northern neighbour. A willingness for conciliation and understanding was frequently shown. As mentioned above, for instance, Germany made no official demands for a revision of its frontier with Denmark. Moreover the repeated moves to produce a bilateral minority protection agreement at the time of the plebiscite and in the early 1920s do not appear to have been sustained in later years. To a certain extent, individuals – and social democrats in both countries – were able to establish a reasonably neighbourly relationship.

Official economic and cultural support of the German minority in north Schleswig by German authorities seemed in principle legitimate and remained within standard international practice of the time. We cannot, however, support the theory put forward by some German historians that these activities did not represent an intervention on the part of the *Reich* in the internal affairs of the German minority or the Danish state.[37] Even taking into account the great caution exercised by German official and semi-official agencies to ensure that their financial support of the Germans in Denmark could not be seen as intervention in the latter's internal affairs, the fact remains that the *Bodenkampf* policy perpetrated by the north Schleswig Germans, for instance, and the rapid growth of the number of German private schools caused irritation in Denmark and led to fierce reactions in places. Nor should it be ignored that the heavy financial dependence of the German minority on the *Reich* removed the group's capacity for autonomous action in crucial political issues. This fact became depressingly obvious after the assumption of power by the National Socialists in Germany.

All those steps taken by groups and agencies within Germany and particularly in the province of Schleswig–Holstein, including those in the cultural sphere, were not merely directed to further the general aim of strengthening the German minority as such and preserving a lively awareness of its ties with the German nation. In all cases the option of reintroducing the question of frontier revision was kept open for when the time was ripe.

Notes

Notes to Section I

1. Name given to Denmark, the duchies and colonial possessions overseas; in German *Gesamtstaat*.
2. Trap, pp. 54 ff.
3. *Departementstidenden*, vol. V; Copenhagen, 1852, pp. 512–14. An overview of the ending of the war is given in Jens Engberg, with an English summary.
4. Himmelstrup and Møller, pp. 76–9.
5. Hjelholt; Bracker.
6. Hjelholt; pp. 182–95 Bracker, vol. 98, pp. 186–95.
7. Rerup (1982), pp. 202–8, 217–21; Scharff, pp. 70 ff. Both peace treaties in de Jessen, pp. 173–80, 309–12.
8. Schultz Hansen, p. 127.
9. See the author's contribution to vol. VI of this series.
10. Schultz Hansen, p. 142.
11. *Sønderjydsk Skoleforening 1892–1942*, Kolding, 1942, p. 276. In the years between 1864 and 1892 2313 youngsters from north Schleswig received schooling in Denmark.
12. Sievers.
13. Fink (1961), pp. 66–83.
14. Jørgensen.
15. Callesen, pp. 46–50.
16. Rerup (1965), pp. 63 ff, 85–95.
17. Friis, vol. I, pp. 106–17.
18. *Ibid*.
19. *Ibid*., vol. III, especially pp. 216–36.
20. Nielsen, pp. 64–80.
21. *Ibid*., pp. 103 ff.

22. *Ibid.*, pp. 131 ff.
23. Fink (1959), pp. 38 ff.
24. Fink (1961), pp. 123–31.
25. Schultz Hansen, pp. 118–23.
26. Fink (1959), pp. 57–64. The text of the convention is given in v. Jessen, vol. I, pp. 26 ff.
27. Hauser, pp. 33–42; Japsen, pp. 7–15.
28. Japsen, *passim.*
29. Tiedje.
30. Leppien, pp. 92–4.
31. Munch, pp. 40 ff, 49, 176.
32. Kaarsted (1975), pp. 143 ff.
33. Callesen, chapters III and IV.
34. Hanssen, pp. 237 ff.
35. Fink (1978), vol. I, pp. 10–15, 57–60; Kaarsted (1975), 145 ff.
36. Fink (1978), vol. I, pp. 61–70.
37. Kaarsted (1968).
38. Callesen, pp. 89 ff.
39. Lassen, pp. 166–79, 193 ff.
40. Forman.
41. Reports of the CIS to the Conference of Ambassadors in Wambaugh, vol. II, docs. 22 and 23; more detailed figures in *Afstemningen i Sønderjylland 10 Febr og 14 Marts 1920*, published 1920 by the Provisional Ministry for Southern Jutland's Affairs; Alnor; v. Jessen, vol. II, with many tables and using the original vote lists; Lassen.
42. Wambaugh, vol. II, pp. 5 ff, 109–14.
43. Lassen, pp. 196–205; Fink (1978), vol. III, pp. 47–54.
44. T. Jessen, vol. I pp. 501–97; Fink (1958), pp. 216 ff, 222–5, 250–7; Mogensen, pp. 28–41; Hjelholt et al, vol. II, pp. 362 ff.
45. v. Jessen, vol. III, pp. 502–8, 526 ff; Mogensen, p. 16.
46. v. Jessen, vol. III, pp. 485–9. The Danish church also had troubles until 1926. *Ibid.*, pp. 490–501.
47. Fink (1958), p. 227.
48. v. Jessen, 1938, vol. III, p. 503; T. Jessen, pp. 507–9 ff. See also v. Jessen, vol. III, pp. 460, 462 for the electoral system.
49. Bogensee, pp. 14–18; Fink (1958), p. 222; Moltesen, p. 421.
50. Mogensen, pp. 58–64.
51. Bogensee, p. 15.
52. Fink (1958), pp. 222 ff.
53. Callesen, pp. 125 ff.
54. Svendsen, pp. 127–46.
55. Bogensee, p. 16.
56. Mogensen, p. 51.
57. v. Jessen, vol. III, pp. 176–82.
58. *Sønderjydsk Skoleforening*, pp. 203–5 ff, 213 ff, 216 ff.
59. v. Jessen, vol. III, p. 489. For the church see *ibid.*, p. 494.
60. Cour, pp. 27 ff, 30 ff.
61. Mogensen, p. 39.
62. Kürstein, p. 239.
63. Mogensen, pp. 34 ff.
64. Broszat, pp. 407–12.
65. *Ibid.*, pp. 423–7.
66. *Ibid.*, pp. 419 ff.
67. Fink (1958), pp. 250–3.
68. Broszat, pp. 430 ff.

Notes to Section II

Place names are given in their standard English versions where appropriate. Danish names are used for places in modern Denmark, with the German version following at first mention, although I have preferred the German version of 'north Schleswig' rather than the Danish 'north Slesvig' (or even 'Sonderjylland': south Jutland) for the region north of the modern German–Danish border.

1. For statistics on the voting and the question of the boundaries in Zones I and II: Jessen, Lassen, Köster, (1921); Köster (1970); Tiedje. Danish accounts mainly reject the plebiscite results by *communes* and cite instead results by *parishes*. A distinction is also made between voters resident in the plebiscite area and non-resident voters.
2. Becker–Christensen (1984), a fundamental study of Danish efforts to integrate the German minority in north Schleswig by legislation, pp. 252 f; Becker–Christensen (1988), pp. 24 f; note 18.
3. Kimminich, p. 14.
4. Guttmann, p. 7.
5. Anonymous (1932).
6. Eibl, p. 337.
7. UN Document E/CN. 4 Sub. 2/L of 21.6.1972.
8. Elklit, Noack, Tonsgaard. This study gives investigations which were of only restricted use for the period dealt with here. Sources used for this purpose for the first time: statistical material in two annual reports (1931–2 and 1933–4) probably of the *Wohlfahrts- und Schulverein für Nordschleswig: Bericht über die deutsche Kulturarbeit in Nordschleswig*, which record the parents' occupation and language at home of around 1800 pupils at German private schools. Further material was provided by a study by E. Hoffmann (see vol. VI, this series, *The Formation of National Elites*).
9. Peter Hopp (1974), pp. 234 f. Synoptic accounts of the history of the German minority, their organisations, political and cultural movements, economic and social activity in Kardel; Tägil; Lenzing; Heuer; Salomon. Detailed chapters on the German minority are also to be found in Fink; Rerup; Brandt.
10. *Schleswigscher Wählerverein* programmes in *Grenzfriedenshefte* 1 (1974); *Deutscher Schul- und Sprachverein für Nordschleswig* (1976),pp. 66–7.
11. See E. Hoffmann, vol. VI, this series.
12. Election results after Thorsen, pp. 86–7.
13. Figures after Jessen, III, pp. 254–6. Here statistical material is only available for market towns (Danish, *købstaeder*) and smaller towns (Danish, *flaekke*), but not for the parish communes (Danish, *sognekommuner*).
14. See Doege (1985), pp. 208 f.
15. *Deutscher Schul- und Sprachverein*, pp. 73 f.
16. Christensen.
17. Becker–Christensen (1984); Dänisches Ministerium des Äusseren; Scavenius, pp. 9 f.
18. Anonymous (1925).
19. On the issue of higher secondary education among the German minority in North Schleswig see Doege (1980).
20. Rühlmann, pp. 1 f.; Kölln; Doege (1980).
21. Doege (1980), p. 185.
22. Kardel, p. 30.
23. Kardel, pp. 86 f, 95; Hopp (1979).
24. Schmidt, p. 107; Hopp (1974).
25. Schmidt, pp. 111 f.
26. Schmidt, pp. 124, 127.

27. Bundesarchiv Koblenz, R 43 I/ (D 695431/32)
28. Tägil, pp. 13 f.
29. *Bericht über die deutsche Kulturarbeit in Nordschleswig*, pp. 4 f.
30. Tägil, p. 14; also: Refslund Thomsen.
31. Doege (1980), chapter II, 2.4; Tägil, p. 16.
32. 'Aktstykker'; Andersen; Jessen, III, p. 189.
33. 'Aktstykker'; Fink, p. 241; Jessen, III, pp. 189, 237.
34. *Satzung des Schleswig–Holsteiner–Bundes* (Constitution of the Schleswig–Holsteiners Union), paras 2–3; Fink, pp. 218f; Tägil, p. 15.
35. Callesen, pp. 125 f; *Deutscher Schul- und Sprachverein* pp. 72-3.
36. Tägil, p. 15.
37. See for example, Lenzing, p. 23.

Select Bibliography

Section I

An overview of Schleswig's history is given by Fink (1946 and 1955), with both volumes appearing in German in 1958. The latest history is written by Gregersen and Rerup (1981–2). A German overview from the same year is provided by Scharff. More specialist works are to be found below. The sources for the period are rich and are kept in the well organised collections of the *Schleswig–Holsteinisches Landesarchiv* in Schleswig, in the *Landsarkivet for de sønderjyske landsdele* in Aabenraa and in the *Rigsarkivet*, Copenhagen. The main libraries are the *Landesbibliothek*, Kiel and *Det kgl. Bibliotek*, Copenhagen.

Alnor, Karl (1926), *Die Ergebnisse der Volksabstimmungen vom 10 Febr. u 14 März 1920*, Flensburg.
Bogensee, Julius (1942), *Det danske Mindretal i Sydslesvig*, Copenhagen.
Bracker, Jochen (1972–3), 'Die dänische Sprachpolitik 1850–1864 und die Bevölkerung Mittelschleswigs' in *Zeitschrift der Gesellschaft für schleswig–holsteinische Geschichte*, 97–8, Neumünster.
Broszat, Martin (1968), 'Aussen- und innenpolitische Aspekte in der preussisch-deutschen Minderheitenpolitik in der Ära Stresemann', in Kluxen, K., et al (eds), *Politische Ideologien und nationalstaatliche Ordnung. Festschrift für Theodor Schieder*. Munich.
Callesen, Gerd (1970), *Die Schleswig–Frage in den Beziehungen zwischen dänischer und deutscher Sozialdemokratie von 1912 bis 1924*, Åbenrå.
Cour, Vilh. la (1956), *Lukkede Døre*, Copenhagen.
Engberg, Jens (1967), *Det slesvigske spørgsmål 1850–1853*, Copenhagen.
Fink, Troels (1978), *Da Sønderjylland blev delt 1918–20.* Aarhus.
Fink, Troels (1958), *Geschichte des schleswigschen Grenzlandes*, Copenhagen.
Fink, Troels (1946), *Rids af Sønderjyllands historie*, Copenhagen.
Fink, Troels (1955), *Sønderjyllands historie siden genforeningen i 1920*, Copenhagen.
Fink, Troels (1959), *Spillet om dansk neutralitet 1905–1909*, Aarhus.
Fink, Troels (1961), *Ustabil balance. Dansk udenrigs- og forsvarspolitik 1894–1905*, Aarhus.
Forman, Jens Christian (1976), *Den internationale Kommissions neutralitetsforanstaltninger ved folkeafstemningen i Sønderjylland 1920*, Aarhus.
Friis, Aage (1921–48), *Den danske Regering og Nordslesvigs Genforening med Danmark*, 3 vols, Copenhagen.
Gregersen, H.V. and Rerup, L. (1981–2), *Slesvig og Holsten*, Copenhagen.

Hanssen, H.P. (1926), *Fra Krigstiden*, Copenhagen.
Hauser, Oswald (1960), *Preussische Staatsräson und nationaler Gedanke*. Neumünster.
Himmelstrup, J. and Møller, J. (1958), *Danske forfatningslove 1665–1953*, Copenhagen.
Hjelholt, Holgeer (1923), *Den danske Sprogordnung og det dankse Sprogstyre i Slesvig mellem Krigene 1850–1864*, Copenhagen.
Hjelholt, Holgeer, et al. (eds) (1955), *Flensborg bys historie*, Copenhagen.
Japsen, Gottlieb (1983), *Den fejlslagne germanisering*, Åbenrå.
Jessen, Franz de (ed.) (1906), *Manuel Historique de la Question du Slesvig*, Copenhagen.
Jessen, Franz von (1938), *Haandbog i det slesvigske Spørgsmaals Historie 1900–1937*, Copenhagen.
Jessen, Tage (1946), 'Mellem to Verdenskrige', in Kamphøvener, Morten, *Sydslesvig gennem tiderne*, Copenhagen.
Jørgensen, A.D. (1882), *Fyrretyve Fortællinger af Fædrelandets Historie*, Copenhagen.
Kaarsted, Tage (1968), *Påskekrisen*, Aarhus.
Kaarsted, Tage (1975), *Storbritannien og Danmark 1914–20*, Odense, 2nd edn.
Kürstein, Poul (ed.) (1969), *Flensborg Avis*, Flensburg.
Lassen, Aksel (1976), *Valg mellem tysk og dansk*, Aabenraa.
Leppien, Jörn-Peter (1981), *Martin Rade und die deutsch–dänischen Beziehungen 1909–1919*, Neumünster.
Mogensen, Carsten (1981), *Dansk i hagekorsets skygge*, Flensburg.
Moltesen, L. (1932), 'De nationale Mindretal efter Verdenskrigen', in *Festskrift til H.P. Hanssen*, Copenhagen.
Munch, P. (1961), *Erindringer 1914–1918*, Copenhagen.
Nielsen, Henning (1977), *Dansk udenrigspolitik 1875–1894 med saerligt henblik på beslutningsprocessen*, Odense.
Rerup, Lorenz (1965), *A.D. Jørgensen*, Copenhagen.
Rerup, Lorenz (1982), *Slesvig og Holsten efter 1830*, Copenhagen.
Scharff, Alex (new edition, Jessen–Klingenberg, M., 1982), *Schleswig–Holsteinische Geschichte im Überblick*, Würzburg.
Schultz Hansen, H. (1985), *Det nordslesvigske landbrug og den dadske bevægelse 1880–1914*, Åbenrå.
Sievers, Kai Detlev (1964), *Die Köllerpolitik und ihr Echo in der deutschen Presse 1897–1901*, Neumünster.
Svendsen, Nic. (1968), *I genforeningens tjeneste*, Copenhagen.
Tiedje, Johs. (1909), *Die Zustände in Nordschleswig*, Marburg, enlarged reprint.
Trap, J.P. (1864), *Statistisk–topographisk Beskrivelse af Hertugdømmet Slesvig*, Copenhagen.
Wambaugh, Sarah (1933), *Plebiscites since the World War*, 2 vols, Washington.

Section II

Scholars working on the subject of the German minority in Denmark will find the main collections in the *Schleswig–Holsteinische Landesbibliothek* in Kiel (Germany) and in *Det kongelige Bibliotek* in Copenhagen (Denmark).
German and Danish archives of special importance are:
Germany: *Bundesarchiv*, Koblenz; *Politisches Archiv des Auswärtigen Amtes*, Bonn; *Schleswig–Holsteinisches Landesarchiv*, Schleswig. Since 1990 admission is also possible to the *Bundesarchiv, Abteilungen Potsdam* (the former *Zentrales Staatsarchiv* of the German Democratic Republic).
Denmark: *Rigsarkivet*, Copenhagen; *Landsarkivet for de sønderjyske landsdele*, Aabenraa and *Archiv der deutschen Volksgruppe*, Aabenraa.

'Aktstykker vedrørende Kreditanstalt Vogelgesangs Tiblivelse' (Files Regarding the Origin of the Vogelgesang Bank) (1946), *Historisk Samfund for Sønderjylland*, 7.

Andersen, H. (1987), *Landevaernet – et tilbageblik* (the Land Protection Association – a Review), Aabenraa.

Anonymous (1925), *Die deutsche Minderheit in Nordschleswig*, probably published by the Schleswig–Holsteiner Bund.

Anonymous (1932), *Der Völkerbund und der Schutz der Minderheiten*, Geneva.

Becker–Christensen, H. (1984), *Dansk mindretalspolitik i Nordslesvig. Udformning af den danske politik over for det tyske mindretal 1918–1920* (Danish Minority Policy in North Schleswig. Formation of Danish Policy Towards the German Minority 1918–1920), Aabenraa.

Becker–Christensen, H. (1988), 'Die Teilung Schleswigs', *Regional Contact*, 1.

Bericht über die deutsche kulturarbeit in Nordschleswig (1931–2).

Brandt, O. (1981), *Geschichte Schleswig–Holsteins*, Kiel.

Callesen, G. (1970), 'Die Schleswig–Frage in den Beziehungen zwischen dänischer und deutscher Sozialdemokratie von 1912–1924', unpublished dissertation, Kiel, see *Schriften der Heimatkundlichen Arbeitsgemeinschaft für Nordschleswig*, 21.

Christensen, Fr. (1971), 'Aufbau deutscher Schulen in Nordschleswig 1919–1940', *Schriften der Heimatkundlichen Arbeitsgemeinschaft für Nordschleswig*, 24.

Dänisches Ministerium des Ausseren (ed.) (1924), *Die deutsche Minderheit in Nordschleswig*.

Deutscher Schul- und Sprachverein für Nordschleswig (ed.) (1976), *Materialen zur Geschichte Schleswigs*, Aabenraa.

Doege, I. (1980), 'Das Deutsche Gymnasium in Apenrade von seinen Anfängen bis 1945', *50 Jahre Deutsches Gymnasium in Nordschleswig*, Aabenraa.

Doege, I. (1985), 'Die deutsche Minderheit in Nordschleswig und ihre dänische Umwelt', *Grenzfriedenshefte*, 4.

Eibl, H. (1933), *Vom Sinn der Gegenwart*, Vienna.

Elklit, J., Noack, J.P., and Tonsgaard, O. (1978), 'Nationale tilhørsforhold i Nordslesvig' (National Affiliation in north Schleswig), *Acta Jutlandica*, 49.

Fink, T. (1958), *Geschichte des schleswigschen Grenzlandes*, Copenhagen.

Guttman, V. (1931), *Die theoretischen Grundlagen der Minderheitenfrage*, Fünfkirchen.

Heuer, J. (1973), *Zur politischen, sozialen und ökonomischen Problematik der Volksabstimmungen in Schleswig 1920*, Kiel.

Hopp, P. (1979), 'Bemerkungen zur Zusammenlegung der deutsch–nordschleswigschen Zeitungen am 1.2.1929', *Schriften der Heimatkundlichen Arbeitsgemeinschaft für Nordschleswig*, 40.

Hopp, P. (1974), 'Johannes Schmidt–Wodder', *Schleswig–Holsteinisches Biographisches Lexikon*, 3, Neumünster.

Jessen, F. von (1938), *Haandbog i det Slesvigske Spørgsmaals Historie 1900–1937.* (Handbook of the Schleswig Question), vols I-III, Copenhagen.

Kardel, H. (1971), 'Fünf Jahrzehnte in Nordschleswig', *Schriften der Heimatkundlichen Arbeitsgemeinschaft für Nordschleswig*, 10.

Kimminich, O. (1985), 'Neuere Entwicklung des Minderheiten- und Nationalitätenrechts' in *Das Parlament*, Beilage B 43.

Kölln, H.J. (1932), *Minderheitenschulrecht in Nord- und Südschleswig*, Leipzig.

Köster, A. (1921), *Der Kampf um Schleswig*, Berlin.

Köster, A. (1970), *Die Volksabstimmungen im Landesteil Schleswig 1920–1970*, Neumünster.

Lassen, A. (1976), *Valg mellem tysk og dansk* (Choosing between German and Danish), Aabenraa.

Lenzing, H. (1973), *Die deutsche Volksgruppe in Dänemark und das nationalsozialistische Deutschland 1933–1939* (dissertation), Bonn.

Rerup, L. (1982), *Slesvig og Holsten efter 1830* (Schleswig and Holstein after 1830), Copenhagen.

Rühlmann, P. (1926), *Das Schulrecht der deutschen Minderheiten in Europa*, Berlin.

Salomon, K. (1973), *Konflikt i Graenseland 1920–1933*, (Conflict in the border region 1920–1933), Copenhagen.

Scavenius, H. (1924), 'Minderheitenfragen in Nordschleswig', *Deutsch–Nordisches Jahrbuch 1924*, Jena.

Schmidt, J. (1951), *Von Wodder nach Kopenhagen, von Kopenhagen nach Europa*, Flensburg.

Tägil, S. (1970), *Deutschland und die deutsche Minderheit in Nordschleswig 1933–1939*, Stockholm.

Thomsen, Kr. Refslund (1946), 'Tysk Udlandsarbejde i Nordslesvig 1936' (German Foreign Activity in North Schleswig 1936), *Sønderjydske Aarbøger*.

Thorsen, S. (1970), *Delt efter anskuelser* (Division according to Opinion), Copenhagen.

Tiedje, J. (1920), *Die deutsche Note über Schleswig*, Berlin.

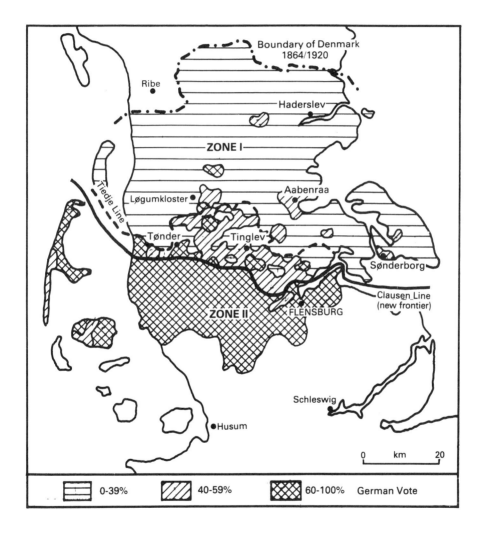

Map 5.1 The Schleswig plebiscite area
Source: Gösta Toft, *Die bäuerliche Struktur der deutschen Volksgruppe in Nordschleswig*,
Flensburg, 1982 (after p. 5).

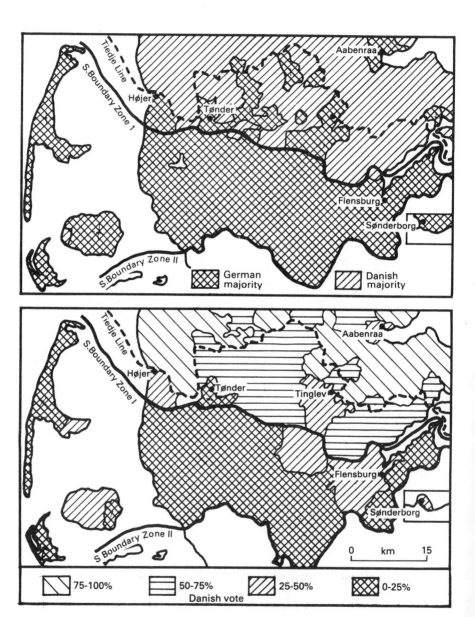

**Map 5.2 Results of the Schleswig plebiscite in part of Zone I
and Zone II**
Source: Sarah Wambaugh, *Plebiscites since the World War*, vol. 1, Washington, 1933,
pp. 47–87.

6 The Frisians (particularly the North Frisians) in Inter- and Trans-state Relations to 1940

THOMAS STEENSEN

Frisians today live in the kingdom of the Netherlands and in the Federal Republic of Germany. In the nineteenth century the Frisian territories belonged at times to as many as four different states: west Frisia was incorporated in the Netherlands; east Frisia belonged from 1815 to Hanover and from 1866 to Prussia; Heligoland from 1807 to the United Kingdom and from 1890 to the German state; north Frisia until 1864 to the Danish *helstat* (Denmark, the duchies of Schleswig, Holstein and Lauenburg, Iceland and colonial possessions overseas; German: *Gesamtstaat*) and from 1864–7 to Prussia. A Frisian state encompassing all Frisian regions has never existed.

The Frisians, therefore, have no Frisian state to which they can relate.[1] This fact has hindered the advancement of a common Frisian identity, besides influencing the attitude of state authorities towards Frisian wishes and demands. Often there is a state on which a minority can call for support (the Danish minority in south Schleswig, for example, can call on Denmark, the German minority in north Schleswig on Germany) and the authorities of the host state are expected to take this factor into account. The Frisians and similar groups have no such support. In Europe the position of the Frisians is comparable, for example, with that of the Bretons in France, the Sorbs in the German Democratic Republic and the Lapps in Scandinavia.

The most important element of Frisian identity is the language.[2] Together with English, Dutch, High and Low German, Frisian belongs to the family of West Germanic languages, rather than being a German dialect, as is sometimes assumed. Nor is there one single Frisian language, but rather three distinct branches: North, East and West Frisian. East Frisian has died out in east Frisia itself and is now spoken only by about 1500 inhabitants of the Saterland in the

Oldenburg district. By contrast, the West Frisian language community in the province of Friesland in the Netherlands numbers more than 350 000.[3] The number of Frisian speakers in north Frisia with its four main dialects (three on the islands, one on the mainland) is estimated at about 10 000; in the mid nineteenth century this figure was around 30 000.[4] The Frisian language communities in Germany are thus among the smallest in Europe.

A Frisian movement can be said to have existed in west and north Frisia since the 1840s, influenced by an earlier Romanticism. The conditions for the movement were by far the most favourable in west Frisia[5], where it could draw on a relatively uniform language, a large community of speakers and a respectable written tradition. In 1844, the *Selskip foar Fryske Tael en Skriftekennisse* (Society for Frisian Language and Literature) was founded, which was to play a significant role in the preservation and advancement of the Frisian language in west Frisia.

In north Frisia, on the other hand, it was not until around 1800 that the first literature of any note appeared.[6] Only a few minor pieces date from earlier centuries. Even during the periods when north Frisia belonged to the Danish *helstat* German was the official language of government, the church and education. From a functional point of view, North Frisian was therefore restricted to the status of a dialect.[7] The first attempts at forming a North Frisian movement, also in the 1840s, were hampered and finally quashed by the growing hostility between Germans and Danes in the duchy of Schleswig[8] – a conflict which was to flare up repeatedly in later years, always overshadowing north Frisian efforts. Neither the inhabitants of German persuasion in Schleswig–Holstein, nor the 'Eider Danes', those who wished to claim the river Eider as Denmark's southern border, were interested in an independent Frisian movement. The vast majority of north Frisians, influenced mainly by their centuries old ties with German as an official language, were in favour of a German Schleswig–Holstein.

The first Frisian organisation in north Frisia was not formed until 1879, when the region was already part of the state of Prussia within the German *Reich*. From 1900 onwards, under the neo-romantic influence of the period, further organisations came into being[9], of which the most important was the *Nordfriesischer Verein für Heimatkunde und Heimatliebe* (North Frisian Association), founded in 1902. This was the first to concern itself with the whole of north Frisia. These organisations were mainly supported by the educated and/or landowning middle classes: teachers and the clergy, fairly wealthy merchants and better off farmers. Agriculture was the most important economic factor in the Frisian regions; their remoteness from the great industrial centres meant that very little industry was able to develop.

The first contacts between the West and North Frisian movements came as early as 1850.[10] Initially, the members corresponded by letter, but in the years before the First World War visits were arranged. At this time, the German and Dutch authorities took little notice of the interFrisian exchanges. Only in the 1920s did they come to be seen as a problem, when the contacts grew stronger and a 'Frisian question' emerged in north Frisia, a development closely connected with international events at the time.

The 'Frisian Question' and the European Congress of Nationalities

With the Schleswig plebiscite of 1920,[11] which was one of the provisions of the Treaty of Versailles, German–Danish territorial differences once again affected north Frisia. Only the northernmost parts of the region were assigned to the second zone of the plebiscite. However, the vote in the second zone brought an 80 per cent majority for Germany, and north Frisia remained undivided as part of the German state.

Some of the Frisians who had voted for union with Denmark in the plebiscite founded in 1923 the *Friesisch–schleswigscher Verein* (Frisian–Schleswig Association) known today by the Frisian name of *Foriining for nationale Friiske* (Association of Nationalist Frisians). This organisation collaborated with the Danish minority, emphasising at the same time the separate identity of the Frisian people and aiming for recognition as a national minority by the German authorities, objectives which should not, however, be confused with the utopian demand for an independent North Frisian state. The nationalist standpoint of the Association was reflected in particular in its demands for instruction in Frisian in schools; acknowledgement of Frisian in all areas of life; and regional self-government in north Frisia. In March 1924 the Frisian–Schleswig Association, which had gained only a few supporters in north Frisia, was involved in the founding of the *Verband der nationalen Minderheiten in Deutschland* (Association of National Minorities in Germany), the first time that the national minorities within one state had attempted to work together. Other member groups were the Polish, Sorbian, Danish and later Lithuanian minorities within the state. The initiative for all this came from the Union of Poles, which also put up the Chairman and General Secretary of the organisation:

> . . . the establishment of a front of national minorities was considered to be an important political factor which would give the Polish movement the possibility of exerting a more effective influence on the policy of the German government and on propaganda in the inter-national arena.[12]

From 1925 on, the Frisian–Schleswig Association applied for membership of the European Congress of Nationalities in Geneva,[13] supported in its application by the Association of National Minorities in Germany. The conveners of the congress, particularly Ewald Ammende, a German from Estonia, had originally intended to invite only the Polish and Danish minorities from the German state. The Association of National Minorities, however, insisted on the inclusion of the Sorbs, who were duly admitted. No representatives of the Frisian–Schleswig Association were invited, but the delegates of the Polish and Danish minorities demanded at the very first meeting on 15 and 16 October 1925 that north Frisian delegates also be admitted in future years.[14] The 'Frisian question' thus emerged, and was to have serious consequences for the Congress in future. The disagreements continued until 1928. At no other time before or since have the north Frisians attracted so much attention on an international scale. The question of whether or not they ought to be represented at the Congress of Nationalities touched on fundamental issues of minorities' policy. It was the first case of its kind to give rise to debate at European level on what actually constitutes a 'national minority'.[15]

In this context, the German authorities were keen to prevent the growth of a Frisian national minority,[16] therefore rejecting or ridiculing the demands of the Frisian–Schleswig Association. This applied to the attitude of authorities in the Prussian province of Schleswig–Holstein and the Prussian state authorities, as well as to the German Foreign Ministry and Ministry of the Interior. The governmental powers in Germany, as in most other countries, tended to regard linguistic and national minorities within their territories as factors for disturbance and sources of unrest best kept under control or suppressed. The national unity of a state was seen as the supreme goal. That national and linguistic variety could be worth preserving and promoting was rarely recognised at this time. The majority of concessions to Polish and Danish minorities in Germany were not granted until the mid 1920s,[17] and then the move was almost entirely prompted by considerations of foreign policy. In particular Germany's Minister of Foreign Affairs, Gustav Stresemann, was keen to accord rights to minorities within Germany as a lever for German demands to grant similar rights to the much larger German minorities in neighbouring states.[18] However, this motive was of no help to the north Frisians: with no Frisian state outside Germany, the Foreign Ministry in Berlin saw no grounds for the recognition of a Frisian minority. Instead it acted for what it saw as the common good of Germany, not wishing the Frisian movement to develop into yet another minority question within the state borders.[19]

A further consideration for the German authorities was the situation at the German–Danish border established in 1920. Although revision of the border settlement was not a current government objective, the 1920 settlement being respected in practice, the new borderline was not officially recognised. A growth of the Danish minority south of the border was the thing to be avoided above all; and to this end it was imperative to strengthen the German front in south Schleswig. It was thus feared that any recognition of a right to claim identity as a Frisian minority in the region would undermine this policy. Besides, the Frisian–Schleswig Association's cooperation with the Danish minority made the former appear to the officials as a Danish organisation in disguise.

There were in Schleswig–Holstein strong forces working towards a revision of the border who supported the German minority's efforts towards this end in the Danish governed region of north Schleswig.[20] For these factions it could be anything but welcome that yet another controversy over minority rights was apparently developing and gradually coming to a head in the western areas of south Schleswig. The most active figure in these German factions was Johannes Schmidt-Wodder, representative of the north Schleswig German minority in the *Folketing* (Danish parliament), as well as at the Geneva Congress of Nationalities. On a broader scale, Schmidt-Wodder was one of the leading political figures among the German minorities abroad between the two world wars.[21]

When the second Congress of Nationalities was held in late August 1926, the Frisian–Schleswig Association was again passed over. The preparatory committee had, however, agreed to a compromise: the Congress was to appoint a commission of enquiry into the Frisian question.[22] In addition, during this second Congress the Polish minority in Germany gave its particular support to the Frisian–Schleswig Association, not least as an instrument of agitation, which could provide fuel for conflict with the German groups. Johannes Schmidt-Wodder countered such moves through the medium of the *Nordfriesischer Verein für Heimatkunde und Heimatliebe* (North Frisian Association), founded in 1902 and the largest organisation in north Frisia.[23] In the 1920s this association worked to further Frisian language and culture, but it differed from the Frisian–Schleswig Association in its attitude to German. The North Frisian Association did not attack the status of the German language, or its function as an official language in the region. Instead it emphasised the close ties of the north Frisians with German and their affiliation with the German people. It was overtly anti-Danish in attitude, which was not the least among the reasons that it received considerable funds at intervals from the German authorities. On 12 September 1926, at the instigation of Johannes Schmidt-Wodder, this organisation issued five principles, known as the *Bohmstedter Richtlinien* (Bohmstedt principles) stressing the German sympathy of the north Frisians. Although they called for the maintenance of a strong Frisian element within the German culture, the principles explicitly renounced all claims to the status of a national minority. A broad based petition showed that these principles were supported by over 13 000 north Frisians – the vast majority, in fact.

In April 1926 the preparatory committee of the Congress of Nationalities had established three criteria for the admittance of new members.[24] The group wishing to join had to be organised; its *selbständiger Kulturwille* (desire for an independent cultural identity) had to be beyond doubt; and the majority of those within the group had to agree to, or at least not oppose, its membership of the Congress. The signatures collected in north Frisia showed that most north Frisians did not want minority status and declined representation in Geneva, so for a while the Frisian question appeared to be solved. But the dubiousness of the majority principle soon became apparent, especially to Josip Wilfan, the President of the Congress of Nationalities and a Slovene from Italy.[25] He justifiably concluded that a decision regarding the existence of a national minority could not be made by majority vote. Instead, the presence of a desire for an independent cultural identity had to be the decisive factor. The majority criterion was later rejected, in March 1928. The Frisian problem had shown it to be an unfit instrument for decisions pertaining to the existence of a national minority.

A few weeks before the third Congress of Nationalities meeting, from 22 to 24 August 1927, the Association of National Minorities in Germany once more requested admittance of the Frisian–Schleswig Association and declared its intention of boycotting further congresses should its request not be fulfilled. Only with considerable reservations did the delegates of the Polish, Danish and Sorbian minorities in Germany take their places in Geneva. Under these circumstances it was the Frisian question which dominated the congress.[26] The issuing of an invitation to the Frisian–Schleswig Association was opposed, particularly by the German minority groups. The immediate response of the minorities within the German state was to declare their withdrawal from the Congress, which was thus split over the Frisian question. All attempts to restore harmony were in vain.

The Frisian question was by no means the only reason for the failure of the third congress, but neither can it be regarded as a mere pretext for the split. Over the course of time it had become a matter of prestige, and it also contained the essence of the fundamental differences in the political orientation of the Congress.[27] These differences were not least a result of the fact that the minorities saw themselves as guardians of the interests of their 'mother countries'. Poland and Denmark strove to preserve the frontiers created after the First World War; likewise, the Polish and Danish minorities in Germany supported the *status quo* and distanced themselves from all irredentist efforts. Germany, on the other hand, desired above all a revision of its eastern borders, seeing the justification for this in the existence of sizeable German speaking minorities in the border regions.[28] In this context Berlin favoured the concept of 'cultural autonomy' as practised in Estonia since 1925, with its major provisions for self-government of minority groups. The Congress of Nationalities took up the demand for cultural autonomy, which gave Germany grounds to rely on the Congress as support for its own foreign policy. But it was the minority groups within Germany who rejected the idea of cultural autonomy out of hand. As 'weak minorities' they would not be able to benefit from its provisions. Their representatives accused the majority of congress delegates of only furthering the interests of 'strong minorities' and turning against the 'weak' groups for reasons of power politics. In this respect, they argued, the Frisian problem was the crux of a fundamental issue. Moreover, the Polish, Danish and Sorbian minorities feared that the congress was being increasingly dominated by the German speaking groups.

The withdrawal of such minorities from the Congress, urged mainly by the Polish minority, was arranged in agreement with the Polish government[29], which had come to regard the Congress as an instrument of German foreign policy. Besides, the restrictions imposed upon minority groups within Poland were a sign that the government was not genuinely interested in an international minorities' forum. Yet the Polish minority does not appear to have aimed deliberately at breaking up the Congress. If an agreement over the Frisian question could have been reached, there would almost certainly have been no split in the Congress, at least at that juncture. The Frisian problem was obviously the spark to a situation that was only too ready to explode, and thus it became the cause of disintegration.

While Poland looked upon the failure in Geneva as furthering its own interests – and had indeed worked towards this end – Denmark reacted with surprise and displeasure.[30] The authorities in Copenhagen considered the Danish minority had been mistaken in surrendering the opportunity offered by an international congress simply because of the Frisians. The Danish Foreign Ministry was sceptical about an independent Frisian movement and kept its distance from the idea. Support for the Frisians could not be in the Danish interest. There was also concern that cooperation between the Danish and Polish minorities could in the long run lead to an undesirable linking of the border issues in the east and in the north. It was felt that the Danish minority should be guided by Danish considerations in its dealings with Poles and Frisians.[31] The Foreign Ministry in Copenhagen thus made cautious attempts to influence the Danish minority in Germany through its consulate in Flensburg, but to no avail.

On 3 July 1928, the committee of the Congress of Nationalities unanimously rejected the application for membership made by the Frisian–Schleswig Association on the grounds that the required collective cultural identity of a lasting nature could not be ascertained for the group at that time.[32] In view of the composition of the committee (it comprised a Slovene, a German, a Catalan and a Jew), it would be a misjudgment to attribute the decision solely to 'pan-Germanism', as the Danish minority declared, but it was indeed the representatives of the German minorities who had been most persistently opposed to Frisian membership. Wilfan, the President of the Congress, had hesitated up to the last. He emphasised that the decision was provisional and not at all hostile to Frisian efforts. The Frisian nationalist movement, he said, was only in the early stages of its development, while the aim of the Congress was to link already existing national communities for the protection of their common rights.[33]

The Association of National Minorities in Germany – the Poles, Danes and Sorbs – objected to this justification and accused the Congress of a lack of solidarity with smaller minorities.[34] The German minorities, on the other hand, also realised that the Frisian problem raised certain fundamental issues, albeit with reversed premises. They wanted representation in Geneva primarily for those groups which, like themselves, were in a position to set the granting of political rights and cultural autonomy as their main goal. They did not believe that the Congress of Nationalities should admit 'weak groups' such as the Frisians, who would drag it down to the level of a 'charitable care organisation'. By admitting unverified and unverifiable groups, they argued, the Congress would be open to ridicule from the League of Nations; indeed from the world in general.[35] The Foreign Ministry in Berlin also had an interest in debarring from the Congress small minorities with a purportedly divisive influence on a state and for which there was no question of cultural autonomy.[36]

The widespread dismissal of north Frisian membership of the Congress may be explained by the general lack of understanding at that period for minorities without a nation-state. In the 1920s very few such groups claimed minority rights. The fact that the Frisian–Schleswig Association was an exception had a lot to do with its links with the Association of National Minorities in Germany, as well as with the nationalist experience of the referendum of 1920. At first only two such groups were present at the congresses in Geneva: the Jews and, after Ammende, the Secretary General, had overcome his doubts, the Sorbs.[37] At the second Congress they were joined by the Catalans from Spain and, in 1930, by the Basques, two groups with a strong corporate identity due, among other things, to the strength of their economic position.

The minorities established in Geneva showed little inclination to support the efforts of newly forming groups. The German minorities in particular spoke of the need to prevent 'atomisation' of the minorities' movement.[38] They held that a vote in favour of Frisian entry to the Congress would lead to 'a thousand other difficulties', for whatever applied to the Frisians, warned Ammende, would also apply to the Bretons and other groups. It was true that the situation of the north Frisians hardly differed from that of groups such as the Bretons. In Brittany, for example, the desire for an independent cultural identity was to be found in only a small part of the population. The majority either did not understand or rejected the efforts. The Congress should not support such groups, declared Ammende. It should seek to avoid the 'artificial creation' of minorities, otherwise it would lose credibility. It was indicative of the situation that the director of the minorities' section in the League of Nations, the Norwegian Eric Colban, also warned against admitting such groups. The Congress should refrain from making itself ridiculous by 'inventing' minorities like the Frisians.[39]

The disagreements between 1925 and 1928 underlined the fact that the 'miniature problem' of the Frisians touched on fundamental questions of European minority policy. Regional and more universal developments were closely related. Johannes Oldsen, the Chairman of the Frisian–Schleswig Association, wrote, not without irony, that the Frisians had played a minor world role during those years.[40] Diplomats and politicians from a number of countries kept themselves informed on the Frisian question,[41] including those in the Netherlands, who were concerned lest the situation influence the attitudes of the west Frisians.

InterFrisian Contacts and Government Attitudes in Germany and the Netherlands

Contacts between the north and west Frisians, which had been broken off during the First World War, were resumed and reinforced during the 1920s and extended to include the east Frisians.[42] It was in east Frisia that representatives of all Frisian and neighbouring regions met in 1925. This first 'Frisian Congress' in the town of Jever was, like its successors in Ljouwert/Leeuwarden (1927); in Husum and on Söl/Sylt (1930) and in Medemblik (1937), of a primarily academic nature. But the congresses also provided opportunity for an exchange of opinion and experience on matters of common interest, and stimulated efforts to preserve the language in west Frisia and north Frisia, with each region in many respects serving as an example and encouragement for the other. A panFrisian concept was frequently hinted at, but this remained vague and undefined. For instance, if a speaker from north Frisia called for 'a strengthening of our community of East, West and North Frisians'[43] none of the listeners thought in terms of political union as a result, which would indeed have been quite illusory.

The contention surrounding the question of the north Frisian minority also left its mark on interFrisian relations. It was conceivable that the west Frisians would also claim minority status and apply for membership of the Congress of Nationalities in Geneva. For this reason, Josip Wilfan, the President of the Congress of Nationalities, made inquiries into the situation in west Frisia in late 1926.[44] He contacted the Dutch pacifist and women's rights supporter, Christine Bakke-van Bosse, who also took an active interest in minority affairs. She addressed herself to the Royal Commissioner in the Dutch province of Friesland, P.A.V. van Harinxma thoe Slooten, who was dismissive and even went as far as to deny the existence of Frisian as a language in its own right. The Commissioner also ensured that at the second Frisian Congress in Ljouwert in 1927 the only representative from north Frisia allowed to give a speech of any length was Rudolf Muuss, chairman of the North Frisian Association, and thus decidedly opposed to the claim of minority status. Delegates of the Frisian–Schleswig Association were not invited to speak.

The German minorities abroad also thought it wise to investigate the situation. In 1928 Carl Georg Bruns, legal consultant to the German minorities and adviser on minority questions to the Foreign Ministry in Berlin, visited west Frisia. In the report which he submitted to the Ministry Bruns concluded that there was no doubt of the west Frisians' fulfilment of the conditions for admission to the Congress of Nationalities.[45] West Frisians of various persuasions told him, however, that they did not wish for representation in Geneva, at least not for the time being. Although many of them were sympathetic to the ideas of the Frisian–Schleswig Association, the very concept of being a minority group was alien to the west Frisians. In contrast to Germany there were no other national minorities in the Netherlands, and they had more faith in the Dutch authorities than the Frisian–Schleswig Association had in the German authorities.

Yet the disagreements in Geneva were not without consequences for west Frisia.[46] The Foreign Ministry of the Netherlands gathered information about the debates on the entry of the north Frisians to the

Congress of Nationalities and the Dutch Cabinet discussed possible effects of this issue on the west Frisians at least twice. The fear of a 'West Frisian inclined Geneva' was perhaps one of the factors which prompted the government in the Hague to comply with the wishes of the west Frisians in setting up a state funded Education Council.

Ties between the Frisian groups in Germany and the Netherlands became more formally defined at the end of the 1920s. In 1928 plans were made for a 'Frisian Council' with representatives from all Frisian regions, which would serve as an organ of liaison in the periods between congresses. The Council eventually came into being in Husum in 1930, where the following tasks were agreed upon: preparation of Frisian Congresses to be held in the different Frisian regions every two to three years; organisation of lectures; exchange of journals; exchange of experience for example in the use of Frisian in schools; publication of a yearbook for the whole Frisian region; promotion of academic research; establishment of contacts with Frisian associations outside Friesland, particularly in towns in Germany and the Netherlands and in America. Political issues were not to be the concern of the Frisian Council. A more radical counterpart to this was created in 1929 by the Frisian–Schleswig Association and representatives of the more radical wing of the west Frisian movement, who established a *Grossfriesischer Kampfbund* (PanFrisian Combat League) which made nationalist demands, although these remained rather vague. These organisations were very probably the first trans-frontier groupings of their kind in Europe.

The governments of Germany and the Netherlands followed these developments with suspicion. The regional authorities in Schleswig, who were responsible for north Frisia, initially regarded the proposed Frisian Council as a possible source of positive support for German foreign policy, but their optimism was not shared by the Prussian government in Berlin. A confidential statement issued by the Minister of the Interior, Albert Grzesinski, a socialist, on 30 January 1929 ran as follows:

> Even if the movement stresses Frisian membership of the Prussian and German state and nation, the dangers which could be involved in the extension of the Frisian movement, particularly across national frontiers should not be overlooked. Any obvious growth in the movement, even in the so-called Frisian home movement (*Heimatbewegung*), can all too easily provide foreign powers with a welcome opportunity to heed assertions of the existence of a separate Frisian national minority in Germany. There is of course no intention of suppressing the so-called Frisian movement. However, the principle of quieta non movere at least must be applied by the authorities to guide their actions, and an artificial nurturing and inflation of

minorities must be avoided. For this reason, no more state funds of any significance may be granted in support of the Frisian movement.[47]

All major support for the 'so-called Frisian movement' was thus to be withdrawn.

Such a policy of mere toleration was destined in the long run to lead to a decline:[48] small cultural minorities depend on state support if their language and culture are to survive. In previous years the Prussian authorities had made certain allowances, such as permission to hold one Frisian lesson each week in schools and occasional grants of money to the clearly loyalist North Frisian Association. It had been hoped by these tactics to cut the ground from under the feet of the Frisian–Schleswig Association and its agitatory activities. But even these subsidies were now to stop, because the aim of the authorities, germanisation of the north Frisians, seemed endangered. Besides, following the decision of the Presidium of the Congress of Nationalities in Geneva in 1928 not to accept the Frisian–Schleswig Association for membership, the German authorities felt that particular risk had abated.

The reservations of the Prussian Minister of the Interior also applied to east Frisia. He was concerned that the cooperation with west and north Frisians would lead to the foundation of an east Frisian minority movement – a quite misplaced fear for which there was not the slightest cause. The efforts of the movements in west Frisia and north Frisia were concentrated primarily on the preservation of their language, whereas Frisian had long died out in east Frisia. Nevertheless, the minister recommended that the local east Frisian *Heimatbewegung* should be made 'appropriately aware of the dangers of ties between west, east and north Frisia' and prevailed upon in future to refrain from attending 'so-called Frisian Congresses'. This aim was not, however, achieved.

The Foreign Ministry in Berlin also recommended the North Frisian Association to exercise caution and reserve in its relations with the Frisians in the Netherlands. It wished to avoid a possible strain on its own relations with the government of the Netherlands, 'with which we desire the best possible relationship'.[49] The Dutch government was for its part suspicious of the ties between Frisians within its own borders and in Germany. In 1928 the Ambassador of the Netherlands in Berlin had followed the instructions of the Dutch Foreign Ministry on the initiative of Provincial Commissioner van Harinxma and asked why in northern Germany there was such a lively interest in the Frisian movement in the Netherlands.[50] In response the German Foreign Ministry arranged a meeting between the Dutch diplomat and the Chairman of the North Frisian Association, Rudolf Muuss, who made it clear during the discussion that the Frisian efforts were nothing more than 'a harmless interest in local history'. A political union of the three Frisian regions was at all events inconceivable and quite out of the question. This meeting allayed the fears of the Ambassador, who sent a report to this effect to the Hague.

Both the German and the Dutch governments therefore followed interFrisian relations with misgiving. They were not seen as an opportunity for trans-frontier *rapprochement* and cultural exchange, and there was no respect for the justifiable Frisian wish to maintain contacts with their fellows in another country. The governments feared unwelcome developments. Admittedly, the dangers envisaged were never specified, but obviously consequences for the border settlements themselves were feared in the long term, and any developments in this direction were to be quashed at infancy.

Due especially to the economic and political crisis in Germany at the beginning of the 1930s, the Frisian Council and the PanFrisian Combat League were never particularly active. Nevertheless, there were meetings, even after the seizure of power by the National Socialists in 1933. The Nazis ensured that the North Frisian Association was brought into line with their ideas (*Gleichschaltung*) and suppressed the minority activities, which the Frisian–Schleswig Association had continued.[51] It appears that the Nazi leaders were at first wary of interFrisian relations, as they were of all international movements. A semi-official statement published in 1934 declared:

> The well being of our peoples (*Stämme*) will not be found in international congresses in the manner of the Jews. We should nurture our identity in fraternity with Saxony and Brandenburg within the glorious and honourable shelter of our *Reich*.[52]

This ideological aversion to any 'international' tendencies soon receded, however, in favour of a pragmatic attitude.

In the mid 1930s, Hitler's Germany was at pains to emphasise its good relationships with its north western neighbours. Early in 1936 a pact of non-aggression with the Netherlands was considered; a year later Hitler counted the Netherlands as 'inviolably neutral territory', albeit only for propaganda purposes as it turned out.[53] To the Nazi authorities, the ties between Frisian groups now seemed a useful medium for improving Germany's image in the Netherlands. The proceedings of the fourth Frisian Congress, held at the end of July 1937 in Medemblik in the formerly Frisian northern part of the province of North Holland, were thus followed with some interest.[54] The Foreign Ministry in Berlin approved the attendance of Germans from the *Reich* with the proviso that the congress should not be political. The *Dienststelle Ribbentrop*, the National Socialist party office for special foreign policy issues in the department of the Deputy

Führer Rudolf Hess, supported the Frisian Congress, as an especially valuable method of promoting friendship between Germany and the Netherlands. Care was to be taken, however, to ensure that only citizens of the *Reich* unquestionably loyal to National Socialism should be allowed to participate.

One member of Ribbentrop's staff took part in the congress, but for obvious reasons did not want to be recognised in Medemblik as a member of a National Socialist department. He was therefore registered as a member of the Germano–Dutch Society. His department maintained 'a certain degree of political caution' with respect to the Frisian movement. Above all, the Nazis wished to check whether political demands might some day be made, cloaked in the mantle of Frisian nationalism. On the other hand, it was quite feasible that Frisian ties could enable 'German influence' to be exercised on the Netherlands. With this in mind, the *Dienststelle Ribbentrop* supported preparations for the next projected Frisian Congress, to be held in 1939 or 1940 in Aurich, east Frisia. This could be portrayed to foreign visitors as a sign that the 'cultural forces of regions' could best unfold within a strong, centrally governed state – a statement which had already been proved false by the Nazis' restrictive policy in north Frisia. The plans for a fifth congress were, however, abandoned after war began.

The departments responsible for foreign policy in the Third *Reich* thus stressed that interFrisian relations were to serve cultural and academic purposes only. They feared that 'unequivocal demands' could otherwise be made on behalf of Frisian language and culture, which would not be at all in their interests. On the other hand, in spite of this emphasis on the cultural aspect, they aimed to exploit interFrisian ties to promote the foreign policy of Nazi Germany. The Frisian Congresses were thus in danger of being robbed of their original goal and also of being misused as an instrument of Nazi propaganda.

Following the occupation of the neutral Netherlands by German troops on 10 May 1940, the attitude of the Nazi authorities to the Frisian movement took on a new dimension.[55] Exploiting the ties formed in the course of the Frisian Congresses, an attempt was made to win over the west Frisian movement to support for the German occupation force. In this way, the Nazis completely perverted interFrisian relations. Nevertheless, a fresh start was still possible after the Second World War, a development that would be aided by the growing desire for European unity. In 1955 a common 'Frisian Manifesto' was agreed upon, containing a reaffirmation of the Frisian language and culture, as well as support for the idea of European unity.[56] In 1956 the 'Frisian Council' reformed, and since then Frisians have met at three yearly intervals, such trans-frontier relations today being tolerated and partly supported by the governments of the Federal Republic of Germany and the Netherlands.

Notes

1. Kloss, especially p. 62. Kloss describes minorities which cannot relate to a national state as *Eigengruppen*, differentiating them from *Aussengruppen*, those which do relate to a state.
2. Reviews of the Frisian language, literature and history are given by Sjölin; Feitsma, Alberts and Sjölin.
3. For a comprehensive sociolinguistic investigation of the situation today see Gorter, Jelsma, Plank, Vos.
4. Steensen (1986a), especially p. 33. For the present situation only estimates can be given.
5. On the Frisian movement in west Frisia see van der Schaaf; Zondergeld.
6. The first book in the North Frisian language was the comedy by Hansen.
7. See Nickelsen, especially pp. 133–4; Hofmann, pp. 7–33, especially p. 24; Århammar, pp. 55–76, especially p. 57.
8. Jensen (1961b), especially pp. 97–112. On the German–Danish conflict up to 1848 see for example Carr.
9. See Steensen (1986a), pp. 42–82.
10. See Jensen (1961b), pp. 168–9; Steensen (1986a), pp. 108–15.
11. See the contribution by Doege and Rerup in this volume.
12. Wrzesiński, pp. 19–43, the quotation on p. 30. On the Frisian–Schleswig Association see Steensen (1986a), pp. 186–229.
13. Michaelsen. For what follows see Steensen (1986a), pp. 229 ff.
14. *Sitzungsbericht der ersten Konferenz*, p. 75.
15. Plesse, p. 47. See also *Neue Züricher Zeitung*, 25 August 1927. The Frisian application for membership 'raised the question as to what should be regarded as a national minority at all'.
16. Steensen (1986a), pp. 313–24.
17. Broszat, pp. 393–445; Fink.
18. See Broszat, especially pp. 394–5.
19. Politisches Archiv des Auswärtigen Amtes, Bonn, Section VI, *Kultur, Deutschtum im Ausland, 10, Friesen*, report from 10 May 1928, printed in Steensen (1986b), pp. 144–5.
20. See for example Tägil, p. 15.
21. See Hopp, pp. 24–35.
22. See Michaelsen, p. 392.
23. See Steensen (1986a), pp. 238–51; Steensen (1986c), pp. 101–7.
24. See Michaelsen, pp. 240–1.
25. See Steensen (1986a) pp. 259–60; Steensen (1986b), pp. 118–21.
26. See Michaelsen, p. 311.
27. See Steensen (1986a), pp. 265–7, 273–8.
28. See Pieper, especially pp. 128–32.
29. See Rothbarth, pp. 187, 165–6. For what follows see Steensen (1986a), pp. 266–7.
30. Comprehensive files on this subject are to be found in the archive of the Danish Foreign Ministry, Copenhagen. For an evaluation see Steensen (1986a), pp. 267–8.

31. Expressed by Denmark's Foreign Minister Laust Moltesen on 4 August 1928, Rigsarkivet, Copenhagen, files of the Danish consulate in Flensburg, 7.C.33.V.
32. See Michaelsen, p. 530.
33. J. Wilfan in a letter to J. Kaczmarek, Secretary General of the Association of National Minorities in Germany, on 13 July 1928, Bundesarchiv, Koblenz, Wilfan papers, no. 31.
34. This view is expressed particularly in several essays which appeared in *Kulturwehr*, the journal of the Association of National Minorities in Germany, for example Jan Skala, ' "Starke" und "schwache" Minderheiten', *Kulturwehr*, 3 (1927), pp. 1–8.
35. The view of the German minorities is expressed particularly in articles in the journal *Nation und Staat*. See also for example Paul Schieman, 'Grundsätzliche Fragen zum Genfer Minderheitenkongress', *Europäische Gespräche*, January 1926, pp. 1–10; Rudolf Brandsch, 'Starke und schwache Minderheiten', *Deutsche Politische Hefte aus Grossrumänien*, 7 (1927), pp. 54 ff.
36. Politisches Archiv des Auswärtigen Amtes, Bonn, Section VI, *Kultur, Deutschtum im Ausland, Nr 10, Minderheitenkongresse*, vol. 6, entry from 10 May 1928.
37. See the list of Congress members 1925–8 in Michaelsen, pp. 575–82.
38. Expressed by the Latvian German Paul Schiemann in *Frankfurter Zeitung*, 26 August 1927. For what follows see Steensen (1986a), pp. 275–7.
39. Quoted in Michaelsen, p. 335.
40. Quoted in Steensen (1986a), p. 278.
41. At least in Germany, Denmark, the Netherlands and Poland. Also the French Foreign Ministry in Paris kept itself informed on the Congresses; Ministère des Affaires Etrangères, Archives, Paris, Section SDN, I E, file 443. Special files on the Frisian question were not to be found.
42. See Steensen (1986a), pp. 279–313.
43. *Reden und Predigten zur 500-Jahr-Feier der Sieben-Harden-Beliebung vom 19. -21. Juni 1925 auf Föhr* (Wyk, 1926), p. 27.
44. See Feitsma, pp. 27–62.
45. See 19 above.
46. See Steensen (1986a), pp. 291–3; on the 'Frisian Council' etc. see pp. 298–308.
47. Landesarchiv Schleswig–Holstein, Schleswig, file 309/35252; printed in Steensen (1986b), p. 146.
48. See Kloss, pp. 122, 142. For what follows see Steensen (1986a), pp. 320–4.
49. See 19 above.
50. Correspondence on this point is to be found in Politisches Archiv des Auswärtigen Amtes, Bonn, Pol. Sect., *IIa, Niederlande, Politik 6*; correspondence of authorities in the Netherlands partly printed in Feitsma pp. 42–5.
51. See Steensen (1986a), pp. 373–413.
52. Heinrich, p. 104.
53. See Jacobsen, pp. 341, 418; Lademacher, pp. 654–74.
54. Described after Politisches Archiv des Auswärtigen Amtes, Bonn, files of the 'Dienststelle Ribbentrop', 21/2, betr. *Gau Weser-Ems 1937–40*, documents of 22 March, 31 March, 16 May, 22 July, 21 October 1937; 20 January 1938.
55. See Schaaf, pp. 319–46; Zondergeld, pp. 286–447.
56. See Ostfriesische Landschaft, pp. 17–18.

Select Bibliography

(All works in German unless otherwise stated)

Århammar, Nils (1976), 'Historisch-soziolinguistische Aspekte der nordfriesischen

Mehrsprachigkeit', *Friesisches Jahrbuch*. (Brief clear study of cause and effect of North Frisian dialect variety).

Broszat, Martin (1968), 'Aussen- und innenpolitische Aspekte der preussisch–deutschen Minderheitenpolitik in der Ära Stresemann', in *Politische Ideologien und nationalstaatliche Ordnung. Festschrift für Theodor Schieder zum 60. Geburtstag*, Munich. (Analyses the interplay of domestic and foreign policy considerations within the Prussian–German minorities' policy, with special reference to the Polish minority in Germany.)

Carr, W. (1963), *Schleswig–Holstein 1815–48. A Study in National Conflict*, Manchester.

Feitsma, A., Jappe Alberts W. and Sjölin, Bo (1987), *Die Friesen und ihre Sprache*, Kgl. Niederländische Botschaft, 'Nachbarn' 32, Bonn. (Brief account of the history and present state of the Frisian language in west, east and north Frisia).

Feitsma, Tony (1986), 'Ut de skiednis fon de Fryske beweging om 1928 hinne', *FRYX*, 7. (Study of political considerations of state authorities in the Netherlands with respect to the Frisian movement in west Frisia, in West Frisian, with many documents).

Fink, Troels (1958), *Geschichte des schleswigschen Grenzlandes*, Copenhagen.

Gorter, D., Jelsma, G.H., Plank, P.H. van der, and Vos, K. de (1984), *Taal yn Fryslân*, Leeuwarden (in West Frisian).

Hansen, Jap Peter (1809), *Die Gidtshals, of di Söl'ring Pid'ersdei (Der Geizhals oder der Sylter Petritag)*, Flensburg.

Heinrich, Gregor (1934), *Wir Friesen!*, Berlin.

Hofmann, Dietrich (1979), 'Die Friesen, das Friesische und das Nordfriesische Wörterbuch', *Nordfriesisches Jahrbuch*, 15. (Useful introduction to the basic historical and linguistic setting of North Frisian with special reference to efforts to collect North Frisian vocabulary).

Hopp, Peter (1976), 'Pastor Johannes Schmidt-Wodder (1869–1959). Ein Forschungsbericht', *Grenzfriedenshefte*, 1.

Jacobsen, Hans-Adolf (1968), *Nationalsozialistische Aussenpolitik 1933–38*, Berlin.

Jensen, Johannes (1961b), 'Die Nordfriesen im Spannungsfeld zwischen Deutschland und Dänemark', *Grenzfriedenshefte*, 2. (Concise account of the effects of the German–Danish conflict in the north Frisian movement).

Jensen, Johannes (1961a), *Nordfriesland in den geistigen und politischen Strömungen des 19. Jahrhunderts (1797–1864)*, Quellen und Forschungen zur Geschichte Schleswig–Holsteins, 44, Neümunster. (Comprehensive account of the effects of liberal and nationalist thought on north Frisia until the end of the Danish *helstat*: describes the first attempt to found a north Frisian movement in the 1840s).

Kloss, Heinz (1969), *Grundfragen der Ethnopolitik im 20. Jahrhundert. Die Sprachgemeinschaften zwischen Recht und Gewalt*, Vienna. (General basic account of the situation of linguistic and national minorities).

Lademacher, Horst (1976), 'Die Niederlande und Belgien in der Aussenpolitik des Dritten Reiches', in Funke, Manfred (ed.), *Hitler, Deutschland und die Mächte*, Dusseldorf.

Michaelsen, Rudolf (1984), *Der Europäische Nationalitäten-Kongress 1925–8. Aufbau, Krise und Konsolidierung*, Frankfurt. (Detailed exhaustive account of the origins and early years of the Congress of Nationalities, drawing on a wide range of sources).

Nickelsen, Hans Christian (1982), *Das Sprachbewusstsein der Nordfriesen in der Zeit vom 16. bis ins 19. Jahrhundert*, Nordfriisk Instituut, Bräist/Bredstedt. (Examines the attitude of north Frisians to their own language as well as to Low and High German).

Ostfriesische Landschaft (ed.) (1955), *Wir Friesen*, Aurich.

Pieper, Helmut (1974), *Die Minderheitenfrage und das Deutsche Reich 1919–1933–34*, Hamburg. (Particularly treats policy towards the German minorities abroad; national minorities within the *Reich* are dealt with only briefly).

Plesse, Herbert (1930), *Organisation und Arbeit der Kongresse der organisierten nationalen Gruppen in den Staaten Europas*, Leipzig. (Earliest study (thesis) of the Congress of Nationalities).

Rothbarth, Maria (1983), 'Der Europäische Minderheitenkongress als Instrument imperialistischer deutscher "Revisionsstrategie". Grenzrevision und Minderheitenpolitik des deutschen Imperialismus (1919–1932)', unpublished PhD thesis, University of Rostock. (The Congress of Nationalities is portrayed one sidedly as a tool in the service of 'imperialistic German minority policy'; the author draws on sources other than those used by Michaelsen).

Schaaf, Sjoerd van der (1977), *Skiednis fan de Fryske biweging*, Leeuwarden. (Comprehensive account of the west Frisian movement; in West Frisian).

Sitzungsbericht der ersten Konferenz der organisierten nationalen Gruppen in den Staaten Europas im Jahre 1925 zu Genf (1925), Vienna.

Sjölin, Bo (1969), *Einführung in das Friesische*, Stuttgart. (Survey of history, characteristics and literature of west, east and north Frisian).

Steensen, Thomas (1986a), *Die friesische Bewegung in Nordfriesland im 19. und 20. Jahrhundert (1879–1945)*, Quellen und Forschungen zur Geschichte Schleswig-Holsteins, 89, Neümunster. (Detailed history of the north Frisian movement from first moves towards organisation up to the Second World War).

Steensen, Thomas (ed.), (1986b), *Die friesische Bewegung in Nordfriesland im 19. und 20. Jahrhundert. Dokumente*, Quellen und Forschungen zur Geschichte Schleswig-Holsteins, 90, Neumünster. (Contains 90 documents on the history of the north Frisian movement).

Steensen, Thomas (1986c), 'Die friesische Frage in historischer Sicht', *Nordfriesland*, 19, no 76.

Steensen, Thomas (1987),*Streifzüge durch die Geschichte Nordfrieslands: Friesische Sprache und friesische Bewegung*, Husum. (Short account of the development of the north Frisian movement, with numerous illustrations).

Tägil, Sven (1970), *Deutschland und die deutsche Minderheit in Nordschleswig. Eine Studie zur deutschen Grenzpolitik 1933–1939*, Stockholm.

Walker, A.G.H. (1980), 'North Frisia and Linguistics', *Nottingham linguistic circular*, 9, no. 1. (A general introduction to the linguistic situation, in English).

Wrzesiński, Wojciech (1968), 'The Union of Poles in Germany 1922–1939', in *Polish Western Affairs*, 9.

Zondergeld, G.R. (1978), *De friese beweging in het tijdvak der beide wereldoorlogen*, Leeuwarden. (Detailed account of the history of the west Frisian movement, particularly in the period of the two world wars, in Dutch).

A comprehensive collection of documents referring to the Frisian movement in North Frisia is to be found in the *Nordfriisk Instituut* in Bräist (Bredstedt). The institute's publications include the journal *Nordfriesland* and the yearbook *Nordfriesisches Jahrbuch*.

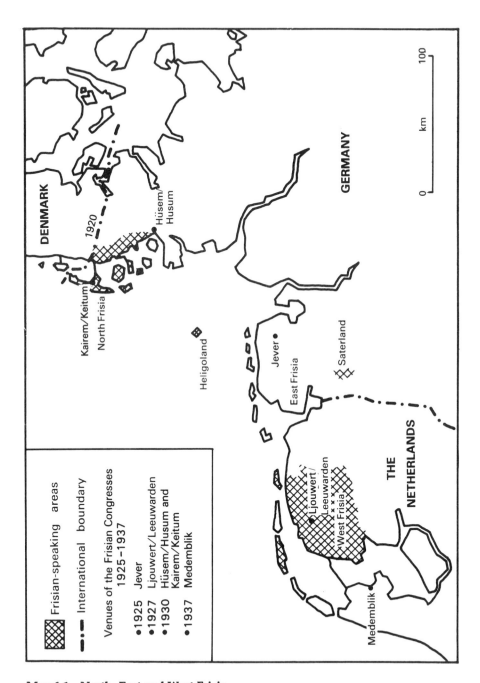

Map 6.1   North, East and West Frisia
Source: T. Steensen, *Die friesische Bewegung in Nordfriesland im. 19 und 20. Jahrhundert*,
Neumünster, 1986, p. 307.

7 The Åland Islands Question
TORE MODEEN

The Historical Background

In 1850, Finland was an autonomous grand duchy ruled by the tsar of Russia. When Finland was incorporated in the possessions of the Russian empire in 1809, it was guaranteed home rule and autonomous constitutional rights. The old Swedish constitution of 1772, amended in 1789, thus continued in force during the whole period of Russian rule in Finland. Under this constitution Finland was divided into *län* (counties) headed by a Governor appointed by the king, and there was no political body or county parliament beside the Governor.

The Åland Islands, situated between the southern part of the Finnish coast and Sweden, were part of the Turku-Pori county. Åland was only a jurisdictional district and a *härad* (district for census and land tax purposes) and as such of minor importance in the judicial and administrative division of the country. However, the Åland Islands were considered of great strategic importance at that time, being at the entrance to the Gulf of Bothnia. For this reason, a considerable number of Russian troops was stationed on the islands. During the years 1836–53 a great fortress, Bomarsund, was constructed where a Russian garrison guarded the security of the islands. During the Crimean War a French–British naval unit destroyed this fortress, and a particular clause was attached to the Treaty of Paris in March 1856. The Åland Islands convention stipulated that no fortifications should be allowed on the islands nor any military or naval establishments.

It was Sweden which, although not a party to the Crimean War, had obtained the Åland Islands convention, which was of only minor value for France and Great Britain but was very important for the security of Sweden. Sweden had tried to keep the islands when Finland was lost in 1809, and now the demilitarisation of the islands was the most Sweden could hope for. Thus, after 1856, the Åland

Islands were in military matters a separate part of the grand duchy of Finland. The civil government, however, was not changed in any way.

The First World War and the Finnish Civil War (War of Independence)

During the First World War, despite the 1856 convention, Russia began to fortify the Åland Islands. With the Russian military defeat on the eastern front and the communist revolution in 1917, Finland saw a chance to free itself from a Russian rule which had over the previous 20 years increasingly ignored Finnish autonomous rights. It was in this chaotic situation that a separatist movement begun to make its mark on the Åland population. The Ålanders were afraid of being involved in any future Finnish–Russian struggles and sought the protection of Sweden. They saw it as a safeguard at a time when Finland's future as an independent state seemed doubtful. This fear was well founded as Finland, soon after having proclaimed herself independent by the end of 1917, became involved in a civil war between the Whites, opposed to communism, and the Reds, supported by Soviet Russia. During this war the Åland Islands were occupied first by military forces coming from Sweden; and then by German forces as Germany, in 1918, extended its military influence to Finland as a whole, while supporting the White forces in the civil war. The importance Sweden attached to these islands from a strategic point of view is emphasised by the limited nature of her intervention: the islands only.

The fear of finnisation in the case of Finland's becoming a sovereign state was another reason for the separatist movement in Åland. Considerable political fighting between Finns and Swedes as to the minority rights given to the Swedish Finns had provided cause for alarm. The Ålanders feared that the Finnish majority would use its numerical strength in a situation of political democracy to oppress the linguistic and cultural rights of the Swedish Finns; but by becoming subjects of the Swedish crown the Ålanders could be sure of maintaining their Swedish language and traditions.

The Ethnic Argument

The First World War was being fought by the western side to free the oppressed nationalities or ethnic groups in Europe and the Ottoman empire. As the European map was redrawn in Paris in 1918–19, the ethnic argument was given much strength. Even states that had not participated in the war could profit by this idea, as when Denmark succeeded in getting back part of its old Slesvig (Schleswig) territories. Slesvig, inhabited by Danish and German ethnic groups, was thereafter divided between Denmark and Germany in a way that took into account the ethnic border, even though that was unclear in many cases.

As Sweden had always looked upon foreign rule of the Åland islands as a threat to her security, she responded positively to the wishes of the Ålanders as ethnic Swedes to be reunited with their mother country. Obviously, however, strategic reasons were more important than ethnic ones in Sweden's attitude, particularly since the experience of the war showed that the demilitarisation prescribed in the 1856 treaty could not be guaranteed.

One problem lay in the fact that while the Ålanders were ethnic Swedes, so too were many other Finnish citizens along the Finnish coast: farmers, fisherman, people engaged in trade and industry, civil servants and judges, and at that time a very considerable proportion of Finland's educated class. Apart from strategic reasons, why should only the Åland Islands be separated from Finland and given to Sweden? The answer lay in the fact that no separatist movement existed among the ethnic Swedes in other Finnish provinces, provided one does not take into account as such any movement for creating a kind of self-governing district that arose during the first years after independence. The Swedo–Finns on Finland's mainland and the islands east of Åland never asked for Swedish rule; only for protection against finnisation in a state with a Finnish majority population.

The Attitude of the Finnish Government

The reaction of the Finnish government during the Åland crises of 1917–21 was to concede self-government of the Åland Islands in order to prevent the loss of the islands to Sweden. This gradually came about through legislative and administrative measures as a result of pressure from abroad. However Finland never agreed to demands to organise an official plebiscite on the islands which undoubtedly, under these circumstances, would have resulted in a large majority for Swedish rule. Finland did not want to lose the sovereignty of the islands to Sweden. But Finland was willing to guarantee the protection of the ethnic character of the islands, by conceding gradually more and more radical autonomous rights, and even the continuing demilitarisation of the islands. The Åland Islands crisis became a factor in the minority question covering the whole of Finland that was debated by the Finnish parliament while drafting a Finnish Constitution. There was considerable international interest focused on Finland in these years, at first in Paris and Versailles in 1918–19, and afterwards in Geneva. The League of Nations there was busy not only trying to solve the Swedish–Finnish conflict over the Åland Islands but also with the implementation and the completion of a minority treaty system for most of the new and even some of the old European states.

The Finnish government necessarily had to take a liberal attitude to the Swedish ethnic question as a means to create an atmosphere of *détente* in the country and on the international scene (and considering also Sweden's interest in the case). Only in a state where the Swedish population group as a whole could feel itself reasonably secure against finnisation, could the Åland Islands hope in the long run to remain Swedish in the ethnic sense of the word.

Yet this need not imply that the other Swedish regions of Finland should enjoy the same kind of home rule as the Åland Islands. The movement for provincial self-government for the Swedish ethnic areas of Finland did not win much support even among the Swedo–Finns in Finland who preferred to remain in a system with Finnish majority rule in most cases, as it gave them, they thought, better possibilities for participating in the national government on an equal footing with the ethnic Finns. In this situation, no Swedish self-governing districts were created on mainland Finland. It is very uncertain whether this idea, even if supported by most of the Swedo–Finns, would have had any possibility of being accepted by the Finnish majority in the state government and in parliament.

The League of Nations and Finland's Membership

The Swedish government tried in Paris to have the Åland Islands question decided by the big powers in connection with the peace treaties. Since this matter did not interest the conference, it was taken to the newly founded League of Nations. The League was simultaneously concerned with Finland's application for membership in the organisation and with the minority protection system in Finland. On 16 December 1920, Finland was accepted as a member of the League, even though the Åland Islands question was still unsolved. Effectively Finland was not willing to consider the Åland Islands question, or her minority protection system in general, in connection with her membership.

Thus it was only after Finland had already become a member of the League that a report was asked for on the minority question. The report on *La Situation juridique et les droits des minorités en Finlande* (The Legal Position and Rights of Minorities in Finland) was drawn up and sent to the Council of the League in 1921. The Council decided, after having studied the report, that Finland should be exempted from any obligation towards the League over the protection of her minorities. This decision was motivated by the fact that the ethnic Swedo–Finns, the only minority of importance, had not asked for such a measure, nor had Sweden's government made such a demand. The Finnish constitution act of 17 July 1919 was considered to be satisfactory in this respect, since the Swedo–Finns enjoyed equal rights with the Finns under the constitution. On 2 October 1921, as this decision was made, the Åland Islands question had already been decided by the Council.

Since many treatises and papers dealing with the minority protection guaranteed by the League of Nations are in error on this point, it is important to stress that Finland did not have to make a minority protection treaty. She did not even have to make a declaration on this subject in general or on the Åland Islands in particular to be accepted as a member of the League. It is worth noting that Lithuania had to conclude such a treaty, while Estonia and Latvia had to make declarations on minority protection. Indeed the Memel convention, to which Lithuania was a party, concerns a situation somewhat similar to that of the Åland Islands.

The Finnish–Swedish Dispute on the Åland Islands at the League of Nations

Against this background, the Finnish–Swedish dispute over the Åland Islands was submitted to the League of Nations. The League, accepting Finland as a member, went so far as to make a reservation over the sovereignty of the Åland Islands, as the conflict was still under the Council's consideration.

The Åland Islands question was discussed for the first time by the Council on 11 July 1920, when Finland was not yet a member of the League of Nations, with the initiative coming from Great Britain. According to article 11 of the Charter of the League, any member of the Council had the right to draw the Council's attention to any international dispute which could disturb mutual understanding among the nations and thus the peace. For the Islands, this was the beginning of a procedure which was to end one year later with the Åland Agreement and the Åland Demilitarisation Convention.

Much has been written on the Åland dispute at the League of Nations, and so it is enough to describe only the main events. Finland tried, without success, to have the case withdrawn from the agenda of the Council, arguing that the sovereignty of the Åland Islands belonged to Finland and that any dispute concerning the islands was thus of an internal character. Sweden's response was based on the desire of the Ålanders to become a part of Sweden:

Il sera permis à la population alandaise de décider immédiatement par plébiscite si l'Archipel Alandais doit rester sous la souveraineté finlandaise ou être réintégré au Royaume de Suède. (The Åland population shall be allowed to decide by plebiscite, immediately, whether the Åland archipelago should remain under Finnish sovereignty, or be reintegrated into the Swedish kingdom.)

The procedural question, that is, whether the Åland Islands question was to be considered an international dispute and thus under the jurisdiction of the Council, was studied by a commission of jurists which also took into account the status of the islands under international law. Because of the fact that Finland had only recently gained independence, the national border question might seem to be still open and thus could be considered by the Council. On the other hand, the commission expressed the opinion that minority groups did not have the right, under international law, to demand to be separated from their state. The state had absolute rights to decide whether or not it would allow a population group, by plebiscite or any other means, to decide for itself on its future, on a possible separation.

As the matter was finally held to fall within the jurisdiction of the Council a new organ was created, the commission of *rapporteurs*, to study how the Åland Islands question should be resolved. This commission reported that it was of the opinion that Finland had sovereign rights to the islands and that they should remain Finnish. But it recommended, on the other hand, that Finland agree to some guarantees for the protection of the Swedish character of the Islands and that the protection system be placed under the supervision of the Council and the International Court of Justice.

In June 1921, the Council discussed this question. Sweden repeated its claim to the islands, which was rejected by Finland. Finland, however, agreed to add new guarantees for the protection of the Swedish character of the islands. Even representatives for the Ålanders were heard during the proceedings, when they supported the Swedish claims. On 24 June 1921 the Council confirmed the opinion of the rapporteurs that the Åland Islands belonged to Finland. They invited the interested parties to settle the dispute by an agreement on guarantees for the protection of the Swedish language and the local culture on the Åland Islands. These guarantees were to concern the provincial autonomy of the Åland Islands; the language of instruction in the schools; the real property rights of the local population; the voting rights of the immigrants to the islands; and the appointment of the governor of the county of Åland.

On 27 June 1921, after a meeting between the Swedish and Finnish representatives had taken place, the agreement reached by the two parties was submitted to the Council. The Council unanimously confirmed the Åland Agreement and decided to add it to its resolution of 24 June 1921. The Council also dealt with the neutrality question on the same date, recommending that a new convention be drafted, in line with a Swedish proposal, which would be concluded by all states concerned and guaranteed by the Council. This ended the League of Nations' handling of the Åland Islands question.

Actions by the Finnish Government to Keep the Åland Islands

When it became obvious that Finland had to take special measures if she wanted to keep the Åland Islands, a series of legislative actions was taken by Finland. The first important decision, made by the Finnish senate was to create the *Ålands län* (county of Åland) by a decree of 13 June 1918 (No 48). On 30 January 1920, before the League of Nations became concerned with the Åland Islands question, but when this question was already under international debate, the Finnish government put before the *Riksdag* (parliament) a bill on the autonomy of the Åland Islands (1919:73). The government referred to a governmental committee created to report on provincial autonomy in general, but also in particular the Åland Islands. The government had decided that the Åland question 'for special reasons' was one that should be treated separately from the other counties. The question of self-government for the counties is still debated in Finland as no legislation on the matter has been passed so far. Finnish counties have remained purely state governmental districts, run by a *Landshövding* (Governor) appointed by the President of the republic.

In its introductory remarks to the bill the government stated that Finland had been inhabited since prehistoric times by *tvenne invid varandra bosatta folk* (two neighbouring peoples) speaking different languages, Finnish and Swedish. The number of Swedish speaking people was about 340 000. Of these 19 613 lived on the Åland Islands, while only 826 Ålanders had Finnish as their mother tongue. The Åland Islands, in the government's view, belonged geographically to Finland as a part of the archipelago. Since time immemorial the islands had historically, belonged to Finland in terms of the government, the judicial system and church administration. Although the Finnish constitution of 17 July 1919 guaranteed several rights to the minority population, the Swedish speaking Ålanders felt insecure and continued trying to separate themselves, with foreign support, from Finland, although they formed only a small proportion of Finland's Swedish speaking population.

The government thus decided to give the aforementioned committee the task of drafting an autonomy act for the Åland Islands, in order to remove reasons for discontent. The government's bill would create a broad autonomy for the province of Åland, insofar as was possible for a unit which was not a state. This was the substance of the government's reasoning. The bill included provisions for the *landsting* (provincial parliament), the *landskapsnämnd* (governmental body), the powers of the Governor, the civil service and defence. The official language of the province was to be Swedish, with rights for citizens also to use Finnish in their dealings with officials. The act could be abolished or amended only with the approval of the provincial parliament, when the particular procedure required for changing Finland's constitution was to be followed by the state parliament.

The opinion of parliament's constitutional law committee and the report of the Grand Committee were given in 1920. The term *län* was changed to *landskap* (province). A provision in the bill, by which the state's officials should master Swedish, was changed to an obligation to master Swedish completely. Although the bill was opposed, it was passed by parliament and confirmed by the President of the republic, K. J. Ståhlberg, on 6 May 1920. The Åland Islands Agreement simply required additional guarantees to the Ålanders to be incorporated into Finnish legislation. This was achieved by a new act, of 11 August 1922, containing additions and amendments to the 1920 act.

The Åland Islands Agreement, 1921

The Åland Islands Agreement of 27 June 1921 is in many ways an exceptional case under (Finnish) international law. It is based on a resolution made by the Council of the League of Nations on 24 June 1921, and was confirmed by the Council on 27 June 1921. But it is still a document containing provisions agreed upon by the representatives of Finland and Sweden. This document was not signed, but only included in the minutes of the Council. It does not appear in the treaty series of the League of Nations, only in its Council minutes series. Nor does it appear in the Finnish or the Swedish official treaty series, being only reprinted in other Finnish and Swedish official documents (in Finland in the bill leading to the act of 11 August 1922).

It was a most unusual procedure, since the normal way of incorporating an international treaty or convention into Finnish law is to reprint it with Swedish and Finnish translations in the official treaty series (*Finlands Fördragssamling*) (the so-called blank procedure), and even to include a reference in the official statute series (*Finlands författningssamling*). However, there were special reasons for this unusual procedure. The agreement concerns only the Åland Islands and since Finland maintained her sovereignty over the islands and Sweden did not obtain any rights, Sweden did not find it necessary to mention the agreement in her treaty series.

The Attitude of the Swedish Government after 1921

Sweden's government thought it wiser to forget the dispute as an obstacle in normalising relations with Finland. Thus the Åland Islands Agreement is hardly mentioned in Swedish textbooks on international treaties concerning Sweden. Having lost its case against Finland, Sweden was not anxious to be reminded of this diplomatic defeat. There have, on the other hand, been many statements by Swedish politicians and scholars agreeing that a take over of the Åland Islands did not really interest Sweden, neither for ethnic nor even for strategic reasons. Sweden was quite satisfied with her territory as it was and had no ambition to acquire a new province which could lead to trouble with its eastern neighbour in the future. The only reason why Sweden started the dispute with Finland was because the Ålanders had seemed so determined to join Sweden, and because Sweden's government thought it was still worth a try to get the islands from Finland. From the beginning of the nineteenth century Sweden's diplomacy has been characterised by moderation and passivity, rather than by aggression. A single exception to this was the annexation of Norway in 1814, but even then Sweden let Norway leave the union without war in 1905.

The Swedish occupation of the Åland Islands in 1918 was abandoned when the German intervention in Finland began. The Åland Islands' dispute at the League of Nations is an exception to the rule and does not fit in well with Sweden's cautious traditions in the international politics game. Sweden put no pressure upon Finland after the conclusion of the Åland Islands Agreement and neither in the League of Nations nor in any other international forum did it attack Finland's handling of the islands' government. Finland's Swedish ethnic group as a whole, and even the Ålanders, did not (and does not) interest Swedish public opinion, which was at first very introvert in its orientation. Later, as Sweden's international consciousness began to develop, under the influence of Prime Minister Olof Palme, it was mainly oriented towards the Third World and America and very little concerned with her neighbours, even those with an ethnic population group of the same character as her own population.

The Attitude of the Finnish Government after 1921

In Finland as a recently independent state, nationalistic feelings were running high in the 1920s and particularly in the 1930s. Any limitation of her sovereignty, not to speak of her losing a part of her territory, was strongly objected to. Some chauvinist circles in Finland even aimed at an enlargement of Finland's territory in the east. Finland's government, however, restricted its actions (such as the Treaty of Dorpat, 1920, between Finland and Soviet Russia) to what concerned autonomous rights for the ethnic Finns of Soviet Russia (eastern Carelia and Ingermanland).

It was only under pressure from abroad that Finland agreed to the special status of the Åland Islands. The very liberal Constitution act of 1919, granting equal rights for Swedish and Finnish speakers, must also be regarded in the light of international politics; the policy of the League of Nations in minority protection matters; and the Åland Islands dispute. When the dispute was settled in Finland's favour, Finland's international obligations remained to protect the Swedish ethnic character of the islands. Finland did not want to emphasise Sweden's role as a party to the agreement, but preferred to see it as only a League of Nations instrument. Finland's obligations were then more readily accepted by domestic opinion than if Sweden was mentioned in this connection. It is for this reason that the agreement was not signed by either side and not published in either treaty series. The League of Nations showed great discretion in this matter, since it did not even ask for its registration with the Bureau of the League, even though despite this the agreement was well-known, having been published in the Official Journal.

However Finland was obliged to include the agreement in her legislation. This was done by translating the text of the agreement into Swedish and Finnish and putting it as a government bill before parliament. Of course, the government could not conceal the fact that the bill was entirely based on the agreement, and some members of parliament opposed the bill because of this. But the majority were fully aware that Finland was bound by the agreement and had no other choice but to confirm it. So the agreement was incorporated into Finnish law in this unusual way.

The Åland Islands Agreement in Finnish and International Legal Literature

In all Finnish textbooks and other comments on the agreement published in this period, the agreement was classified merely as a decision of the Council of the League of Nations. Even the well-known scholar, Professor S.R. Björksten, who published a paper on this matter, deemed it wise to maintain the stance that the agreement between Finland and Sweden on the guarantees for the protection of the ethnic character of the Åland Islands was transformed into a League of Nations act, when confirmed by the organisation. Thus, Finland did not have to face the unpleasant fact that the very broad autonomous rights of the Ålanders depended on a Finnish obligation not only towards the League of Nations but also towards Sweden, as a party to the agreement of 27 June 1921.

However, in the international literature concerning the minorities' protection system after the First World War, the Åland Agreement was usually seen as a treaty concluded between Finland and Sweden under international law. When the question of the validity of these treaties was subject to a study by the Secretary General of the United Nations after the Second World War, the Åland Islands Agreement of 27 June 1921 was still considered as valid, binding Finland and Sweden. The same point of view was maintained by the Swedish government when a new autonomy act for the Åland province was drafted in Finland after the Second World War. Sweden then demanded that the guarantees for the protection of the Swedish language and culture on the islands be observed as stated in this agreement. In my study of the question, published in 1973, I acceded to the view that the agreement was still valid between Finland and Sweden, even though the international guarantee had ceased with the termination of the League of Nations.

The Åland Autonomy Act

The original Åland Islands Autonomy act of 1920 had given the provincial parliament large legislative powers, particularly in the field of administrative law (municipal law, planning and building law, fire protection, order and security, social welfare, schooling, roads, farming, fishing, environment matters etc.) and had also granted rather considerable powers to the provincial government. Thus, the Ålanders were given the opportunity to govern themselves on a provincial level: the municipal administration being relatively autonomous in Finland, this meant that the Åland Islands administration was competent to deal with most local matters. Finland believed that this would be sufficient to protect the Swedish character of the islands, particularly since the number of ethnic Swedes was so great, and also Swedish was to be the only language of the state authorities.

The Åland Islands Agreement of 27 June 1921, reaffirmed in the Finnish act of 11 August 1922, contained several important additional rights for the Swedish population of the islands. Swedish was to be the language of instruction in all schools. In elementary schools Finnish was not even to be taught as a 'foreign' language without the permission of the municipality concerned. Finnish speaking immigrants were thus placed at a disadvantage in maintaining Finnish as the language of their children. Finnish citizens coming into the province were not to receive voting rights there until they had been resident for five years. As additional security the province, or the municipality, or a person resident in the province, was given a 'right to buy' in dealings in any real estate sold to an outsider.

This ensured that land could remain in the hands of the Ålanders, and was a major guarantee for its population particularly as farming was the main trade (together with fishing and shipping) of the islanders and the ownership of landed property is regarded as very important for any ethnic group in a minority position. The five years' residence voting qualification for immigrants guaranteed that political power would remain in the hands of the original population. After five years of residence even an outsider was supposed to become 'naturalised', that is, to adopt the Swedish attitudes and language of the Ålanders. The agreement and the act also contained provisions for the appointment of the Governor and for the right of the provincial government to obtain tax derived income from the state. The last article contained the right to call the attention of the Council of the League of Nations to disputes arising from the implementation by the Finnish government of these guarantee provisions, and opened the possibility of asking the opinion of the Permanent International Court of Justice on legal questions pertaining to the agreement and the act. The threat of finnisation present in some bilingual districts of Finland was thus avoided.

The Implementation of Ålandish Autonomy

The first 20 years of implementation of the Åland Autonomy act and the additional Guarantee act were marked by a correct and law abiding, if not always enthusiastic, attitude on the side of the Finnish government. Finland had accepted the particular status of the Åland Islands only under outside pressure and was thus not very happy to sponsor it. The Ålanders were equally disappointed when their dream of being incorporated into the 'motherland', Sweden, did not materialise. It was not self-government but separation that had been requested, said their leaders, who thus retained a certain bitterness towards the Finns. Their attitude was further hardened by resentment at having been accused of treason by Finnish authorities during one early period of the separatist movement.

The first provincial elections took place on 8 May 1922. On 9 June of the same year the provincial parliament had its first session, with Mr Julius Sundblom, one of the two leaders of the separatist movement, being elected as the *Landsting's* first speaker, remaining so until his death in 1945. The provincial government began work on 1 August 1922, headed by the other separatist leader, Mr Carl Björkman. The Ålands Delegation, a body headed by the Governor and with equal representation for the Finnish government and the provincial government, operated from January 1923. All the Governors during the first 20 years of Åland's autonomy were Swedish–Finns. From 1948 the province of Åland has been a constituency with the power to elect a member to Finland's parliament. But even prior to this arrangement the Åland Islands were, for certain periods, represented in parliament by members with an interest in their cause.

If there was no enthusiasm for the autonomy on either side in the beginning, it did work, even though the application of the statutes concerning self-government and the ethnic guarantees raised many questions. One difficult problem was the jurisdiction of the provincial authorities. Under the act it was only those affairs which were under the jurisdiction of the state authorities that were defined. But gradually the situation became clarified, after hard work done both by Finnish and provincial authorities. No dispute between the state and the province was ever of such importance that it was taken to the League of Nations. This shows that a reasonably good atmosphere prevailed during the period when such a measure was possible.

The provisions of the Autonomy act, repeated in the Guarantee act, prevented any change, let alone abolition of the acts without the consent of the provincial parliament. This made it impossible for Finland, even if its government had been so inclined, to abolish or restrict the autonomy of the Ålanders and their ethnic rights. Thus though the 1930s in particular were characterised by virulent attacks against Swedish ethnic rights in Finland, supported by important groups in and out of parliament, the constitution was not amended. Indeed no government even proposed such measures. However the Language act and Officials' Language Proficiency act were changed in these years, together with the Helsinki University act, in a way that was generally unfavourable to Swedish ethnic interests.

The Ålanders and Sweden

During the First World War there were many restrictions on travelling between Finland and Sweden which also involved the Ålanders. After the war many young men from Åland went to

Sweden to avoid being drafted into the Finnish army. But as the Ålanders became exempted from military service this emigration soon ceased. After the war communications between the Åland Islands and Sweden were reestablished. Ålanders resumed their sailing trips to the Stockholm market with fresh fish and other commodities. Sweden was not a country that attracted immigrants at this time, so the emigrants from Åland mostly went to the USA, though there were cases of Ålanders going to work on Swedish farms and having other jobs in Sweden. For Swedes to come and work or settle in Åland Islands, however, was a very rare occurrence.

Between the wars the tourist industry on the Åland Islands began. Many people from Stockholm came to pass their holidays in boarding houses in Mariehamn or other places on these beautiful islands. Sweden always had a Consul in Mariehamn. Occasionally this official was sent from Stockholm by the Swedish government, but often he was an Ålander with only honorary consular powers. By contrast, not many Ålanders went to study in Sweden. Mainland Finland was still the place for them to go to college or to other institutes of higher learning. Moreover some of the Ålandish students remained on mainland Finland having found jobs there. As a result some Ålanders became liable for military service in the Finnish army, and such men later fought in the Soviet–Finnish wars of 1939–40 and 1941–4.

The Demilitarisation Question

The demilitarisation question was linked to the guarantees for preserving the Swedish ethnic character of the Åland Islands. On 20 October 1921, a convention was concluded between the Baltic states, Great Britain and Italy, though excluding Soviet Russia. One consequence of the treaty, guaranteed by the League of Nations, was that the Ålanders were exempted from military service in Finland. With the international situation in 1938 leading towards war, Finland joined with Sweden to plan a fortification of the Åland Islands. It was not carried out, however, because of opposition from the Soviet Union, a non-party to the 1921 convention.

This demilitarisation convention was duly observed by Finland until the outbreak of the Second World War when Finland's security demanded a military presence on the islands. This move was not opposed by the other parties to the treaty when notified. However, after the Russo–Finnish war of 1939–40, the Soviet Union demanded that the Åland islands return to a demilitarised status (treaty of 11 October 1940). These demands were renewed after the armistice between Finland and the Soviet Union in 1944 (see also the treaties of 2 February 1947 and 17 April 1948). The Åland Islands have thus remained demilitarised, with their status controlled mainly by the Soviet Union. The 1921 convention is, however, still regarded as valid, although a matter between Finland and Sweden, and without any guarantee by an international organ.

Concluding Remarks

Was the 1921 Åland Islands Agreement successful in providing guarantees for the protection of the Swedish ethnic character of the Åland Islands? If the answer relates to the situation until 1940, the period of this study, the answer must be in the affirmative. Although the Åland Autonomy act of 1920 was incomplete in many ways it did serve as a basis for the creation of a Home Rule for the Åland Islands. This act together with the additional guarantees given by the 1922 Guarantee act (1921 Åland Islands Agreement) provided the Ålanders with an organisation able to develop both Home Rule and minority protection for the islanders.

It is hard to tell whether a lack of these international and municipal instruments would have resulted in a greatly different situation, from the ethnic standpoint. In the 1920s and the 1930s the ethnic situation in Finland as a whole did not change substantially and one might suppose that the Åland Islands, somewhat isolated from the mainland, would anyway have had a good chance of remaining predominantly Swedish during this whole period.

In terms of later, post-1945, developments, however, in years marked by considerable movement of population in Finland, the constitutional and administrative special status of the Åland Islands was of great value. The Åland Autonomy act was completely renewed in 1951, but in the spirit of further strengthening rather than restricting the autonomy and the minority protection aims of the Åland constitution. The international law aspect of the legal situation of the islands had been substantially changed after the disappearance of the League of Nations, and after it had become obvious that the United Nations did not want to go on guaranteeing the Åland Islands treaties. But Sweden still remains a party to these treaties and, if needed, is able to intervene in favour of Swedish interests, both ethnic and military. In practice, however, this remains a purely theoretical hypothesis.

Select Bibliography

Bibliographical Note

The most important scholarly study of the demilitarisation question is written in French by Söderhjelm. Three studies of the recent history of the Åland Islands merit mentioning in this context. That by Johannes Salminen covers the career of Julius Sundblom, the leader of Åland's political life for many decades. The former Governor Martin Isaksson has published two books on the military history of the Islands during the Russian period: *Kring Bomarsund* and *Ryska positionen Ålandskaja*. While James Barros has published a book on this topic, the most recent work, dealing more thoroughly with the Åland Islands case before the League of Nations from the point of view of international politics is by Tore Modeen, *De folkrättsliga*. A shorter version in English is to be found in *Scandinavian Studies in Law*, 1973, pp. 175–210. An 'official' history of the first 25 years of Ålandish autonomy was written by Matts Dreijer who has subsequently published further with *Ålands självstyrelse 1947–1972*. For the sixtieth anniversary of Ålandish autonomy a book was published by the *Landsting* with various essays written by experts on the Åland Islands (Matts Dreijer, Tore Modeen, and others). Of particular interest is volume 51 of the *Nordic Journal of International Law* (*Nordisk Tidsskrift for International Ret*) 1982 which contains papers from a seminar held in June 1980 in Mariehamn and dealing mainly with legal subjects. See also the articles of Björksten (1931), Modeen (1977), and Rotkrich (1986). The author's interview with former Governor Martin Isaksson in April 1987 has been of use for the section on the Åland Islands and Sweden in this chapter.

Åland i utveckling. Festskrift utgiven av Ålands landsting med anledning av självstyrelsens 60-års jubileum den 9 Juni 1982 (1982), Mariehamn.
Barros, J. (1968), *The Åland Islands Question*, New Haven.
Björksten, S.R. (1931), 'Finland och det folkrättsliga minoritetsskyddet' (Finland and the Minorities Protection under International Law), *Tidskrift, utgiven av Juridiska Föreningen i Finland*.
Dreijer, M. (1947), *Ålands självstyrelse 25 år*, Mariehamn.
Driejer, M. (1972), *Ålands självstyrelse 1947–1972*, Mariehamn.
Isaksson, M. (1981), *Kring Bomarsund. Tio försök att skildra åländska verkligheter 1808–1856* (About Bomarsund. Ten Essays on Events in Åland 1808–1856), Helsingfors.
Isaksson, M. (1983), *Ryska positionen Ålandskaja. En översikt av Ålands militära historia åren 1906–1918.* (The Russian Position in the Ålands. A Survey of the Military History of Åland 1906–1918), Helsingfors.
Modeen, T. (1973), *De folkrättsliga garantierna för bevarandet av Ålandsöarnas nationella karaktär*, (The Guarantees under International Law for Preserving the Ethnic Characteristics of the Åland Islands), Mariehamn.
Modeen, T. (1977), 'Völkerrechtliche Probleme der Åland-Inseln' (The Åland Islands in International Law), *Zeitschrift für ausländisches öffentliches Recht und Völkerrecht*, 37.
Rotkrich, H. (1986), 'The Demilitarisation and Neutralisation of the Åland Islands: A Regime in "European Interests" Withstanding Changing Circumstances', *Journal of Peace Research*, 23.
Salminen, J. (1979), *Ålandskungen* (The King of Åland), Helsingfors.
Söderhjelm, J.O. (1928), *Démilitarisation et neutralisation des Iles d'Åland en 1856 et 1921*, Helsinki.

8 The German Minorities in Poland and Czechoslovakia in the Interwar Period

RUDOLF JAWORSKI

On the eve of the Second World War, the German minorities in Czechoslovakia and Poland became the focus of international attention as they became the flimsy pretext for German National Socialist expansion in eastern Europe. The connection thus provided has remained a central point of reference in many subsequent considerations of the events; the Germans of Poland and Czecho-slovakia have been interpreted either as a 'fifth column' or as the abused victims of National Socialist foreign policy, depending on one's political point of view.

Whether the examination starts with National Socialist aggression against both countries or with the postwar order created at Versailles, ultimately it always comes down to the role of the German minorities within the sphere of National Socialist foreign policy. This is equally true of those interpretations in which the minority provisions after 1918 are viewed as having inevitably laid the basis for the disaster of the 1930s. The Germans in Poland and Czechoslovakia appear in this perspective as two-fold victims: the repressed minorities of the interwar period and those who at the end of the Second World War had to pay the price of National Socialist imperialism with the loss of their homeland.

No less problematic than the above-mentioned interpretation, primarily stemming from representatives of the German minorities involved, is the sweeping suggestion that the Germans in Poland and Czechoslovakia acted as the habitual and obliging accomplices of the Third *Reich*, an interpretation found in many relevant Czech and Polish publications. Postwar consciousness of the suffering experienced during the German occupation, as well as the necessity of justifying historically the forced removal of millions of Germans were the most important motives in this form of argument. Meanwhile, in Polish, as well as non-official Czech, historiography differentiated methods of approaching this problem have become possible. The vanguard positions in German historical research have begun to broaden their approach as well. It should be noted, however, that the exact evaluation of this question is still a delicate theme in the relations between the Federal German Republic and its two eastern neighbours.

If one is to avoid falling back into the conventional trench fighting and so reviving old sensitivities, two established approaches recommend themselves. Above all, the German minority question in Czechoslovakia and Poland should be considered as a *sui generis* problem and, on this basis, deeper investigations should take place in an international context. Moreover, the topic can be deemotionalised through comparison with other minorities in the same country or – as in this study – through the contrast of two German minority groups, living in different countries. On these premises, the international aspects and implications of the German minority question in Poland and Czechoslovakia in the period from 1918 to 1938–9 can be discussed from the following focal points:

- Initial position and attitude of the German minorities in Poland and Czechoslovakia after 1918;
- The approach and policy of the dominant population *vis-à-vis* the German minority;
- The minority and national policy of the German *Reich*;
- The National Socialist challenge.

Initial Position

The Germans in Poland and Czechoslovakia were the most numerous, and, in terms of their political weight, also the most significant of the German minorities in Europe. Both *Volksgruppen* (national groups) were located immediately on the German border. Further, a majority of this German population had in each case first been reduced to minority status within a state context by the delimitation of borders that followed the First World War. The overwhelming majority of Germans living in Poland during the interwar period were to be found in what had formerly been Prussian Poland, having become part of the newly founded Polish state. The Sudeten Germans, almost like local bankruptcy assets left over from the shattered Habsburg monarchy, had been incorporated into the Czechoslovak successor state. In both cases, the assignment of new citizenship took place against the will of those concerned. As a result, the 'borderland Germans' as they were known in contemporary usage, were, almost from the beginning, involved to a much greater degree in international politics than many other German minorities who had lived in linguistic enclaves or remote nationally mixed situations for centuries. This distinction is valid for some of the other German settlements in Poland and Czechoslovakia themselves: in the eastern and south eastern regions, where scattered German settlements of the latter type dominated. They, along with the compact Lódz region in central Poland and the German settlement groups of Poznania–Pomerania, east Upper Silesia and the outlying regions of the Bohemian lands, can for the most part be excluded in the problem under discussion here, because they took on foreign political significance only during the 1930s, and, for the most part, became politically mobilised to a significant extent at this point.

Thus, the German minorities in Poland and Czechoslovakia did not represent enclosed and exclusive settlement areas, but were to be found in a variety of mixed relations in various regions of both states, as Tables 8.1 and 8.2 show.

The differences in scale between the two minorities are immediately apparent. What, however, cannot immediately be discerned from the figures below is the much larger fractionalisation of the German settlement areas in Poland as compared to Czechoslovakia. Two factors caused this: numerous waves of emigration over the course of more than 300 years; and the separate development of the Polish territories after Polish partition in the eighteenth century. This was illustrated, for example, in a clear west–east decline of economic capacity and in the degree of political organisation. On the whole, party political activity had only developed in Poznania–Pomerania and Silesia. The post–1918 attempt to create an overlapping national agency of interests was unsuccessful, and not only because of outside hindrance. Among the Germans of Poland, it was characteristic that the further east they had moved, the less the feeling they had retained of belonging to the German 'mother country'. If, for example, the Germans in Poznania–Pomerania, as one time German citizens, had reacted to their separation from Germany with a mass exodus, the Germans in the farming settlements of Volhynia reacted differently. For them their 'Germanness' became simply a cultural question of language and customs following their inclusion in the new Polish state.

While the interwar history of the Germans in Poland was marked by an attempt to create a new common consciousness, the political leaders of the Germans in the Bohemian lands merely had to embrace an already established regional structure. Their self-designated collective name of Sudeten Germans which was quickly accepted even by their national opponents, bears witness to a greater ethnic

Table 8.1:   The regional distribution of the German minority in Czechoslovakia based on the 1930 census

Area	German Population	Percentage of the Population
Bohemia	2 270 943	32.3
Moravia–Silesia	799 995	22.8
Slovakia	147 501	4.5
Sub-Carpathian Ruthenia	13 249	1.8
Czechoslovakia	3 231 688	22.3

Source: Alfred Bohmann, *Menschen und Grenzen*, vol. 4 (Cologne, 1974), p. 97.

Table 8.2:   The regional distribution of the German minority in Poland based on the 1931 census

Area	German Population	Percentage of of the Population
Poznania–Pomerania	298 000	9.4
Silesia	91 000	7.0
Galicia	40 000	0.5
Central and Eastern Poland	312 000	1.7
Poland	741 000	2.3

Source: Bohmann, *Ibid.*, vol. 1, pp. 44 ff.

uniformity in comparison to the German minority in Poland. In contrast to the still overwhelmingly agrarian character of the Germans in Poland, the Sudeten Germans were strongly socio-economically differentiated, with a clear preponderance in the area of trade and industry. This condition was reflected in an extensive press and associational system as well as in a complete spectrum of political parties. As far as the *gesamtdeutsches Denken* (panGerman thinking) of the Sudeten Germans was concerned, the relevant initial steps had originally been taken at the end of the nineteenth century. What was new after the First World War was a general withdrawal of focus from Vienna and a stronger orientation toward Germany itself.

As different as the German minorities in Poland and Czechoslovakia were in numbers and in their political and economic significance, one common feature still bound them together, or at least that part of the population living directly on the German and Austrian borders. Before the First World War they had been able to count themselves as members of the dominant national group, with all the resulting privileges and a corresponding conscious superiority, even if, in purely numerical terms, they were already a minority in their immediate *milieu*. Their Czech and Polish neighbours were frequently considered both socially and culturally inferior. One neither cultivated them socially nor learned their language, for example. It was precisely these neighbouring Slavic peoples that had now risen at the end of the First World War, to become the dominant national group in the state. All at once, the Germans were completely dependent on these Slavic groups, and were henceforth to be subordinate to them as minorities. This abrupt exchange of roles was perceived by the German side as discrimination and came as a shock to both the Sudeten Germans and the Germans in the former Prussian provinces of the east.

Undoubtedly the Germans living in the former Prussian provinces had been more helpless following the downfall of the German empire than the Sudeten Germans, who were already experienced in helping themselves. In Poland, the situation of the Germans was certainly more difficult and complicated than in Czechoslovakia. Violent ballot battles, the exposed situation of the 'corridor', the domestic and econo-political instability of the new Polish state, and not least, the rapid unrelenting pace of Polish minority politics, made the German minority more insecure and put them under far greater pressure than the Sudeten Germans experienced at that time. The direct link between the German minority in Poland and the controversy over the revision of the western border of Poland had by the beginning of the 1920s already made them an important factor in relations between Poland and Germany.

The situation in Czechoslovakia was different to that in Poland: the question was one not merely of insuring the survival of the German minority, but also of its political position in the state. Further, in contrast to the Germans in Poland, the majority of the Sudeten Germans did not consider themselves as a minority, but rather as a third, frustrated, national group alongside the Czechs and the Slovaks. A visible sign of their predominantly internal orientation was the weak commitment of the Sudeten Germans to the European minority movement. Sudeten Germans primarily sought opportunities for the improvement of their lot through the Prague parliament, rather than through the League of Nations or Germany. This basic attitude limited expectations *vis-à-vis* the German state, and during the 1920s and even at the beginning of the 1930s these remained limited mainly to an ideal cultural–political level.

This did not preclude an attentive Sudeten German observation of political and economic developments in Germany or the hope that the strengthening of Germany would indirectly have a positive effect on their own situation. On the whole however, it was more a question of orientation than one of direct support. Sudeten German closeness to Germany was expressed less in a dependent relationship, such as has been distinguished to a much larger degree for the Germans in Poland, than in the similarity of the socio-political structure and tendencies of development.

Policy Towards the German Minority

As a result of the Versailles system, Poland and Czechoslovakia had minority protection obligations enforced on them as a constituent element of their new statehood. From the beginning – and more strongly in Poland than in Czechoslovakia – this was perceived as an infringement of the newly achieved sovereignty. In both cases, a very rigid sense of the nation–state idea was responsible for the reaction.

Poland and Czechoslovakia had had to wait too long for their own independence to be willing to share it with other national groups. Minorities were conceded, at most, individual equality as citizens, but were not accorded collective group rights. The Poles and the Czechs, who before the First World War had been the standard bearers of the idea of national equality, in their function as state peoples after 1918 became themselves the masters of other nationalities. Yet neither Czechoslovakia nor Poland formed an ethnically self-contained nation–state as the following tables show:

Table 8.3:   The nationality structure in Poland based on the census of 1931

Nationality	Persons	Percentage of the Population
Poles	21 993 000	68.9
Ukrainians	4 442 000	13.9
Jews	2 733 000	8.6
Byelorussians	1 697 000	5.3
Germans	741 000	2.3
Russians	139 000	0.4
Lithuanians	83 000	0.3
Czechs	38 000	0.1
Others	50 000	0.2
Total	31 916 000	100.0

Source: Bohmann, *ibid.*, vol. 1, p. 44. Compare Map 9.2 below, p. 210.

Table 8.4:   The nationality structure in Czechoslovakia based on the census of 1930

Nationality	Persons	Percentage of the Population
Czechs	7 406 493	51.1
Slovaks	2 282 277	15.8
Germans	3 231 688	22.3
Poles	81 737	0.6
Jews	186 642	1.3
Magyars	691 923	4.8
Ruthenians	549 169	3.8
Others	49 636	0.3
Total	14 479 565	100.0

Source: Bohmann, ibid., vol. 4, p. 96.

What emerges from these figures is that in purely numerical terms, the Czechs were in a worse national–political starting position than their Polish neighbours. This had concrete effects on their minority policy; they were of necessity more willing to compromise than the Poles. The figures also make it clear that the German minority in both Poland and Czechoslovakia was only one among many nationality problems, with foreign political implications, as for example the question of the Lithuanians in Poland or the Magyars in Czechoslovakia. Nevertheless, the relationship of the new state peoples to their German minorities, because of the previously mentioned national transfer of power was particularly explosive, and it received an added charge because of the geographic proximity of the two German states. However, due to the particular nature of affairs, a closer connection was seen between the German minority and the foreign policy of the German *Reich* in Poland than in Czechoslovakia.

The only seemingly contradictory domestic and external portrayal of the German minority was similar in both states. In domestic political disputes, the nationalist press and organisations of the state peoples branded the Germans as a dangerous element, and could not warn strongly enough against their disproportionate influence. In official Polish and Czechoslovak statements for consumption abroad, an attempt was made to present the Germans as a 'disappearing minority' in the truest sense of the word. The goal was the same in each case: the Polish and the Czech nation–state was to be achieved as soon as possible and as far as possible should be presented as untroubled.

For Poland the following points of view were of decisive importance in the attitude toward the German minority:

- The preservation of the territorial integrity of the new state, which in view of the external demands for revision, was given absolute priority.
- The reparation of historic injustices in former Prussian territories of partitioned Poland.
- The avoidance of possibilities of external influence on the domestic nationality problems in Poland.

The last two points were certainly applicable to Czechoslovakia, although to a lesser degree. The historical experience of the Czechs under Austrian domination had been less dramatic than that of the Poles in the Prussian part of partitioned Poland and thus the conception of sovereignty was less rigorously developed. A connection between territorial integrity and the German minority question did not exist in earnest for Czechoslovakia until 1938, at least not as an immediately perceptible threat from the German state or Austria. There were nevertheless great misgivings with regard to the idea of a German–Austrian *Anschluss*, which was current throughout the entire interwar period. The otherwise rather conciliatory Czechoslovak foreign policy took an uncompromisingly harsh position in relation to this idea, due to fear of the indirect, but noticeable effect of the formation of this sort of united German *bloc* on the Germans in Czechoslovakia. Subsequent history proved this fear to have been accurate.

One cannot speak of a uniform attitude toward the German minority within either state. The government, officials, political parties, associations and press had to a certain extent divergent views on this subject. Those voices which recommended *Ausgleich* (settlement on equal terms) did not have an easy time obtaining an adequate hearing from the public, due both to the national euphoria which followed the First World War and to the increasing external threat in the second half of the 1930s. It should also be noted that the German minorities discussed here were neither seen as, nor treated as, a monolithic unit by the state peoples.

The mistrust of the Polish officials and the Polish public was particularly directed against the Germans living in western Poland and not at the scattered German settlements in eastern and south eastern Poland. In the two last mentioned areas, the numerically larger and in part irredentist Ukrainians and Byelorussians constituted the greater challenge. In Czechoslovakia, the Sudeten Germans and not the Germans of Slovakia were perceived as a threat to national unity. In Slovakia it was the Hungarian minority that was exposed to particular repression. In each of the constellations cited, the situation primarily involved a border problem with neighbouring states which were represented within the country by conational groups, thus adding a factor of foreign political threat to the minority question.

The role of protecting power and advocate that the German state claimed for the Germans of Poland and Czechoslovakia was occasionally countered from both sides, though more often the Polish side, by attempts to make valid analogous mandates for the 120 000 Sorbs as well as for the approximately 800 000 Poles living in Germany. The comparatively limited political and economic significance of these Slavic minorities, however, prevented their successful use as a compensatory balance to the German state minority policy in east central Europe.

On the whole, a far more moderate tone can be ascertained in the relevant debates between Czechoslovakia and Germany throughout the entire period. If Polish reaction to the political initiatives of the German state on minority issues was always more acute, this can be explained above all by the immediate perplexity of Poland and the determined designs of its western neighbouring state. This different degree of concern about the foreign and minority policy of the German state, together with the long term rivalry between Poland and Czechoslovakia over the leadership of east central Europe prevented a common defence strategy. Although both countries belonged to the same camp in European politics, they were isolated from each other on the minority question which was so important to both domestic and foreign policy – a situation which was to have disastrous effects for both countries in the 1930s.

The *Reich* Minority and National Policy

The new national–governmental order of Europe which followed the First World War could by no means lead to final solutions pleasing to all sides, due to the complicated ethnic situation in east central Europe. Numerous minority and border problems arose. For the militarily defeated and territorially shrunken postwar Germany such issues became a central topic of public interest and foreign policy. In particular, the large scale transfer of land to the reconstituted Polish state – 42 918 square kilometres of land with a population of 2 961 754 – without a plebiscite, made the Weimar Republic a natural pleader of the minority question. This task was energetically taken up immediately after the end of the war, although the methods and instruments used were subject to sundry changes during the course of the 1920s.

There were various motives for this commitment. Benevolent

motives certainly played a role, but equally, there was the desire to
escape international isolation via the representation and protection of
the German minorities and at least in this area to preserve something
of lost international reputation. The fact that Germans represented
the largest number of the minorities in Europe – contemporary
German estimates were some nine million – gave these efforts a
certain plausibility and prospect of success. Different social and
political groups in Weimar made *Pflege des Grenz- und Auslandsdeutschtums* (looking after the interests of German culture in the
borderlands and abroad) a high profile concern in public life.
Numerous documentation and information centres like, for example,
the *Deutsches Auslandsinstitut* (German Institute for Foreign
Countries) in Stuttgart; a large number of associations such as the
Verein für das Deutschtum im Ausland (League for German Culture
Abroad), with two million members in 1929; and a flood of pertinent
publications which even the specialist could hardly ignore, together
made it clear that the problem of the German minorities had abruptly
moved into the public consciousness of the Germans – including
social democratic circles.

From the beginning, the 'German brother outside the borders of
the *Reich*' was the focus. This included the Germans in Alsace–
Lorraine; north Schleswig; Poznania–Pomerania; and Upper Silesia
and sometimes, the Germans on the perimeter of Austria – the
Südtirol and the Sudetenland – were included as well. These
German minorities were considered the 'unredeemed' brothers, who
together with the Austrians had been unjustly prevented from
unification with 'Mother Germania'. If these groups were arranged in
order of importance, then the Germans of east central Europe took
first place with the Germans in the areas ceded to Poland at the very
head.

Although activity undertaken in the name of *Volkstum* or *Deutschtum* (national or German identity) fulfilled above all a propaganda
function, it also represented an important complement in numerous
ways to the official minority policy of the German state. In diplomatic
negotiations with lands which had German minorities, the German
side could invoke the pressure of public opinion. Further, the
compromising allocation of money for the German minorities abroad
could in part be facilitated via these private associations and
institutions. In view of the political balance of power in Europe, these
sorts of manoeuvre were not to be abandoned. Particularly at the
beginning of the 1920s, Germany still lacked the international
influence to enable it to take the offensive in this matter. Thus only a
cautious policy of support for the German minorities was possible.
This was in part developed below the diplomatic level and again
showed a clear emphasis on support for the Germans in the

territories of western Poland. In this case, it was to some extent a matter of the pursuit of the former *Ostmark* (eastern Marches) policy of Prussia. The stated goal was the stopping of rapid German migration from western Poland, in order to strengthen the ability of the German elements in this region to survive, but the underlying aim was to safeguard the political requirements in terms of population size for the reacquisition of this area.

This cultural and econo-political support was provided in the form of secret subventions for the German cultural establishments in Poland, including schools, societies, and newspapers, as well as the provision of credit to German businesses (cooperatives, banks). The funds raised annually, amounting to millions, flowed particularly into agriculture and throughout the entire Weimar period created the twofold basis of German state minority policy *vis-à-vis* Poland. Without these massive support measures, the Germans in Poland would have, during the world economic crisis at least, lost the material basis of their national independence. This meant that the political independence of the German minority was not directly encouraged. Their permanent position as supplicants exposed them in a not insignificant degree to actual and potential influences from the German state.

Although the Sudeten Germans were not excluded from the unofficial *Förderung des Deutschtums im Ausland* (work for the advancement of German culture abroad), the financial means available to them were only a fraction of that spent on the Germans in Poland. In addition, there was no even approximately comparable system or continuity in the analogous governmental allocations to the Sudeten Germans. There were many reasons for this unequal treatment. The economically secure Sudeten Germans had certainly no need of such far reaching help and were not so easily influenced from outside, due to their political diversity, even if some of their spokesmen sometimes wished they were.

More important, however, were the varying interests of the German state as concerned the Germans in Poland and Czechoslovakia. The border revision question was clearly of fundamental significance in these differing levels of attention of German governments and officials. After the reconstruction of the Polish state, there had been determined territorial demands *vis-à-vis* Poland which had the support of the majority of public opinion in Germany. These demands were again indissolubly linked to a claim for the protection of the German population which had fallen under Polish sovereignty in what had become western Poland. This determined the great significance of the German minority question in Poland for German foreign policy. It was thus an independent factor in Germany's Polish and foreign policy, part of the overriding 'struggle against Versailles'.

The Sudeten Germans did not have the same outstanding significance during the interwar period, with the omission of the
artificially inflated 'Sudeten crisis' in the period just before the
Munich agreement. From the foundation of the Czechoslovak
republic, the Germans in the Bohemian lands had been looked upon
by the government and by a large part of public opinion in the
Weimar Republic as an integral part of that country. There were no
valid territorial demands as concerned Czechoslovakia. Since the
Sudeten German territories had not been part of prewar Germany,
this was not a case of former German citizens. In contrast to
Poznania–Pomerania and Upper Silesia, the Sudeten lands could not
be the object of active German revisionist politics. Thus, for a long
time, the Sudeten German question did not influence the general
relations of Germany with Czechoslovakia in the way that the
minority question dominated Germany's relations with Poland. It
was clearly desirable that the Sudeten Germans defend their national
individuality in the interest of *gesamtdeutsche Kultur* (the 'whole
German culture'), but it was to be done within Czechoslovakia and as
good Czechoslovak citizens, to summarise briefly the basic maxim of
German state Sudeten policy until the mid 1930s. It is not difficult to
recognise here a continuation of Bismarckian expectations of the
Germans of the Habsburg monarchy.

The 1925 Locarno Conference and the admission of Germany to the
League of Nations the following year provided the preconditions for
Germany to be able to pursue openly and effectively its minority
policy as an internationally recognised mandate and to place it within
the framework of a far-reaching German European policy. The
fundamentals and plans of action of German state minority policy
which had been set out at the beginning of the 1920s were by no
means given up. As the conscious non-guarantee of the German
eastern borders clearly demonstrates, Germany left open – peacefully
for the time being, to be sure – the demand for revision *vis-à-vis*
Poland. Similarly, the positive German reaction to the entry of two
Sudeten German political parties into the Prague coalition in 1926
demonstrated that here too German minority policy had not undergone any fundamental change.

The National Socialist Challenge

The establishment of the National Socialist dictatorship in Germany
was a domestic political event, which one could not immediately
assume would bring with it a reassessment of the groups discussed
here. The National Socialists had not previously played a role in the
Pflege des Grenz- und Auslandsdeutschtums. Instead they took over the

proven apparatus of the official and open *Deutschtumspflege* with its coordinated connections to the German minorities abroad. The ideological vocabulary also remained the same, so that it aroused no attention when in his first *Reichstag* speech on 23 March 1933, Adolf Hitler stressed the special responsibility of the new 'national government' for the fate of the Germans living outside the borders of the state.

Behind the scenes, however, well organised changes were taking place, the old leadership was successively thrust aside and measures were taken for the *Gleichschaltung* ('bringing into line') of the German minorities abroad. At the same time, the purely instrumental character of the minority question for the National Socialists from the outset was demonstrated. The National Socialist power strategists thought in large scale terms and not of small scale border corrections in defence of a single settlement group in eastern Europe. The absolute priority of the *Lebensraum* (living space) ideology over the *Volkstum* ideology was not, however, immediately evident to contemporaries.

The positive echo that the National Socialist seizure of power found among most of the German minorities abroad and especially in east central Europe, should not be too hastily interpreted as a general pro-Fascist disposition on their part. The majority of the Germans in Poland and Czechoslovakia felt themselves disadvantaged, if not openly oppressed and discriminated against, in these states. In this context, what counted was the fact that this feeling existed and not so much the question of how justified it was. The feeling of discontent was great and had built up considerable potential for conflict. That under these circumstances everything that looked like an increased display of power in the German mother country was welcome, goes without saying, because an improvement in their own situation was expected from a more united, stronger and influential German state.

The years of the internally divided and internationally humiliated Weimar Republic appeared finally to have passed and Germany shone with a new lustre. It was that and not the National Socialist label that impressed the German minorities. This dazzle also deceived the majority of Germans in Germany and, initially, even a large number of non-German foreign countries. Thus, it was not to be expected that the German border minorities whose picture of Germany was in any case coloured by wishful thinking, would react with greater vision or reserve. In addition, the fact that the Third *Reich* made some successful foreign policy moves on national–political grounds as, for example, the return of the Saarland in 1935, fostered corresponding visions of release among the Germans in Poland and Czechoslovakia.

Conditions for the spread of National Socialism were particularly auspicious among the Germans in Poland. The continuing pressure from Polish officials and the national Polish press, the weakness of the political organisation and leadership of the German minority there and not least, the habit of allowing themselves to be influenced and directed by Germany, provided really ideal conditions for winning this minority over to Fascism and for its *Gleichschaltung*. Since, however, almost all of the influential political forces of the Germans in Poland, with the exception of the smaller catholic and social democratic circles, wanted to enlist in the service of the 'new idea', rival camps of necessity developed, with their rivalry reinforced by the effects of the different positions taken by the *Reich*.

The major contender in this dispute was the *Jungdeutsche Partei* (Young German party), the first National Socialist organisation in Poland, coming out of Silesia. This party, founded in 1930 as a radical renewal movement, announced a policy of relentlessly pressing for a settlement of accounts with the old German leadership and promised to bring about finally the overdue unification of German settlement groups in Poland on the National Socialist pattern. The *Deutsche Vereinigung* (German Union), founded in Poznania–Pomerania in 1933, particularly opposed this claim, which was supported by the traditional *Volkstum* leaders and followers of the National Socialist idea. In Central Poland, the *Jungdeutsche Partei*, on the contrary, came up against the opposition of the *Deutscher Volksverband* (German People's League), which had undergone a *völkisch* (nationalist) revitalisation under the influence of the 'national revolution'. In summary, it can be assumed that the National Socialist 'renewal' had mobilised the Germans in Poland, first in western Poland, spreading to central and eastern Poland, but it did not lead to a unification comparable to that in the German *Reich*. Up to the beginning of the Second World War, there was no formal *Gleichschaltung* of the Germans in Poland. It was not considered opportune for the new powers in Germany to encourage an open conflict with Poland during the 1930s.

In the Sudeten lands, the influence of the National Socialists took a less turbulent, and above all, a more gradual path. The political life of this minority was far too complicated and too independent to succumb easily. True, under the influence of events in Germany, as in Poland, there was a sharp dispute between the young National Socialists and the old *Volkstum* leaders. Indeed, there was an observable breakdown in the Sudeten German party system. However, all of this still took a much calmer and more orderly course. The 'national revolution' was achieved by way of a protracted consensus building and disputes with the strong anti-Fascist forces including, for example, the Sudeten German social democrats.

'Henlein Fascism' was not imported from the Third *Reich*. It had its ideological and organisational roots in the Sudeten lands and in Austria. As is known, the idea of a 'national socialism' actually came from there. The Sudeten German national socialist party was older than the German one. In addition to this direct line of tradition, there was the *völkisch* tinged wealth of experience of the tested *Volkstum* organisations. It was therefore no accident that in 1933 the *Deutscher Turnverband* (German Gymnastic Association) became the crystallisation point for the all-party *Sudetendeutsche Heimatfront* (Sudeten German Homeland Front) and that a gymnastics instructor from Asch, Konrad Henlein, was able to assume the leadership of the Sudeten Germans. This mass movement quickly developed into the strongest Sudeten German political party. In the 1935 parliamentary elections, it received more than 1.2 million votes. This original collective movement, however, only moved into the narrow horizon of interest of National Socialist Germany in the following years. In the Sudeten German case, in contrast to the Germans in Poland, one cannot simply speak of an external seduction or mobilisation by the Third *Reich*. That the Henleinist movement later became an instrument of National Socialist expansion is no justification for overlooking the independent beginnings of the movement.

The mood of political awakening among the German population in Poland and Czechoslovakia as well as the visible lines of connection to the Third *Reich* caused increasing nervousness among Polish and Czech officials. The prohibition of meetings, the dissolution of organisations, the seizure of printed matter, the trials for high treason and the prevention of group travel to Germany, among other things, followed each other at ever shorter intervals, making clear the official desire to eliminate both local German identification with the National Socialists and possible factors of German state influence on the German minorities in Poland and Czechoslovakia by means of every possible draconian measure. It is easy to imagine that these actions produced exactly the opposite effect. The hysterical comments in the nationalist press of both countries also had an escalating effect. Local Germans were pilloried as *provocateurs*, enemies of the state and agents. The propensity for seeing every German, simply on the basis of nationality, as a potential *hitlerowiec* (Hitlerite) or *hakenkrajcler* (Swastika bearer) was scarcely designed to strengthen the loyal feelings of these minorities to their country.

Despite the similar reactions of the national peoples of Poland and Czechoslovakia to National Socialist provocations, there were still certain differences in each country due to the differing domestic and foreign policy situation in each. In Czechoslovakia, a firm position, with a broad political and social basis, was taken early against National Socialism. In Poland, with its semi-authoritarian government, which had further been bound to National Socialist Germany by several bilateral agreements (the 1934 Non-aggression Pact and the 1937 Minorities Declaration), such a position was not possible to the same degree. In the end, however, National Socialist aggression *vis-à-vis* Poland and Czechoslovakia levelled these nuances, just as it made the differing processes of winning the German minorities in the two countries over to Fascism meaningless.

Select Bibliography

General

Alexander, Manfred (1978), 'Die Politik der Weimarer Republik gegenüber den deutschen Minderheiten in Ostmitteleuropa 1918–1926', in *Annali dell'Istituto storico italo-germanico in Trento*, IV.

Batowski, Henryk (ed.) (1971), *Irredenta niemecka w Europie środkowej i południowowschodniej przed II wojną światową*, Katowice.

Czubiński, Antoni (ed.) (1984), *Rola mniejszości niemieckiej w rozwoju stosunków politycznych w Europie 1918–1945*, Poznań.

Fuchs, Gerhard (1968), 'Von Locarno nach München. Zur Kontinuität der aggressiven Politik des deutschen Imperialismus gegenüber der Tschechoslowakei und Polen', in *Jahrbuch für Geschichte der UdSSR und der volksdemokratischen Länder*, 12.

Jacobmeyer, Wolfgang (1986), 'Die deutschen Minderheiten in Polen und in der Tschechoslowakei in den dreißiger Jahren', in *Aus Politik und Zeitgeschichte*, 31.

Komjathy, Anthony and Stockwell, Rebecca (1980), *German Minorities and the Third Reich: Ethnic Germans of East Central Europe between the Wars*, New York.

Pearson, Raymond (1983), *National Minorities in Eastern Europe 1848–1945*, London.

Pieper, Helmut (1974), *Die Minderheitenfrage und das Deutsche Reich 1919–1933/34*, Hamburg.

Sierpowski, Stanislaw (1986), *Mniejzości narodowe jako instrument polityki miedzynarodowej 1919–1939*, Poznań.

Szefer, Andrzej (1967), *Mniejszość niemiecka w Polsce i w Czechosłowacji w latach 1933–1938*, Katowice.

Poland

Breyer, Richard (1955), *Das Deutsche Reich und Polen 1932–1937*, Würzburg.

Chojnowski, Andrzej (1979), *Koncepcje polityki narodowościowej rządów polskich w latach 1921–1939*, Wrocław.

Grünberg, Karol (1970), *Niemcy i ich organizacje polityczne w Polsce międzywojennej*, Warsaw.

Hauser, Przemysław (1981), *Mniejszość niemiecka w województwie Pomorskim w latach 1920–1939*, Wrocław.

Heike, Otto (1955), *Das Deutschtum in Polen 1918–1939*, Bonn.

Heit, Siegfried (1980), 'National Minorities and their Effect on Polish Foreign Relations', in *Nationalities Papers* VIII.

Krekeler, Norbert (1973), *Revisionsanspruch und geheime Ostpolitik der Weimarer Republik. Die Subventionierung der deutschen Minderheit in Polen 1919–1933*, Stuttgart.

Potocki, Stanisław (1969), *Położenie mniejszości niemieckiej w Polsce 1918–1938*, Gdansk.

Riekhoff, Harald von (1971), *German–Polish Relations 1918–1933*, Baltimore.

Wynot, Edward (1972), 'The Polish Germans 1919–1939: National Minority in a Multinational State', in *The Polish Review*, XVII.

Czechoslovakia

Campbell, Gregory (1975), *Confrontation in Central Europe. Weimar Germany and Czechoslovakia*, Chicago.

Brügel, Johann Wolfgang (1967), *Tschechen und Deutsche*, Vol. 1 1918–1938, Munich.

César, Jaroslav and Černý, Bohumil (1962), *Politika německých buržoazních stran v Československu v letech 1918–1938*, 2 vols, Prague.

Jaworski, Rudolf (1977), *Vorposten oder Minderheit? Der sudetendeutsche Volkstumskampf in den Beziehungen zwischen der Weimarer Republik und der ČSR*, Stuttgart.

Kural, Václav (1985), 'Tschechen und Deutsche im tschechoslowakischen und im deutschen Staat (1918–1945)', in *Zur Geschichte der deutsch-tschechischen Beziehungen. Eine Sammelschrift tschechischer Historiker*, Berlin.

Lemberg, Eugen and Rhode, Gotthold (eds) (1969), *Das deutsch-tschechische Verhältnis seit 1918*, Stuttgart.

Leoncini, Francesco (1976), *La Questione dei Sudeti 1918–1938*, Padua.

Novák, Otto (1978), 'Počátky henleinovského hnutí a československo-německé vztahy', in *Acta Universitatis Carolinae. Phil. et Hist. 2, Studia Historica XVIII*.

Smelser, Ronald (1975), *The Sudeten Problem 1933–1938. Volkstumspolitik and the Formulation of Nazi Foreign Policy*, Clinton, Mass.

Welisch, Sophie (1980), *Die sudetendeutsche Frage 1918–1928*, Munich.

9 The Ukrainian Problem in Interwar Poland
PAWEL KORZEC

Introduction

This study concerns itself with the south east of Poland as defined by the frontiers of 1939. This was a region mainly inhabited either by a Ukrainian population or by Slav populations without clearly defined national consciousness, but inclining towards the Ukrainian people by reason of affinities of language and religion (Lemkos, Boikos in southern Galicia, and the Polesians). These territories are here designated as the western Ukraine, as distinct from the Soviet Socialist Republic of the Ukraine bisected by the Dnieper within its pre–1939 frontiers.

From a geographico-historical point of view, western Ukraine has to be divided into two regions:

- eastern Galicia, before 1918 part of the Habsburg empire, whose population was Greek Catholic in religion; and
- north western Ukraine (Volhynia, Polesia, the Chelm region and southern Podlachia), belonging to the Russian empire before the First World War, whose population was Orthodox.

In all, western Ukraine covered an area of about 120 000 square kilometres, nearly a third of the area of interwar Poland, and had nearly eight million inhabitants. According to the official census, Poles constituted a small minority in these territories: 14.5 per cent in the province of Polesia; 16.6 per cent in Volhynia, 22.4 per cent in Stanislawow; 42.3 per cent in Lwow/Lemberg.[1]

The Situation of the Ukrainians before the First World War

The historic destinies of these two provinces of western Ukraine were different. Even when they found themselves parts of the same state after 1918, the Polish authorities, for political reasons, did everything to prevent their unification. The maintenance on the old frontier between the two empires of what was called the Sokal cordon (from the name of the frontier town of Sokal) was intended to constitute a barrier against the penetration into the other Ukrainian lands of political ideas from Galicia, which had a more developed national and political consciousness.

In the tsarist empire, the Ukrainians like the other non-Russian peoples were subject to a system of national oppression and russification. Nor did the powerful influence of the Orthodox clergy, who gave way to centralising and russifying pressures, favour the awakening of national consciousness. It was only the occupation of these regions by the armies of the central powers in 1915 which provoked the upsurge of the Ukrainian national movement. The Russian revolution and the treaty signed at Brest–Litovsk in February 1918 between the Ukrainian state which had come into being and the central powers stimulated a hectic process of development of Ukrainian national life. Amongst other things, the schools were immediately ukrainianised. Hundreds of primary, secondary and professional schools were set up. This state of affairs lasted until the conquest of these lands in 1919 by the Polish army.

The Ukrainian national consciousness and culture of the population of eastern Galicia were incomparably more strongly developed. Thus Lwow had become an important cultural and political centre for the Ukrainians. The Ukrainian press often referred to Galicia as the Piedmont of the Ukraine.

Specific socio-economic factors had a major influence on the development of political relationships. Galicia, the only province of the old Polish state which enjoyed political autonomy and complete potential for the development of Polish national life and culture, remained economically a very retarded region, virtually set apart from the great movement of capitalist takeoff which affected other Polish regions and other lands of the Habsburg monarchy. Deprived of flourishing economic contacts with the other Polish provinces, Galicia failed to become economically integrated into the body of the Austro–Hungarian monarchy.

The explanation for this lies in a whole series of causes. The geographical factor played a certain role. Open to the north, Galicia was in a fashion cut off from the other lands of the monarchy lying to the south by the chain of the Carpathian mountains, which made communications and exchange of goods difficult. Despite the proximity of the rich coal mines of neighbouring Silesia and of what were then significant petroleum deposits (at Boryslaw and Drohobytch), industry was hardly developed and the roads were in a wretched condition. Politico-strategic considerations had a not inconsiderable influence on this situation. The government in Vienna was mindful of the fact that in the event of war Galicia would fall easily into the hands of the Russian army.

However, the decisive factor in this state of affairs was the system of economic and socio-political relations at local level. It has already been mentioned that Galicia enjoyed autonomous status. In this region inhabited by two nationalities, power had however passed into the hands of the culturally more advanced Poles: more precisely, it was held by the conservative class of Polish nobles and magnates, closely linked to imperial court circles in Vienna. Similarly the administration of the province was provided by a bureaucratic apparatus which was recruited essentially among the Polish nobility.

An agricultural and heavily populated region, Galicia had an exceptionally archaic agrarian structure. Great landed estates were still very significantly represented there in the twentieth century. By contrast, the size of smaller farms was falling over time as a result of subdivision. There was very little differentiation in the condition of the peasantry. Medium sized properties (ten to 20 hectares) constituted only 4 per cent of the total of peasant farms. On the other hand the proportion of small farms (two to two-and-a-half hectares) was 37.5 per cent and of 'dwarf' farms (under two hectares) 42.5 per cent.[2] Thus in circumstances of economic backwardness 80 per cent of Galician peasants were unable to feed their families from their land and had to look for work in the big agricultural enterprises. The very low wages and the absence of industry led to definitive or seasonal emigration. Hundreds of thousands of Polish and Ukrainian peasants emigrated to the USA, Brazil, and other overseas countries to find a living. Ukrainian sources estimate the number of Ukrainian emigrants before 1914 at two and a half million.

Economic polarisation brought bitter social and class antagonisms. In the western, Polish part of Galicia, a process of radicalisation of the masses was coming to fulfilment at the end of the nineteenth and the beginning of the twentieth century. The peasant parties made large strides, as did the socialist movement among the urban workers. In eastern Galicia, on the other hand, social and class antagonisms were intertwined with the circumstances of the struggle for national independence. Among the Ukrainian peasantry, poor and exploited by the landed proprietors as well as by the Polish bureaucracy, the anti-Polish nationalist movement spread easily. The growing conflict manifested itself in quarrels between Polish and Ukrainian students, increasingly frequent in the years just before the First World War. During the election campaign for the Galician diet in 1908, the Governor of Galicia, Count Potocki, a member of one of the leading families of Polish magnates, fell victim to a terrorist attack perpetrated by the Ukrainian student Siczynski. Ukrainian aspirations to freedom found some support in certain Viennese political circles, especially among the military. Here the traditional Austrian policy of *divide et impera* (divide and rule) held sway. What is more, when, with war looming, certain Polish political and nationalist groups began to exhibit slavophile and pro-Russian tendencies, the Ukrainian national movement remained patently loyal to the Habsburg monarchy. The emperor Franz Josef expressed his gratitude to the Ukrainian population for its fidelity to the crown, calling the Ukrainians the Tyroleans of the east.

From the end of the nineteenth century, Ukrainian political groups had been forming. The aspirations of the peasant masses were voiced by the Rutheno–Ukrainian Radical party, founded in 1890 and headed by, amongst others, the famous ideologist and political militant, Ivan Franko. In their review, *Narod* (The Nation), the radicals formulated a radical–democratic programme close to socialism, looking to expropriate the big landowners for the benefit of peasant agricultural cooperatives. In the political sphere, they demanded a major democratisation of the whole life of the state. At the outset, the Ukrainian radicals established flourishing contacts with the Polish populists, extolling the principle of a common front of Polish and Ukrainian peasants in the struggle against the control of the landed proprietors in Galicia. At the Lwow Congress of 1895 the principle of the independence of the Ukraine was proclaimed. However, the party soon underwent a considerable change. Under the influence of the chicanery and repression handed out by the Polish bureaucracy, many of the radical leaders, including Ivan Franko, departed from the solidarity line and began to proclaim the principle of strict national concentration in the conflict with the Polish ruling classes. They came together with the powerful group of *Narodowtsy* (populists) led by Romantchouk and Oleśnicki to form in 1899 the National Democratic party. This new party had already a nationalist and anti-Polish character. It visibly represented austrophile leanings. In a long term perspective, the National Democrats saw the solution of the problem of the Ukrainian nation to lie in separating the eastern Ukraine from Russia and uniting it with the western Ukraine to form an autonomous Ukrainian state within the framework of the Austrian monarchy.

Meanwhile, the left wing of the Radical party formed itself in the last years of the nineteenth century into a Ukrainian Social Democratic party, which offered a socialist, anti-aristocratic, and anti-clerical programme. Some party militants, for example Mykola Hankiewicz, kept up close contacts with the Polish Socialist party in Galicia. There were also so-called 'Moscalophile' tendencies among the Ukrainians. The Moscalophiles idealised the political and social system of tsarist Russia and combated the radical leanings of the Ukrainian countryside. In contrast with the other groups, the Moscalophiles rejected the programme of national autonomy.

The revolutionary events of the years 1905–7 in Russia and Poland reinforced Ukrainian political activity. At the same time, given the threat of war with Russia, the central authorities of the Habsburg monarchy were increasingly interested in gaining the sympathy of the Ukrainian population. By dint of struggling against polonisation, the Ukrainians succeeded in securing equality for the Ukrainian language in the courts, administration, and schools. Chairs of Ukrainian language and culture were created at the University of Lwow. Grants to Ukrainian cultural and social groups were increased. Altogether, before the First World War, the Ukrainians of Galicia obtained more than 3000 elementary schools, six state secondary schools, and 15 private secondary schools. They set up nearly 3000 reading rooms of the *Proświta* organisation for culture and public education; nearly 500 cooperatives; numerous credit institutions; and sporting organisations, etc. The biggest achievement in the field of culture was the creation of the scientific society *Sewčenko*, through which scientists from all the Ukrainian provinces worked.

The deputies to the national diet in Lwow carried on a fierce battle to change the voting and administrative systems in Galicia, not hesitating to employ parliamentary obstruction as well as sabotaging the decrees of the Polish majority. Some Polish politicians grasped the need for a Polish–Ukrainian understanding, but the nationalism of most of the Polish deputies was opposed to it. The actions of the conservatives, the governor, Bobrzynski, and Leo Bilinski, nevertheless resulted in a fiasco in this sphere. The elections to the diet in 1913 saw a Ukrainian success. Thirty deputies of Ukrainian national and russophile persuasion were elected, whereas at the previous elections in 1908 only 12 Ukrainians and eight russophiles had been returned. The efforts of the Ukrainian deputies and the instructions of the Vienna government brought about a vote in favour of changing the status of the province and the electoral system. The outbreak of war, however, prevented the implementation of these changes favouring the Ukrainian population.

Western Ukraine during the First World War

Western Ukraine was badly hit by the war. The military front passed over it several times as it moved back and forth. The passage of the Austrian, Hungarian, German, Russian and Polish armies caused terrible devastation. The leaders of the main political parties formed the Central Ukrainian Council under the eminent parliamentarian Kost' Lewyckyj. On 3 August 1914 the Council published a manifesto, summoning the Ukrainian people to the struggle against Russia. The Council also set about organising a separate Ukrainian military force. When, soon afterwards, the Russian army occupied eastern Galicia, these manoeuvres brought a wave of brutal repression. The Ukrainian organisations were broken up, and thousands of young people and intellectuals (including eminent militants like the metropolitan Count Andrij Sheptytsky) were deported deep into Russia.

Some of the political militants took refuge in Vienna and there continued animated political activity. On 5 May 1915, the General Council of the Ukraine was set up in Vienna, grouping the leaders of the parties as well as the parliamentary representatives of Galicia and Bukovina. The *Rada* (Council), which constituted during the war the principal organ of the Ukrainian nation in the Habsburg monarchy, postulated the formation of an independent Ukrainian state adjacent to the Dnieper with the assurance for western Ukraine of autonomous status within the framework of the Austro–Hungarian monarchy. The *Rada* also began to form two Ukrainian divisions, volunteers for which were recruited from the Ukrainians among the prisoners taken from the Russian army. As the war dragged on, and after the defeats suffered by the dual monarchy, opposition to excessive ties to governmental circles in Vienna appeared among certain Ukrainian politicians. It was Eugen Petrušewicz, a deputy to the parliament in Vienna, who became the spokesman of those demanding a more independent policy.

On 5 November 1916, a manifesto of the emperors of the two central powers was published, announcing the formation of an independent Polish state. This produced uneasiness in Ukrainian political circles. On 30 May 1917, Petrušewicz laid before parliament a declaration in the name of the Ukrainian deputies stating that the Ukrainians opposed the union of Galicia and Volhynia with the new Poland and that the Ukrainian nation would regard such an act as a violation of the principle of the right of nations to self-determination.

The outbreak of revolution in Russia initially gave rise to political conditions favourable for the Ukrainians. The central powers inspired the creation of the People's Republic of the Ukraine. During the peace negotiations at Brest–Litovsk, this republic, by virtue of the treaty with the central powers signed on 9 February 1918 secured the territories of the Chelm region and of southern Podlachia. Given that these regions had been regarded as part of the kingdom of Poland up to their direct annexation by Russia in 1912, this led to a bitter conflict between Polish political circles and the governments of the central powers, which also produced a deterioration in Polish–Ukrainian relations. According to Ukrainian sources, there had been a secret understanding aiming at the creation of an autonomous crown territory made up of the lands of eastern Galicia and northern Bukovina. On 20 February 1918, Kost' Lewyckyj, in the name of the parliamentary representatives of the Ukrainians in Vienna, demanded the division of Galicia into two autonomous regions, Ukrainian and Polish. In September 1918, a representative body for the whole Ukrainian nation in Austria, the Interparty Council, was established.

The Creation of the People's Republic of Western Ukraine and the Polish–Ukrainian War 1918–19

The disintegration of the Austro–Hungarian monarchy in October 1918 opened the way for the foundation of national states out of its ruins. On 18 and 19 October 1918, the congress of parliamentary representatives and delegates of political parties of the Ukraine deliberated at Lwow. It was then decided to set up the Ukrainian National Council (the Constituent), and Petrušewicz was elected to head it. At the same time, a *Delegatura Rady* (provisional government) was formed under Kost' Lewyckyj. The congress came out for a Ukrainian state encompassing all the ethnographically Ukrainian lands of the Habsburg monarchy (eastern Galicia, transCarpathian Ruthenia, and northern Bukovina). Talks were commenced with the Vienna government: the Ukrainians were at that point the only Slav nation wishing to retain political links with Austria.

The rapid succession of events, however, called for equally rapid decisions. On 28 October 1918, the Polish Liquidation Commission was set up in Cracow, claiming to be the competent body for the liquidation of Austrian authority in Galicia. The commission agreed to place Galicia under the central Polish government in Warsaw and so quickly assembled armed forces and prepared to take possession of the whole of Galicia including Lwow. In these circumstances, the Ukrainian politicians decided to act without delay to set up the People's Republic of Western Ukraine. During the night of 31 October to 1 November 1918, Ukrainian units established garrisons in the greater part of Lwow and throughout eastern Galicia up to the river San. At Lwow the Ukrainian forces encountered armed resistance from Polish divisions formed on the spot under Captain Maczyński. A bloody and savage conflict began between the two sister nations, which went badly for the Ukrainians. After three weeks of fierce battles, the Polish armies captured Lwow with the aid of heavy artillery, on 23 November 1918, but they were not strong enough to occupy the whole of eastern Galicia. The government of the people's republic took refuge at Stanislawow, from where it continued to direct military and political action.

The outbreak of the Polish–Ukrainian war was an unpleasant surprise for the governments of the victorious powers, who were about to set out at the Paris Peace Conference to deal with the many thorny problems concerning the future peace treaty. The Polish–Ukrainian conflict muddled an already extremely complicated situation in eastern Europe. The strategic position of eastern Galicia in relation to Soviet Russia and, after March 1919, to the Hungarian Soviet republic also, was an important consideration. Western political leaders feared, not without reason, that the armed conflicts and the chaos prevailing in eastern Europe might facilitate the penetration of Soviet influence. Moreover, the Galician quarrel brought out a difference of opinion between Britain and France. Whereas the British strove to secure a ceasefire and a compromise solution at all costs, the French government, for a variety of reasons, supported the Polish position in the questions at issue. In Paris, it was the Polish National Committee which represented Poland's interest with the allied powers.

The efforts of the Entente towards ending the war in eastern Galicia had scarcely any success. The military missions sent to Galicia and Poland (Noulens and Barthélémy) were unable to secure direct Polish–Ukrainian negotiations any more than a lasting agreement. Nationalist tendencies on both sides were too powerful. Moreover, the Ukrainians, who had the upper hand militarily in the early months, looked to resolve the conflict by military means.[3] The decisive factor in the Polish–Ukrainian war was the arrival in Poland of Haller's very well equipped troops, who had been assembled and armed in France. Although the Polish government had undertaken not to use them against the Ukrainians, this condition was taken seriously neither on the Polish nor on the French side. The Polish offensive which began in April 1919 rapidly broke through the Ukrainian front, and after fierce battles the armies of the People's Republic were forced in July 1919 to retreat across the river Zbrucz (the old Russo–Austrian frontier). The fate of the Republic of Western Ukraine was sealed. The French military wanted a rapid end to the Polish–Ukrainian conflict so that the Polish armed forces would be free to fight against Soviet Russia. Under these circumstances, the Council of Foreign Ministers, reinforced by the influence of the French government, authorised the Polish government, on 25 June 1919, provisionally to occupy eastern Galicia to the Zbrucz with the aid of all its troops, including those under Haller. At the same time the decision of the great powers called on Poland to guarantee territorial autonomy to eastern Galicia as well as all political, cultural, and religious liberties for its inhabitants. The ultimate decision on the future of eastern Galicia was to be taken by the powers on the basis of a plebiscite of the population.

The international and legal position of the second province of western Ukraine, in other words the regions which belonged before the First World War to the Russian empire, was quite different. On 21 April 1920 on the eve of the Polish army's assault, the Polish government and the directorate of the People's Republic of the

Ukraine, headed by the *ataman* Petliura, signed the Treaty of Warsaw, by which Petliura ceded to Poland eastern Galicia, Volhynia, and some other areas inhabited by a Ukrainian population. This treaty between Pilsudski and Petliura produced vehement protests in Ukrainian political circles in Vienna.

The Treaty of Riga of 18 March 1921 finally gave Poland the territories of Volhynia, Polesia, the Chelm region and southern Podlachia. Two years later the fate of eastern Galicia was also settled. In conformity with the decision of the Council of Ambassadors of 15 March 1923, the province was definitively annexed to Poland. The destiny of five or six million Ukrainians thus became an internal problem for the Polish state.

The Policy of the Polish State and the International Implications of the Ukrainian Problem in Poland

The armed struggle with the Republic of Western Ukraine ended after nine months in an indisputable victory for the young Polish republic, which in the next four years, was able to add political and diplomatic victories too. Yet not only did all these successes fail to extinguish the conflict between the two peoples, they even extended it beyond eastern Galicia, so that it spread to all the other provinces of the Polish state inhabited by Ukrainians or by an ethnically mixed population. Moreover, it did not remain localised within the frontiers of Poland, but also had a bearing on the international position of the Polish state, and in particular on Polish–Russian and Polish–German relations, Russia and Germany being two powerful neighbours and traditional enemies. Also, Poland's hostile policy towards her southern neighbour meant that the relatively weak Czechoslovakia turned the Ukrainian problem skilfully to her advantage. Prague took a hand in the Polish–Ukrainian conflict above all in the first years, before the decision of the Council of Ambassadors.

The potential danger lay in the fact that a Ukrainian republic existed, albeit dependent on Moscow, in which the majority of the Ukrainian people lived. Although the dominant tendencies among the Ukrainians in Poland were nationalist and anti-Soviet, the anti-Polish feeling which grew year by year nevertheless caused certain groups to look towards the Soviet Ukraine (the attitude of Petruševicz and his group in the *Rada* may be mentioned as an example). It was indeed beyond question that Galicia, formerly the political and cultural centre of the Ukraine, was dropping behind. By contrast, the Soviet Ukraine was experiencing in the 1920s an exceptional era marked by growing 'ukrainisation' of political and cultural life.

Moscow's interest in the problem of eastern Galicia increased step by step with the worsening of the Polish–Ukrainian conflict. The main difficulty was to find a suitable interlocutor: the only valid one was Petruŝewicz's government in exile. In the summer of 1921, the Polish government received disturbing reports from its diplomatic representatives about contacts between the Soviet governments of Moscow and Kharkov and that of Petruŝewicz. The independence of eastern Galicia and its entry into the Soviet Ukraine as an autonomous province were under discussion. Apparently, these tendencies were not confined to Petruŝewicz's group. During a visit to the capitals of western Europe, Sheptytsky, the metropolitan of the Greek Catholic church of eastern Galicia, in an interview with the Pope and with the French Prime Minister, Raymond Poincaré, categorically opposed granting Poland sovereignty over eastern Galicia. He also suggested that, in the absence of other solutions, the province might be integrated into the Soviet Republic of the Ukraine. It is not difficult to imagine the astonishment of his hearers at these words.

In order to foil possible agreement with the Soviet governments, Warsaw made approaches aimed at an understanding with Petruŝewicz. The latter, however, made the withdrawal of Polish troops from eastern Galicia a precondition of negotiations, which was tantamount to a refusal. This intransigence made it plain to the Polish government that an agreement between Petruŝewicz and Moscow was on the cards, all the more so since the government of the Soviet Union, dropping its tactic of disinterestedness in the affairs of the western Ukraine, presented a note of protest against the decision of 15 March 1923 of the Council of Ambassadors. But Petruŝewicz's talks with the Soviet diplomats did not lead to a real understanding. His initiative was not supported by other groups, and the Soviet government, convinced of his political isolation, held aloof from committing itself officially. Yet despite this failure, his government kept up its contacts with Moscow and Kharkov even after its move from Vienna to Berlin. It was only at the end of the 1920s, after the collapse of ukrainisation and the Kremlin's shift to a policy of state centralism in 1929, that the pro-Soviet tendencies in certain Ukrainian circles foundered. The rise of anti-Soviet feeling among the Ukrainian intelligentsia put paid to the role of Petruŝewicz in Ukrainian political life.

It was, however, Germany which was the main factor of external interference in Polish–Ukrainian affairs. Given the generally bad relations between Poland and Germany, and the revisionist tendencies holding sway in German military and political circles, it is not surprising that the Weimar Republic and later the Third *Reich* gave vigorous support to the Ukrainian irredentist movement. After 1923 Berlin became the principal centre of anti-Polish activity, and the

Ukrainian question the pivot of its eastern policy. The process whereby the Ukrainian nationalists drew together with Germany and accepted her arbitration was entirely understandable. The traditional bonds of sympathy between the Ukrainian and Austrian peoples stretched indirectly to Austria's ally, Germany. Germany was the first to show support for the creation of a Ukrainian sovereignty, although that stemmed from an estimate of her own interests. An important point, finally, was that Germany was the main opponent of the treaty of Versailles, which had also dashed the Ukrainians' hope of independence.

In spite of the serious international implications of the Polish–Ukrainian conflict, it would be a mistake to follow Polish propaganda in seeing foreign influence as the prime motor of that conflict. In fact, it was Polish internal policy, especially national policy, which had a decisive influence on the further development of the problem of the western Ukraine. A wise and measured policy could have gone far to relieve the bitterness of the Ukrainians stemming from their defeat and disappointed ambitions. The anti-Russian, and especially anti-Soviet, leanings of most Ukrainians could have been turned to large account in a skilful political game. But Polish policy took a diametrically opposite direction and deepened the divide between the two peoples year by year.

In inheriting the Ukrainians and many other minorities from the Habsburg monarchy, Poland inherited also in some sense the thorny nationality problems which had in the end brought about the empire's fall. Interwar Poland, with 31 per cent of its population ethnically non-Polish, had become the main multinational country in Europe (excepting the Soviet Union), and for a multiplicity of reasons could not, and did not want to find a solution to this problem. Whereas in other countries which found themselves in similar situations such as Czechoslovakia, or Yugoslavia, attempts were made with more or less success to moderate and resolve the nationality problem, the most influential Polish political circles, and the governments they ran, put into effect in this sphere the strange tactic of *non est* – the denial of the real facts. Thus the existence of the Ukrainian people was obstinately denied, and the effort made to replace the notion of 'Ukrainian' by that of 'Ruthenian', an archaic concept spurned by those involved. The Ukrainian language, in which a body of original scientific, literary, and artistic work was developing, was dubbed the 'Ruthenian dialect'. A people with aspirations to independence and a history of parliamentary struggles and organised political parties found itself treated as 'ethnic raw material', capable of undergoing rapid Polonisation. The Ukrainians were dealt with as objects of unreasonable imperio-colonial ambition, and not as partners with whom a *modus vivendi* in a common state could and should be found.

The reaction which was produced in Ukrainian nationalism, though more understandable from a psychological point of view, was guilty of a corresponding lack of political realism and hence did a great deal of harm to the Ukrainian population. The Ukrainians of Galicia expressly refused to acknowledge their membership of the Polish state. Thus, up to 1923, awaiting the verdict of the great powers, they boycotted all national activities, like the elections to the diet and the senate, and they held to that political line after the famous decision of the Council of Ambassadors. They regarded Polish sovereignty over the lands of western Ukraine as an occupation and pursued a policy of irredentism which drove them to collaborate with the enemies of the Polish state, for whom the Ukrainian problem was merely a trump card in their anti-Polish manoeuvres on the international plane.

The decision of the Council of Ambassadors marked a turning point in Polish–Ukrainian relations. The definitive attribution of eastern Galicia to Poland removed the international control which had existed up to that point and had been impossible for the Polish government to ignore. There then commenced an uncompromising anti-Ukrainian policy, deriving from the fact that from 1923 the government was in the hands of a coalition of right wing nationalist parties headed by National Democracy. Growing resistance on the part of the Ukrainian and Byelorussian population served as a pretext for an offensive against these Slav minorities. There were changes also in the sphere of Ukrainian politics. The hopes of Petruśewicz's government in exile for settling the problem of eastern Galicia by diplomatic means were summarily destroyed. Immediately after 15 March 1923, Petruśewicz and his political entourage left Vienna for Berlin.

The change of location of the government in exile reflected a complete change in its outlook. Petruśewicz continued his diplomatic activity at international level, especially at the League of Nations, but he moved to a pro-German position, while keeping up his Soviet contacts. The decision of 15 March had serious consequences also for the attitude of Ukrainian political émigrés, among whom feelings of discouragement and resignation achieved the upper hand and produced a massive outflow to the USA and, above all, to Canada, where large concentrations resulting from former Ukrainian emigration already existed. The accession of the intelligentsia contributed to the political activism of these Ukrainian centres on the other side of the Atlantic. Many émigrés, on the other hand, took advantage of the amnesty proclaimed in Poland to return to their homeland, including the eminent parliamentarian and ex-Prime Minister of the government of western Ukraine, Kost' Lewyckyj. Such arrivals swelled the ranks of the legal and clandestine Ukrainian organisations active in the country.

Eastern Galicia was a theatre of major political upheavals as the hitherto indisputable authority of Petruševicz slowly dissolved. In concentrating his attention on diplomatic questions, he was failing to recognise new aspects to the relationships and problems with which the Ukrainian population in Poland had to live. Many of his opponents openly accused him, though without justification, of having enlisted with the Soviet Union. In fact his historic short-comings boil down to his profound political idealism. Brought up in the parliamentary and liberal traditions of pre-war Vienna, he was unable to foresee that the great international decision makers could violate in cold blood the fundamental principles of the Paris peace conference and of the League of Nations, embodying the right of non-dominant peoples to self-determination and freedom.

The oppressive policy of the Polish government reinforced movements in Ukrainian society towards political consolidation. On 11 July 1925 the Ukrainian National Democratic Union was set up in Lwow, under the leadership of an eminent politician, Dmytro Levytsky. The National Democratic Union brought together several existing political parties with differing socio-economic programmes, and thus became the most influential political grouping of the Ukrainian minority in Poland. Its platform formulated the principle of the unity of the Ukrainian people without respect to differences of class. Its ultimate goal was the creation of an independent state from all the lands which were ethnographically Ukrainian. As for the line to be followed within the Polish state, its programme looked to the achievement of national aspirations by every possible means of struggle, 'without conceding any legal status to a foreign power in these territories' – which meant refusal to recognise Polish sovereignty in the Ukrainian lands.

To turn to its relations with the Ukrainian Soviet Republic, the Lwow Congress stated in one of its resolutions that, though it did not accept either the principles of communism or the republic's system of government, it did see the republic as one of the embryos of an independent Ukrainian state in the future. Indeed it emphasised that, despite the 'dictatorship of the proletariat', the Ukrainian people had the benefit of national and cultural rights there. This programme, ratified by the second National Democratic Union congress in November 1926 on the basis of a draft from the centre group, thus reveals a shift of attitude towards the Ukrainian Soviet Republic, which was no longer recognised as a Ukrainian state. The point dealing with 'representation abroad' was also annulled, signifying a break with the group led by Petruševicz, who left the National Democratic Union and founded the *Trudowaja Partija* (Ukrainian Labour Party), which rejected Polish sovereignty over the western Ukraine but, in spite of its anti-communism, kept its links with the Soviet Republic. At the same time, the autonomist group, headed by Dr Wolodymir Baczynski, founder of the National Democratic party, was eliminated from the National Democratic Union. Baczynski opposed the terrorism of the Military Organisation (see below) and tried to secure autonomy on an equal footing with the Jewish minority by agreement with the Polish progressive groups. In that same year of 1926 he committed suicide, doubtless because of the violent accusations levelled at him by his nationalist adversaries.

After this reshaping, the National Democratic Union took on the character of a national unity movement with nationalist and pro-clerical leanings. That did not preclude a degree of political opportunism, consisting in agreements with the Polish government side by side with tolerance of anti-Polish extremism and collaboration with the Germans most hostile to Poland. Despite an atmosphere of growing antisemitism, the National Democratic Union cooperated with the Jews to create in 1928 the second *bloc* of national minorities, on the occasion of the Polish parliamentary elections, in which it obtained a major success.[4] This political conformism was the pretext for fierce criticism from the left wing and communist groups: the Social Democratic party, the Ukrainian Social Radical party, and the Communist party of western Ukraine. But the main political opponent of the National Democratic Union was the extremist terrorist group, the Organisation of Ukrainian Nationalists.

An important element in Ukrainian–Polish relations during the 20 years between the wars was the terrorist activity of the Ukrainian Military Organisation, to whose origins and operation it is therefore appropriate to give some attention. By the end of 1919, and above all during the Polish–Soviet war, the Ukrainian population was beginning to meet the repression exercised by the Polish authorities with resistance activities. Thus at the end of 1920, on the initiative of Petruŝewicz's government in exile and with the support of the key elements of the old army of western Ukraine, it was decided to set up a clandestine Ukrainian military organisation. It was modelled, to begin with, on the fighting organisations of the period of the 1905 revolution, notably the Russian social revolutionaries. From that source the Ukrainian Military Organisation picked up a whole collection of undesirable conspiratorial practices: agents, acts of provocation, terror, etc. Alongside the central command, a political college was set up, including the representatives of the two main legal parties, the National Democrats and the Radicals. The commander of the Military Organisation was Konowaletz, colonel of the *Siczowe Strilcy* (Sicz Sharpshooters), an elite regiment of the army of western Ukraine, who later on, with what was left of his regiment, joined Petliura's army, fighting alongside the Poles against the Red Army.

The Military Organisation had few members and was poorly armed in its early years. However, year after year, the policy of repression and the destruction of Ukrainian public education and culture drove thousands of young people to the Ukrainian universities in Czechoslovakia (Prague, Podiebrady), where they easily came under the influence of exiled nationalists, returning to their country well adapted from a military and political point of view to join the organisation. Because of lack of money, the Military Organisation launched a series of raids on the mails, landed estates, etc. These exploits, after the fashion of the old Polish Combat Organisation led by Pilsudski, roused the enthusiasm of the young, but contributed to internal demoralisation. The Military Organisation degenerated into an authoritarian and ultra-nationalist organisation, which cut it off from more progressive organisations. The older radical militants, unable to accept an often senseless terrorism, resigned from the organisation and its political leadership.

In 1921, in an attempt to show the world that the Ukrainian people were keeping up the struggle against Polish occupation (especially in face of the decision expected from the great powers on the subject of eastern Galicia), the Military Organisation's leadership commenced a terrorist campaign against the Polish administration and against Ukrainians who collaborated with the authorities, a campaign which was particularly violent during the election period. Amongst other things, the Military Organisation laid it down that the arrival of the Polish head of state in occupied eastern Galicia amounted to a provocation against the Ukrainian nation, and that that demanded a suitable response. In line with that stand, on 25 September 1921, a student, Stefan Fedak, made an unsuccessful attempt on the Head of State, Jozef Pilsudski, who had arrived in Lwow, and the Governor of Lwow, Grabowski. Three years later, there was another unsuccessful attempt, aimed this time at the Polish President, Stanislaw Wojciechowski, who had come to Lwow for the opening of the Eastern Fair.

Something else which decisively marked the character and the internal situation of the Ukrainian Military Organisation was its collaboration with the intelligence services of neighbouring countries hostile to Poland. The leader in this sphere, Ehven Konowaletz, was a controversial figure, and not overburdened with scruples when it came to finding ways of financing his group's activity. In 1922, threatened with arrest, he fled Poland for Germany, where he immediately formed links with the German army and the *Abwehr* (intelligence service). The entry into the leadership of the Military Organisation of Richard Riko Jaryj, who had had little previous involvement in the Ukrainian movement but was indisputably an official of the *Abwehr*, dates from the same period. He became the liaison man between the *Abwehr* and the organisation and, indeed, the major leader of the Military Organisation alongside Konowaletz.

Seeing that the Ukrainian Military Organisation was in close touch with part of the leadership of the National Democratic Union, it can be said without exaggeration that the Ukrainian movement was heavily infiltrated by German politico-military organisations hostile to Poland. This, obviously, was not unfamiliar to the Polish counter-espionnage services, which used every means to intercept documents compromising for the National Democratic Union and Military Organisation. The German archives contain many interesting and top secret documents on the history and activity of the latter organisation, as well as of the powerful organisation which grew out of it, the Organisation of Ukrainian Nationalists. In fact, the Military Organisation was, almost from the start of its life, linked to German military circles which prompted and financed it. Among the other items can be found an extensive and interesting report on the beginnings of the Military Organisation by Osyp Dumin.[5] Dumin was an officer of the Ukrainian army and one of the principal leaders of the organisation, who later became the historian of the Ukrainian army, and, disillusioned by the inner workings of the organisation and especially by the attitude of his commander, Colonel Konowaletz, drew up a detailed memorandum for the benefit of the German authorities. Though tendentious, the document contains vital material for the history of the Military Organisation. As a consequence of this report, and probably because of the intrigues of the Organisation's leadership, the German army intended to arrest Dumin as an agent of the Polish secret service, but the Foreign Ministry preferred to avoid this step, in case a trial should demonstrate the connections between the German authorities and the Organisation. Dumin subsequently worked at the Koenigsberg Scientific Institute. After Soviet troops took the town in 1945, all trace of him was lost.

In January 1929, while the Polish–Ukrainian conflict was becoming sharper and Polish–German relations were deteriorating, the Congress of Ukrainian Nationalists was held in Vienna. The result was the creation of the Organisation of Ukrainian Nationalists, the leadership of which was entrusted to Konowaletz, already commander of the Ukrainian Military Organisation. This new political movement spurned legal methods and preached the armed struggle for the liberation and unification of the Ukrainian lands. It also kept up close contacts with the German army and extreme right. The Lithuanian government was another supporter, first of the Military Organisation and then of the Organisation of Ukrainian Nationalists. Financial help was rather moderate. On the other hand, the Lithuanian intelligence agencies rendered priceless services in the shape of false passports for Ukrainian militants and travel facilities under false names for Ukrainian propagandists going to the USA, Canada, France, or Britain. The latter had no chance of getting entry visas under their real names. The Lithuanians also harboured the Military Organisation's journal, *Surma*, which was published from Kowno.

One of the figures most influential in the policy of the Ukrainian Military Organisation and Organisation of Ukrainian Nationalists was the theoretician behind Ukrainian nationalism, Dmytro Doncew. His main work, entitled *Nationalism*, became a sort of bible for Ukrainian youth. Doncew took his inspiration from the ideology of Italian Fascism, then of German National Socialism. He proclaimed the principles of nationalist extremism – the rejection of all ethical and moral rules in the struggle against the political opponents of the Ukraine, and the physical extermination of communists and Jews. By contrast he showed relatively little virulence in regard to Poland. Among other things, he regarded as advantageous the Treaty of Warsaw of 1920 made between Pilsudski and Petliura before their common attack on the Soviet Union. This was doubtless related to the fact that, after repatriation to Poland in 1923, he was able to carry on his political activities there until 1939.

In the autumn of 1930, the head of the Polish government, Pilsudski, carried out a kind of *Putsch*. On 29 September, a presidential decree dissolved the two chambers of parliament, three years before the normal expiry of the legislature. At the same time, the government arrested the opposition leaders, deputies, and senators, sending the prisoners to the fortress of Brest, where they endured an extremely severe regime of detention, going as far as the use of physical torture. During the weeks following, most of the Ukrainian deputies and senators as well as a hundred or so of the leaders of the different Ukrainian organisations were arrested. On the personal order of Marshal Pilsudski, there began a barbarous 'pacification' which stained the Ukrainian territories with blood. The principle of collective responsibility was applied in the course of the military operations, which lasted three months. Four hundred and fifty villages were systematically ransacked and devastated. Thousands of peasants were arrested and tortured. A large part of the population sank into extreme poverty. The political effect of the pacification was disastrous. It was mounted on the pretext of combating the growing terrorism and sabotage of both the Ukrainian Military Organisation and the Organisation of Ukrainian Nationalists, but the counterterror given out to the peasantry, far from doing harm to the Ukrainian extreme right, on the contrary served its ends. The Polish state, by its irresponsible policy, aroused a fierce hatred among the Ukrainian masses. Terrorised, the Ukrainians remained calm, but waited with growing impatience for the right moment for revenge.

The anti-Ukrainian pacification nevertheless shocked world public opinion. Demonstrations against the Polish regime were organised in France, Britain, and the USA. The world press published extensive reports on the tortures administered by the Polish army and police. It is clear that this campaign was largely inspired by the Ukrainian *émigré* organisations hostile to Poland. The German press made a substantial contribution to this effort, publishing numerous articles and commentaries on events in Poland. During the months following, the Ukrainian centres put out in several languages a 'black book' on the pacification, illustrated with photographs of devastated villages and tortured men, as well as with horrifying eye-witness accounts.[6]

The Ukrainian organisations in the USA, Canada, and Britain, supported by the liberal parliamentary parties of those countries, issued appeals to their respective governments as well as to the League of Nations, demanding the despatch of an international commission of enquiry to the territories affected by the pacification. Protests came in from all quarters. Petruševicz, backed by the German delegation, pursued diplomatic action at the League, which was simultaneously receiving petitions against the oppressive policy of the Polish government presented by the Ukrainian parliamentary club and other organisations. Poland, however, mounted a diplomatic counteroffensive, seeking to show that the pacification had been merely a reply to the terror carried on by the Ukrainians against the Polish population and to their collaboration with the fiercest enemies of the Polish state. To support this contention, a mass circulation Cracow paper, *Ilustrowany Kurier Codzienny*, published secret reports from the German consul in Cracow on his contacts with the National Democratic Union. In these circumstances, the League of Nations passed a resolution relatively favourable to Poland.

These reverses in the forum of the League, as well as Poland's conclusion of non-aggression pacts with the Soviet Union in 1932, and Germany in January 1934 drove the moderate group of the National Democratic Union under Vasyl Mudry and Vladimir Tselevitch to look for a *modus vivendi* with the Polish government. Some Polish politicians also favoured the cooling down of the Polish–Ukrainian conflict. Secret negotiations ended in success on the eve of the parliamentary elections of September 1935, boycotted by most Poles because of the anti-democratic electoral system. In this situation, the 'normalisation' of Polish–Ukrainian relations represented an undeniable success for the government. It was for that reason that, in an unprecedented move, Warsaw supported the Ukrainians' electoral campaign. Twenty Ukrainian deputies were elected to the Polish diet and senate. Vasyl Mudry, who, in October 1935, replaced the intransigent Dmytro Levytsky as President of the National Democratic Union was elected Deputy President of the parliament. Following an amnesty, the majority of Ukrainian political prisoners were set free from the prisons and the famous concentration camp of Bereza Kartuzka. The Ukrainian minority also obtained undertakings in the fields of the economy and education. In exchange for these concessions, the Ukrainian parliamentary group ceased to make self-determination a prerequisite and showed its willingness to respect the existence of the Polish state by supporting the budget bill.

This *rapprochement* with the government, known as Polish–Ukrainian normalisation, nevertheless encountered the opposition of groups on the left and on the extreme right, and even of an influential group of the National Democratic Union, centred around the journal *Dilo*. Moreover the policy of understanding did not have a long life on the Polish side. Warsaw's liberal declarations were sabotaged by the local administration. In step with the deterioration of the international situation, and on the pretext of state security, the Ukrainian and Byelorussian territories were subjected to the control of chauvinist military quarters. A wave of brutal measures in the economic, national, and confessional spheres, such as, for example, the forcible conversion of Orthodox into Catholic churches, provoked spontaneous resistance by these minorities. Hence normalisation came officially to an end at the beginning of 1938. On 23 February, Vasyl Mudry announced that the National Democratic Union deputies would not vote for the budget because of the anti-Ukrainian policy being carried out by several ministries. On 7 May 1938, the National Democratic Union's central committee published an official statement according to which, in view of the failure of the normalisation policy, it seemed that Polish–Ukrainian relations could be put on a regular footing only on the basis of territorial autonomy guaranteed by Poland. This idea was taken up again on 9 July 1938 by the Ukrainian parliamentary group. It meant that the National Democratic Union had shifted to an overtly anti-Polish policy. Even the hitherto moderate Ukrainian papers moved under the pressure of public opinion to an extreme anti-Polish nationalism. The Ukrainian question in Poland became in some sort analogous to that of the Sudeten Germans in Czechoslovakia. Of course, the promptings came from the same source.

The higher ranks were in a state of considerable commotion, as were the extreme right wing youth. On 23 May 1938, the head of the Organisation of Ukrainian Nationalists, Ehven Konowaletz, was assassinated in Rotterdam. His successor was his brother-in-law, Colonel Andrij Melnyk, who possessed neither his popularity nor his political abilities. In this crucial period, Melnyk subordinated himself totally to his German protectors, mainly from the *Abwehr*. This policy caused strong internal opposition and even a schism in the Organisation of Ukrainian Nationalists. The Czechoslovak crisis, the Munich conference, and the creation of an ephemeral mini-state, Transcarpathian Ukraine, whipped up great enthusiasm among Ukrainian nationalists. Legal and illegal propaganda reinforced the popular belief that the Munich conference had brought the problem of national minorities to a head, and that National Socialist Germany envisaged the creation of new national states in eastern Europe, and in particular the rebirth of a united and independent Ukraine. In this atmosphere in the autumn of 1938, thousands of young Ukrainians began to flee across Czechoslovakia to Germany, where they joined the various Ukrainian military organisations set up under the guidance of the *Abwehr*. After training in spying and political subversion, some of these volunteers returned to Poland with particular missions. Thus, from autumn 1938, sabotage and political subversion intensified in eastern Galicia. Terrorist action was particularly directed at Polish colonists and the Jewish rural population. The Ukrainian nationalists were in this way implementing their programme of eliminating the non-Ukrainian population and their watchword: 'the Poles across the San!'.[7]

The Polish authorities were not slow to react. Tens of thousands of Ukrainians, especially the supporters of the Organisation of Ukrainian Nationalists, were locked up. A new military 'pacification' brought bloodshed to the Tarnopol region. On the eve of the Second World War, a state of something like a Polish–Ukrainian war reigned in Poland's south eastern territories.

Postscript

During the Second World War, Poland, terribly martyred by its occupiers, experienced a bloody supplementary drama. After 20 months of Soviet occupation, in June 1941, Poland's Ukrainian territories saw the arrival of the Germans. The massacre of the Jewish population and of the Polish intelligentsia began immediately, but it was not the exclusive work of the SS and of the special squads of the *Wehrmacht*. Alongside the German army came Ukrainian Fascist detachments, specially formed and equipped by the Germans. The occupying power was also able to find on the spot volunteers among the fanaticised youth for service in the auxiliary police. The Ukrainian commandos distinguished themselves by their cruelty in the concentration camps as well as the Jewish ghettos. The metropolitan Sheptytsky's pastoral letters against these crimes were ignored. In

1943, the Ukrainian National Committee formed a division, *SS Galizien*, and in the same year the massacres of the Polish rural population in Volhynia began, organised by the Ukrainian extreme right. Units of the Polish secret army replied by burning Ukrainian villages. It is unnecessary to add that all this took place with the tacit approval of the occupying power.

This state of civil war between two sister nations endured for the first years of the Polish People's Republic, ending in the total devastation of the Ukrainian regions and the exile of the population. Today, what remains of the Ukrainian population can be found in the former German territories annexed by Poland in 1945. It is a matter of historical paradox that the great majority of the Polish population repatriated from the Western Ukraine after its annexation by the Soviet Union dwells in these same territories. Nowadays, no responsible Polish politician continues to assert the sovereignty of Poland over the territory of the Ukraine or of western Byelorussia.

An eminent Ukrainian historian, descended from a family of leaders of the National Democratic Union, summed up his study of Polish–Ukrainian relations in this way:

> I will not attempt to discuss the history of Polish–Ukrainian relations during the interwar era. So far no scholarly studies have appeared on the policies of the Second Polish Republic towards its involuntary Ukrainian citizens, and on the internal developments of the Ukrainian community in Poland between 1919 and 1939. The subject is too important and too painful to deal with in a casual manner; rather, it must be left to the labors of future historians and political scientists. I cannot, however, refrain from quoting Talleyrand's well known *bon mot*: 'this is worse than a crime, it is a stupidity'. These words could well serve, I believe, as a motto to a history, still to be written, of Polish–Ukrainian relations between the treaty of Riga and the end of World War II.[8]

Notes

1. Kubijowicz and Kuzela (eds), pp. 165–70.
2. *Historia Polski*, vol. 3, pt 1, pp. 631–2.
3. Kutchabsky.
4. Korzec (1975a); Korzec (1977); Korzec (1975b)
5. Dumin.
6. *Polish Atrocities in Ukraine* (New York, 1931); *La plus sombre Pologne* (Lausanne, 1931).
7. Hanusiak.
8. Rudnytsky, p. 26.

Select Bibliography

Dumin, O. 'Die Wahrheit über die ukrainische Organisation', Berlin, May 1926. Politisches Archiv, Bonn: Polen-Ukraine, Geheim Akten, vol. 2. Text published in Polish translation by Korzec, P. in *Zeszyty Historyczne*, 30 (1974), pp. 98–137.

Hanusiak, M. (1979), *Ukrainischer Nationalismus Theorie und Praxis*, Vienna.

Historia Polski (1963), vol. 3, pt 1, Warsaw.

Korzec, P. (1975a), 'Der Block der nationalen Minderheiten im Parlamentarismus Polens des Jahres 1922', *Zeitschrift für Ostforschung*.

Korzec, P. (1975b), 'Polen und der Minderheitenschutzvertrag 1919–1934', *Jahrbücher für Geschichte Osteuropas*, 2.

Korzec, P. (1977), 'Der zweite Block der nationalen Minderheiten im Parlamentarismus Polens 1927–28', *Zeitschrift für Ostforschung*.

Kubijowicz, W. and Kuzela, Z. (eds) (1949), *Encyklopedija Ukrainoznawstwa*, vol. 1, pt 2, Munich.

Kutchabsky, W. (1934), *Die Westukraine im Kampfe mit Polen und dem Bolchewismus in den Jahren 1918–23*, Berlin.

Rudnytsky, I.L. (1980), 'The Burden of History', in Potichnyj, P.J. (ed.), *Poland and Ukraine, Past and Present*, Edmonton.

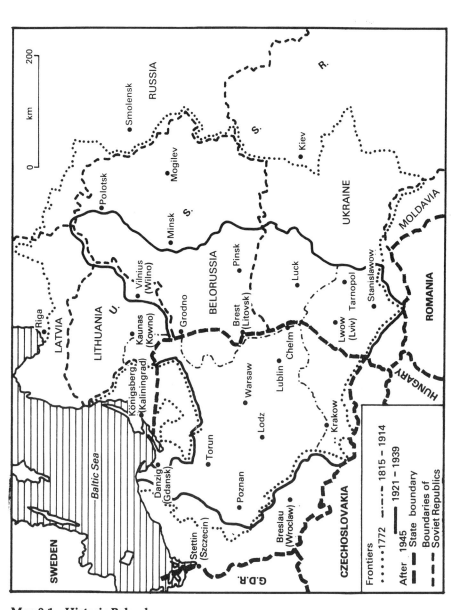

Map 9.1   Historic Poland
Source: G. Castellan, *Dieu garde la Pologne. Histoire du catholicisme polonais 1795–1981*,
Paris, 1982.

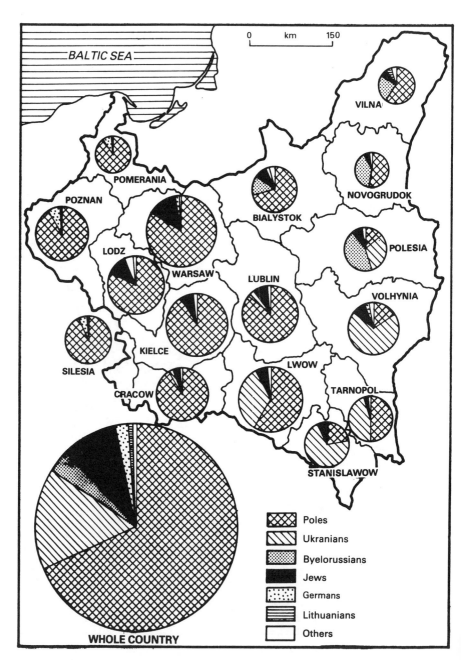

Map 9.2   Poland's national minorities in 1931
Source: Histoire de Pologne, Warsaw, PWN, 1971

10 Nationality Problems in Upper Silesia, 1918–1922

BOGDAN KOSZEL

I

The territory of Upper Silesia endured various vicissitudes throughout its history. The Slavic tribes living there were conquered by Bohemia in the tenth century. In 990, Mieszko, the Polish duke who founded the Piast dynasty, recovered Silesia from Bohemia and merged it with the Polish state. In 1009, a diocese was set up for Silesia with its seat in Wrocław/Breslau. During the feudal disintegration of the state, the Piast dukes in Silesia maintained close ties with the dynasty, even though they brought in German colonists and founded towns in accordance with German law (Magdeburg law).

At the end of the thirteenth century Silesia came again under the rule of the Bohemian kings of the Luxemburg dynasty. This process began in the time of Duke Henry the Bearded and continued without a break until 1369, when the entire territory of Silesia became part of Bohemia. The Polish kings Władysław the Short (1261–1333) and Casimir the Great (1333–70) endeavoured to regain the lost territories by both diplomatic and military means, but after several setbacks, Poland renounced her claims to Silesia at Namysłów/Namslau in 1348.[1]

The gradual germanisation of Silesia started in 1526, when the Austrian Habsburgs took over power in the Silesian duchies. However this primarily concerned Lower Silesia with Wrocław, Legnica/Lignitz and Głogów/Glogau while Upper Silesia remained Polish from the cultural and linguistic points of view. This situation continued until 1740, when the Prussian king, Frederick II, seized Silesia. From that time this territory formed part of the Brandenburg Prussian state. Silesia was then swept by a second systematic wave of germanisation which led first and foremost to the germanisation of towns. The Polish element was in the majority in the Upper Silesia countryside and the borderlands between Silesia and *Wielkopolska* (Greater Poland).[2] The third partition of Poland carried out in 1795 by Austria, Prussia and Russia

211

erased the Polish state from the map of Europe. A gradual process of russification or germanisation of the Polish population started in the territories annexed by Russia and Prussia.

The process of denationalisation in Upper Silesia was particularly strong during the chancellorship of Otto von Bismarck. One of his first moves was the elimination of the Polish language from schools in eastern Upper Silesia, which was inhabited mainly by Poles. An ordinance issued by the president of the Opole/Oppeln regency in 1872 banned the use of the Polish language in schools, except for religious instruction; Polish could be used as an auxiliary language in lower forms. After Bismarck's dismissal the Poles gained new opportunities for development. Some of them became involved in the activities of the German Catholic Centre party; others – mostly workers – joined the Polish Workers party of the Prussian part of Poland, which was set up in 1903. In the elections to the *Reichstag* held in the same year, a representative of the Polish national–radical camp, Wojciech Korfanty, was elected.

Polish cultural life flourished. Many economic, cultural and sports organisations were set up. The Society of People's Libraries, founded in Greater Poland, included Upper Silesia in the scope of its activities, spreading education and opening Polish libraries. Silesia had a gymnastic society, *Sokół* (Falcon), as well as various economic institutions, especially people's banks. Shortly after the outbreak of the First World War, Upper Silesia had 21 Polish periodicals, of which four were dailies; five were weeklies; two were bi-weeklies, two were monthlies, and eight papers were published every second day.[3]

At the end of the First World War, Upper Silesia presented a complex picture of politics, nationalities and social relations. Trends towards unification with Poland were strong, but equally strong was a gravitation toward Germany. The centuries long period of German colonisation in Upper Silesia led to the formation of a specific population structure. Even with the best of wills, it was impossible for politicians to lay exact border lines between Polish and German centres because the two populations were so intermixed. Hence it was impossible to apply there those criteria of division into national minorities which were usually used in international politics. German statistics gave some idea of nationality relations in this area before the First World War: but they were not always honest and accurate. According to official pre-First World War German sources (population censuses and records of children of school age) there were 1 258 186 Poles and 884 045 Germans in Upper Silesia in 1910. German school records of 1911 put the number of Poles at 1 548 500 and Germans at 588 000.[4]

There is not a shadow of doubt that the sharp conflict that developed after the First World War between Poland, Germany and also to a lesser extent, Czechoslovakia over Upper Silesia, a conflict in which the Entente powers interfered, was due mainly to the economic importance of this territory. It was a region with enormous natural resources: hard coal, zinc, lead and iron ore. It had a powerful industry which before the First World War had employed nearly 250 000 workers, of which 192 000 had been involved in mining and the iron and steel industry and 58 000 had been employed in the metal industry.[5] The military defeat of the German *Reich* in 1918 and the establishment of the Polish state led to a dynamic development of organisations and societies which demanded the return of Upper Silesia to Poland. The main decisions were taken at the Paris Peace Conference, which opened its debates in January 1919. Deep differences of opinion arose among the Allies over Poland's western and northern frontiers. France wanted Poland to be an economically and militarily strong state in order to act as a check on Germany from the east. If Poland was to replace France's former ally, tsarist Russia, and perform this function effectively, her territory would have to be increased accordingly. The opinion on the Seine was that the Upper Silesian industrial region in particular should be part of the Polish state.[6] Great Britain, on the other hand, did not want German hegemony on the continent to be replaced by French hegemony and consequently was of the opinion that Paris should have a counterweight in Europe in the form of undiminished power for Germany.

In spite of these differences between the Allies, the Polish delegation in Paris, led by Roman Dmowski, succeeded in winning French support for the Polish plans to incorporate nearly the whole of Upper Silesia into the Polish state. The original text of the peace treaty handed to the German delegation on 7 May 1919 included the main Polish demands, worked out by a commission for Polish questions chaired by Jules Cambon, the French Ambassador to Berlin. It assigned to Poland the Opole regency with the districts of Grodków/Grottkau and Nysa/Neisse but without the western parts of the Niemodlin/Falkenberg and Prudnik/Neustadt districts. This decision was the best achievable one, and was in line with the ethnic character of Upper Silesia. It took into account the economic connection of these territories with the rest of Poland, which was important for France as such a division would undercut to some extent the roots of German expansionism, a constant threat to the peace of Europe.

On 29 May 1919, the government in Berlin replied to the peace terms for Germany in a document entitled 'Remarks of the German Delegation on the Peace Terms'. It was stated in the document that the terms 'constituted an absolutely unjustified inroad into the geographical and economic structure of the German *Reich*'. The German government expressed the view that, after 1163, Upper Silesia had had no political connexion whatever with Poland, and was thus of the opinion that 'There were no Polish national traditions in Upper Silesia, no memory of Polish history; nor had Upper Silesia participated in the liberation struggle'. Germany further denied that Upper Silesia was inhabited by a clearly Polish population. It relied, as evidence of this, on election results and on the fact that, even after the collapse of Germany, barely 22 per cent of the school children were entered for instruction in any language other than German. The Upper Silesians did not speak literary Polish, but *Wasserpolnisch*, a Polish dialect that was a mixture of German and Polish, which was not used for literary purposes. They argued that this dialect did not constitute a national characteristic and was not incompatible with German national consciousness. Besides, the whole development, intellectual and material, of Upper Silesia was the result of German efforts. Leaders in science and the arts, in trade and industry, in agriculture and labour organisation were exclusively German. Poland could dispense with Upper Silesia, but Germany could not. Neither would its cession to Poland be in the interests of peace, for Germany would not be able to reconcile herself to the loss, which would leave her unable to fulfil her financial obligations arising out of the war.[7]

The well constructed German arguments gave the British Prime Minister, David Lloyd George, an opportunity to resume discussions on the national status of Upper Silesia, starting on 2 June 1919, at the first meeting of the Supreme Council which considered the German reply to the draft peace treaty. Lloyd George came out against the cession of Upper Silesia to Poland. He shared the view of the German delegation that the imposition of severe peace terms on Germany would lead to the growth of revolutionary sentiments in the *Reich*. In his opinion it was Germany, and not Poland, which was best suited to play the role of a *cordon sanitaire* separating Soviet Russia from the rest of Europe. However, in the expectation of determined opposition from the Poles and dissatisfaction from France, he explained that his stand was inspired by a wish to guarantee the right of self-determination to nations. Counting on the support of President Wilson, an ardent advocate of the idea of self-determination, he proposed that a plebiscite be held in the disputed territory. In addition to the USA's support he succeeded in securing that of Italy for his plans.[8]

After heated discussions by the Big Four, the decision was taken to hold a plebiscite.[9] Poland's chances of regaining Upper Silesia decreased dramatically. One could hardly expect that given Poland's strong involvement in the east when its frontiers were being established, and Germany's large opportunities in terms of economic and administrative pressure in Upper Silesia, the plebiscite would be in Poland's favour.

At the same time Czechoslovakia, taking advantage of Poland's weakness, put forward claims to some parts of Upper Silesia. These claims, which were certainly greatly exaggerated, were not met.

Czechoslovakia was granted only the Hlučin territory at this time.[10]

The voting procedure was set down in article 88 of the Versailles Treaty, together with the annex, and Article 5 of this annex stated:

> On the conclusion of the voting, the number of votes cast in each commune will be communicated by the Commission to the Principal Allied and Associated Powers with a full report as to the taking of the vote and recommendation as to the line which ought to be adopted as the frontier of Germany in Upper Silesia. In this recommendation regard will be paid to the wishes of the inhabitants as shown by the vote, and to the geographical and economic conditions of the locality.[11].

The plebiscite was to be held in an area of 10 782.6 sq km, under the supervision of an international commission. German troops and some of the higher levels of German state government were to leave the area. Order was to be maintained by allied military detachments and police units drawn from the local population. All citizens who were over 20 and had either been born in Upper Silesia or had settled there no later than 1 January 1919 were entitled to vote in the plebiscite.

The decision to hold a plebiscite in Upper Silesia might have appeared justified, but it ignored the evidence of the German population censuses and did not take into account the fact that many Upper Silesians had voted for Polish candidates in the elections to the parliament of the *Reich*. Nor did it take into account the low level of state consciousness among the Upper Silesian population, which resulted from the fact that Poland had not existed as a state for over a century and that all manifestations of Polishness had been severely suppressed by an efficient Prussian administration during much of that period. The granting to persons born in upper Silesia but not resident there of the right to vote was a tactical error on the Polish part. The relevant clause of Article 88 of the Versailles Treaty was included at the request of the Polish delegation, which counted on the vote of Poles who had left Silesia for the Ruhr. But these expectations were not fulfilled.[12]

II

The Versailles decision on a general vote in Upper Silesia aroused the indignation of the Polish population and was one of the main reasons for the outbreak of the first Silesian uprising in 1919. The disputes at the peace conference showed the Germans that in their endeavours to retain Upper Silesia they could count on international approval. This spurred them to still greater efforts and bolder actions, guaranteeing them victory in the plebiscite. In the summer of 1919, armed incidents between Poles and Germans began to multiply. The Polish population organised mass demonstrations and strikes, demanding the restitution of the freedom of speech and the press, the withdrawal of the *Grenzschutz* units and the incorporation of Upper Silesia into Poland. The Germans replied with acts of terror; they stepped up the arrest of Polish activists and forbade the publication of Polish texts without the previous consent of the police authorities. More and more Poles from Upper Silesia sought refuge in Piotrowice/Petrowitz in Cieszyn/Teschen Silesia, in Sosnowiec/Sosnowitz and Oświecim/Auschwitz.[13]

It was among these refugees and in the ranks of the Polish Military Organisation of Upper Silesia, set up at the beginning of 1919, that the idea arose of starting an armed uprising in order to put an end to the German terror. The example had been given by neighbouring Greater Poland where in December 1918 an anti-German uprising broke out, ending successfully in the incorporation of that territory into Poland. In June and July 1919, the Polish Military Organisation, commanded by Józef Grzegorzek, quickly grew in strength. Many Silesians joined this organisation, among them many soldiers demobilised from the German army. Before the uprising the Polish Military Organisation had several thousand sworn members, but it had few weapons. The number of officers was insufficient since very few Silesians had succeeded in getting promotion to higher ranks in the German army.[14]

The Germans, however, also strengthened and reorganised their forces. As early as the end of November 1918, the 117th Infantry Division, commanded by General Karl Höfer, arrived in Silesia. It was later transformed into *Grenzschutz* units and next into a small *Reichswehr* Brigade No 32. There were also many organisations which sought to combat Polish national aspirations. The most important was the *Freie Vereinigung zum Schutze Oberschlesiens* (Voluntary Association for the Protection of Upper Silesia) with its seat in Opole, as well as the so-called *Bürgerwehren* (Citizens' Guards) which supported the police. In January 1919, the 117th division, weakened by revolutionary tendencies among its soldiers, was strengthened by the *Oberschlesiches Freiwilligenkorps* (Upper Silesian volunteer corps). It was composed of German officials and workers who were released from their work but continued to receive pay. This corps numbered 4000 and, as a part of the *Grenzschutz*, its role was to combat the Polish national movement and the radical German working class movement. When in July 1919 the members of the *Grenzschutz* began to return to their factories the other workers protested. This led to many incidents and demonstrations, culminating in a strike held on 14 August 1919, in which about 140 000 workers took part. The following day *Grenzschutz* units opened fire on workers in front of the Mysłowice colliery, killing ten people.

The news of the massacre aroused indignation in Upper Silesia, and an uprising broke out spontaneously in this tense atmosphere. A group of Polish Military Organisation activists staying in a camp at Piotrowice gave the district commanders at Rybnik and Pszczyna/ Pless an order to start action. On the night of 16 August fighting started in the Pszczyna district and on the next day in the districts of Rybnik, Katowice/Kattowitz, Bytom/Beuthen and Tarnowskie Góry/ Tarnowitz. Military operations were spontaneous guerilla actions, in a densely populated industrial region. On 1 August 1919 the Polish Military Organisation had 23225 members armed with 3788 rifles, 2523 revolvers, 34 machine guns and 3685 grenades.[15] After the first period of surprise, the Germans concentrated their forces and, taking advantage of their superiority in arms and men, passed on to a systematic dislodging of the insurrectionaries towards the east. From 19 August, the Germans began to achieve superiority, driving the insurgent units towards the Polish frontier.[16]

On learning about the events in Upper Silesia, the Entente powers set up a special military commission to go at once to the disturbed territory. The head of the commission was General C.J. Dupont, chief of the French military mission in Berlin; the other members were Colonel Goodyear (USA); Lieutenant Colonel Tidburg (Great Britain); Major Vaccary (Italy) and Captain Poupart (France). The commission arrived in Upper Silesia on 24 August with the aim of putting an end to the uprising, which was in any case already dying out. The last insurgent units crossed the Polish frontier on 25 August. Some 20000 refugees were placed in six camps: at Sosnowiec, Grodziec, Szczakowa, Oświecim, Jaworzno and Zawiercie.

This first uprising ended in a Polish military defeat in Upper Silesia. It was not a detailed or carefully thought out operation but rather a spontaneous outbreak covering only a part of the plebiscite territory. Given the great disproportion in the forces, it was easily suppressed. However, it strengthened Germany in the international forum. The uprising was presented to the western powers by German propaganda as an act contrary to the Versailles Treaty and as the result of the work of the communist movement. Such an interpretation could be sure of a favourable reception from the Entente powers.[17]

III

Polish–German negotiations on controversial problems arising out of the Versailles Treaty had opened in July 1919, but were interrupted when the uprising broke out and the Polish delegation left Berlin. They were resumed on 25 September 1919, as a result of pressure from the Entente powers. On 1 October a Polish–German agreement was concluded on the basis of which the refugee insurgents could return to Upper Silesia without running the risk of penal reprisals.[18] This Polish–German agreement was of great importance, as it calmed people's minds in Upper Silesia and averted, at least for the time being, the danger of new disturbances. It also led to a short lived détente between Warsaw and Berlin, and was followed by the signing of a number of accords and economic agreements.

Yet as early as August 1919, when the Polish side was depressed by the collapse of the uprising, the German authorities ordered the holding of local elections in Upper Silesia on 9 November, in order to secure convincing proof that the German element was in the majority in that area. The Polish side expected another setback. Rather unexpectedly, thanks to the strenuous work of local activists, nearly 60 per cent of the voters cast their votes for Polish candidates. Out of the 11 255 newly elected councillors, 6822 were of Polish nationality and 4373 were German. Out of the 22 districts of the plebiscite area, in 12 the Poles won an overwhelming majority.[19] Both sides regarded the local elections as a general rehearsal for the plebiscite. Thus official Polish propaganda struck an exaggeratedly optimistic note, regarding the results as a guarantee of Polish victory in the plebiscite. The general opinion was that the plebiscite would be advantageous for Poland and should be held immediately after the arrival of an Allied commission.

The Versailles Treaty came into force on 10 January 1920. A month later the Inter-Allied Plebiscite Commission arrived in Upper Silesia and took its seat in Opole. Its Chairman was the French General Henri le Rond. Great Britain was represented by Colonel Harold F.P. Percival, and Italy by General Andreo de Marinis Stendardo de Ricigliano. The Commission had a staff of officials and military men who were to set up an administration which would see to it that the voting was properly conducted and prepare the technical side of the plebiscite. After the resignation of the USA from the Commission, the most important posts in the administration and armed forces were taken by the French, which was of great importance for the further development of the situation in the plebiscite area.[20]

The Commission had military units of the three powers at its disposal, numbering 15–20 000 men, most of them French. The German *Grenzschutz* units left the plebiscite area along with Joseph Bitta, President of the regency, who left Opole, and Otto Hörsing, who left Katowice. Senior officials, district presidents, mayors, teachers and the *Sicherheitspolizei* (German secret security police) numbering about 5000 functionaries remained on the spot. Moreover, the Germans organised *Selbstschutz* (underground fighting squads) numbering about 30000 men, as well as many anti-Polish organisations, the most important of these being the *Vereinigte Verbände Heimattreuer Oberschlesier* (United Unions of Upper Silesians Faithful to the Homeland). German political party activity was coordinated by the *Schlesischer Ausschuss* (Silesian Department), set up in Wrocław in December 1919. Its task was to create a German national front to fight for German retention of Upper Silesia; conducting the plebiscite campaign, overseeing the propaganda and any agitation, securing financial resources and directing intelligence activities. Officially, the German side was represented by the Plebiscite Commissariat with its seat in Katowice headed by Kurt Urbanek.[21]

The government in Warsaw appointed Wojciech Korfanty as Polish Plebiscite Commissioner. From his headquarters in the Lomnitz hotel in Bytom Korfanty rallied representatives of all the Polish political parties active in Upper Silesia, from the right wing National party to the workers' Polish Socialist party. A Polish Plebiscite Commission was set up in every district town. *Kate* (secret Polish cells) were established in the plebiscite area, to report on the mood of the population and to conduct propaganda activity.

In the spring of 1920 the Polish and German governments started large scale activity in the plebiscite area. Countless brochures and books were published in both languages; publications were also brought out in French for the occupation forces. The film industry and radio were included in this campaign, which was on both sides inspired by an extreme nationalist spirit and was permeated with hatred for the adversary. Frequent conflicts occurred between Poles and Germans. There were also clashes with the occupation units. The French did not conceal their sympathy for the Poles, while the Germans could count on the favourable attitude of Great Britain and Italy.

From April 1920, the Polish side demanded ever more categorically that the German *Sicherheitspolizei* and German officials be withdrawn from the plebiscite area and that combined law and order forces and a combined administration be set up. These demands, which were in accordance with the Versailles Treaty, were presented at many meetings and demonstrations, especially on 24 April 1920, when mass meetings were held in 13 localities. At the beginning of May 1920, clashes took place between Poles and Germans in Lubliniec/ Lublinitz, Olesno/Rosenberg, Opole and Racibórz. The Polish side proclaimed a 48 hour strike from 10 May until 12 May 1920, to promote Polish national aspirations. In reply to these demonstrations the Germans attacked the Lomnitz hotel in Bytom, the Polish consulate in Opole and the seat of the Polish Plebiscite Commissariat at Koźle. The *Sicherheitspolizei* arrested Polish activists, broke up meetings, supplied German organisations with arms and ammunition and conducted an openly pro-German agitation. The vexed question of the withdrawal of the *Sicherheitspolizei* was gradually becoming the spark setting off a new uprising.[22]

Throughout the plebiscite campaign Poland was conducting a war in the east against Soviet Russia. After the initial successes of the Polish army and capture of Kiev, a Soviet counteroffensive forced the Polish troops to retreat. At the beginning of August 1920 the front line ran not far from Warsaw and the survival of the state was at stake. Germany, wishing to take advantage of Poland's difficult situation, proposed to the western powers that it would stop the Soviet advance towards the west if Upper Silesia was left within the frontiers of the *Reich*.

Between 5 and 16 July 1920, the Entente powers held a conference at Spa, which rejected the German proposal and kept the provisions of the Versailles Treaty in force. However, weakened by the war, Poland had to make concessions at the conference over the Polish–Czechoslovak frontier in Teschen Silesia. Under pressure from western politicians, the Polish government had to give up its demand for a plebiscite in that area. On 28 July 1920, the Council of Ambassadors, made up of representatives of the USA, Great Britain, France, Italy and Japan, divided the territory unfavourably to Poland. Poland was allocated a territory of 1009 sq km, inhabited by 143 000 people, while Czechoslovakia was accorded 1 273 000 sq km with 283 500 inhabitants. The frontier line was to run along the Olza river, which divided the town of Cieszyn into two parts.[23]

Polish–German relations were gradually worsening when the President of the *Reich* proclaimed Germany's neutrality in the Polish–Soviet war on 20 July 1920 and five days later put a ban on the export and transit of military supplies to Poland. This was meant mainly to halt the supplies of French and Italian arms to the Polish units fighting along the Vistula line. German nationalists tried to use the Polish–Soviet war for their own purposes and with Soviet Russia growing in strength on the European continent were increasing cooperation with the Soviets. German nationalists also tried to use the issue of the war in their plebiscite propaganda in Upper Silesia, warning the Silesians not to vote for a state involved in a protracted war, the result of which was uncertain. This argument created a following among many Silesians, and led to a drop in pro-Polish feeling.

The tension in Upper Silesia reached its climax in August 1920. Fierce fighting was then going on very close to Warsaw, and on 14 August the first French units, which were to protect military transports to Poland, arrived in the plebiscite area from Teschen

Silesia. This led to the formation of a German resistance to French intervention in the Polish–Soviet war. Clashes with the French occurred in many places. On 17 August when the Polish–Soviet fighting was in its crucial phase, German units attacked Polish plebiscite premises. The seat of the District Plebiscite Commissariat in Katowice was demolished, and Andrzej Mielęcki, a well known Polish activist, was killed. In this situation Polish inhabitants in the eastern districts began on 18 August spontaneously to protest against the German police and fighting squads.

The leadership of the Polish Military Organisation regarded the attack staged by German units on 17 August as an attempt to liquidate Polish propaganda centres and kill Polish independence activists. Two days later, on 19 August the Polish Military Organisation command in Upper Silesia gave the order for an uprising. At the same time the Polish Plebiscite Commissariat proclaimed a general strike and Korfanty issued a proclamation to the population.[24]

The order to start armed operations was received by the Polish Military Organisation commanders in the districts of Bytom, Gliwice/Gleiwitz, Katowice, Lubliniec, Pszczyna, Racibórz, Rybnik, Tarnowskie Góry, Toszek/Tost and Zabrze/Hindenburg. The insurgents did not attack large towns, where allied troops were stationed. They stuck to destroying German security police stations and administrative centres. Fierce fighting was waged at Mysłowice/ Myslowitz in the Baildon and Pokój iron and steel works, in Chorzów/Königshütte and in the German colliery of the Hołduns in the Pszczyna district.

The outbreak of the second Silesian uprising was connived at by French representatives on the InterAllied Commission. The weakening and curbing of German influence in Upper Silesia and the destruction of the *Sicherheitspolizei* were also in French interests. Thus its representatives did not hamper the distribution of Polish appeals, and supplied the insurgents with important information and even explained away the fighting to the European public.[25] The aims of this armed struggle were completely different from those which had inspired the previous year's insurrection. Whereas the year before the aim had been to invalidate the Versailles verdict and create a *fait accompli* through the incorporation of Upper Silesia into Poland, the second uprising had more limited aims: the destruction of the *Sicherheitspolizei* and its replacement by policing forces, composed in equal numbers of Poles and Germans.

This second uprising lasted five days. On 24 August 1920, the InterAllied Commission decided to accept Polish demands. An order was given for the *Sicherheitspolizei* to assemble in Gliwice, Rybnik and Opole, where it was disarmed and disbanded. In its place an *Abstimmungspolizei* (plebiscite police), half Polish and half German, was set up. Polish propaganda greatly overestimated the result. It promulgated the view that the uprising had weakened the German element in the area and that the plebiscite would thus end in success.[26] In this situation endeavours were made to bring forward the date of the plebiscite to take advantage of the rise in pro-Polish sentiments, while the Germans were interested in putting the plebiscite off in order to mobilize their forces. On 28 August the Polish and German Plebiscite Commissioners and leaders of Polish and German organisations reached an agreement and issued a joint appeal calling on the population of Upper Silesia to keep the peace and not to provoke incidents.

IV

After the end of the second Silesian uprising both sides started an intensive propaganda campaign to secure for themselves the most favourable conditions for the plebiscite and to win over the majority of the future voters. The Allies did not approve of the Polish voting regulations which divided the plebiscite area into two parts; eastern and western, with the voting to be held first in the industrialised and overwhelmingly Polish area, which would have greatly influenced the inhabitants of the western part.[27] Nor did the InterAllied Commission agree to bring forward the date of the plebiscite, a demand put forward by the Polish side in view of the ruined state of their economy following the Polish–Soviet war and the costs of a prolonged plebiscite campaign.

When the InterAllied Commission announced the rules of the plebiscite those entitled to vote were divided into four categories:

- people living in Upper Silesia and born there
- people born in the plebiscite area but not resident there
- people who had arrived in Upper Silesia before 1 January 1904
- people born in Upper Silesia or resident there on 1 January 1904 and expelled by the authorities

Men and women who had reached the age of 20 by 1 January 1921 were entitled to vote, and were to cast their ballot cards with the inscription Polska–Polen or Deutschland–Niemcy into the ballot boxes. In every constituency a mixed Polish–German committee was set up to receive the votes under the protection of the allied forces and establish the results of the voting.[28]

Both sides made wide use of the assistance of their states and communities. All over Poland many committees of help for Upper Silesia were set up. Their activity was coordinated by the Central

Plebiscite Committee headed by Wojciech Trampczyński, President of the Polish parliament. A training centre for plebiscite activists and agitators was founded in Cracow. The local committees organised many collections, received visits from groups of Upper Silesians, worked out propaganda publications and popularised knowledge of Upper Silesia among Polish people. Control over these activities was in the hands of Korfanty and the Polish Plebiscite Committee.[29] The German side had its directing centres outside the plebiscite area, in Berlin and Wrocław, and the governments of the *Reich* and Prussia provided large sums for the plebiscite campaign. All efforts were concentrated on bringing over from Germany on voting day the largest possible number of emigrants who had been born in Upper Silesia.

The plebiscite was held on 20 March 1921. According to the data published in Poland, out of the 1 028 000 people entitled to vote, 993 000 (96.5 per cent) took part in the voting. The Germans brought over 182 000 emigrants for the voting while the Polish side brought only about 10 000. This was in accordance with the provisions of the Versailles Treaty. Including the emigrants, 1 185 000 people cast their votes, 706 000 of them voting for Upper Silesia remaining with Germany, and 479 000 (that is 40.4 per cent) for its return to Poland. Out of 1474 communes, 682 (that is 46.3 per cent) voted for Poland and 792 (that is 53.7 per cent) for Germany.[30]

The results of the plebiscite call for comment. If the emigrants' votes had been disregarded, the proportion would have been 47.3 per cent for Poland and 52.7 per cent for Germany. The Germans obtained a decisive majority mainly in the small communes and landed estates belonging to Germans whose owners exerted pressure on the Polish agricultural labourers they employed. The inclusion of the Głubczyce district in the plebiscite also had a negative effect on results, since Poland did not have a chance there.

The plebiscite did not automatically determine the fate of Upper Silesia, for in accordance with article 88 of the Versailles Treaty, the final decision was to be taken by the Entente powers. The division of Upper Silesia was a difficult task for them as the communes which voted for Poland were scattered. Moreover, the industrial nature of the region made division undesirable. The population of the main industrial region generally voted for Germany, but the people living further west generally cast their votes for Poland. If the industrial region were to be ceded to Poland, a large number of Germans would come under Polish rule. If it were to be allocated to Germany, many Poles would be left in Germany.

Germany, supported in the InterAllied Commission by the British and Italians, took the view that it had won the plebiscite and that the whole region should remain within the frontiers of the Weimar

Republic. Poland and France were of the opinion that close attention should be paid to the Versailles Treaty which envisaged that the decision would be made on the basis of the results by communes. In the view of Poland and France, the only justifiable solution was the division of Upper Silesia. A heated discussion developed among the members of the InterAllied Commission. Colonel Percival and General de Marinis proposed in this case that Poland should only receive two districts, those of Pszczyna and Rybnik, and small parts of the Katowice district. This meant that practically the entire industrial region would have remained in the *Reich*. General le Rond put forward a completely different proposal. On the basis of an exact analysis of the plebiscite results he proposed that the industrial region, together with the territory between Gliwice and Strzelce Opolskie/Gross Stremlitz, where Poles were in the majority, should be returned to Poland. The two proposals were incompatible and in spite of endeavours no compromise solution could be reached. After a discussion which lasted a month, the British–Italian and French proposals for the division of Upper Silesia were sent to the Supreme Council in Paris on 30 April 1921.[31]

The Supreme Council, convened in London in the first days of May 1921, had two important questions on its agenda: payments for war damage and reparations by Germany, and the division of Upper Silesia. Warsaw realised that France would be in a difficult situation and, seeking first and foremost to win the support of Great Britain and Italy over the question of reparations and damages, might be ready to sacrifice Upper Silesia. It was necessary to have an additional strong argument, in the form of a new armed uprising which would settle the question of dividing Upper Silesia in favour of Poland.

V

Following the setback suffered in the plebiscite and the British–Italian proposal for the division of Upper Silesia, the leaders assembled in Bytom on 30 April 1921 and took the decision to arrange an uprising. On being informed about this decision, the government in Warsaw did not at first give its consent, fearing the outbreak of a Polish–German war, for which Poland was not prepared, and the reaction of the Entente powers. The intention of Korfanty, who commanded the entire action, was to stage a short-lived armed operation, to demonstrate the Polish position and exert pressure on the western powers. This concept finally won the approval of the government in Warsaw, which supplied arms and ammunition, means of transport, money and qualified commanders.

The concept of a new uprising met with a favourable reception from the French: Generals le Rond and Gratier thought an uprising was advisable and necessary. It was also said to be supported by military circles in Paris, which were thinking of a joint French, Polish and Czechoslovak action against Germany and the occupation of the territory of the *Reich* to force it to pay reparations.[32]

The third Silesian uprising broke out on 3 May 1921. Its command, called the Supreme Council of the Insurrectionary Forces, was headed by Lieutenant Colonel Maciej Mielżyński (pseudonym: *Nowina-Doliwa*). The insurgent forces were divided into three groups: group North, group West and group South. They had medical and transport units at their disposal as well as the *gendarmerie*. About 60 000 people as well 2000 volunteers from outside Silesia joined the insurgent ranks.[33] The German forces, composed mostly of volunteer units from Germany, were commanded by General Karl Höfer. Like the Polish forces, the German troops were divided into three operational groups, *Nord, Mitte, Süd*/(North, Centre, South). They numbered about 30 000 men but were better trained and well supplied with arms and ammunition.

The insurgents, taking advantage of the element of surprise, had great successes in the first phase of the fighting. By 10 May they had captured the territories along the so-called Korfanty line, which corresponded to the French plans for the division of Upper Silesia. On 21 May the German forces started a determined counteroffensive. The fiercest fighting took place near St Anne's mountain, where the Germans tried to break through the insurgents' lines and to encroach upon the Upper Silesian industrial region. Although the Poles lost St Anne's mountain in fierce fighting, the Germans did not succeed in breaking through the front line at that place, nor did they succeed in breaking through at Zebowice/Zembowitz and Olesno.

From the beginning of June the fighting gradually abated. Polish–German negotiations were started and the InterAllied Commission began to bring its troops into the area involved in the fighting and to separate the two sides. The Polish side accepted a plan for the withdrawal of its forces from the plebiscite area on 11 June and the German side on 25 June. The last units were withdrawn on 5 July and the uprising came to an end.[34] Compared with previous uprisings, the third one was the longest, lasting about two months. It also occurred over a wider region. It was on the Polish side, better prepared and better organised, but in the last phase it was the intervention of the InterAllied Commission that saved the insurgents from defeat.

This third Silesian uprising exacerbated relations between Paris and London. During the first phase of a vehement discussion Britain wanted the uprising recognised as a rebellion against the law, which would have justified its immediate suppression and the severe punishment of its initiators. France, on the other hand held to the view that the uprising was an act of despair on the part of the Polish population in Upper Silesia which was threatened with the prospect of remaining under German rule. After frantic consultations at the highest level, accompanied by a vociferous press campaign, the scales of victory tipped in favour of Paris.

Various proposals for the delimitation of Upper Silesia were put forward during the negotiations which lasted from May until August 1921, the one unwavering element being that the industrial region should be accorded in its entirety either to Poland or to Germany. In the light of the arguments put forward and the efforts to resolve two contradictory concepts of a division of the region, it became increasingly clear that none of the great powers was taking into account the interests of national forces in Upper Silesia, and that they were only interested in which side would possess the industry of the region.[35]

In the middle of 1921 France's international position was visibly strengthened. The Germans tried to fulfil the reparation obligations imposed on them. The internal crisis was eased, and Paris recorded many significant successes in other areas (for example the establishment of the Little Entente, and the Turkish victories over the British–supported Greeks). In this situation France was able to press its plans for solving the Upper Silesian question, all the more so as in the international arena it held the trump card in its hand, namely, the Silesian uprising.

London realised the situation and was ready to make concessions. The first manifestation was the recall of its representative on the Inter Allied Commission, Colonel Harold F.P. Percival, and his replacement by an unassertive Foreign Office official, Sir Harold Stuart. Another manifestation of the changed attitude of London political circles towards the question of Upper Silesia was the sending of Scottish troops to the plebiscite area: these took a more neutral stand than the English forces.[36]

From 8 to 13 August 1921 the Supreme Council, with the participation of the Prime Ministers of France, Great Britain and Italy, discussed the question of establishing a final Polish–German frontier in Upper Silesia. The extremely stormy debates, during the course of which the western powers once again presented a whole list of well known arguments which in their opinion justified their respective theories on dividing Upper Silesia, ended with the transfer of the problem to the League of Nations.[37] So the final decision was again put off. The only real achievement of the August talks was that for the first time the possibility of dividing the industrial triangle was posed by a French expert, Louis Loucher. In the heated atmosphere of the

Supreme Council's debate the proposal left no impression, but it became the basis of the discussion at the League of Nations.

On 12 October 1921, after two month's debates, the Council of the League of Nations made a decision on the division of Upper Silesia, which was approved by the Conference of Ambassadors on 20 October and so was able to be put into force. Under the terms of the decision, Poland received an area of Upper Silesia covering 3214 sq km with about 900 000 people. This constituted 29 per cent of the plebiscite area with 46 per cent of its population and meant that Poland was allocated the most densely populated regions of Upper Silesia and the largest part of the industrial region. However, the area granted to Poland was inhabited by 260 000 Germans, while 532 000 Poles remained on German territory. As regards population, Poland received more than the percentage of Polish votes in the plebiscite, but as regards area, she received considerably less. This loss was compensated for by the value of the recovered territory. Out of 67 collieries Poland obtained 53, out of 15 zinc and lead mines she was granted ten, out of 14 steel works nine passed to Polish control, and out of 37 blast furnaces 27 were allocated to Poland. As a condition for the transfer of territory, the Conference of Ambassadors demanded that Poland and Germany conclude an agreement on the protection of national minorities and on the economic division of Upper Silesian industry.

The decision on such a division of Upper Silesia, which was undoubtedly a success for French policy, aroused great indignation in Berlin. The government of Chancellor Karl Wirth resigned in protest. Sharp statements against Poland and France were made in the *Reichstag*. It looked as though Germany would never agree of its own free will to these frontier changes.[38] The situation was appraised much more calmly in London. Great Britain relied on the clause which made the division of Upper Silesia dependent on the conclusion of a German–Polish agreement defining the legal norms that were to be in force in the whole plebiscite area for a 15 year transitional period.

On 23 November 1921 Polish–German talks opened at the League of Nations in Geneva. In accordance with the regulations adopted, the negotiations were conducted by 12 subcommissions each dealing with definite subjects and composed of Polish and German representatives in equal numbers. They held their meetings in various Upper Silesian towns: for example the group dealing with railways, monetary questions, the coal industry, trade unions and social insurance met in Katowice; the group concerned with water and electricity held its meetings in Zabrze. The two most important subcommissions, which were to establish legal norms guaranteeing the protection of national minorities and to define the powers of the Mixed Commission for Upper Silesia and the Upper Silesian

Arbitration Tribunal, held their meetings in Geneva. All disputes were settled, without the right of appeal, by the chairman of the debates on behalf of the League of Nations, the former Swiss President, Dr Felix Calonder.[39]

It was only after prolonged and stormy debates that a convention regulating the political, social and economic life of Upper Silesia for 15 years (the *Convention Germano–Polonaise rélative à la Haute Silésie*) was signed in Geneva on 15 May 1922. This extensive document containing 606 articles precisely defined the principles of Polish–German co-existence in Upper Silesia. It was divided into six parts:

- general provisions
- residence and citizenship
- protection of national minorities
- social and insurance questions
- economic questions
- the rules of the activity and competence of the Mixed Commission for Upper Silesia and the Upper Silesian Arbitration Tribunal.

The most important provisions of the Geneva Convention guaranteed full equality to all people living in the former plebiscite area. This applied to cultural and economic as well as political rights. The national minorities were given the right to use their mother tongue in primary and some secondary schools, and to set up social, cultural and sports organisations. In the economic sphere, the Convention curbed the state's right to expropriate, even with compensation, landed estates and businesses belonging to citizens of the other state.

The final part of the Geneva Convention provided for the setting up of a Mixed Commission for Upper Silesia, with its seat in Katowice. The Commission was given wide powers in the settlement of Polish–German disputes. It was composed of two representatives from Poland and two from Germany and a chairman to be appointed by the Council of the League of Nations.[40] The signing of the Geneva Convention and its ratification by Poland and Germany marked the implementation of the last element on which the realisation of the division of Upper Silesia depended. From 4 May until 14 June 1922, negotiations were held in Opole on the way in which General le Rond was to transfer the plebiscite area to the Polish and German authorities. In accordance with the agreement reached then, the withdrawal of Allied forces was completed between 18 June and 9 July and Polish and German offices started work.

On the last day of the withdrawal, demonstrations were held on both sides of the frontier; they abounded in speeches and statements of a nationalistic and *revanchiste* character. The attitude of both sides gave the impression that the division of Upper Silesia was a temporary solution which could not be maintained in the long run. It was clear that the solution satisfied neither the Poles nor the Germans. It was a result of disputes and differences of opinion among the great powers which were not inspired by a desire to divide the territory according to ethnic principles, unrealistic as this would have been, but by cold political calculations. Paris supported the return of the territory to Poland only because its interests coincided with the Upper Silesian Polish population's aspirations for national liberation.

The period of the uprisings and the plebiscite led to an aggravation of Polish–German relations and fanned vehement nationalistic propaganda on both sides of the frontier. As a result, Upper Silesia, along with Gdańsk and Pomerania, was to be a trouble spot in Polish-German relations throughout the twenty years between the two world wars.

Notes

1. Gravert-May,
2. Labuda, pp. 3–32.
3. Popiołek, p. 445
4. Weinstein, p. 29
5. Jedruszczak (1981), p. 13.
6. Przewłocki (1975), p. 10.
7. Text in *Akty i dokumenty* (1925), vol. II.
8. *Foreign Relations of the United States* (1943), vol. VI pp. 139–43.
9. *Conférence de la Paix 1919–20*, pp. 1217–27.
10. Szymiczek; Szklarska-Lohmanowa.
11. Kaeckenbeeck, pp. 12–14.
12. Krasuski, p. 52.
13. Przewłocki (1969), p. 78, Laubert.
14. Dabrowski, p. 10.
15. Jedruszczak (1958), p. 122.
16. Hörsing, p. 43.
17. Hawranek, p. 285.
18. Smogorzewski, pp. 341–4.
19. Jedruszczak (1981) p. 38.
20. Wambaugh, vol. II, pp. 232–3.
21. Laubert, pp. 48–9.
22. Hawranek, p. 291.
23. Szymiczek, p. 78.
24. Hawranek, p. 294.
25. Przewłocki (1973), p. 165.
26. Dabrowski, p. 34.
27. Przewłocki (1975), p. 32.
28. Wambaugh, vol. II, pp. 243–57; Hawranek, p. 298.
29. Hawranek, p. 298.
30. Frich, Table No. III.

31. Text of British–Italian proposal in Wambaugh, vol. II, pp. 243–57.
32. Höltje, pp. 29–33.
33. Mielżyński, p. 17; Ryżewski.
34. Wrzosek, p. 186.
35. Korczyk.
36. Przewłocki (1975), p. 41.
37. Korczyk, p. 216.
38. Kulak.
39. Société des Nations. Journal Officiel, 1922. vol. III, pp. 53–5, 117.
40. Kaeckenbeeck, pp. 18–25; Göppert, pp. 171–97.

Select Bibliography

Bibliographical Note

The problem of Upper Silesia, in the years 1918–1922, is well covered by scholarship and has given rise to an extensive bibliography (see E. Wyglenda; H. Rister, especially vol. 1, pp. 307–331). The archival records on the Upper Silesian plebiscite, the division of territory, and the Silesian uprisings are located in the Record Office of New Documents in Warsaw, and the Provincial State Record Offices in Katowice, Wrocław and Opole, respectively.

Interesting collections of documents are deposited in the Silesian Institute in Opole, and the Silesian Research Institute in Katowice, which coordinate research studies on Silesia. The most important synthetic works dealing with the general history of Upper Silesia are the books of Hawranek, and of Popiołek, Historia Śląska. They include detailed information on the population circumstances of Polish and German citizens residing in Upper Silesia, especially at the end of the nineteenth and the very beginning of the twentieth centuries. The condition and levels of economic and cultural life are also included.

The outstanding book in terms of special issues is Zieliński, which shows the mechanism of Polish and German propaganda in the pre-plebiscite period. Another publication is by Höfer, who was one of the most important participants in the developments.

The military side of the Silesian uprisings is described by Jedruszczak, Powstania śląskie, and by Ryzewski, Trzecie powstanie. The activities of German military units have been written up by Biały and Szymański. The general policy of the Polish government and society vis-à-vis the problems of Upper Silesia is described by Jedruszczak, Polityka polska.

The policy of the European powers towards the state status of Upper Silesia is presented in Przewłocki's Francuskie zainteresowanie, describing the French point of view. Other works of the same author are on the general policy of the great powers, Mocarstwa zachodnie, and on the InterAllied Commission, Miedzysojusznicza Komisja.

British policy is well described by Cygański. Another author dealing this subject is Libal–Bertram.

The division of Upper Silesia, the plebiscite and the Upper Silesian Convention are very well documented. The legal aspect is presented by two authors, Kaeckenbeeck and Wambaugh. Additionally, from the Polish point of view, the plebiscite and convention are discussed by Smogorzewski. His book was generally addressed to international public opinion in western Europe.

Akty i dokumenty dotyczace sprawy granic Polski na konferencji pokojowej w Paryzu 1918–1919 (1925), vol II. Paris.

Biały F. (1976), *Niemieckie ochotnicze formacje zbrojne na Slasku*, Katowice.

Conférence de la Paix 1919–20, Recueil des actes de la Conférence, Partie IV, Commission de la Conférence (1928), Paris.

Cygański, M. (1976), *Polityka Wielkiej Brytanii w sprawie Górnego Ślaska w latach 1919–20*, Opole.

Cygański, M. (1977), *Poltiyka interwencyjna Wielkiej Brytanii w sprawie Górnego Ślaska w 1921 i poczatkach 1922*, Opole.

Dabrowski, W. (1923), *Górny Ślask w walce o zjednoczenie z Polska (źródła i dokumenty z lat 1918–22)*, Katowice.

Foreign Relations of the United States, The Paris Peace Conference 1919 (1943), vol. VI, Washington.

Frich, K. (1921), *Polskość Górnego Ślaska według urzedowych źródeł pruskich a wyniki plebiscytu*, Warsaw.

Gravert–May, G. (1971), *Das staatsrechtliche Verhältnis Schlesien zu Polen, Böhmen und dem Reich während des Mittelalters*, Aalen.

Göppert, H. (1925), *Das deutsch–polnische Abkommen über Oberschlesien vom 15 mai 1922 und seine Grundlagen. 'Oberschlesien und der Genfer Schiedsspruch'.*

Hawranek, F. (ed.) (1984), *Dzieje Górnego Ślaska w latach 1816-1947*, Opole.

Höfer, General K. (1938), *Oberschlesien in der Aufstandszeit 1918–21, Erinnerungen und Dokumente*, Berlin.

Höltje, Ch. (1958), *Die Weimarer Republik und das Ostlocarno-Problem 1919–34. Revision oder Garantie der deutschen Ostgrenze von 1919*, Würzburg.

Hörsing, O. (1938), *Oberschlesien in der Aufstandszeit 1918–21*, Berlin.

Jedruszczak, T. (1981), *Powstania ślaskie 1919–21*, Katowice.

Jedruszczak, T. (1958), *Polityka Polska w sprawie Górnego Ślaska 1918–22*, Warsaw.

Kaeckenbeeck, G. (1942), *The International Experiment of Upper Silesia. A study in the working of the Upper Silesian Settlement 1922–37*, New York.

Korczyk, H. (1962), 'Sprawa górnoślaska w polityce mocarstw sprzymierzonych w drugiej połowie, 1921 r. (VII 1921-X 1921)', in Popiołek, K. (ed.), *Studia i materiały z dziejów Ślaska*, vol. V, Wrocław.

Krasuski, J. (1985), *Między wojnami. Polityka zagraniczna II Rzeczypospolitej*, Warsaw.

Kulak, T. (1971), 'Parlament Rzeszy niemieckiej wobec decyzji Rady Ambasadorów i postanowień Konwencji Górnoślaskiej', in Chlebowczyk, J. and Popiołek, K. (eds), *Studia i materiały z dziejów Ślaska*, vol. XI, Wrocław.

Labuda, G. (1985), 'Die polnische Westgrenze in der tausendjährigen Geschichte des Staates und Volkes', in *Polnische Weststudien*, IV.

Laubert, M. (1938), *Die Oberschlesische Volksbewegung. Beitrag zur Tätigkeit der Vereinigung Heimattreuer Oberschlesier 1918–21*, Breslau.

Libal-Bertram, G. (1972), *Aspekte der britischen Deutschlandspolitik 1919–22*, Göttingen.

Mielżyński, M. (1931), 'Wspomnienia i przyczynki do historii III powstania górnoślaskiego, Mikołów.

Popiołek, K. (1984), *Historia Górnego Ślaska od pradziejów do roku 1945*, Katowice.

Przewłocki, J. (1973), *Francuskie zainteresowanie Górnym Ślaskiem*, Katowice.

Przewłocki, J. (1970), *Miedzysojusznicza Komisja rzadzaca i plebiscytowsa na Górnym Slasku w latach 1920–22*, Wrocław.

Przewłocki, J. (1975), *Mocarstwa zachodnioeuropejskie wobec problemów Górnego Ślaska w latach 1918–33*, Katowice.

Przewłocki, J. (1969), *Pierwsze powstanie ślaskie*, Katowice.

Rister, H. (1987), *Schlesische Bibliographie 1971–80 mit Nachträgen aus früheren Jahren*, 3 vols, Marburg.

Ryżewski, W. (1967), 'Organizacja i siła bojowa wojsk powstańczych w III powstaniu ślaskim', in *Zaranie Ślaskie*, no. 3.

Ryżewski, W. (1977), *Trzecie powstanie ślaskie 1921*, Warsaw.

Smogorzewski, K. (1932), 'Le plébiscite et la partage de la Haute Silésie', in *La Silésie Polonaise*, Paris.

Sociéte des Nations (1922), *Journal Officiel*, vol. III.

Szklarska–Lohmanowa, A. (1967), *Polsko-czechosłowakie stosunki dyplomatyczne w latach 1918–25*, Wrocław.

Szymański, Z. (1969), *Niemieckie korpusy ochotnicze na Górnym Ślasku 1918–22*, Opole.

Szymiczek, F. (1938), *Walka o Ślask Cieszyński w latach 1914–20*, Katowice.

Wambaugh, S. (1933), *Plebiscites since the World War*, 2 vols, Washington.

Weinstein, J. (1931), *Oberschlesien, das Land der Gegensàtze*, Paris.

Wrzosek, M. (1969), *Trzecie powstanie ślaskie*, Warsaw.

Wyglenda, E. (1981), *Górny Ślask 1918–22, Bibliografia*, Opole.

Zieliński, W. (1972), *Polska i niemiecka propaganda plebiscytowa na Górnym Ślasku*, Warsaw.

Map 10.1 Upper Silesia after delimitation 1921
Source: R. Machray, *The Problem of Upper Silesia*, London 1945.

11 According to the Principle of Reciprocity: the Minorities in Yugoslav–Austrian Relations 1918–1938

ARNOLD SUPPAN

The new states, the 'republic of Austria' and the 'kingdom of Serbs, Croats and Slovenes' (from 1929 onwards the 'kingdom of Yugoslavia'), that were created out of lands of the Habsburg empire after its disintegration at the end of October and the beginning of November 1918, should ideally have sought and brought about continued collaboration, even under the new, changed conditions, as a result of the centuries old political, economic, social and cultural relations of their constituent peoples. In fact their relations between 1918 and 1938 were characterised by confrontation rather than cooperation, for many reasons.

There were conflicts over the determination of borders in southern Carinthia and southern Styria between 1918 and 1920, which were waged in the political–diplomatic and the military spheres. These ended with the determination of the border near Radkersburg (Radgona) in August 1920 and with the Carinthian plebiscite on 10 October 1920 (see Map 11.1). Conflicts existed also over the confiscation of property (land, houses, enterprises) belonging to Austrian citizens and societies in Yugoslavia or belonging to Yugoslav citizens in Austria between 1918 and 1923. A solution was only provided by the sequestration agreement between the heads of government, Pašić and Seipel, on 24 February 1923. There was the question of tolerance of Croatian émigrés in Austria and of Austrian National Socialist émigrés in Yugoslavia at the beginning of the 1930s; there was police cooperation only against the communists who had been pushed underground in Yugoslavia in 1921. Finally there was competition in the international arena of alliances. Whereas Yugoslavia committed itself to preserving the *status quo* after 1919 through alliances with Czechoslovakia, Romania and France, in initially non-aligned Austria the question of '*Anschluss*' was discussed again and again (particularly in 1921, 1925 and 1931). From 1932 on a process of *rapprochement* with Italy and Hungary took place (Rome Protocols in 1934), and with the July agreement of 1936 *rapprochement* with National Socialist Germany began.[1]

Apart from these and other disturbing factors in bilateral relations between Yugoslavia and Austria (mention must be made of bomb attacks on international express trains on the line from Salzburg to Belgrade and of the assassination of King Alexander in Marseilles in 1934) discussion on the minorities' issue played a dominant role not only in the policies of both state Chancelleries throughout these 20 years, but also on the regional level in Carinthia, Slovenia and Styria. The main issues throughout were clearly the conflicts over the situation of the Slovenes in southern Carinthia, followed by the problems of the Germans in southern Styria and the Gottschee. In the 1920s the fate of the Germans in the Vojvodina aroused the interest of the government in Vienna, although Germany increasingly assumed the function of a protecting power after its entry into the League of Nations. The situation of the Croats in the Burgenland hardly stood in the limelight of bilateral politics, a fact for which the calm development of the Burgenland as well as a lack of interest on the part of political circles in Zagreb can be held responsible.

Statistics, Positions and Rights

According to the Austrian and Hungarian censuses of 1910, when evaluations had been made according to categories based on the colloquial or mother tongue, the determinations of borders in 1919–20 created the following national minorities:

- 577 000 German speakers in Yugoslavia, particularly in Slovenia (southern Styria, Miesstal, Gottschee, Ljubljana/Laibach, Prekmurje), in Croatia and Slavonia (with Medjimurje and Syrmia), in the Vojvodina (Banat, Batschka, Baranja) and in Serbia, Bosnia and Dalmatia
- 118 500 Slovene and Croat speakers in Austria, including 74 200 Slovene speakers in southern Carinthia, Styria and Vienna; 44 300 Croat speakers in the Burgenland, Vienna and Lower Austria.

Of course, these figures had changed by 1920. Although the losses of the war had largely been compensated for by a surplus of births,

Table 11.1: German speakers in Yugoslavia and Slovene and Croat speakers in Austria

Territory	Austrian or Hungarian census of 1910	Yugoslav census of 1921 Austrian census of 1923	Yugoslav census of 1931 Austrian census of 1934
German speakers in:			
Yugoslavia	577 000	505 500	500 000
Slovenia	106 000	41 500	29 000
Croatia–Slavonia (including Syrmia)	134 000	124 000	129 000
Vojvodina	312 000	316 500	311 500
Serbia, Bosnia, Dalmatia (including Belgrade)	25 000	23 500	30 500 (including Zemun/Semlin and Pančevo/ Pantschowa)
Slovene and Croat speakers in:			
Austria	118 500	(no figure)	67 700
Slovene speakers in Carinthia	66 500	34 600	25 000
Croat speakers in the Burgenland	43 600	41 700	40 000
Slovene speakers in Styria	5 700	(no figure)	1 000
Slovene and Croat speakers in Vienna, Upper and Lower Austria, Salzburg, Tyrol and Vorarlberg	2 700	1 100	1 700[2]

the political changes since 1918 had led to migrations of the population, affecting not least the new national minorities in border regions:

- the politically forced exodus of many public sector employees (civil servants, teachers, railway employees, professional soldiers);
- exodus to the national state (after opting for citizenship);
- emigration overseas.

Moreover, on the occasion of the censuses in the new national states, administrative and social pressure was increased on people to declare their loyalty to the majority population, in other words, to the new nation of the state. The numerical changes between the censuses of 1910 and the Yugoslav ones of 1921 (see Map 11.2) and 1931, on the one hand, and the Austrian ones of 1923 (see Map 11.3) and 1934 on the other, document the extent of the migratory and assimilatory processes that were either voluntary or the products of force (see Table 11.1 above).

These census statistics already demonstrate the problem areas of the conflict over national minorities between Yugoslavia and Austria: southern Carinthia with its Slovene speaking minority and southern Styria with its German speaking minority. Since both minorities settled in new border areas, all economic, social and cultural questions were aggravated on national and political grounds up to the point of accusations of irredentism and revisionism.

In particular the economic and social positions of the four main minority groups – 'Danube Swabians' and southern Styrians in Yugoslavia, Carinthian Slovenes and Burgenland Croats – played a major role in bilateral minority policy. There were approximately 400 000 'Danube Swabians' settled relatively compactly in the Vojvodina, eastern Slavonia and Syrmia who could draw strength from membership of a prosperous farming class (only 36.6 per cent of the farms were less than ten hectares) along with a well trained stratum of craftsmen, whereas the professions of the intelligentsia were chiefly confined to doctors, chemists, priests and teachers. Despite there being a strong cooperative movement with German entrepreneurs in the agricultural sector, and consumer goods industry, the number of German industrial workers remained limited, and the percentage of municipal officials and civil servants was infinitesimally small. As the old upper and middle class, the southern Styria Germans were strongly represented in the urban middle class with houses and landed property, in many industrial companies and in the professions. However, their position was worse in the agricultural sector for while the inhabitants of the Abstaller Feld were able to live from agriculture and forestry, the Gottschee farmers in the south of Slovenia were not. In Slovenia and Slavonia the Germans were still represented among the big landowners, but they had suffered from several land reforms.

In comparison with the southern Styrians and Danube Swabians the Carinthian Slovenes and Burgenland Croats were economically and socially much worse off, having chiefly small holdings (with exceptions being Heideboden in the north east of the Burgenland and the Völkermarkt judicial district). There was an already large number of industrial workers and agricultural labourers, led intellectually by the Catholic priests and some teachers. The professions were only poorly developed and there were only isolated representatives in the stratum of employees and civil servants. Representatives from the big landowning or industrial classes were not found either among the Carinthian Slovenes or among the Burgenland Croats. Of course, these fundamental differences as regards socio-economic position between the Germans in Yugoslavia and the southern Slavs in Austria influenced national as well as bilateral minority policy, affecting the utilisation of minority rights, the school system and even political participation.[3]

As the Germans in Yugoslavia and a section of the southern Slavs in Austria (the Croats completely, the Slovenes to a lesser extent) had been denied the right of self-determination, the peace conference in Saint-Germain – on the one hand in the peace treaty with Austria, on the other, in the minorities' treaty with the kingdom of Serbs, Croats and Slovenes – had conceded articles protecting their minority interests, admittedly though without adding a reciprocity clause as in the Upper Silesia agreement of 1922. However, these minorities received only rights as individual members of a minority, and were granted no group rights and hence no recognition as juridical persons. Nevertheless, Yugoslavia and Austria undertook:

- to guarantee the complete protection of their lives and their liberty;
- to guarantee free private and public religious observance;
- to acknowledge the right to acquire citizenship and to opt for a particular citizenship;
- to practise equality in safeguarding civil and political rights;
- to practise equality in the admission to public services, offices and honorary posts;
- to practise equality when issuing licences for different professions and trades;
- to acknowledge the right of every citizen to use 'any language' freely;
- to introduce fitting measures facilitating the oral and written use of minority languages in court;
- to acknowledge the right of minorities to found, run and control private institutions in the fields of education and charity;
- to build state primary schools teaching in a minority language in 'towns and districts where a relatively substantial number' of citizens speaking a minority language lived;
- to earmark for the minorities a suitable percentage of the sums paid out from the public budgets for education, religion or welfare.

The obligations of Austria and Yugoslavia towards their minorities were the same as regards their content, but different in terms of international law. Under her peace treaty Austria was responsible to all the signatory powers, including Yugoslavia. The Yugoslav Minority Treaty, on the other hand, had not been presented to Austria of signature, so Vienna could not intervene in the case of violations of the treaty by Belgrade. Only the German minority itself could do this through the Council of the League of Nations, a possibility that was also open to the Croatian and Slovene minority in Austria.[4]

From the very beginning legislation and legal practice in both states tended to interpret and handle the articles for the protection of minorities restrictively. As early as 1919 an agricultural reform was introduced in Yugoslavia, which was aimed at the big landowners of German, Magyar and Turkish background in particular. Still more unjust was the fact that members of the minorities, with the exception of Russian immigrants to Yugoslavia were not allowed to vote in the first parliamentary election in 1920. The most serious measures, however, resulted in the dismissals of German civil servants, judges, notaries, professors, teachers, officers, railway and postal employees in Slovenia, against which the Foreign Ministry in Vienna and the Styrian diet protested repeatedly but in vain. Extensive confiscations of the property of 'foreign' societies, and their dissolution or sequestration, were just as little in keeping with the Minorities Treaty. The most heated conflict took place over the *Deutsches Haus* in Celje (Cilli), where a compromise solution was only reached in 1930, after a southern Styrian lawyer had filed a suit with the Council of the League of Nations and Germany had demonstrated support. In the early years the Republic of Austria took revenge by freezing Yugoslav bank accounts and confiscating property, albeit on a much smaller scale since many more Austrians had property and other investments in Yugoslavia than Yugoslavs in Austria.

However, in 1921 when the Austrian ministerial bureaucracy discussed the implementation of the new articles for the protection of minorities, they regarded many provisions as already fulfilled by the constitutional laws of 1867. The ones concerning the use of language in court and the establishment of private schools – soon to be a controversial subject in southern Carinthia – provide an example. They did not want to accept the idea of a 'relatively substantial proportion' of citizens speaking foreign languages as long as there were no exact statistical data to control their actions. So the most positive measures in Yugoslavia and Austria remained the continuing licensing of political societies: the *Schwäbisch–Deutscher Kulturbund* (Swabian–German Cultural Union) in Novi Sad (Neusatz) in

1920; the *Politično in gospodarsko društvo za Slovence na Koroškem* (Political and Economic Society for Slovenes in Carinthia) in Klagenfurt (Celovec) in 1921; the *Politischer und wirtschaftlicher Verein der Deutschen in Slowenien* (Political and Economic Association of Germans in Slovenia), licensed with the same statutes in Maribor (Marburg) in 1922; and the *Hrvatska stranka* (Croatian Party) in the Burgenland, which did not have any success with its own ethnic group. In association with these organisations developed the newspapers *Deutsches Volksblatt* in Novi Sad; *Koroški Slovenec* in Vienna (*sic!*); *Marburger Zeitung* and *Hrvatske Novine*, also published in Vienna.[5]

Schools, Societies and Cultural Autonomy

While there were problems over a whole series of property issues in the 1920s it was disagreements over schooling for the minorities that caused the greatest friction in bilateral relations. The major focus was on the question of continuation of the *utraquist* (bilingual) schools; the prevention of the establishment of Slovene private schools in southern Carinthia; the dissolution of all German private schools in southern Styria; and the restriction of German secondary schools in the Vojvodina. On 22 January 1922 the *Slovensko šolsko društvo v Celovcu* (Slovene School Association) in Klagenfurt addressed a petition to the General Secretariat of the League of Nations. The closure of two Slovene private schools in St Ruprecht near Völkermarkt (Št Rupert pri Velikovcu) and in St Jakob in the Rosental (Št Jakob v Rožu) violated article 67 of the Treaty of Saint-Germain. Moreover, the school system for the Carinthian Slovenes had been governed since the times of the Austro–Hungarian empire in a way *'qui est sans pareille dans tout le monde civilisé'* ('which has no equal in the civilised world'). However complaints to the School Inspectorate for Carinthia, to the social democrat head of the provincial government, Gröger, and to the Christian Social Federal Chancellor, Dr Mayr, had remained without effect.

In accordance with the procedure of the League of Nations the petition was conveyed to the Austrian government for comment. The Department for International Law at the *Ballhausplatz* acknowledged the complaint as 'undoubtedly justified', as 'the Carinthian provincial government really does not permit the establishment of Slovene private schools in Carinthia'. However, 'on the other hand, it is known to the Federal Foreign Ministry that the Slovene provincial government has also closed all German private schools in Slovenia'. The Ministry of Education in Vienna, though, was not prepared to admit flaws in the minority school system for the Carinthian

Slovenes, and referred to the willingness of the School Inspectorate for Carinthia to open even public Slovene primary schools in Völkermarkt and St Jakob and defended the institution of the *utraquist* school, claiming it met the wishes of the Carinthian Slovenes who were, economically, 'absolutely dependent on constant and close contact with the Germans in Carinthia and with the rest of the German speaking area of Austria'.[6]

There was of course no adequate answer to the Slovene School Association's reproach that the establishment of Slovene private schools was being hindered and the investigation committee of three, set up by the League of Nations, demanded further information from Vienna. When no such information was forthcoming, despite repeated demands, the Norwegian Director of the Minorities Commission, Colban, personally enquired at the *Ballhausplatz*, but in March 1923 received the information that both heads of government had meanwhile discussed the issue, so the petition was laid aside. During the negotiations between the Prime Minister, Pašić, and the Federal Chancellor, Seipel, and both Foreign Ministers, Ninčić and Grünberger, in Belgrade on 24 February 1923 the minorities' question really had been discussed. However, when the Yugoslav Foreign Minister had drawn attention to 'how much worse the Slovenes in Carinthia were treated regarding schools than the Germans in the Kingdom of Serbs, Croats and Slovenes', the Austrian Foreign Minister presented 'sufficient counter material' and 'justified complaints about the behaviour of many Slovene leaders and organisations'. When the Austrian side stressed that all the German schools in Yugoslavia had been closed and that Austria could hence 'hardly give permission for the founding of Slovene private schools in Carinthia', the Yugoslav hosts contented themselves with the mutual assurance to respect the rights of the minorities in the field of culture. The principle of reciprocity had prevailed.[7]

In his report to the *Skupština* (the Belgrade parliament) Ninčić, concerned about the Slovene opposition, let himself be carried away and made a comparison that was by no means objective. 'Whereas 37 primary schools with 81 classes and 3340 pupils and two German grammar schools exist for 40 000 Germans in Slovenia and Prekmurje, 70 000 Slovenes in Austria cannot obtain a single school'. The Carinthian provincial government and the panGerman *Freie Stimmen* in Klagenfurt countered by mentioning the circumstances surrounding the German school system in Slovenia. In the Miesstal, ceded in 1919, all 11 primary schools had been transformed 'into purely Slovene ones against the will of the parents'; in the German communities in the Abstall area there was no longer a single German primary school; and both former German grammar schools in Maribor and Ljubljana were being turned Slovene 'from the bottom up' (that is starting with the first form) every year. Moreover, Ninčić quoted figures for the Carinthian Slovenes that dated from 1910, but for the Germans in Slovenia those of 1921.[8]

The *Ballhausplatz* did not consider a 'public, polemical discussion between government and government as befitting the existing good relations between Vienna and Belgrade' and made do with detailed information conveyed to Foreign Minister Ninčić by the Austrian *chargé d'affaires*, Hoffinger: the significant drop in the number of those who professed to be Slovenes in Carinthia had an analogy in the decrease in the number of Germans in Slovenia. 'Both here and there those who have changed their ethnic allegiance since 1910 presumably wished to express explicitly that they consider themselves loyal citizens of the new national homeland.' For 50 years the primary schools of the mixed language parts of Carinthia had possessed in the *utraquist* schools an institution guaranteeing the learning of the German and Slovene languages in the same measure.

> The fact that this school form meets the political and economic needs of a small ethnic minority in a predominantly German country better than a purely Slovene school with 'German' as a compulsory subject, is clear.

On the basis of the election results in 1921 it was also possible to establish that among the Carinthian Slovenes there was only a minority of about 15 000 persons 'whose political aims stood in seemingly irreconcilable opposition to Austrian state interests and the idea of the Austrian state' and who, supported 'by influential circles across the border', were fanning irredentism in southern Carinthia.[9]

When Foreign Minister Ninčić came to Vienna in July 1924 on a return visit, four of the 14 items on the agenda of his host, Minister Grünberger, were concerned with the problem of minorities and irredentists in southern Carinthia. As far as the school conditions for the Carinthian Slovenes were concerned, Grünberger wanted to refer to 85 *utraquist* schools which began with reading lessons in Slovene and to two Slovene public primary schools in St Jakob and Zell (Sele). However, after the fall of the empire and the plebiscite a large proportion of Slovene teachers had emigrated to the kingdom of Serbs, Croats and Slovenes 'for national reasons and to gain financial advantages', and the Carinthian provincial government had denied reemployment to teachers 'who had taken high Yugoslav positions during the campaign for the plebiscite'. Grünberger's detailed preparation proved to be a piece of work requiring much diligence. During the talks between the two Ministers, in the presence of the envoys Pogatscher and Milojević, Ninčić refrained from making any allusion to the *gravamina* of the Slovenes in Carinthia, obviously quite intentionally. On the other hand, he spontaneously mentioned the

attitude of Germans in Yugoslavia and criticised the German parliamentarians sharply, particularly deputy Kraft, who had joined the
Democratic Party opposition in a situation especially favourable for
the Germans, when Pašić's government had needed the votes of the
Germans and Turks to create a majority. So feelings against the
Germans in government circles were 'furieuses'. However, in accordance with his plan, Grünberger referred to the dissolution of over 200
German cultural and social associations in Slovenia, to the abolition
of the majority of German schools in Slovenia, to the analysis of the
names of schoolchildren admitted to the few German parallel classes
in state schools, to violent disruptions of German events in Southern
Styria and to the dissolution of the Swabian–German Cultural Union,
ostensibly as a reprisal for the suppression of the Carinthian
Slovenes.[10]

As a matter of fact the German school system in Yugoslavia had
developed along completely different lines. In what had been
southern Hungary (now the Vojvodina), the Hungarian language,
which had been dominant since 1907, was replaced by German in the
primary schools of predominantly German villages and in the
grammar schools of predominantly German towns. By contrast in
Slovenia uncompromising measures were taken to make the public
primary and secondary schools (about 60 schools) Slovene and to
abolish the German private school system (34 schools in all). This
different treatment was justified by the different assessment of the
loyalty of the two German ethnic groups. 'Whereas there could still
be talk of an irredentist danger near the Austrian border, this is
completely out of the question on the Hungarian border.' This
differentiation changed from 1922 onwards, when the new Minister
of Education, Pribićević, a Serb from Croatia and an enthusiast for an
integral Yugoslavism, nationalised all private educational institutions belonging to the minorities (not just the German ones in other
words), confiscating their property at the same time, and only let
'minorities' departments' be formed in the four junior classes of the
now state owned primary schools, if there were enough (30) children.
According to a decree by the same minister enrolment in these
minorities' departments had to be made on the basis of the ethnic
allegiance established by the school authorities in analyses of names;
children with Slav surnames (even if only the name of one grand-
parent) were enrolled in separate Serbian, Croatian or Slovene
classes and so did not learn one word in their native language at
school![11]

There were several protests made in the Austrian parliament
'concerning the suppression and persecution of the German minorities in the kingdom of Serbs, Croats and Slovenes', particularly in
southern Styria. However at the beginning of 1924 both the Political–

Economic Association in Maribor and the Swabian–German Cultural Union in Novi Sad warned against intervention by the Austrian government, since they feared a further deterioration of the situation would be the only result. Even after the temporary dissolution of the Cultural Union as a result of the opposition stance of the German Deputies' Club (eight members), in 1924 the Club Chairman Kraft expressly requested the government in Vienna not to adopt stricter administrative practices towards, or even take any retaliatory measures against, the Carinthian Slovenes. On the other hand, Pribićević did not shrink from referring to 'the bad treatment of the Carinthian Slovenes' as the reason for the dissolution, which was, of course, a pretext.[12]

After successful parliamentary elections in February 1925 Pribićević decreed the closure of the remaining fifth to eighth forms of the German secondary schools in Novi Vrbas (Neu-Werbas) and Vršac (Werschetz) and of the first to fourth forms of the German secondary schools in Pančevo and Novi Sad. His Ministry declared that

> this decree has been issued as an administrative measure against the Austrian federal government which is said not to have observed the provisions of the treaty for the protection of minorities concerning the Slav school system in Austria, particularly in Carinthia.

The German *Skupština* deputies suspected that the Foreign Minister Ninčić was also behind this reprisal, and the *Ballhausplatz* considered not only an appeal to the League of Nations, but also 'reprisals against the Carinthian Slovenes'. But the Austrian *chargé d'affaires* in Belgrade, Hoffinger, immediately raised 'serious misgivings':

> The thought that the ethnic minorities in themselves should become the objects of reprisals because of the treatment of other minorities should be prevented from gaining ground by the German states (*sic!*), which have to protect so many minorities against malevolent governments, as the tables would immediately be turned and all foreign governments would outlaw the German minorities 'as a reprisal'.

Moreover, retaliatory measures could hardly be efficiently developed because of the small number of Slovene schools in Austria.[13] The Austrian negotiator-in-chief for trade agreements, departmental head Professor Schüller, added an even more stringent argument to the discussion within the government. The current negotiations over a trade agreement with the Belgrade government were in danger, and with them the export of Austrian industrial products and the entire trading situation of Austria. For: 'Yugoslavia is today the most important market for Austrian industry' and Austria could not afford to lose the best market 'we have today'. 'As a result, any worsening of our relations with Yugoslavia for formal reasons or out of consideration for public opinion will have to be paid for by us financially.'[14]

The warning by an eminent foreign trade expert was taken seriously by Chancellor Ramek, and he made only a diplomatically cautious declaration to parliament. So the two weeks' discussion in the government and parliament had produced a clear sequence of priorities in Austrian foreign policy: foreign trade policy had precedence over minorities' policy, even if the latter should be pressed by public opinion! Pribićević immediately reacted to this policy in an active fashion.

He justified the closure of some German parallel classes in Yugoslav secondary schools on the grounds of the growing interest on the part of the German population in lessons in the national language, Serbo–Croat, 'so that the young Germans this way (and all the earlier) acquire that knowledge of the national language which is necessary for administrative and economic reasons. . .'. In addition Pribićević now tried to draw a positive picture of the German minorities' school system in the kingdom of Serbs, Croats and Slovenes. In Yugoslavia there were 200 German primary schools with 623 departments; in additional there were five German secondary and municipal schools with 53 departments. The Germans also possessed 49 nursery schools with 62 nursery school teachers. However, the remark that only 79 German teachers were appointed to the German schools shows that it was not 'German schools' that were meant, but only minorities' departments in state schools in which German was also taught. It was not least these figures that suggested there was a glaring lack of German speaking teachers.

By contrast, Pribićević criticised the minorities' schooling system in Austria since the 'Croats in the Burgenland and the Carinthian Slovenes did not have a single primary school with the mother tongue as the teaching language'. This reproach was incorrect as far as the majority of the predominantly Croat speaking communities in the Burgenland in the middle of the 1920s was concerned, but was true of the senior primary school classes in Carinthia in which Slovene was only taught as a school subject. Pribićević's criticism was aimed particularly at the *utraquist* school system in southern Carinthia and he threatened to transfer this system to the Germans in Yugoslavia so that they too could learn their national language perfectly.[15]

In his statement Minister Pribićević had, above all, replied to a parliamentary declaration made by Chancellor Ramek, himself of Sudeten German origin, who had defended the minorities' school system in Carinthia on 3 March 1925:

It is understandable that it is of the greatest importance for the Slovene children who will become citizens of an almost purely German state and country [sic!], also from the viewpoint of the economic advantages derived, that they learn German at school more perfectly than would be possible by learning the German language as a compulsory subject in a purely Slovene school. This advantage of the *utraquist* school has also become clear to the Slovene population. Only an 'infinitely small fraction' of Slovenes was of a different opinion, the protagonists of southern Slav agitation in the struggle surrounding the plebiscite, who were now trying 'to cultivate a kind of irredentism among our Slovene population that is loyal to Carinthia'; but Austria could not confide the education of its Slovene children to such persons . . .[16]

With these statements, tacit agreement in bilateral relations had been temporarily reached: minorities' issues were now increasingly treated as internal questions.

However, this did not put an end to the discussions, as the year long deliberations on 'Slovene cultural autonomy in Carinthia' were soon to show. Discussions were opened in 1926 on the initiative of the Carinthian social democrats and led to a joint bill on the part of social democrats, the Christian social group, the *Landbund* (Land League) and the *Grossdeutsche* (panGermans) in the Carinthian diet a year later. Following the example of the 'cultural autonomy of the ethnic minorities in Estonia', a 'Slovene National Community' was to be formed as a public corporation consisting of a 'People's Council' elected by all people registered in a 'Slovene Ethnic Book' and the 'Slovene school communities'. The Slovene People's Council was to be allowed to collect community fees, establish cultural and social institutions and found schools. The model conceived for the relatively wealthy German minority in Estonia would also have contained possibilities for an autonomous development for the Carinthian Slovenes. However, the Slovene negotiators were of the opinion – and actual events corroborated this – that the Slovene farmers and workers could only afford such 'cultural autonomy' in five or six communities. So they demanded that all the *utraquist* schools in southern Carinthia be handed over to the Slovene National Community, which the German Carinthians only wanted to allow in school communities with more than two-thirds Slovene parents of school children. Such a concession to the Slovene National Community would again have turned out to the disadvantage of the Slovenes because of the experiences with the census of 1923.[17]

The Carinthian discussion surrounding 'cultural autonomy' also affected bilateral minorities' policy, since the model would have suited the southern Styrian Germans and the majority of the Danube Swabians. From the start Carinthian politicians had had such reciprocity in mind, both Germans and Slovenes. When the social democrat member of the Carinthian provincial government, Zeinitzer, thought that 'cultural autonomy' could be a precursor for German minorities in other states, the Slovene member of the diet, Petek, simply pointed to the social and economic differences. The Germans in Yugoslavia could afford such 'cultural autonomy' as they were city dwellers, big landowners and factory owners. As matters stood the Political and Economic Association of the Germans in Slovenia was very interested in the Carinthian project, but the Carinthian head of government, Schumy, did not wish for a direct fusion of bilateral minority problems, and nor did Petek.

Nor were the government agencies in Vienna of one mind. Whereas the *Ballhausplatz* expected favourable results from this policy for relations with other countries and their German minorities, officials of the Ministry of the Interior and the Ministry of Education warning against the formation of a 'state within a state' which might become the starting point for irredentism. At best they could only agree to school autonomy for the Carinthian Slovenes 'if Yugoslavia simultaneously issued a similar decree in the form of a state treaty and on the basis of a reciprocal relationship'. The Minister for Education, Schmitz, did not share the misgivings of his civil servants to this extent, but Chancellor Seipel wanted to wait for reactions from Belgrade.[18]

Yet government circles in Belgrade were remarkably reticent, something to which growing tensions in the structure of the government since 1926 and the deterioration of the foreign policy situation with Italy certainly contributed. Besides, as had been the case in earlier years, Belgrade gave Ljubljana precedence over Carinthia. Nevertheless, Slovene public opinion considered the intended cultural autonomy for the Carinthian Slovenes as a 'veritable Greek gift'. The introduction of a voluntary national register would reduce artificially the numbers of the Slovene minority in order to confirm the result of the 1920 plebiscite. Apart from that there should be negotiations not about the numerically 'insignificant' German minority in Slovenia (*sic!*), but about the Germans in the Vojvodina, whose situation was 'today much, much more satisfactory' than that of the Slovenes in Carinthia. So the Carinthian cultural autonomy project did not particularly please either the Slovene or the Serbian politicians because a positive settlement would, of course, have had to produce positive results for the Germans in Yugoslavia.

It was only the *Slovenec* in Ljubljana, the newspaper of the Slovene People's Party that tried to make the principle of reciprocity work both ways:

In Yugoslavia we have incomparably more Germans than there are

Carinthian Slovenes; nevertheless, the principle of reciprocity has often been stressed in parliament and by ministers: what the Carinthian Slovenes enjoy, our Germans should also get without hesitation. We think that a more honest principle cannot be propounded, but it is up to the Germans to implement it fully.[19]

In the spring of 1929 the *Ballhausplatz* – against the background of the minorities' discussion in the *plenum* of the League of Nations – was quite prepared to accept a treaty for the protection of minorities with Yugoslavia modelled on the treaty with Czechoslovakia signed in Brno (Brunn) in 1920. However, Belgrade was preoccupied with its own state reform and negotiations in Carinthia itself were broken off for lack of further willingness to compromise between majority and minority. Curiously enough, shortly afterwards two leading Croatian economists asked the Austrian envoy in Belgrade to describe the progress of the Croatian school system in the Burgenland and even documented it with the aid of the *Ballhausplatz*.[20]

In the wake of Germany's admission to the League of Nations and the Council of the League, it had, as a renewed great power, increasingly become the protecting agency for the Germans in Yugoslavia, especially the Danube Swabians in the Vojvodina. Thus the latter were ruled out as an element in any bilateral minorities' policy between Yugoslavia and Austria, as was demonstrated for the first time in 1929–30 when the draft of a new Yugoslav primary school law was widely discussed. At the same time, a lawyer from Celje sent a petition to the League of Nations because of the confiscation of the *Deutsches Haus*. In the late summer of 1929 German deputies approached Foreign Minister Stresemann and Undersecretary Schubert, who for their part intervened with the Yugoslav government. In the late summer of 1930 a change took place in the Yugoslav minority policy towards the Danube Swabians, particularly in the fields of schools and societies. All the while Austria was only an observer and the *Ballhausplatz* recapitulated:

> Before signing a bilateral minority treaty both states should have codified the minority law in their legislation and would have to be politically consolidated enough to be able to guarantee the constancy of their minorities policy.[21]

Of course, during the world economic crisis a consolidation of both states was out of the question and the contacts of the Danube Swabians with Austria contracted greatly. On the other hand, German influence became stronger, particularly from 1933 onwards, as the Austrian envoy noted:

> As a result of considerable resources National Socialism is making

great progress among the eastern Swabians, a fact which, in the long term, must create a hostile attitude towards Austria and also badly harm our economic relations with the Vojvodina, the richest part of Yugoslavia.[22]

It was not just in the relatively remote Vojvodina that National Socialism made great progress from 1933 onwards. An even tighter organisational network came into being in southern Styria. The majority of the German townspeople there and also those in the Gottschee took the side of Berlin and Munich in the Austro–German conflict in 1933–4. Vienna retained only a certain protective function for old Austrian circles now integrated in the Patriotic front, and reciprocity considerations were no longer discussed.

The Slovene senator Rožič had returned to such reciprocity considerations in the general debate on the budget bill in Belgrade on 26 March 1933 and had contrasted the allegedly 'privileged' situation of the Germans in Yugoslavia with the ostensibly disadvantaged position of the Carinthian Slovenes. He argued that the Yugoslav government's economic policy now took account of the interests of the German minority; that politically they were now integrated in a large organisation; and that since 1929, 154 primary schools with 570 departments and 572 teachers had been at the disposal of the Germans, in which 33 304 children were taught. They also had six municipal schools and the grammar school in Novi Vrbas. There were already 415 cultural and social societies, including about 120 subsidiary societies of the Cultural Union. At the 74 *utraquist* schools in southern Carinthia there was, because of attendance at Slovene lessons in religion, a linguistic ratio of 84 to 16 in favour of the pupils with Slovene as their mother language, but the German (?) teachers were pushing German lessons with gothic writing and by distri- buting the juvenile literature of the German school association *Südmark*. By contrast, only 28 Slovene cultural societies were still active, and the Hermagoras Society had had to move first to Prevalje and then further to Celje in 1919–20.[23]

Neither the *Ballhausplatz* nor the Carinthian provincial government reacted to this speech in parliament, a clear departure from the practice of reciprocity in the 1920s. When towards the end of 1936 the Gottschee Germans took the initiative, and compared the national cultural situations of the Carinthian Slovenes and the Germans in the Gottschee (Kočevsko) to make them the object of bilateral negoti- ations, a bilateral settlement again came up for discussion. The *Koroški Slovenec* welcomed the 'solidarity of the minorities'. The *Ponedeljski Slovenec* in Ljubljana expressly advocated a policy of mutual agreement, as every state authority should, in the interests of domestic order and peace, be concerned 'that the residents of border areas [can] be satisfied with the *status quo* and have no reason to seek the fulfilment of their wishes and demands with the neighbour across the border'. Thus 'on judicious treatment' the minority might 'form a natural bond between two cultures and two peoples and bring them closer together'.[24]

However, the *Ballhausplatz* considered the demands of the Carinthian Slovenes as presented in Ljubljana in May 1937 as a private arrangement, and the people of the Gottschee did not fare much better in Belgrade. Both Chancelleries waited for the other to take the initiative and contented themselves with gathering material. Indeed political relations, as opposed to economic ones, were so cool that a swift settlement seemed to have receded into a dim distance. This paved the way for more radical solutions, which were soon sought.

Irredentists and Revisionism

The conflicts over the determination of borders, the confiscation of property and dismissals from employment had so strained the situation of both border minorities, the southern Styria Germans and the Carinthian Slovenes, from the very beginning, that only a judicious long term state minority policy towards both minorities could have formed 'a natural bond between two cultures and two peoples'. Of course, there were German and Slovene farmers who cultivated their fields on both sides of the border, family and friendly relations across the border, contacts between cultural societies and sports clubs, Austrian newspapers in Slovenia and Slovene newspapers in Carinthia and Styria and the border was also open for bilateral shopping. But state policy in Vienna and Belgrade, and even more so provincial policy in Klagenfurt, Ljubljana and Graz, was not only concerned with trade, cultural and social relations. It was also repeatedly concerned with the Slovene irredentists in southern Carinthia and the German irredentist in southern Styria and with a possible border revision in the area of Carinthia, Styria and Slovenia. So it was a question of the agitation in favour of unifying an ostensibly 'unredeemed' area with a conational mother country, linked with the revisionist demand for cession of this territory.[25]

A few days after the announcement of the result of the plebiscite in southern Carinthia the opinion in Slovene and Belgrade government circles was that the 'Carinthian question' would be renewed the moment Austria formed a union with Germany. Nevertheless, as an ally of France the government in Belgrade opposed all revisionist considerations as a matter of principle as they were not in keeping with the Parisian system of order; and on the other hand, the Serbs had to exercise restraint towards Hungary, Romania and Bulgaria as far as the successful delineation of their borders was concerned. The majority of the Slovene public – expressing itself above all in newspapers and national societies – was bound, justifiably, to feel discriminated against as regards the determination of the borders, primarily in favour of Italy. Thus it did not want to acknowledge that the result of the plebiscite had already been confirmed by international law on 10 October 1920 and began to hope for a possible connection of the question of *Anschluss* and the issue of the northern frontier of Slovenia.[26]

Therefore, as early as November 1920 the Austrian Foreign Ministry instructed its representative in Laibach 'to report all his observations concerning the organisation of an incipient irredentist movement in Slovenia on behalf of the Slovenes in Carinthia'. The Legation Councillor addressed, Kohlruss, immediately reported on the activities of a society recently founded in Ljubljana, *Gosposvetski zvon* (The Bell of Maria Saal), which wanted initially to expose the alleged injustice of the plebiscite and also aspired to liberate 'all unredeemed territories'. Carinthia was given the same importance for Yugoslavia that Alsace and Lorraine had had for France between 1871 and 1918. The Slovene priest Arnejc, who had fled from southern Carinthia, formulated the goal of the society: 'Just as the Serbs are working for their *Kosovo polje*, we must do the same for our *Gosposvetsko polje* (Zollfeld, the area round Maria Saal). The conscious Slovene and Yugoslav must be familiar with the essence of the irredentist idea.'[27]

Of course, the Carinthian provincial government soon learned of such revisionist wishes and the head of the government, Lemisch, made the following unequivocal threats before the diet:

> We consider it our national and patriotic duty to draw the attention of the diet to this conspiracy against the law and peace and to demand that measures be taken at once – at the same time respecting the protection of the minorities – to render ineffective the subversive activities of Slovene traitors![28]

Only Carinthian Slovenes could be meant by the term traitors, currently the priests and teachers who had fled to Slovenia after the plebiscite, but soon potentially all the 15 279 people who had voted for union with the kingdom of Serbs, Croats and Slovenes on 10 October 1920 (41 per cent of the voters in the plebiscite area). Since it was, above all, persons from this group that demanded the new minority rights, the majority in the province made a very quick connection between the demand for minority rights and a latent bent for irredentism and revisionism.

The 'Carinthia question' did not just remain a bone of contention between Carinthia and Slovenia, but again assumed international dimensions as early as the spring of 1921. A Belgrade commission had investigated the deficiencies of Slovene supervisory boards in the area of the plebiscite and the president of the province of Slovenia, Brejc, a lawyer and the political leader of the Carinthian Slovenes between 1903 and 1918, had resigned as the politician mainly responsible for the plebiscite. Yet in January 1921 the Slovene provincial government had requested the government of the king-dom of Serbs, Croats and Slovenes to revive the 'Carinthian question' at the Conference of Ambassadors in Paris, so as at least to be granted the region south of the Drau (Drava). A well-known newspaper in Ljubljana tried to connect the revision of the frontier with the question of Western Hungary and the issue of the *Anschluss*. However, influential Slovene politicians considered the plebiscite in Upper Silesia, which on 20 March 1921 had produced a result of 59.6 per cent to 40.4 per cent in favour of Germany, a result comparable to the Carinthian one (59.04 per cent to 40.96 per cent in favour of Austria), to be a better starting point for a revival. The former Trieste deputy to the *Reichsrat* and current expert on international agree-ments in Belgrade, Dr Otokar Rybář, took a lead and demanded from his government that it take immediate diplomatic steps with the main Allied powers, without, however, referring to the different plebiscite provisions in the Treaties of Versailles (article 66) and Saint-Germain (article 50). The former provided for a partition of Upper Silesia, taking into account to a large extent the results of the local plebiscite, a partition which the Council of the League of Nations carried out on 20 October 1921. The latter enabled the whole area of the plebiscite in southern Carinthia to be assigned according to the overall result.[29]

On 26 March 1921 Pašić's government did indeed send a note to the Conference of Ambassadors with the request to assign the plebiscite area on the right bank of the Drau (the region between the Drau, the lake of Faak and the Karawanken) to the kingdom of Serbs, Croats and Slovenes. The majority of votes for Yugoslavia on the right bank of the Drau and the partitions of other plebiscite areas (Upper Silesia, Northern Schleswig) were given as reasons. Austrian diplomats in Paris and London reported that the *Quai d'Orsay* and the Foreign Office regarded the Carinthian question as a *res judicata* (closed issue) but warned against possible allied measures against the *Anschluss* movement in several Austrian provinces. All the same, official provincial policy in Carinthia was remarkably cautious in order to offer no provocation. On 2 June the Conference of Ambassadors rejected the request of the kingdom of Serbs, Croats and Slovenes over the Drau border as being contrary to the formal agreements of the Treaty. Nevertheless, a top secret clause was agreed upon, according to which the great powers would reconsider Yugoslavia's frontier claims in the case of Austrian–German unification.[30] While the Austro–Yugoslav frontier was being marked along the main ridge of the Karawanken in the summer of 1921, and Slovene leaflets suddenly appeared calling for the removal of the Demarcation Commission's boundary stones, the Austrian *chargé d'affaires*, Hoffinger, called on Prime Minister Pašić and requested that the royal government take suitable measures 'to put an end to these activities that undermine mutual trust and constantly fan national overexcitement in border areas'. For the Austrian government no 'Carinthian question' existed and it was endeavouring with all its energy to eliminate any old prejudices and memories that stood in the way of a reconciliation of their peoples. 'Nothing stands in the way of this except the activity of hypernationalists on both sides.' Pašić agreed to administrative and penal intervention against any such agitation. On 23 January 1922 he announced before the *Skupština* that the 'Carinthian question' was settled:

> Our border with Austria has been drawn, and to our disadvantage, but, I must say that we are at fault. . . Zone A, in which we had the majority, unfortunately voted for Austria and so we have lost this important region, but we are to blame that certain elements took material interests rather than national ones into account and voted for German Austria.[31]

This attitude on the part of the Belgrade government was fully in keeping with the foreign policy strategy of the *Ballhausplatz*, whose political division had, in a memorandum to Chancellor Schober on 2 December 1921, written that a 'liberation' of the German 'diaspora' living in the successor states and their union with Austria did not lie within the scope of political realisation. Thus their effective protection could be provided only by a foreign policy which, based on normal and neighbourly relations between states, increasingly guaranteed an enforcement of the laws protecting minorities that went beyond the provisions of the peace treaty. If Austria sought a *rapprochement* with its neighbours, a good relationship between Austria and the Little Entente would be the most effective policy to protect the German minorities living in the successor states.[32]

In 1922–3 Yugoslavia and Austria were indeed interested in forming neighbourly relations and were also in a position to curb irredentist or revisionist tendencies and ambitions in the short term. New unrest arose only in Carinthia when in Guštanj (Gutenstein) in the Miesstal, Carinthian until 1919, a monument was unveiled to the Slovene lieutenant Malgaj, who had been killed there at the beginning of May 1919, in the presence of political and military representatives from Ljubljana and Maribor. It bore the following inscription on its pedestal:

> Oh, I am not sleeping, I am biding time and expect us to go together to our brothers beyond St Veit to drink the waters of our Gail![33]

A (military) liberation of the Slovenes in Southern Carinthia reaching as far as the Gailtal was thereby implied.

When in spring 1925 the discussion of the *Anschluss* flared up anew in Austria, Slovene politicians and publicists again became vocal and tried to make a connection between the issue of the *Anschluss* and the Carinthian border question. Deputy Smodej, until 1918 an editor of the *Mir* in Klagenfurt, interrogated Foreign Minister Ninčić, demanding to know the attitude of the Belgrade government towards the question of Austria's union with Germany and what concrete proposals it had if the relevant powers conceded the *Anschluss* to Austria. Ninčić said that a union between Austria and Germany not in accordance with the peace treaties would mean a grave violation of those treaties and was impossible. Ninčić also confirmed to the panGerman Vice Chancellor Waber in Vienna that Yugoslavia would not tolerate steps of any kind against Austrian integrity and, if needs be, would intervene with ruthless severity.[34] This was of course aimed at Slovene and German revisionism.

However irredentist agitation, with blatant revisionist demands, increased again. At the end of 1925 the *Slovenski Narod* sketched a programme for propaganda on behalf of 'our unredeemed brothers on the other side of the Karawanken' and demanded that history books and maps be distributed among schoolchildren at home and abroad, 'as the French did over 47 years as far as the stolen provinces of Alsace and Lorraine were concerned'. In geography textbooks there was talk of 'unredeemed homeland' in Italy, Austria and Hungary and a Slovene national awareness was mentioned which would reincorporate the 'unredeemed ethnic comrades', under circumstances that would include an 'exchange of property'. The most obviously revisionist programme was presented at the beginning of 1927 by the former Provincial President, Brejc, in the Laibach periodical *Čas*, which listed four territorial 'suggestions' for a partition of Austria among its neighbouring countries. In all cases Yugoslavia was to obtain southern and south eastern Carinthia including Klagenfurt and Villach; possibly also central and eastern Carinthia; Styria without the Ennstal; and central and southern Burgenland. The 'Austrian problem' was to be solved by partitioning Austria between Germany, Yugoslavia and Czechoslovakia, taking the possibility of a 'free state of Vienna' into account. On the other hand, the head of the Carinthian provincial government Schumy made clear 'the viewpoint of the indivisibility of Carinthia' in the case of *Anschluss* in Vienna and Berlin.[35]

On the orders of the Carinthian *Heimatbund* the director of the provincial records office, Wutte, began the analysis of Slovene publications for possible irredentist content around 1930. He criticised a 'dialect map of the Slovene language' drawn up by the

Laibach slavist Ramovš; an anniversary issue of 1930 of *Slovenski Korotan;* and a 'report on the situation of the Slovene people in Carinthia' at the annual meeting of the *Družba sv Ciril in Metod* (Society of Saints Cyril and Methodus). Wutte even conceded that after 1925 Slovene propaganda against Carinthia had 'generally grown more moderate and peaceful in its external form', but its aim was still the 'liberation' of the territory lost on account of the plebiscite. So 'an exhaustive scholarly study of Southern Carinthia' was necessary on the part of the German Carinthians, for which it was 'essential that young persons learn Slovene'. In the future scholarship would also have to be 'put in the service of the national defence of Carinthia'.[36]

Yugoslavia had growing domestic and foreign policy problems such as criticism by the Slovene public of the dictatorial regime in Belgrade (see the punctations of Ljubljana): increased tension with Italy with the danger of war, Austria's *rapprochement* with Italy under Dollfuss and the emergence of an encirclement syndrome in Yugoslavia. In this atmosphere Yugoslav and Austrian discussion of irredentists and revisionism flared up anew from the summer of 1932. Indeed even British newspapers published revision plans that worked in favour of Slovenia. In the late summer of 1932 the Carinthian provincial government protested against the revival of the old Slovene ceremony instituting the duke of Carinthia in the Zollfeld at a congress of Slav national costumes in Ljubljana, because the Slovenes' claim to southern Carinthia was stressed in it 'and the incorporation of this area in a Greater Slovenia was presented as the yearning and aim of all Slovenes'. When the Director of the Vienna Imperial, Court and State Record Office, Hofrat Bittner, spoke of an 'excellent means of propaganda for the irredentists' when giving an expert opinion for the Foreign Affairs section of the Federal Chancellery, the *Ballhausplatz* intervened with Foreign Minister Jevtić. The preparatory committee for the congress in Ljubljana then omitted the planned ceremony 'on its own initiative'.[37]

The irredentist aims of some societies and newspapers in Slovenia were clearer, particularly in the *Klub koroških Slovencev* (Club of Carinthian Slovenes) and in the nationwide *Narodna odbrana*. Whereas the *Klub*, under the leadership of the Carinthian born lawyer Felaher, tried to register 'all putative attempts on the part of the Carinthian provincial government to germanise the Slovene population', the Ljubljana section of the *Narodna odbrana* had as its statutory aim 'to maintain cultural contacts with all our fellow nationals, especially in Italy and Austria, to ensure their national existence'. Moreover, the newspaper of the Slovene People's party, whose chairman Korošec had just been exiled to the Dalmatian island Hvar, called on the Belgrade government of Uzunović in April

1933, in the face of the revisionism of the enemies of Yugoslavia, to make its own revisionist demands which 'would unite the over 100 000 Slovene Carinthians and 60 000 inhabitants of the coastal territories with the motherland'. The *Slovenec* did not shrink from suggesting the tactics that should be used. 'If our official policy cannot take this course because it must reject any form of revisionism as a matter of principle, we will seek the indirect course and proceed to make propaganda for our soil still under alien rule.' For, 'we, too, are in favour of an alteration of the peace treaties for there is no Slovenia without Gorica, without Trst and without Celovec'.[38] The revisionist programme of the Slovene People's party was rarely worded so clearly, although at this time it conformed with the mood of the Slovene leadership, as a meeting of the Chamber of Trade and Commerce in Ljubljana with over 400 industrialists, businessmen and traders proved.

During important *Sokol* celebrations in Ljubljana at the end of June 1933 a minorities' exhibition drew particular attention to the border questions that concerned Austria and Italy. Even a map with the Czech–Yugoslav corridor plan of 1919 was hung up. On the other hand, the Carinthian *Heimatbund* sensed irredentist propaganda on the part of the 'Yugoslav Academic Society Triglav' during the visit of the 73 year old former Slovene deputy to the *Reichsrat*, Franc Grafenauer, to the Gailtal. The directorate for public security attached to the Federal Chancellery warned 'that Slovene nationalist circles took every opportunity to make propaganda for union with Yugoslavia in Carinthia'. So in December 1933 the *Ballhausplatz* decided to make a 'determined' intervention with Foreign Minister Jevtić, as the Austrian government could no longer tolerate 'these constant, planned intrigues against the integrity of Austria'. Moreover, Vienna might be forced 'to broach the subject of these constant threats to Austrian property with the powers interested in this question or in the international forum' (League of Nations). The revisionist slogan, 'Austria belongs to Germany, but Carinthia belongs to us', was published again in the December issue of the *Omladina*, the monthly journal of the *Narodna odbrana*; and the *Reichspost* in Vienna reported about secret negotiations between the Foreign Affairs office of the NSDAP (Rosenberg) and representatives of Slovene organisations. Jevtić then immediately tried to calm matters with a denial in the semi-official *Prager Presse*:

> The policy of the Yugoslav government consists of respect for the treaties and rejection of any territorial revision in any direction, including Austria. It has no contact with the Slovene irredentists and will do everything in its power to suppress such a movement. It only desires the integrity, independence and prosperity of Austria.[39]

The *Narodna odbrana*, however, did not give in. On 2 February 1934, during a National Socialist wave of terror in Austria, a very clear policy statement appeared in its mouthpiece *Pohod* in Ljubljana:

> Carinthia belongs to us and if things were different in Austria we would be fully entitled to obtain with peaceful means and under possibly changed circumstances what the shameless plebiscite agreement [*sic!*] took away from us.[40]

For the Carinthian and Austrian authorities the question was now the extent to which leading Carinthian Slovenes were involved in this irredentist movement. Whereas police stations in Klagenfurt and Villach were not prepared to differentiate between Slovene associations and irredentist activity and labelled priests, doctors and businessmen who were Carinthian Slovenes as 'well known Yugoslav agitators' and 'irredentists fighting for the separation of the Slovene part of Carinthia'; the state police bureau of the General Directorate for Public Security in Vienna made clear distinctions between the loyal behaviour of the Carinthian Slovenes and the irredentist activity of different societies in Slovenia:

> The Carinthian Slovenes adopted a strongly disapproving attitude to the Austrian National Socialists and frequently openly supported the police authorities against the National Socialists. . . . In contrast to this development is the increased activity of Slovene circles abroad who are more and more vehemently advocating a separation of large areas of Carinthia and Styria in favour of Yugoslavia . . . The Slovene movement in Carinthia is organised and funded from Laibach.[41]

The head of the Political Department at the *Ballhausplatz*, Hornbostel, discerned a tacit agreement between this Slovene propaganda against Carinthia and the National Socialist propaganda in southern Styria against Austria. Both clearly grew after the visit of the Prussian Prime Minister Göring to Belgrade in June 1934 and the assassination of Chancellor Dollfuss on 25 July 1934, especially as thousands of Austrian National Socialists had fled to Yugoslavia after the abortive July *Putsch*. It was only after their transportation to Germany and after the assassination of Yugoslavia's King Alexander by *Ustaša* and *VMRO* in Marseilles, though there was presumably also a connection with Chancellor Schuschnigg's efforts to develop a new minority policy in Carinthia, that the irredentist propaganda noticeably decreased.[42]

The Yugoslav public was now preoccupied by the diplomatic conflicts with Hungary and Italy over support of the assassins of the king and among the Slovene public changes in opinion became visible which 'disassociated themselves from inopportune speculations about possible political events'. In an open letter to the *Slovenija* at the beginning of spring 1935 a clear warning even was given to the revisionists:

> Any playing with the thought that the Slovene part of Carinthia could be liberated by means of a political deal with Hitlerism is a childish political notion. This speculation belongs to the same category of political trivia as the dream of the restoration of the Habsburg empire. Hitler flags on the Karawanken would mean the end of small independent nations in the area of the Danube; would mean the war.[43]

But not everybody heeded this almost prophetic warning.

In the mining town of Trbovlje in April 1935 a *Legija koroškíh Slovencev* (League of Carinthian Warriors) was founded, which, following the nationalist aims of the *Narodna odbrana*, was allegedly to devote itself to the 'liberation of the unredeemed Slovene brothers in Carinthia'. The fears of the Austrian consulate in Laibach and the Carinthian Director of Security proved to be exaggerated. But even the influential Catholic educational Society of Saints Cyril and Methodus could not refrain from expressing a mythologising point of view during the celebrations of its fiftieth anniversary:

> Aging German civilisation had come to a halt on the appearance of the young Slav civilisation . . . until the time comes when the Slavs will return over their third frontier to their second in the Hohe Tauern and over the Semmering and the territory populated by the Burgenland Croats and extend their hand to the brother Czechs and Slovaks in the north. . . . It is not a utopia, but rather an objective calculation: the great family of Slavs will, in a veritable *Völkerwanderung* of its fresh forces, find its way into the heart of Europe where it will continue and end its cultural mission.[44]

On the whole, however, the 'usual clearly irredentist statements' diminished noticeably in 1936–7.

Even the general meetings of the Club of Carinthian Slovenes took a much more moderate tone. In 1937 it was explicitly stressed that this club was 'not an irredentist organisation, but one that only wanted to maintain as profound cultural relations as possible with the Slovenes in Carinthia'. Nevertheless, the myth of Slovene Carinthia was upheld, as was proved by a calendar page supplement to the new year's issue of *Slovenec*. There was a photograph of Maria Saal with its famous cathedral with the following caption: '*Slovenska zemlja – Gospa sveta na Koroškem – Zibelka našega naroda*' ('Slovene soil – Maria Saal in Carinthia – The cradle of our people').[45] The *Ballhausplatz* reacted surprisingly sharply to this calendar page – probably because of the approximately simultaneous deportations of members of the (Austrian) Patriotic Front from southern Styria.

Criticisms were made of the anti-Austrian attitude of the editorial staff of the *Slovenec* and of Slovene nationalist and irredentist tendencies. The deputy minister in Belgrade, Ivo Andrić, who had been spoken to on the subject by the Austrian envoy, Wimmer, was less worried by the calendar than by the general vehement style of the *Slovenec* against the National Socialist regime in Germany, for in Berlin on 17 January 1938 Stojadinović, Yugoslavia's Prime Minister and Foreign Minister, had assured Hitler that he viewed the Austrian question 'as a purely internal matter for the German people' and had in turn received an assurance from Hitler that he would respect the inviolability of Yugoslavia's borders. So on 15 March 1938, just after the *Anschluss*, Stojadinović warned Slovene critics of such moves that the principle of reciprocity now held highly unpleasant implications for Yugoslavia:

> We can neither invade Carinthia, nor can we demand a plebiscite for our 90 000 people, of whom 40 000 are already estranged from their people, for the Germans might demand a plebiscite for our 400 000 Germans.[46]

On 16 March 1938 Stojadinović was asked about guarantees for the Carinthian Slovenes in the Belgrade senate, while National Socialist demonstrations in Graz were already calling for a 'German Marburg'. Such a revisionist demand had been raised here and there in the German nationalist press up to the *Anschluss* but had never received the support of Austrian government agencies. The general clause formulated by the Political Department of the *Ballhausplatz* in December 1921 was typical of their outlook:

> The liberation of the German diaspora living in the succession states and their union with Austria do not lie within the scope of political realization.[47]

However, it was not only German nationalist historians, geo-politicians and ethnographers like Helmut Carstanjen, Otto Maul, Hans Bruckner, Hans Volkmar, Werner Schneefuss and Manfred Straka that described southern Styria in their work as a 'German southeastern *Mark*' (district) and drew the border of German 'ethnic soil' broadly, in the Bacher Mountains, south of Maribor and across the Windische Büheln (Slovenske gorice) as far as Oberradkersburg (Gornja Radgona). At a conference of the influential society *Südmark* in Graz in 1924, while severe criticisms were being made of Slovene minority policy, the altering of the frontier between Styria and Slovenia had also been discussed.[48]

In the same year the Austrian *chargé d'affaires* in Belgrade, Hoffinger, presented the *Ballhausplatz* with a 'memorandum about certain future possibilities being prepared in the south-east of Austria and their effects on Austria'. The widening gap between the Serbs on one hand and the Croats and Slovenes, on the other, obliged Serbian statesmen to deal with the possibility that they would, in the future, more or less voluntarily have to part with the north western part of the country and think in terms of a reconstruction of a Balkan Greater Serbia. But a Croat and Slovene state ran the risk of being penetrated politically and economically by Italy. As Germany 'did not come into account for active positions against a major power for some time', it was in the interests of Austria and Czechoslovakia to include the Croat–Slovene region in an economic *rapprochement* with the successor states of the Austro–Hungarian empire.[49]

When the leader of the Slovene clericals, Korošec, went to Austria and Germany for consultations in 1927 and 1929 – the second time certainly on the order of King Alexander – the spectre of a Catholic restoration immediately appeared in Belgrade which could go as far as a plan to create a Bavarian–Austrian–Hungarian–Slovene–Croat state, possibly under Habsburg leadership. However, there could be no question of this as the contacts between Korošec and the Austrian Christian Social party under Bishop Seipel were as cool as could be imagined.[50]

The sensitivity of the Slovene and Yugoslav public towards possibly revisionist statements from Austria was, at any rate, no less than the sensitivity of the Carinthian and Austrian public. When after a conversation with Prime Minister Briand in Paris in May 1930, Chancellor Schober was asked about Austrian plans for the construction of an 'eastern railway' between south east Carinthia and south west Styria, Schober replied in a somewhat nonchalant way: 'The shortest route from Graz to Klagenfurt at present leads through Yugoslavia, through Marburg. . . . They should give Marburg back to us, then we will not have to build this stretch.' The *Narodna odbrana* in Belgrade reacted with irritation:

> Did we take away Maribor from the Republic of Austria? Does Maribor not legally belong to us? Was Maribor not freed from the former Austrian empire by the outcome of the war and on the basis of a great principle adopted by the peace conference and on which the League of Nations is based?

Responsible statesmen had to observe certain forms of expression in bilateral relations.[51]

A concrete desire to alter the border between Spielfeld and Radkersburg – here the border ran along the Mur – in favour of Austria was expressed in April 1933 by the District Committee of Radkersburg; the District Chamber of Agriculture and Forestry situated there; the town of Radkersburg itself and the market towns of Spielfeld and Strass. In a petition to the Austrian government they referred to the disruptions in economic relations since the 'unnatural determination of the border' in 1919, and also to the alleged wish of the German population of the Abstall area and the mixed language and Slovene population as far as Maribor to be reunited with Styria and Austria. The petitioners called to mind the plebiscite that was not carried out in 1919–20 and the Four Power Agreement now introduced by Mussolini, which provided for limited, peaceful revisionism.

Hornbostel in the Political Department of the *Ballhausplatz* gave a cautious answer to the 'Austrian Work Group for the Revision of the Peace Treaties', which was intervening with Chancellor Dollfuss on behalf of the three southern Styria border communities:

> Nothing can be undertaken in the matter at present because
> 1) the so-called Four Power Pact, which has caused such a stir in the press, has to our knowledge not yet been concluded;
> 2) it seems more than doubtful whether adequate legal grounds for the practical opening of border revision questions will remain in the Four Power Pact;
> 3) it would be contrary to overall Austrian interests if, in opposition to the policy of the greatest reserve pursued by all governments, including the present one, the Austrians of all people were the first to announce a *concrete* revisionist desire to the world public. The moment when this and other wishes can be submitted to the appropriate authorities we hope will come in the course of time (*sic!*). So we have for the moment no choice but to study concrete wishes, as far as they are serious, and keep them on file for the above-mentioned moment.[52]

So were there secret revisionist wishes at the *Ballhausplatz*, too? On consulting the Imperial, Court and State Record Office the English writer and journalist William Harbutt Dawson was told that there was no literature on possible 'Austrian revisionist claims': 'such works are all written from the panGerman point of view'.

In a confidential item of information sent to Franckenstein, the envoy in London, the *Ballhausplatz* conceded 'that the peace Treaties of Versailles and Saint-Germain contained provisions that must be revised'. What was meant was the elimination of the obligation to pay reparations that was obtained in the Hague negotiations in 1930 and not so much frontier revisions. For

> in the interests of maintaining good relations with all European states, Austria avoids taking the initiative in the question of revisions and particularly as far as a revision of the borders of today's Austria is concerned.[53]

The Slovene administration of the Banovina in Ljubljana must have heard of revisionist rumours in the Abstall area, because on 21 September 1934 Banus Marušič presented a detailed report on economic and national–political conditions on the northern border between Slovenia and Styria to the Presiding Committee of the Yugoslav Council of Ministers and the Cabinet of the Minister of the Interior. In the Abstall area and in the surroundings of Gornja Radgona the German farmers were still economically stronger than the Slovene landowners and the Germans were supported intellectually and financially by their 'Austrian brothers'. Apart from that, in southern Styria many Austrians were still the owners of twin holdings in Austria and Yugoslavia. 'All these Austrian Germans are *Hitlerjanci* (supporters of Hitler), and with these of all people our Germans have the best relations, so that all of them, from the first to the last will soon be Hitler supporters.' Everywhere on the border the Yugoslav Germans had their representatives in the area committees of the *Jugoslovenska narodna zajednica* (Yugoslav National Community) and had obtained some successes in local council elections with the aid of the Austrian owners of twin holdings in Austria and Yugoslavia. So local groups of the *Narodna odbrana* demanded the liquidation of twin holdings, the end of political pacts with the Germans, the exclusive employment of nationally uncompromising officials on the border and a prohibition of the sale of real estate to foreigners; and Banus Marušič endorsed these demands to a large extent.[54]

The *Narodna odbrana* justifiably feared the great danger of the Hitler movement on the border, 'for it stimulates our Germans and prepares them for a determined struggle'. So the administration of the Dravska Banovina also stiffened its attitude towards the southern Styria Germans, particularly after Korošec took office as Minister of the Interior in Stojadinović's government in June 1935. Most local groups of the Swabian–German Cultural Union were again dissolved in the course of 1936 and the German envoy, von Heeren, who had vainly intervened with Prime Minister Stojadinović, could only complain to Berlin:

As is known there, Korošec, as the leader of the Slovene Clericals has always been prepared for a struggle against the Germans in Slovenia. Just as he fanned Slovene irredentism against the government in Vienna before the collapse of Austria–Hungary, today he sees behind any German activity in Slovenia aims that are ultimately irredentist. In addition, as a Catholic priest, Korošec has the deepest distrust of any possibility of the Germans in Slovenia being influenced by propaganda from the new Germany.[55]

In October 1937 the *Banus* of the Dravksa Banovina already saw the security of the state endangered by 'panGerman expansionist efforts', 'particularly on the north western border'. The Slovene authorities took little action against National Socialist subversive activity in Southern Styria, but at the beginning of 1938 deported four members of the (Austrian) Patriotic Front from Maribor, amongst other things on the grounds of having made irredentist propaganda for the separation of southern Styria from the state of Yugoslavia. Deputy Minister Andrić admitted the absurdity in the reproach of propaganda for union with Austria, but saw no possibility of influencing the Slovene public to this effect.[56]

Conclusion

In summary the following paradox can be established. Since losing the plebiscite in 1920, nationalist societies and newspapers in Slovenia had tried to foment irredentism and revisionism in southern Carinthia. On the one hand, they made use of the Slovene minority in Carinthia and, on the other, of National Socialist *Anschluss* propaganda, and wanted to make the 'Carinthian question' the subject of international discussion again. German nationalist circles and societies in Graz promoted irredentism and revisionism in southern Styria. But both activities met with relatively little response from those directly addressed, the Carinthian Slovenes and the southern Styrian Germans, even if the Carinthian and Slovene authorities reacted with exaggerated reports and restrictive measures. When National Socialism was able to gain a foothold among the Germans in Slovenia with its anti-Austrian propaganda in 1933–4, and was tolerated by the Slovene authorities, the Slovene public belatedly noticed that the National Socialist agitation was not just aimed at the regime of the corporative state, but was also beginning to release German nationalist revisionist claims. This danger was only recognised by the left wing intelligentsia in opposition to the government in March 1938 and was soon to end in the catastrophe of the war in April 1941.[57]

Notes

(For abbreviations used in references to archives, see p. 270)

1. For Yugoslav–Austrian relations between the world wars see Maur, vol 2; Krizman, pp. 5–24; Zorn, pp.40–6; Suppan, (1984) p. 222–404.
2. *Ergebnisse der Volkszählung 1910* (1912); *A magyar szent korona országainak 1910. évi népszámlálása*, VI/64 (1924); *Definitivni rezultati popisa 1921; Ortsverzeichnis von Österreich 1923; Gli derung der Bevölkerung des ehemaligen Jugoslawien 1931; Ergebnisse der österreichischen Volkszählung 1934.*
3. Biber, pp. 11–41; Wehler, pp. 17–20; Suppan, (1983) pp. 96–115, 143–68.
4. Flachbarth, pp. 46–57, 159–259; Viefhaus, pp. 189–94; Miller, XIII, pp. 299–302, 337–449, 508–46; Mandelstam.

5. Ermacora, pp. 526–7; Veiter, pp. 477–80; Mitrović, pp. 200–6
6. Union scolaire Slovène à Klagenfurt, No 102, au Secrétariat de la Ligue des Nations à Genève, Vienna, 22 January 1922; Governor of Carinthia to Federal Ministry of Foreign Affairs, 4 March 1922; Federal Ministry of Interior and Education to Federal Ministry of Foreign Affairs, 24 March 1922; Superior Councellor Leitmaier to Minister Pflügl in Geneva, 29 April 1922; Minister Pflügl to Secretary General Drummond, 1 May 1922, HHStA, BKA, Abt. 15/VR, Kart. 103.
7. Suppan, (1984), pp. 288–9; Gütermann, pp. 216–17, 352; *Slovenec*, 24 February 1923; *Slovenski Narod*, 27 February 1923.
8. *Samouprava*, 9 June 1923; *Stenografske beleške Narodne skupštine Kraljevine SHS*, 8 June 1923, I, p. 423; Vinaver, p. 234; *Freie Stimmen*, 16 and 22 June 1923 (Martin Wutte).
9. Governor of Carinthia to Federal Ministry of Foreign Affairs, 15 July 1923; Consul Bischoff to Chargé d'affaires Hoffinger, 4 Aug. 1923, HHStA, BKA/AA, Abt. 15/VR, Kart. 104.
10. Interview between Foreign Minister Grünberger and Foreign Minister Ninčić, 15 July 1924, HHStA. NPA Südslavien I-III, Kart 694.
11. Grassl, pp. 793–810; Chargé d'affaires Hoffinger to Foreign Minister Grünberger, 20 Oct. 1923, HHStA, NPA Südslavien, Kart. 817 (alt).
12. Consul general Kohlruss to Foreign Minister Grünberger, 11 Feb. 1924, HHStA, BKA/AA, Abt. 15/VR, Kart. 113; *Zgodovina Slovencev*, pp. 636–7.
13. Ministry of Foreign Affairs of the Kingdom of the Serbs, Croats and Slovenes, II. political department, to Ministry of Education, 20 February 1925, Arhiv Jugoslavije, Ministarstvo prosvete, kut. 66; *Stenographische Protokolle*, II/2, pp. 2000–1; Minister Hoffinger to Foreign Minister Mataja, 23 February 1925, HHStA, NPA Südslavien, Kart. 784 (alt).
14. Department head Schüller to Federal Chancellor Ramek, 25 February 1925, HHStA, NPA Südslavien, Kart 784 (alt).
15. *Stenographische Protokolle*, II/2. pp. 2013–15; *Neue Freie Presse*, 4 March 1925; *Belgrader Zeitung*, 12 March 1925; *Stenografske beleške Narodne skupštine Kraljevine SHS*, 1925–6, III, p. 166.
16. Declaration of the Federal Chancellor Ramek in the Federal Parliament, 3 March 1925, HHStA, NPA Südslavien, Kart 784 (alt).
17. Petek, pp. 127–42; Einspieler, pp. 32–84; Hass and Stuhlpfarrer, pp. 53–66; Moritsch, pp. 329–37.
18. H. Wendel, 'Kärnten als Beispiel', *Sozialdemokrat*, 21 Aug. 1927; L. Epstein, 'Estland, Kärnten, Tschechoslowakei', *Bohemia*, 6 September 1927; 'Korutanský vzor?' *Národni listy*, 24 September 1927; Foreign Minister Schmitz, 3 March 1927, AVA, BMU, 18A, Kärnten in genere, Fasz. 4333.
19. *Slovenec*, 22 March 1928; *Jutro*, 14 July 1927.
20. Federal Ministry of Education: 'Das kroatische Schulwesen im Burgenlande', 13 March 1931, HHStA, NPA Südslavien, Kart. 300 (alt).
21. 'Petition an den Völkerbundrat wegen Verletzung von Rechten der deutschen Minderheit im Königreiche Jugoslawien durch instehende Verfügungen und Entscheidungen der jugoslawischen Behörden', Dr Walter Riebl, Cilli, June 1930; order BKA AA, Abt. 13/pol. to Minister Ploennies, 29 March 1930, HHStA, BKA/AA, Abt. 15/VR, Kart. 113.
22. Yugoslav Ministry of Interior, Department of State Security, to Ministry of Education, 12 December 1933, Arhiv Jugoslavije, Ministarstvo prosvete, fond 66, 70–183; Minister Ploennies to Federal Chancellery, 12 June 1933 (secret), HHStA, NPA Jugoslavien, Kart. 785 (alt).
23. 'Lage der deutschen Minderheit in Jugoslawien und Lage der Slowenen in Österreich. Aus der Rede des Senators Dr Valentin Rožič im Senat des

Königreiches Jugoslawien am 26. März 1933 in der Generaldebatte über die Budgetvorlage'; *Stenografske beleške Narodne skupštine Jugoslavije*, 1932–3, III, pp. 67–74.

24. *Kärntner Tagblatt*, 8 November 1936; *Ponedeljski Slovenec*, 7 December 1936; *Koroški Slovenec*, 6 February 1937; *Gottscheer Zeitung*, 1 April 1937; *Ponedeljski Slovenec*, 24 May 1937; 'Die Forderungen der slowenischen Minderheit in Kärnten auf kulturellem, wirtschaftlichem und politischem Gebiete', 16 June 1937, HHStA, NPA Jugoslavien, Kart. 785 (alt); 'Forderungen der deutschen Minderheit im Draubanat auf kulturellem, wirtschaftlichem und politischem Gebiet', June 1937, Biber, pp. 117–19.

25. Carinthiacus; Wutte and Lobmeyr.

26. Wambaugh, vol. I, pp. 203–4; Wutte (1985), pp. 403–15; Rožič; Rumpler; Pleterski, Ude and Zorn.

27. Consul Kohlruss to Foreign Ministry, 1 December 1920, HHStA, NPA Südslavien 2/3, Kart. 702.

28. *Villacher Tagblatt*, 4 December 1920.

29. *Slovenski Narod*, 19 December 1920, 8 February, 13 February, 18 February, 6 March 1921; *Slovenci v desetletju*, p. 204; *Slovenec*, 23 March 1921; Foreign Ministry to provincial government of Carinthia, 28 February, 1921, Kärntner Landesarchiv, Landesregierung/Präsidium, Fasz. 623, 1–4/62–1921.

30. Report of Ambassadors Eichhoff and Franckenstein to Foreign Ministry, 20 and 21 April 1921, HHStA, NPA Südslavien I/20, Kart. 696; reply of Prime Minister Pašić in the *Skupština*, 18 May 1921; telegram, Hoffinger to Foreign Ministry, 20 May 1921; Foreign Ministry instruction to Ambassadors in Paris, Rome, London, Belgrade, 31 May 1921; telegram Hoffinger to Foreign Ministry, 13 June 1921, HHStA, NPA Südslavien 2/12, Kart. 708.

31. *Samouprava*, 26 January 1922.

32. Memorandum by Ambassador Egger and Consul Bischoff, 2 December 1921, HHStA, NPA Tschechoslovakei, Kart. 822 (alt); see Kerekes, p. 342.

33. *Slovenec*, 23 March 1921; Meško.

34. *Slovenski Narod*, 14 and 26 June 1925; Wutte (1925), p. 11; *Stenografske beleške Narodne skupštine Kraljevine SHS*, 1924–25, 13 July 1925, pp. 458–63.

35. *Slovenski Narod*, 30 December 1925; Brejc, pp. 1–25; provincial government of Carinthia to BKA/AA, 4 March 1927, HHStA, NPA Südslavien, Kart. 798 (alt).

36. Ramovš, *Slovenski Korotan/Das slovenische Kärnten/La Carinthie slovène*, 12 October 1930; Wutte, 'Bericht über den Stand der wissenschaftlichen Arbeiten zur Kärntner Frage' (text of lecture, end May 1932).

37. *Manchester Guardian*, 24 December 1932; provincial government of Carinthia to BKA/AA, 4 August 1932; Counsellor Bittner to BKA/AA, 9 August 1932; BKA/AA to director Hügel, 10 August 1932; note of the Austrian legation in Belgrade, 14 August 1932; report of Consul General Orsini-Rosenberg to Federal Chancellor Dollfuss 10 September 1932; Foreign Ministry of the Kingdom of Yugoslavia, verbal note to the Austrian Legation, 14 September 1932, HHStA, NPA Südslavien, Kart. 787 (alt).

38. Consul General Orsini-Rosenberg to Federal Chancellor Dollfuss, 7 March 1933, HHStA, NPA Südslavien, Kart. 787 (alt); *Slovenec*, 20 April 1933.

39. Arhiv JAZU, ostavština Trumbića 140/9, French papers; *Slovenski Narod*, 3 August 1933; Order of Secretary General Peter to Minister Ploennies, 9 December 1933, HHStA, NPA Südslavien, Kart. 787 (alt); *Omladina*, December 1933: 'Naš iredentizem'; *Reichspost*, 22, 27 and 29 December 1933; *Prager Presse*, 5 January 1934.

40. *Pohod*, 3 February 1934.

41. Federal police offices in Klagenfurt and Villach to central executive board of public security, 19 February 1934 and 12 April 1934, HHStA, NPA Südslavien,

Kart. 787 (alt); Bureau of State police to Federal Chancellery, department 13, April 1934, HHStA, NPA Südslavien, Kart 787 (alt).

42. Minister Hornbostel to chief editor Funder, 24 April 1934, HHStA, NPA Südslavien, Kart. 787 (alt); Ormos, pp. 322–23, 337.

43. *Slovenija*, 29 March 1935.

44. Report of the Consulate in Ljubljana to Federal Chancellery, 30 April 1935, HHStA, NPA Südslavien, Kart. 788 (alt); *Koledar Družbe Sv Cirila in Metoda* (Ljubljana 1936).

45. *Slovenec*, 1 January 1938; order of Federal Chancellery, Department 13, to Minister Wimmer, 18 January 1938, HHStA, NPA Südslavien, Kart. 798 (alt).

46. Report of Minister Wimmer to Federal Chancellery, 17 February 1938, HHStA, NPA Südslavien, Kart. 798 (alt); record of Prime Minister Stojadinović, completed by Minister Cincar-Marković, 17 January 1938, Arhiv Jugoslavije, zbirka Stojadinovića, F 24; *Aprilski rat*, pp. 17–20.

47. Memorandum of Minister Egger and Consul Bischoff, 2 December 1921, cited above, n. 32.

48. Biber, pp. 93–103, 343–9; Rumpler and Suppan, pp. 198–210.

49. Memorandum of Chargé d'affaires Hoffinger to Federal Ministry of Foreign Affairs, 18 December 1924, HHStA, Gesandtschaft Belgrad, Fasz. 3.

50. Private letter Consul General Kronholz to Minister Wildner, 5 December 1929, HHStA, NPA Jugoslavien 7/1, Kart. 721.

51. *Narodna odbrana*, 11 May 1930.

52. Letter of District Committee Radkersburg etc. to Federal Government and Government of Styria, 5 April 1933; private letter of Minister Hornbostel, 28 April 1933; HHStA, NPA Österreich, Kart. 379 (alt).

53. Order of Secretary General Peter to Minister Franckenstein (London), 28 April 1933, HHStA, NPA Österreich, Kart. 379 (alt).

54. Report of the Government of Slovenia to the Council of Ministers in Belgrade and to Ministry of Interior, 21 September 1934, Arhiv Jugoslavije, Ministarstvo prosvete, ONBr 1366, fond 66, 3–6.

55. Report of the German Minister von Heeren to Foreign Ministry in Berlin, PA Bonn, VI A, Bd. 14, E 540560–2; see Biber, pp. 57–8, 113–15.

56. Rumpler and Suppan, pp. 230–5.

57. See Grafenauer, pp. 34–45; Ferenc, pp. 9–20.

Select Bibliography

Official Publications

A magyar szent korona orszagainak 1910. évi népszámlálása. VI: Végeredmények össze-foglalása (Budapest, 1924).

Definitivni rezultati popisa stanovništva od 31 jan. 1921. god. Résultats définitifs du recensement de la population du 31 janvier 1921 (Sarajevo, 1932).

Die Ergebnisse der Volkszählung vom 31, Dezember 1910 in den im Reichsrate vertretenen Königreichen und Ländern 1/1: Die summarischen Ergebnisse der Volkszählung (Vienna, 1912).

Die Ergebnisse der österreichischen Volkszählung vom 22. März 1934. Bundesstaat – Textheft (Vienna, 1935).

Die Gliederung der Bevölkerung des ehemaligen Jugoslawien nach Muttersprache und Konfession. Nach den unveröffentlichten Angaben der Zählung von 1931 (Vienna, 1943).

Ortsverzeichnis von Österreich. Bearbeitet auf Grund der Ergebnisse der Volkszählung vom 7. März 1923 (Vienna, 1930).

Protokolle des Ministerrates der Ersten Republik. Kabinette Dr Seipel, Dr Dollfuss und Dr Schuschnigg (Vienna, 1980–88).
Stenografske beleške Narodne skupštine Kraljevine Srba, Hrvata i Slovenaca (Belgrade, 1921–29).
Stenografske beleške Narodne skupštine Kraljevine Jugoslavije (Belgrade, 1932–39).
Stenographische Protokolle über die Sitzungen des Nationalrates der Republik Österreich (Vienna, 1921–34).

Documentation

Ferenc, Tone (ed.), *Quellen zur nationalsozialistischen Entnationalisierungspolitik in Slowenien 1941–1945/Viri o nacistični raznarodovalni politiki v Sloveniji 1941–1945* (Maribor, 1980).
Jedlicka, Ludwig and Neck, Rudolf (eds), *Vom Justizpalast zum Heldenplatz* (Vienna, 1975).
Petranović, Branko and Zečević, Momčilo (eds), *Jugoslavija 1918-1988. Tematska zbirka dokumenata* (Belgrade, 1988).
Vojnoistorijski institut (ed.), *Aprilski rat 1941* (Belgrade, 1969).

Books and Articles

Barker, Thomas, and Moritsch, A. (1984), *The Slovene Minority of Carinthia*, New York.
Biber, Dušan (1966), *Nacizem in Nemci v Jugoslaviji 1933–41*, Ljubljana.
Brejc, Janko (1925–6), 'Avstrijski problem. Le problème d'Autriche', *Čas*, 20.
Carinthiacus (Stanko Erhartič) (1925), *Die Lage der Slovenen unter Österreich und jene der Deutschen im Königreiche der Serben, Kroaten und Slovenen*, Ljubljana.
Einspieler, Valentin (1980), *Verhandlungen über die der slowenischen Minderheit angebotenen Kulturautonomie 1925–30*, 2nd edn. Klagenfurt.
Ermacora, Felix (1963), *Handbuch der Grundfreiheiten und Menschenrechte*, Vienna.
Flachbarth, Ernest (1937), *System des internationalen Minderheitenrechtes*, Budapest.
Grafenauer, Bogo (1946), 'Narodnostni razvoj na Koroškem od srede 19. stoletja do danes', *Koroški zbornik*, Ljubljana.
Grafenauer, Bogo (1987), *Slovensko narodno vprašanje in slovenski zgodovinksi položaj*, Ljubljana.
Grafenauer, Bogo, Gestrin, Ferdo, Melik, Vasilij, and Mikuž, Metod et al. (eds) (1979), *Zgodovina Slovencev*, Ljubljana.
Grassl, Georg (1927–8), 'Das Schulrecht der Deutschen in Südslawien', *Nation und Staat*, I.
Gütermann, Christoph (1979), *Das Minderheitenschutzverfahren des Völkerbundes*, Berlin.
Haas, Hanns and Stuhlpfarrer, K. (1977), *Österreich und seine Slowenen*, Vienna.
Hoptner, Jacob B. (1962), *Yugoslavia in Crisis 1934–41*, New York.
Institute for Contemporary History (ed.) (1977), *The Third Reich and Yugoslavia*, Belgrade.
Karsten, Hans (1929), 'Die Deutschen in Südslawien', *Das Deutschtum des Südostens im Jahr 1928*, Graz.
Kerekes, Lajos (1979), *Von St. Germain bis Genf*, Vienna.
Krizman, Bogdan (1977), 'Jugoslavija i Austrija 1918–1938', *Časopis za suvremenu povijest*, 9.
Mandelstam, André N. (1931), *La protection internationale des minorités*, Paris.
Maur, Gilbert in der (1936), *Die Jugoslawen einst und jetzt*, vol. 2, Leipzig.
Meško, F.X. (1922) *Mladim Screm*, Prevalje.

Miller, David Hunter (1924), *My Diary at the Conference of Paris. With Documents*, 22 vols, New York.
Mitrović, Andrej (1969), *Jugoslavija na konferenciji mira 1919-1920*, Belgrade.
Moritsch Andreas (1978), 'Das Projekt einer Kulturautonomie für die Kärntner Slovenen im Jahre 1927', *Österreichische Osthefte*, 20.
Neumann, Wilhelm (1980), *Kärnten 1918–1920*, 2nd edn, Klagenfurt.
Ormos, Maria (1969), *Franciaország és a keleti biztonság 1931-1936*. Budapest.
Petek, Franc (1979), *Iz mojih spominov*, Ljubljana.
Petersen, Carl, Scheel, Otto, Ruth, Paul Hermann, and Schwalm, Hans (eds) (1933–8), *Handwörterbuch des Grenz- und Auslanddeutschtums*, 3 vols, Breslau.
Pleterski, Janko, Ude, Lojze, and Zorn, Tone (eds) (1970), *Koroški plebiscit*, Ljubljana.
Podgorc, Valentin (1937), *Die Kärntner Slowenen in Vergangenheit und Gegenwart*, Klagenfurt.
Ramovš, Fran (1931), *Dialektološka karta slovenskega jezika*, Ljubljana.
Rožič, Valentin (1925), *Boj za Koroško*, Ljubljana.
Rožič Valentin (1933), *Lage der deutschen Minderheit in Jugoslawien und Lage der Slowenen in Österreich*, Belgrade.
Rumpler, Helmut (ed.) (1981), *Kärntens Volksabstimmung*, Klagenfurt.
Rumpler, Helmut, and Suppan, A. (eds) (1988), *Geschichte der Deutschen im Bereich des heutigen Slowenien 1848–1941/Zgodovina Nemcev na območju današnje Slovenije 1848–1941*, Vienna.
Suppan, Arnold (1983), *Die österreichischen Volksgruppen*, Vienna.
Ujevič, Mate (1934), *Gradišcanski Hrvati*, Zagreb.
Veiter, Theodor (1970), *Das Recht der Volksgruppen und Sprachminderheiten in Österreich*, Vienna.
Viefhaus, Erwin (1960), *Die Minderheitenfrage und die Entstehung der Minderheitenschutzverträge auf der Pariser Friedenskonferenz 1919*, Würzburg.
Vinaver, Vuk (1985), *Jugoslavija i Francuska izmedju dva rata*, Belgrade.
Vinaver, Vuk (1971), *Jugoslavija i Madjarska 1918–1933*, Belgrade.
Wambaugh, Sarah (1933), *Plebiscites since the World War*, 2 vols, Washington.
Wehler, Hans-Ulrich (1980), *Nationalitätenpolitik in Jugoslawien. Die deutsche Minderheit 1918–1978*, Göttingen.
Wuescht, Johann (1969), *Jugoslawien und das Dritte Reich*, Stuttgart.
Wutte Martin (1925), *Der Kampf um Süd-Kärnten*, Graz.
Wutte, Martin (1985), *Kärntens Freiheitskampf*, 3rd edn, Klagenfurt.
Wutte, Martin and Lobmeyr, Oskar (1926), *Die Lage der Minderheiten in Kärnten und in Slowenien*, Klagenfurt.
Zorn, Tone (1974), 'Kulturna avtonomija za koroške Slovence in nemška manjšina v Sloveniji med obema svetovnima vojnama, *Zgodovinksi časopis*.
Zwitter, Fran (1979), *Die Kärntner Frage*, Klagenfurt.
Zwitter, Fran (1937), *Koroško vprašanje*, Ljubljana.
Zwitter, Fran (1938), 'Nemci na Slovenskem', *Sodobnost*, 6.

Theses

Suppan, Arnold (1984), 'Nachbarschaft zwischen Kooperation und Konfrontation. Politik, Wirtschaft, Minderheiten und Geschichtsbild in den bilateralen Beziehungen Österreichs und Jugoslawiens zwischen den beiden Weltkriegen, 1920–1938', PhD, University of Vienna.

Archives

Arhiv Jugoslavije = Archives of Yugoslavia, Belgrade
AVA = Allgemeines Verwaltungsarchiv = Record Office of General Administration, Vienna.
BKA/AA = Bundeskanzleramt/Auswärtige Angelegenheiten = Federal Chancellery/Foreign Affairs, Vienna.
BMU = Bundesministerium für Unterricht = Federal Ministry of Education, Vienna.
HHStA = Haus-, Hof- und Staatsarchiv = Imperial, Court and State Archives, Vienna.
JAZU = Jugoslovenska akademija znanosti i umjetnosti = Yugoslav Academy of sciences and arts, Zagreb.
Ministarstvo prosvete = Ministry of Education, Belgrade.
NPA = Neues Politisches Archiv = New Political Record Office, Vienna.
PA = Politisches Archiv = Political Record Office, Bonn.
VR = Völkerrecht = law of nations.
zbirka Stojadinovića = collection of the papers of Prime Minister Stojadinović, Belgrade.

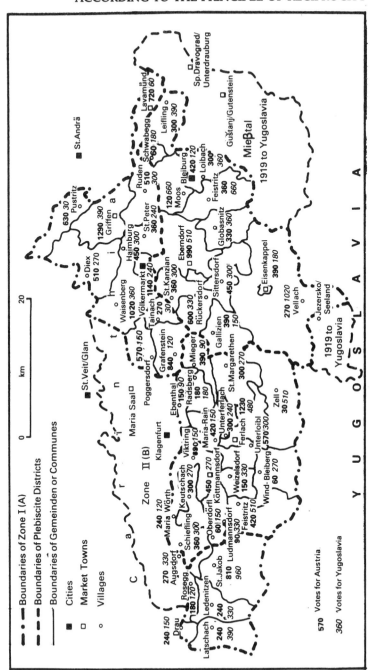

Map 11.1   The result of the plebiscite in Zone I (A) of the Klagenfurt Basin from 10 October 1920

Source: Sarah Wambaugh, *Plebiscites since the World War*, 1933 (based on map in M. Wutte, *Kärntens Freiheitskampf*, Klagenfurt, 1922).

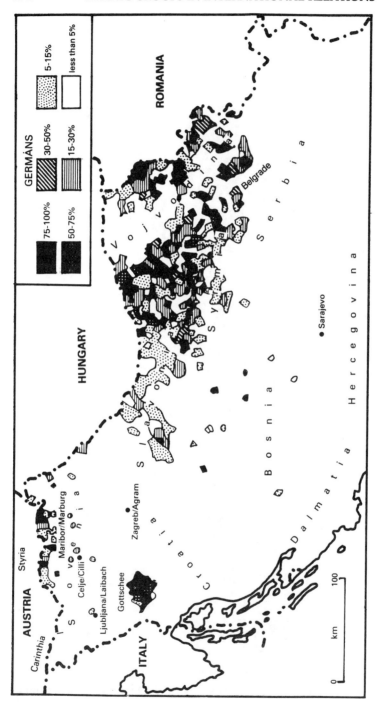

Map 11.2   Germans in Yugoslavia 1921
Source: Ivo Banac, *The National Question in Yugoslavia – Origins, History, Politics,* 1984.

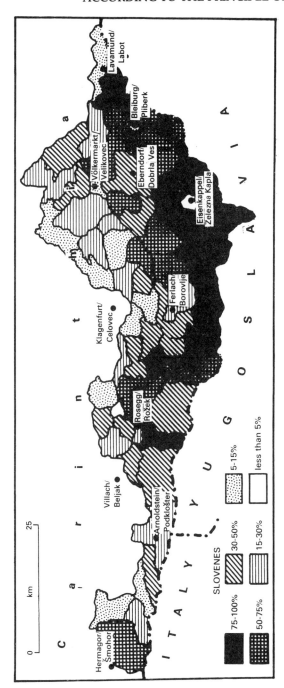

Map 11.3   Slovenes in Austrian Carinthia 1923
Sources: Die Slovenen in Kärnten/Slovenci na Koroškem (Celovec 1974), *Kärntner Weissbuch* (Klagenfurt 1980).

12 The Compulsory Exchange of Populations Between Greece and Turkey: the Settlement of Minority Questions at the Conference of Lausanne, 1923, and its Impact on Greek–Turkish Relations

KALLIOPI K. KOUFA and
CONSTANTINOS SVOLOPOULOS

Introduction

There are several methods used in inter- and trans-state relations to solve the problem of 'non-dominant ethnic groups', as a constant source of racial, linguistic, religious, etc. discrimination or unfair conditions of life, and as a potential cause of foreign intervention or the outbreak of war. Among these methods, international law has devised the so-called compulsory transfer of national minorities, in other words an obligatory uprooting or transplantation of populations from one country to another. It is a most drastic method, used for the physical elimination and discontinuance of the coexistence within the same state of mixed populations possessing different ethnic consciousnesses and, possibly, ethnic affiliations. This particular method was used to solve the thorny problem of Greek and Turkish minorities after the end of the First World War and the reestablishment of peace between Greece and Turkey, in 1923.

The compulsory exchange of Greco–Turkish populations, based on a formal international agreement and followed by certain elementary guarantees with a view to the recovery of abandoned property, commanded much attention in the interwar period, and remains very controversial to date. It has been fiercely criticised as contrary to human dignity and as a flagrant violation of international public order and international morality, which resulted in a human tragedy.[1] It has also been praised as a very effective, and realistic means of evacuating the unassimilated masses or fragments of the populations of the two states concerned and eliminating those troublesome differentiations which obstructed their paths towards ethnic homogeneity.[2]

The complexity and interest of the controversy is enhanced by the difficulty of producing a neat answer to the basic theoretical issue involved in the subject.[3] If efforts to protect the 'non-dominant ethnic groups' in inter- and trans-state relations have their ultimate socio-political and legal justification in the right of national self-determination, of human freedom or – at least – of toleration, the very method of compulsory transfer and enforced migration is based precisely on the refutation of all these.[4] From this standpoint, it could be argued that the obligatory exchange of populations between Greece and Turkey is undoubtedly a test case for any discussion of the broader problem concerning the degree of homogeneity and cohesion necessary to state society and the relevance of compulsion or constraint which may be used to achieve them in the framework of democracy and international institutions.

The compulsory mass transfer of the Muslim population from Greece and of the Greek Orthodox population from Turkey was effected on the basis of the convention concerning the exchange of Greek and Turkish populations and the annexed protocol of 30 January, 1923. This convention was signed together with an agreement relating to the restitution of interned civilians and the exchange of prisoners of war between Greece and Turkey, and both were completed by a declaration relating to the amnesty with the annexed protocol and a declaration relating to Muslim properties in Greece, signed on 24 July, 1923. All these acts form part of the peace settlement with Turkey reached at the Conference of Lausanne (20 November 1922 to 24 July 1923).

The ensuing compulsory uprooting of Greek and Turkish minorities and the compulsory liquidation of property left behind raised immense problems of economic and human readjustments in both states. On the face of it, the price was heavier for Greece, which, in a period of severe economic difficulties, had to accept more than 1 100 000 refugees from Asia Minor and eastern Thrace, equivalent to 20 per cent of her population.[5]

Moreover, the application of various stipulations of the formal agreements raised serious difficulties which for some time continued to poison Greco–Turkish relations.

The purpose of this study is not only to recount and interpret the exchange of national minorities between Greece and Turkey agreed at Lausanne but also to provide the political framework within which this (in)human transaction and exchange – almost unique in international practice – took place and, then, to assess its impact on Greco–Turkish relations in the interwar period.

The Choice of Compulsory Exchange Before the Opening of the Lausanne Conference.

If one looks for the underlying reason which led Greece and Turkey to the compulsory exchange, it appears that this act was intended to resolve a problem that was growing constantly more acute, in that the two nations, while employing completely different methods to cope with it, were both moved by a mutual concern to attenuate the centrifugal trends inside them and to assist the process of national integration. More specifically, almost half a millennium of Greek Orthodox and Turkish coexistence within the Ottoman empire had had all the characteristics of the juxtaposition of two different national entities. Efforts to introduce a liberal, constitutional regime designed to promote equality and fraternity between the different races within the framework of a unitarian, multinational state, had been thwarted by the reaction of the conservative Muslim party in the second half of the nineteenth century and the nationalist wing of the Young Turks' movement from 1908 onwards. During the First World War chiefly, the latter clung to the concept of a Turkish national state and practised massive persecution and forced displacement of Asia Minor's Christian populations.[6] On the other hand, although the Muslim presence in Greece, which, since the country's territorial expansion, was concentrated mainly in the north, under Ottoman domination until the Balkan wars of 1912–13, had never been so important nor had it led the authorities to resort to such arbitrary measures, it was nonetheless a source of constant concern for the Hellenic government. An approximate assessment of the size of the relevant ethnic minority living in either country illustrates the case quite well: immediately before the events leading to the decision to carry out the exchange, the Muslims in Greece numbered 450 000, while the most plausible estimates put the number of Greeks living in Turkey at over one and a half million.[7]

Apart from the underlying causes, the decision to carry out the compulsory exchange also sprang from current events and their resultant pressures. The military disaster of 1922 and the Hellenic army's evacuation of Asia Minor had necessarily created a new situation in the geographical area in which Greece and Turkey had for so long opposed each other and also coexisted. The dream of a powerful Hellenic national state, that would (at least partially) replace the Ottoman empire as a factor for balance and stability in the two continents of Europe and Asia, had collapsed. At a stroke, the treaty of Sèvres, which, having become a dead letter, was now null and void, had to be replaced by a new act, whose provisions would reflect the two parties' power balance.[8]

Nonetheless, before the negotiations to establish peace had begun, the Turkish nationalists, strong in their success, demonstrated their implacable determination to rid themselves once and for all of the numerous Greeks living in the territories they controlled. In the first two months following the Kemalist troops' entry into Smyrna, an overwhelming proportion of the Christians (nine-tenths, according to reliable evidence) were massacred or forced to abandon their ancestral homes in Asia Minor and flee to Greece, stripped of all they possessed.[9] Another case of uprooting of the Greek population from their native land occurred in eastern Thrace after the armistice was signed at Moudania on 11 October 1922 and the region's Hellenic authorities and military and their Entente allies were due to retreat and be replaced by the Turks.

It was then that Eleftherios Venizelos, who had just been nominated as the head of the Greek delegation in the imminent negotiations over the terms of peace, and was now powerless to reverse the tide of events, once again demonstrated his ability to adapt to *faits accomplis*. Anxious to ensure provision for the retreat of the Muslim population from Greece before the Christian element was completely evacuated from Turkish territory, he proposed the immediate implementation of a compulsory exchange of populations between Greece and Turkey. Specifically, on 13 October 1922, in a reply to Fridtjof Nansen, the League of Nations' High Commissioner for refugees, Venizelos, advanced the following proposition:

Two weeks ago, the Ankara government's Minister for the Interior announced that the Turks were determined not to put up any longer with the Greeks' presence on Ottoman soil. At the forthcoming conference, I shall therefore propose compulsory recourse to the exchange of Greek and Turkish populations. Winter is approaching, and this will make the problem of housing the refugees even harder to solve than that of feeding them. I make so bold as to beg you to take all possible steps to ensure that the refugees begin to move before peace is signed. In view of the fact that there are some 350 000 Turks at present in Greece, and since they could be assigned the houses and land abandoned by the Christians of Asia Minor or those that are now being abandoned by the Christians of Thrace, it would thus be possible to ensure homes for a corresponding number of Greek refugees.[10]

In his text, without actually stating it in so many words, Venizelos had essentially adopted the term 'compulsory exchange'. After this, Nansen undertook to promote the solution that had been proposed by Venizelos but actually *imposed* by the Turkish government's action of expelling the Greeks from Turkish territory.

The prospect of a compulsory exchange between Greece and Turkey was favourably received by the four Allied powers and by the relevant bodies of the League of Nations. However, despite its insistence on being relieved once and for all of its Christian minorities, the Ankara government adopted a dilatory attitude. The most likely hypothesis is that, since they wanted to carry out in full their policy of *faits accomplis*, the Turkish leaders were disposed to delay the final resolution of the problem until after the Peace Conference that was to take place in Lausanne before the end of November. As no official relations existed between Turkey and the League of Nations, the Ankara government refused to participate in the talks the High Commissioner (whom they regarded simply as a private individual) attempted to initiate on the subject. It was only under the pressure of all the other interested parties that the problem of the ethnic minorities (by now inseparably bound up with that of the refugees) was brought before the conference a few days after it had begun, without even being included on the official agenda.[11]

The Formulation of the Decision for Compulsory Exchange at the Lausanne Conference

On 20 November 1922, the peace conference was opened at Lausanne, by the President of the Swiss Confederation, Robert Haab. The Turkish delegation led by General Ismet Pasha Inonü arrived as victors and on an equal footing with the principal Allied powers (Great Britain, France, Italy and Japan) represented at the conference by a range of important personalities as delegation heads. The Greek delegation was led by E. Venizelos, Prime Minister during the First World War and the Paris peace conference. The Romanian Foreign Minister and that of the kingdom of the Serbs, Croats and Slovenes were also present, and the USA sent as observer its Ambassador at Rome. Bulgaria and the Soviet Union were also invited and duly represented while Belgium and Portugal were admitted to participate in some of the discussions.

The peace conference was divided into three main commissions, each to be presided over by a delegate of one of the three inviting powers. Thus, the first commission on territorial and military questions and on the regime of the Straits was chaired by Lord Curzon, the British Foreign Secretary; the second commission on the regime of foreigners and minorities in Turkey was chaired by Marquis Garroni the Italian Ambassador at Istanbul and the third commission on financial and economic questions, on ports and railways, and on sanitary questions was chaired by M Barrère, the French Ambassador at Rome.

Following Turkish disagreement on a number of issues, in particular with regard to the judicial guarantees for foreigners in Turkey and certain economic questions, the conference was suspended and negotiations discontinued from 5 February to 23 April 1923. The long and laborious negotiations were then resumed and continued until 24 July 1923, the date when the treaty of Lausanne was finally signed together with another 15 diplomatic instruments, including a Final act. In the meantime, on 30 January 1923, just before the suspension of the negotiations, a separate convention concerning the (compulsory) exchange of Greek and Turkish populations and an agreement between Greece and Turkey relating to the reciprocal restitution of interned civilians and exchange of prisoners of war were signed by the two states, antedating by six months the general peace treaty to which these two instruments were also affixed.

The comprehensive peace treaty thus reached at Lausanne was in appearance quite different from the other peace treaties concluded after the end of the First World War, in that it consisted of a whole series of different diplomatic instruments constituting an integral whole.[12] Besides the main peace treaty (comprising 143 articles dealing with various questions) it encompassed five special conventions (among which the above-mentioned exchange convention), an agreement, four declarations, six protocols, the Final act and a number of explanatory letters and agreements (attached but not mentioned in the Final act and related to various stipulations of the above instruments).[13]

The question of the exchange of populations between Greece and Turkey was discussed within the Territorial and Military Commission between 1 December 1922 and 27 January 1923. The members of the Commission were invited by its President, Lord Curzon, to discuss this question of immediate importance, which 'closely affected the interests of both peoples' and called 'for an early solution, because the livelihood of the people and the cultivation of the crops for next year were involved'. The British delegate's proposition was immediately taken up by E. Venizelos who emphasised that a solution was urgently required. It was in the interests of both peoples – he stressed – that a solution should be devised as quickly as possible. The head of the Turkish delegation,

Ismet Pasha, initially suggested that this question was bound up with the solution of the question of minorities in his country and, in any case, that it was to be discussed at a later meeting. But he finally agreed with the generally prevailing opinion in favour of the immediate confrontation of the problem. A mixed sub-commission was immediately constituted in order not merely to explore the subject, but also to draw up a draft convention for signature by the two parties with as little delay as possible. Dr F. Nansen, after having read to the Commission a report referring to his own experience on the subject 'obtained on the spot', was designated to help the sub-commission in its task.

In view of the common decision of the parties immediately interested to proceed to the exchange solution, two important political questions were mainly discussed before such an agreement could be made. First, whether the future treaty should be based on the principle of compulsory or of voluntary emigration; and second, what would be the area of its application.[14]

In the first case, Venizelos, having consented to the method of compulsory exchange before the opening of the conference, though he accepted it only under stress of necessity, was still willing to consider another solution of the problem based on principles which were more humane and more in accordance with the natural rights of populations. Specifically, he declared that compulsory exchange was repugnant to the Greek delegation. From his side, he did not wish to oblige the Turkish population to leave Greece. The Greek government was ready to give up the idea of compulsory exchange on condition that the Turkish government allowed the Greeks who were at present expelled from Turkey to return to their homes. In view of these considerations, he made a proposal to the effect that the population remaining in Constantinople or in Anatolia, as well as the Turkish residents in Greece, should not be compelled to abandon their regular homes and that any Greek inhabitants of Anatolia or of eastern Thrace who had taken refuge in Greece should be allowed to return to their homes.

The new initiative taken by the Greek representative gave the opportunity to the President of the Commission to express also his deep regret

> that the solution now being worked out should be the compulsory exchange of populations – a thoroughly bad and vicious solution, for which the world would pay a heavy penalty for a hundred years to come.

Ismet Pasha, in the name of all that concerned the existence, independence and rights of the Turkish people, pointed to the danger of 'minorities becoming weapons in the hands of foreigners, capable of being utilised for subversive purposes'. He thus constantly stressed that compulsory exchange had become unavoidable. The final adoption by the sub-commission of this obligatory principle, was definitively accepted – as a great but inevitable 'misfortune', at its meeting of 27 January 1923.

In the meantime, the members of the Territorial and Military Commission adopted the solution given by the sub-commission to the problem concerning the area of application of the projected exchange. At the first meeting of the Commission, on 1 December 1922, Venizelos had stressed that he could not agree that thousands of Greeks should be obliged to leave Istanbul. Such an expulsion would amount to an unprecedented political, economic and social catastrophe. The Greek delegate's position had also been strongly supported by Lord Curzon. The Greek population was vital to the existence of Istanbul as a great centre of commerce and industry and without it, that city would be in danger of losing its authority, wealth and trade. After the reservation he had initially expressed, Ismet Pasha agreed to the exclusion from the exchange of the Greeks born in Istanbul, 'because the Allied delegations had urged that the elements which constituted a factor of commercial and economic importance should not be removed all of a sudden from a city such as Constantinople' [Istanbul]. As early as 10 January the President of the sub-commission announced that an agreement had been reached on the principle of a general exchange except as regards the Greek Orthodox element in Istanbul and the Muslim one in western Thrace.

In these circumstances, although most serious difficulties had arisen in connection with the framing of the convention relating to the exchange of populations, by dint of mutual sacrifices – according to the statement of the President of the sub-commission – it had proved possible to reach agreement on all points before the end of January 1923.

The Exchange of National Minorities Between Greece and Turkey Agreed at Lausanne

Although it constitutes a novelty, in that it is admittedly the very first international transaction of its sort in the history of mankind,[15] the Convention of Lausanne for the compulsory exchange of populations was not contrived in a vacuum but was worked out in due sequence according to a series of other international agreements. These now need to be briefly referred to for the better understanding of its conception and origins. In other words, it has some direct historical precedents, all aiming at the evacuation or uprooting of minority populations from their land and social *milieu* by transfer to another homeland dominated by their ethnic kinsmen. Thus we shall see that the implementation of the idea and policy of transfer and exchange of national minorities had its own history in the foreign relations of both Turkey and Greece. Accordingly, it will be useful (if not essential) to note these direct precedents or earlier attempts at exchanges of minority populations by the two states, before proceeding to the interpretation and analysis of the contents of the Exchange Convention of Lausanne itself.

Direct Historical Precedents and Genesis of the Exchange Convention

The first explicit provision for a reciprocal exchange of populations can be found in the protocol annexed to the Treaty of Constantinople, of 16–29 September 1913, between Bulgaria and Turkey. According to section C of this protocol, voluntary exchange of Bulgarian and Muslim populations and their properties would be facilitated by the two governments within a zone of 15 kilometres either side of the entire common frontier. The exchange was to take place on the basis of whole villages. Rural and urban properties were to be exchanged under the auspices of the two governments and mixed commissions appointed by the two governments were to proceed to the exchange and eventual indemnification.[16]

On the other hand, according to article seven of the treaty, the Muslims inhabiting the territories ceded to Bulgaria were granted the right to opt either to remain thereafter as Bulgarian subjects in these territories or to declare their national allegiance to the Ottoman empire and leave the ceded territories within four years.[17] Using this right of option, the Muslim populations left Bulgaria in masses and came to eastern Thrace where they established themselves in the districts of Kirk-Kilisse and Adrianople upon the properties of Bulgarian minority communities. To improve the established state of affairs, and force the transfer of the Bulgarian minority communities to the abandoned Muslim villages ceded to Bulgaria – and precipitate, as well, the reciprocal emigration of the remaining Bulgarian and Muslim national minorities in Turkey and Bulgaria respectively – the two states signed, on 2–15 November 1913, a Convention concerning the Exchange of Populations.[18]

According to this convention, the Bulgarian peasants of the districts of Kirk-Kilisse and Adrianople were to be settled in the abandoned Muslim villages of Thrace ceded to Bulgaria, inasmuch as the Bulgarian villages of the above districts had been occupied by the Muslim refugees who came from Thrace. The Turkish government was to provide the means of transport for the Turkish subjects of Bulgarian origin leaving Turkey, whose dwellings had been forcibly occupied, to the villages recently ceded to Bulgaria and abandoned by the Turkish population, situated within a zone of 20 kilometres at most from the border. The rights of property were to be respected and indemnities, fixed by agreement or on the basis of an appraisal made by an *ad hoc* commission, were to be paid to the emigrants. This convention was never ratified by the Bulgarian Chamber of Deputies, although a mixed commission consisting of Turkish and Bulgarian delegates, later divided into two sub-commissions, met and worked to implement it from May to October 1914, when Turkey entered the First World War.

Some rather similar difficulties which arose between Greece and Turkey, also in the years 1913–14, led to a somewhat different agreement between these two countries as to the solution of their national minority problems through an exchange of populations. There were the massive displacements of Greek populations caused by the Second Balkan War plus the migrations of Muslims from the Balkan countries as a response to the propaganda invitation addressed to them by the Young Turks, and the systematic expulsion and deportation by the Ottoman government of the Greeks from Turkish eastern Thrace and the western coasts of Asia Minor. In early 1914, therefore, the Greek government was led into negotiations with the *Porte* with a view to an exchange of national minority populations.[19]

The negotiations started with a proposal made to the Greek Prime Minister, Venizelos, by the Turkish Minister at Athens for an exchange of 'the Greek rural populations of the district (*Vilayet*) of Smyrna with the Muslims of Macedonia'.[20] This proposal was favourably received by the Greek government, anxious, on the one side, to end the unilateral Turkish expulsions and deportations of Greeks and the confiscation of their properties and, on the other side, to avoid eventual hostile clashes with the Muslim emigrants voluntarily establishing themselves in the regions of western Anatolia, from which the Greeks were massively and forcibly displaced by the Ottoman government.

According to the Greek counterproposals and the informal agreement, reached after subsequent diplomatic correspondence, the forced emigration of the Greeks was to cease and the populations of the Greek villages in Thrace and in the district of Smyrna were to be exchanged against the Muslim peasants of Macedonia and Epirus. The desire of the people to emigrate was to be spontaneous and officially ascertained by a mixed commission consisting of four members appointed by the two governments and including a neutral arbiter from a European country for the final settlement of differences. The mixed commission was also to proceed to the appraisal and liquidation of the properties of the emigrants. This informal agreement started to be applied with the establishment and a number of meetings of the mixed commission in June to July 1914. It was discontinued, however, and failed in its desired effect. The expulsions of the Greeks continued while Turkey joined the Central powers in the First World War and, later on, Greece joined the Allied powers against Turkey.

Had the Treaty of Sèvres, of 10 August 1920, between the Allied powers and Turkey come into effect, Turkey would not only have had to recognise the principles of reciprocal and spontaneous emigration of the individuals belonging to ethnic minorities dictated by the Allied powers but would also have had to conclude with Greece a special agreement providing for the reciprocal and spontaneous emigration of the Greek and Turkish populations in the territories transferred to Greece or remaining in Ottoman possession respectively (article 143). Moreover, according to that same treaty (article 149), the Ottoman government would have had to facilitate the repatriation of Ottoman subjects of non-Turkish race who had been expelled since 1 January 1914, and to restore their confiscated property.[21]

It is, however, necessary to recall at this point, that the above stipulations of the abortive Treaty of Sèvres were only following the very model which a previous treaty, the Treaty of Neuilly, between the Allied powers and Bulgaria, had already devised almost a year earlier, on 27 November 1919. By the terms of article 56, paragraph 2, of this treaty, Bulgaria undertook to recognise such provisions as the principal Allied and Associated powers might consider best with respect to the reciprocal and voluntary emigration of national minorities. It was in this light that a special convention between Greece and Bulgaria concerning reciprocal emigration was signed by these two governments on the same day, at Neuilly, as part of the whole peace settlement reached there.

This special convention respecting reciprocal emigration[22] provided for the right of the subjects of the contracting parties who belonged to ethnic, religious or linguistic minorities to emigrate freely to their respective territories and the corresponding duty of the contracting states to facilitate by all means at their disposal the exercise of this right. A mixed commission composed of four members – one member appointed by each contracting state and two members of another nationality, one of whom would be acting President, appointed by the Council of the League of Nations – was to survey this emigration and liquidate the immovable property of the emigrants. Emigrants were entitled to take with them, or to have transported, their movable property of every kind exempt from customs duties of any kind. They were to exercise their right of emigration within a period of two years from the constitution of the mixed commission, before the commission or before its representatives. The exercise of the right of emigration entailed an automatic change of nationality.

This convention, ratified by both states by 9 August 1920, regulated the voluntary Greco–Bulgarian minority transfer on rather broad lines, leaving to the mixed commission the ultimate power on all questions of detail and execution. Its operation lasted until 31 January 1932 and, according to the statistics of the mixed commission, the numbers of emigrants who availed themselves of its terms were 92 000 Bulgars and 46 000 Greeks.[23] Although liberal and voluntary, in principle, this major international experiment in reciprocal exchange of populations produced good results only after it became in practice to a great extent compulsory and simply regulatory of the established facts.[24] An attempt to describe in this context the administration of its provisions – the methods used for supervising and facilitating the emigration and for evaluating and liquidating the properties and payments – or to account for the extraneous elements and circumstances which affected its application and execution would certainly carry us beyond the province of our topic. Suffice it only to mention that of the number of emigrants just referred to above who availed themselves of the terms of this convention, 39 000 Bulgars and 16 000 Greeks had already left their homes before the convention became effective in 1920.[25] Also that initially and even for some time, the prospect of emigration was attractive or desirable to neither ethnic minority. Between November 1922 and 1 July 1923, only 166 Bulgarian families and 197 Greek families declared for emigration. The sudden and abrupt increase in the number of declarations for emigration on both sides during the succeeding months has been explained by authoritative opinion as due largely to the systematic settlement – following the Lausanne convention of 1923 for compulsory exchange of Greco–Turkish populations – of Greek refugees from Turkey in Greek Macedonia and Thrace among Bulgarian minority villagers who were thereby prompted to depart; and due also to the respective establishment of these Bulgarian refugees from Greece upon Greek minority villages in southern Bulgaria prompting, in turn, the Greek minority to leave Bulgaria.[26]

Against this background of previous international agreements, the convention of Lausanne of 1923, hereafter to be dealt with extensively, appears as the last and most radical in its endeavour to solve the minority problem between Greece and Turkey. It contains, indeed, the dominant elements of all the previous arrangements just referred to: (a) expulsionist thought implemented by the physical removal and resettlement of minority populations; (b) the process to be achieved on the basis of international legal provisions and international organisational devices. In addition, compared to its direct historical precedents, it marks a formal and drastic advance, insofar as political realism and effectiveness, on the one hand, and ruthless disregard of elementary human rights and lack of humanitarianism, on the other hand, were concerned.

Before turning our attention to the provisions and the administration of the system of compulsory exchange instituted by the Lausanne convention, it is important to refer again to the basic facts and conditions surrounding its genesis. As already mentioned, the Greco–Turkish war ended in 1922 with the overwhelming defeat of the Greek armies in Asia Minor. The disorderly retreat of the Greek armies was followed by a vast movement of Greek populations from Asia Minor and Thrace. People fled to Greece in order to escape from religious and political persecution in Turkey. Moreover, large migratory movements of Greeks from Turkish territory had already taken place before, in the previous decade, as a result of the two Balkan Wars of 1912–13 and the First World War, when the new policy of 'ottomanisation' was applied by the Young Turks in their efforts to eliminate the national minorities of the Turkish empire and achieve a homogeneous Turkish state. With the reestablishment of peace, it was all too obvious that among the conditions surrounding any viable or durable settlement of Near Eastern affairs there had to be, on the one hand, a scheme for the protection or transfer of the remaining national minorities which could not or would not emigrate and, on the other hand, a mechanism for the liquidation of all the personal properties hurriedly abandoned or left behind by the successive waves of emigrants.

It was for these reasons that at the peace conference on Near Eastern affairs which opened at Lausanne on 20 November 1922, such issues had to be considered and resolved. In the meantime, the precarious, lamentable state of the successive masses of refugees continually arriving in Greece, and the burdens placed upon Greece in taking care of them and settling them, led the third assembly of the League of Nations, at its session of 19 September 1922, to authorise Dr F. Nansen, High Commissioner of the League for Russian refugees at Istanbul, to assist also in the relief of the refugees from the Greco–Turkish war. It was in the framework of this mission of Dr Nansen and after his exchange of views with the Greek and Turkish governments that the proposal for the adoption of a separate convention concerning the exchange of Greek and Turkish populations came up and was put forward at the conference of Lausanne, the result being the final drafting of the exchange convention, signed on 30 January 1923.

Content and Analysis of the Provisions of the Lausanne Exchange Convention

Scope and Nature of the Agreement Article one of the Lausanne convention not only established the principle of a compulsory exchange of populations but also defined the exchangeable persons. The actual terms of this provision stated that:

> As from 1 May 1923, there shall take place a compulsory exchange of Turkish nationals of the Greek Orthodox religion established in Turkish territory, and of Greek nationals of the Muslim religion established in Greek territory. These persons shall not return to live in Turkey or Greece respectively without the authorisation of the Turkish Government or of the Greek Government respectively.

In other words, according to the first stipulation of this international agreement, each of the two contracting parties undertook the obligation to exchange a number of its own citizens against a number of the citizens of its counterpart without taking into consideration the desires of the citizens involved, that is without making any allowance for any possible disagreement by the individual persons who were to be subject to the exchange.[27] According to the first paragraph of article 3 of the agreement, those Greeks and Muslims who had already 'since 18 October 1912, left the territories of which the Greek and Turkish inhabitants are to be respectively exchanged' were also to be considered as included in this exchange.[28]

There has been extensive discussion about the lack of humanity involved in this obligatory repatriation or mutual deportation of populations, and about its contravention of minority rights and of all principles of international law regarding fundamental individual rights theretofore established and recognised.[29] The fact that this compulsory exchange was in contravention of previous developments in international law in the area of territorial changes, whereby the will of the population was to be explored through an option or a popular vote, has also rightly been stressed.[30] These points do not therefore need to be laboured here in particular.

It is interesting, however, to observe that this compulsory exchange of Greco–Turkish populations was based primarily, but not exclusively, upon the criterion of the religious affiliation of these peoples.[31] However, whereas article one uses the expression 'Turkish nationals of the Greek Orthodox religion' and 'Greek nationals of the Muslim religion', in order to define the citizens to be exchanged by the two contracting parties, it is all too obvious from the very title of the exchange agreement ('Convention concerning the Exchange of Greek and Turkish Populations'), from the simple reference to 'Greeks' and 'Muslims' in the following articles, and from the drafting and the discussion of the relevant stipulations in the framework of the Sub-commission on Minorities at the Conference of Lausanne,[32] that the criterion of religious affiliation was to be considered and determined within the broader context of the ethnic appurtenance or the national consciousness of those exchanged.[33] This, of course, had to be the same as that of the contracting parties, either Greek or Turkish. In other words, there were obvious ethno-political limits to the applicability of religion or faith as a criterion for the exchange.

In effect, a literal interpretation and application of article one would have had to include in the exchange such other ethnicities as were established in the territories of the two contracting parties, like the Serbs, Romanians, Russians, Albanians, Arabs etc., who were coreligionists but who had no ethnic affiliation or common loyalty to either the Greek or the Turkish nation as such. This illogical consequence would have betrayed the whole spirit of this bilateral convention and the main purpose of its drafters, namely to get rid of each other's national minority by expelling it from their territories and repatriating it to its 'proper' homeland.

The date of 18 October 1912, set by the aforementioned first paragraph of article three,[34] with a view to considering as included in the obligatory exchange 'those Greeks and Moslems who have already . . . left the territories the Greek and Turkish inhabitants of which are to be respectively exchanged', is the date of the declaration of war between Greece and Turkey in the first Balkan war of 1912. The reason for this retroactive provision, extending the application of the exchange agreement to previous emigrations between the two contracting parties, was the desire to clear up at least a substantial number of situations created by the preceding successive migratory movements between Greece and Turkey. It was for this reason that the terms of article three, first paragraph, did not encompass all former emigrants and refugees but only those who had left after the beginning of the first Balkan war and only from those Greek and Turkish territories which were included in the exchange.[35]

According to the second paragraph of article three, 'the expression "emigrant" in the present convention includes all physical and juridical persons who have been obliged to emigrate or have emigrated since 18 October, 1912'. Moreover, the second paragraph of article eight, regulating the free transport of the movable property of those to be exchanged, made a special reference to 'the members of each community (including the personnel of mosques, *tekkes*, *medresses* (schools with a religious base), churches, convents, schools, hospitals, societies, associations and juridicial persons, or other foundations of any nature whatever)' who would leave the territory of one of the contracting parties and would have the same rights as the individual emigrants. Thus, the extension of the relevant provisions of the agreement to those juristic persons who had left Greek and Turkish territories respectively after the beginning of the first Balkan war was especially provided for; and under the term, 'juristic persons', communities including the personnel of mosques, churches, schools etc. were to be understood as included in the exchange.[36]

Extent of and Exceptions to Exchangeability Article two of the agreement in its first paragraph provides for the non-exchangeability of

(a) the Greek inhabitants of Constantinople and (b) the Muslim inhabitants of western Thrace.

It further defines in its second and third paragraphs these two categories of persons, as follows:

All Greeks who were already established before 30 October 1918, within the areas under the Prefecture of the City of Constantinople, as defined by the law of 1912, shall be considered as Greek inhabitants of Constantinople. All Moslems established in the region to the east of the frontier line laid down in 1913 by the Treaty of Bucharest shall be considered as Moslem inhabitants of western Thrace.

The correct interpretation of this provision, which expressly exempts a number of Greeks and Muslims from the obligatory exchange, caused many controversies and strained relations between the two contracting parties over a prolonged period of time, as we shall presently see.

The date of 30 October 1918 was the day of the armistice of Moudros,[37] and the use of this date excluded from the exemptions under article two a large number of Greeks who had arrived in Istanbul after that date. The Treaty of Bucharest after the end of the second Balkan war, signed by Greece and Turkey on 10 August 1913 had pushed the Greek frontier line to the east as far as the river Nestos (Mesta). This eastern frontier of Greece, also marking the western boundary of the region of western Thrace, surrendered by Bulgaria in 1919 and granted by the Treaty of Lausanne to Greece, was contested as the boundary of western Thrace by Turkey, at the Conference of Lausanne. According to the Turkish argument it was not the river Nestos (Mesta) but the river Strymon (Struma) which formed the western boundary of the region in question. With the stipulation then of article two, third paragraph, of the exchange agreement, the Greek definition of the western boundary of western Thrace, as that frontier line laid down by the Treaty of Bucharest and mostly formed by the Nestos, was finalised and accepted by Turkey.

The main controversy, however, was over the term 'established' and the definition of Greek inhabitants of Istanbul in the second paragraph of article two. It necessitated years of patient effort and a recourse to the Permanent Court of International Justice before it could be settled. As already said,[38] the second paragraph of article two defines the Greek inhabitants of Istanbul as 'all Greeks who were already established before 30 October 1918, within the areas under the Prefecture of the city of Constantinople, as defined by the law of 1912'. If at first reading the meaning of this stipulation appears to be rather simple, repeated reading will reveal the uncertainty involved as regards the definition of the Greeks 'established' in Istanbul and, in particular, the ambiguities arising from the lack of any reference to the rules to be applied in order to determine the *status* of the 'established' people.[39]

Thus, according to the Greek interpretation, covered as 'established' were the persons who were, regardless of any Greek or Turkish law prescribing the conditions of transfer or acquisition of domicile, continuous residents in a certain place and centred their activities and business there. It was clear from the Greek point of view that, under the terms of the convention and the preparatory work of the Conference of Lausanne, all persons who had been resident in Istanbul before 30 October 1918 and had the manifest intention of remaining there for a considerable period, fulfilled the conditions prescribed by article two of the agreement and were entitled to be exempted from the exchange.

In the Turkish definition, the word 'established' was to be understood in reference to Turkish legislation; that is, the status of 'establishment' depended on the fulfilment of those legal formalities which were prescribed by the existing Turkish law, insofar as that law had not been modified or suspended by the provisions of the Lausanne convention. In Turkish eyes, those who were 'established' in a particular place were those who resided there with the intention of remaining there permanently. The Turkish law of 14 August 1914 provided for the fulfilment of certain formalities of registration by all persons leaving their place of origin in order to establish a domicile in another place. The Greek inhabitants of Istanbul resident there from before 30 October 1918, but who had not complied with the local legislation or whose families were established in regions of Turkey subject to exchange and who did not come with the intention of remaining in Istanbul permanently, were not to be considered as 'established' in Istanbul and, therefore, were not to be exempted from the exchange.[40]

The two contracting parties adhered to their own interpretations and counterarguments, and the arrest and internment for evacuation from Istanbul by the Turkish authorities, in October 1924, of 4452

Greeks, a considerable number of whom were clearly not subject to the exchange terms, intensified the crisis in relations between the two states. It culminated in an appeal by the Greek government to the Council of the League of Nations. On 13 December 1924, the Council finally decided to request the Permanent Court of International Justice to give an advisory opinion on the Greco–Turkish dispute and the interpretation of article two of the Exchange convention:

> What meaning and scope should be attributed to the word 'established' in article two of the convention of Lausanne of 30 January 1923 regarding the exchange of Greek and Turkish populations, in regard to which discussions have arisen and arguments have been put forward . . . ? And what conditions must the persons who are described in article two of the convention of Lausanne under the title of 'Greek inhabitants of Constantinople' fulfil in order that they may be considered as 'established' under the terms of the convention and exempt from compulsory exchange?

In its unanimous advisory opinion of 21 February 1925,[41] the court proceeded 'to consider firstly the meaning and scope of the word *établis* [established] in general and, secondly, the question of whether the situation contemplated by this word should be determined according to the laws in force in the two countries concerned'.[42] From the fact that the agreement was drawn up in French, the Court considered the meaning of the French word *établissement* as embracing both the factor of residence and stability, that is an intention to continue residence in a certain place for an extended period. It decided that

> the word 'established' having been used to describe a portion of the Greek inhabitants of Constantinople naturally embraces those inhabitants who, on 30 October 1918, were already residing at Constantinople with the intention of remaining there for an extended period.[43]

The Court therefore did not approve the Turkish thesis that to determine the question of 'establishment' it was necessary to resort to Turkish legislation. In the opinion of the Court

> it might well happen that a reference to Turkish and Greek legislation would lead to the division of the population being carried out in a different manner in Turkey and in Greece. This again would not be in accordance with the spirit of the convention, the intention of which is undoubtedly to ensure, by means of the application of identical and reciprocal measures in the territory of the two states, that the same treatment is accorded to the Greek and Turkish populations.[44]

Hence, the Court maintained that the purpose of the word 'established' in article two was to refer to a situation of fact constituted by residence of a lasting nature, and that 'Greek inhabitants of Constantinople' exempted from the exchange were those residing within the boundaries of the prefecture of the city of Istanbul as defined by the Turkish law of 1912, having arrived from any other place prior to 30 October 1918, with intention to remain for an extended period.[45]

Although this Court decision seemed to have settled the question, in practice negotiations and controversies over the status of the Greek population in Istanbul continued, and it affected relations between the two states down to the year 1930. By the terms of article 16, second paragraph, (to be reviewed later)[46] Greece and Turkey both undertook an obligation not to place any obstacle 'in the way of the inhabitants of the districts excepted from the exchange under article two exercising freely their right to remain in or to return to those districts and to enjoy to the full their liberties and rights of property in Turkey and in Greece'. The infringement by both contracting parties of articles 16 and two, and the expulsion of the Ecumenical Patriarch Constantine VI from Istanbul in 1925 on the grounds that he was an 'exchangeable' Greek, led to another period of agitation and crisis in Greco–Turkish relations.

Indeed, Greece violated the above provision of article 16 due to her difficulty in resettling the Greek refugees from eastern Thrace, who occupied the land and property of many Muslims not liable for exchange in western Thrace. Turkey violated both articles two and 16. This was partly as a retaliatory action against Greece and partly as a result of her unwillingness to consent to the return of many absent Greeks not liable to exchange and who wished to return and to regain their abandoned property, which had been seized by the Turkish authorities along with some of the property of Greeks legitimately remaining in Istanbul.[47] Thus, another period of direct negotiations and mutual desire to improve political relations started in early 1925, which resulted in the signing by the respective governments of another two conventions of limited application,[48] before the matter was finally to be settled by the convention of Angora of 10 June 1930.[49]

By the terms of article ten of this convention, Turkey recognised as 'established' all Orthodox Greeks who were Turkish subjects actually present in the area of Istanbul excepted from the exchange, whatever the date of their arrival or the place of their birth. The same quality of 'established' was accepted for those eligible Greeks who had already left Istanbul with passports issued by the Turkish authorities. In reciprocal terms, article 14 provided for the recognition by Greece as 'established' of all Muslims who were Greek subjects actually present in western Thrace excepted from the exchange, whatever the date of their arrival or the place of their birth.

The same quality of 'established' was accepted for the eligible Muslims who had already left western Thrace with passports issued by the Greek authorities. Under article 28, however, those Greek Orthodox Turkish subjects or Muslim Greek subjects who were not liable for exchange, but who were absent, and had left Istanbul or western Thrace respectively without being provided with passports issued by the relevant Greek or Turkish authorities, were deprived of the right to return to Istanbul or to western Thrace as appropriate. It is, finally, worth noting, that these stipulations affected about 30 000 Greeks who had left after the occupation of Istanbul by the Allies with English, French and especially Greek passports, not to mention those Greeks who, having already left with Imperial Turkish passports before the government of Ankara was represented in Istanbul, were in practice included in the obligatory exchange.[50]

Attention should further be drawn in this section to some other important classes of Greeks and Turks who, either through interpretation of the terms and conditions of the Exchange convention of Lausanne or by some other means, were also to be excluded from the obligatory exchange. The first such category encompasses, on the one hand, the Greek subjects established in Turkey and the Turkish subjects established in Greece, and, on the other hand, the Greeks who were Turkish subjects, but who professed a different religion to Greek Orthodox. In effect, the exclusion from the obligatory exchange of these two classes of Greeks and Turks is easily deduced from the definition of those liable to exchange under article one[51] as 'Turkish nationals of the Greek Orthodox religion established in Turkish territory, and Greek nationals of the Muslim religion established in Greek territory'. It is obvious that by implication the Greek nationals established in Turkey and the Turkish nationals established in Greece were not to be included in the exchange,[52] and, moreover, that the Greeks of Catholic or Protestant or any religion other than the Orthodox were also not to be included in the exchange.[53]

The second category includes the Albanian Muslims in Greece, as well as the Greek inhabitants of the islands of Imbros and Tenedos. Thus, with regard to the first class of the above, by virtue of an oral commitment made by the Greek delegation at the Sub-commission on Minorities, during the Conference of Lausanne, the Muslims of Albanian origin established in Greece were to be excluded from the exchange on the grounds that even though they were coreligionists with the Turks, they were not by any means their compatriots.[54] However with regard to the Greeks of the Aegean islands Imbros and Tenedos – which were both granted to Turkey by the main Treaty of Lausanne[55] – their exemption from the obligatory exchange was expressly provided for by article 14, paragraph two, of that treaty in the following terms: 'The stipulations entered into or to be entered into between Greece and Turkey concerning the exchange of Greek and Turkish populations shall not be applicable to the inhabitants of the islands Imbros and Tenedos.'[56]

Provisions in Favour of the Exchangeables Article six of the convention provided that no obstacle was to be placed for any reason whatever in the way of the departure of a person belonging to the populations which were to be exchanged. It will be observed that the wish of both the Greek and the Turkish governments to precipitate the exchange definitely guaranteed the execution of this stipulation. Yet another guarantee of practical importance was further provided for in that same article six, in the terms of which, in the event of a conviction or trial for crime of an emigrant, the emigrant should be handed over to the authorities of the country of destination either to serve the sentence or to be brought to trial. In other words, both contracting parties undertook the obligation to avoid punishing crimes committed in their territories by those liable to be exchanged for reasons of justice and also in order to avoid the possible arbitrary retention of such persons, particularly problematic if unfairly prosecuted or condemned.

It is important to note also in this context the stipulation of article four, providing that the 'first instalment of Greeks' to be sent to Greece was to consist of 'all able bodied men detained . . . in Turkey' who belonged to the Greek population and whose families had already left Turkish territory. In this respect, the protocol annexed to the Exchange convention,[57] contained the declaration by the Turkish plenipotentiaries promising to release and provide for the departure of 'the able bodied men referred to in article four of the said convention', without waiting for the coming into force of the Exchange convention.[58]

Emigrants lost the nationality of the country which they were leaving and automatically acquired the nationality of the country of their destination upon their arrival in the territory of the latter country, according to the first paragraph of article seven. Moreover, according to the second paragraph of article seven – which was obviously aimed at the great numbers of Greeks and Turks who had migrated as far back as 1912 and the Balkan wars[59] – 'such emigrants as have already left one or the other of the two countries and have not yet acquired their new nationality shall acquire that nationality on the date of signature' of the Exchange convention – that is on 30 January 1923.

It is interesting to observe that this provision does not take into consideration the existing municipal legislation of the contracting parties; and that it is incomplete, in that it does not envisage or provide for those emigrants who did not establish themselves in Greece or in Turkey but in a third country, either prior to or after the signature of the Exchange convention. As a consequence, Greece arranged for the naturalisation of Greeks who were formerly Turkish subjects, now emigrating to Greece, by issuing the legislative decree of 21–25 August 1923. It was not until later on that the Greek law 3098 of 17–24 July 1924 made provision for the naturalisation of such people who had emigrated to a place other than Greece.[60]

Another series of provisions and measures to aid those exchanged was to be carried out or facilitated through the agency of a mixed commission – itself to be dealt with in the next section. Thus, according to article eight, the emigrants as well as the members of 'each community' as described earlier[61] were to be free to take away with them all their movable property, without being liable to any duty or tax. The fullest facilities for transport were to be provided, under the terms of the third paragraph of article eight, by the authorities of the two countries, upon the recommendation of the Mixed Commission. According to the last paragraph of that same article, in those cases where all or part of the movable property could not be taken away, an inventory and valuation of the property left behind would serve as a basis for the liquidation entrusted to the Mixed Commission.[62] Particular mention should also be made, in this connection, of article five providing for the rights of property and monetary assets of the emigrants, which were not to be prejudiced in consequence of the exchange – meaning, of course, that the persons subject to exchange could collect debts owed to them before their departure.[63]

As regards the rural and urban immovable property of the emigrants and of the communities, article nine also entrusted to the Mixed Commission its liquidation and, moreover, provided for the extension of the same measure of liquidation to property situated in the districts to which the compulsory exchange applied which belonged to religious or benevolent institutions of communities established in districts where the exchange did not apply.[64]

In order to guarantee the rights of the people to be exchanged and also avoid the arbitrary estimation of their properties by the two contracting parties, article 13 provided for the valuation by the Mixed Commission of the movable and immovable property to be liqui-dated, 'the interested parties being given a hearing or being duly summoned so that they may be heard'. Nonetheless, according to article ten, in the case of any measures taken by Greece or Turkey since 18 October 1912, which had resulted in any restriction on rights of ownership over the property of the exchangeables, such as confiscation, forced sale, etc., its value was to be fixed by the Mixed

Commission as if the measures in question had not been applied. Expropriated property was to be freshly evaluated and compensation which would repair injuries ascertained by the Mixed Commission was to be fixed. Analogous solutions were provided, by the third paragraph of article ten, in favour of the property owners to be exchanged who were deprived of 'the enjoyment . . . in one way or another' of their property income.[65] Particular mention should also be made in this connection of the stipulation in the second sentence of article 14, paragraph two, that emigrants should be entitled to receive, as representing the sums due to them, in the country of their destination, property of a value equal to and of the same nature as that which they had left behind.[66]

Finally, according to article 16, in order to help those to be exchanged, the two governments undertook the obligation of coming to an agreement with the Mixed Commission over a plan for the evacuation of the emigrants, in other words, in the terms of the first paragraph of this article: 'concerning the notification to be made to persons who are to leave the territory of Turkey and Greece under the present convention, and concerning the ports to which these persons are to go for the purpose of being transported to the country of their destination'. They undertook also the following obligations under the terms in paragraph two: (a) not to exercise any direct or indirect pressure on the relevant populations with a view to making them leave their homes or abandon their property before the date fixed for their departure; (b) not to impose special taxes or dues on the emigrants who had left or who were to leave the country; (c) not to place any obstacle in the way of the inhabitants of the districts excepted from the exchange under article two freely exercising their right to remain in or return to those districts, and to enjoy to the full their liberties and rights of property in Turkey and Greece. This provision was not to be invoked as a motive for preventing the free alienation of property belonging to inhabitants of the said regions which were excepted from the exchange, or the voluntary departure of those among these inhabitants who wished to leave Turkey or Greece.

Allusion has already been made to the difficulties involved over articles two and 16 of the Exchange convention.[67] The problem of the interpretation of the status of those 'established' in Istanbul and the problem of the liquidation of the property of those forced to leave and of their indemnification became closely related. Greece was, on the one hand, confronted by demands from Turkey for the surrender of all property of the Muslims who were to stay and, on the other hand, by the demands of her own nationals, both eligible and ineligible for exchange, for indemnification for their properties left behind in Turkey.[68] The ensuing period of dispute and recriminations over the appraisal, liquidation and restoration of properties, effectively ended, as already noted,[69] with the Greek–Turkish convention of Angora in 1930.

The Mixed Commission   The provisions concerning the creation and function of a Mixed Commission, to assist in the execution of the Exchange convention, reflected beyond any doubt the intention to guarantee impartiality and to give a distinctive international institutional aspect to the carrying out of the emigration and liquidation envisaged in the agreement.

Thus, by the terms of article 11, within one month from the coming into force of the Exchange convention, a mixed commission was to be set up in Turkey or in Greece consisting of four members representing each of the contracting parties, and three members chosen by the Council of the League of Nations from among nationals of powers which did not take part in the war of 1914–18. The presidency of the Commission was to be exercised in turn by each of these three neutral members. Moreover, the Commission was to have the right to set up, in such places as might appear necessary, Sub-commissions working under its orders. Each Sub-commission was to consist of a Turkish member, a Greek member and a neutral President designated by the Mixed Commission. The Mixed Commission was to decide the powers to be delegated to the Sub-commission.[70]

The Mixed Commission was set up on 17 September 1923, less than a month after the Exchange convention came into force, immediately after the ratification of the treaty of Lausanne by the two contracting parties. Turkey had ratified this on 23 August 1923, and Greece on 25 August 1923. Within a month of its setting up, the Mixed Commission held its first meeting, in Athens, on 8 October 1923.

Article 12 of the Exchange convention provided for the duties and the powers of the Mixed Commission. Its duties, according to the first paragraph of this provision were twofold: (a) 'to supervise and facilitate the emigration' and (b) 'to carry out the liquidation of the movable and immovable property'. Its powers, according to the following paragraphs of that same provision, included: settling the conventions to be followed, full power to take the measures necessitated by the execution of the Exchange convention and to decide all questions to which the convention might give rise; power to decide by majority vote; and the power to settle definitely 'all disputes relating to property, rights and interests' which were to be liquidated.

These broad powers of the Mixed Commission were, of course, qualified within the framework of the provisions already discussed which formed the basis of the very procedure of emigration and liquidation,[71] for example, in articles eight, nine, and ten. So, in effect, was its power to decide by majority vote. The fact that its neutral members constituted by themselves a minority *vis-à-vis* the members representing the two contracting governments (article 11, first paragraph), and the fact of their absolute dependence on the views of the latter when these were in agreement occasioned, when the latter were in disagreement, the taking of all important decisions by unanimous vote.[72]

Finally, according to article 13, the Mixed Commission was also entrusted with the power 'to cause the evaluation to be made of the movable and immovable property' which was to be liquidated, on the basis of the value of the property in gold currency and after duly summoning and hearing the interested parties. Article 14 provided for the transmission by the Mixed Commission to the dispossessed owners of declarations stating the sums due to them; the total sums due on the basis of these declarations constituting 'a government debt from the country where the liquidation takes place to the government of the country to which the emigrant belongs'. When the process was completed, if a sum remained 'due from one of the governments to the other government' after a balance had been struck, the debit balance should be paid in cash. The Mixed Commission had, however, the power to postpone payments and to 'fix the interest to be paid during the period of postponement'. Articles 15 and 17 provided for the funds designed to facilitate emigration, to be advanced to the Commission by the states concerned, under conditions laid down by the Commission, and for the expenses entailed by the maintenance and working of the Mixed Commission and of the organisations dependent on it, which were to be borne by the two states concerned in proportions to be fixed by the Commission.[73]

The Impact of the Exchange on Greek–Turkish Relations

Perspectives for the Development of Greek–Turkish Relations After the Exchange of Populations

In his statement made after the submission of the final draft of the sub-committee dealing with the exchange of populations problem, Lord Curzon, President of the Territorial and Military Commission in the Lausanne Conference, repeated, for the last time, that he felt sure all the delegates viewed with abhorrence and almost with dismay the principle of compulsory exchange.

One need only read the papers to realise how widely this feeling of dissatisfaction had spread; and the conference had only yielded to the demand that the exchange should be compulsory because all those who had studied the matter most closely seemed to agree that the suffering entailed, great as it must be, would be repaid by the advantages which would ultimately accrue to both countries from a greater homogeneity of population and from the removal of old and deep rooted causes of quarrel.[74]

The British statesman's observations were to prove accurate in connection with the new general situation arising from the Lausanne Conference. The purpose of the Conference had been to restore peace and organise it on a new basis in the geographical area between the south eastern extremity of the continent of Europe and the north western boundary of the Middle East. The Conference's decisions had a decisive effect both on the development of the new territorial profile and, by extension, of the balance of relations between Greece and Turkey; and on the two countries' internal equilibrium and composition. In connection with this new *status quo*, there was a general rearrangement of the Greek and Turkish elements' roles in that part of the world in which they had been at loggerheads and co-existed for centuries.

Contemporary observers and later researchers discerned in the decisions of the Lausanne Conference the general influence of Kemalist Turkey's position. The frustration of the creation according to the terms of the Sèvres Treaty of an independent Armenia and an autonomous Kurdish state, as also of the cession of part of Asia Minor to Greece; the scrapping of the capitulations and the blanket imposition of the national legislation on the new Turkish state; and finally the broad coincidence of the extreme bounds of Turkey's territorial sovereignty with the predetermined terms of the Ankara National Contract all made up the gist of the new treaty. This not only definitively revoked the earlier Treaty of Sèvres but also matched the basic desires of the Turkish government. Realistic in the conception and execution of his programme, Mustafa Kemal had rejected once and for all any notion of adopting bygone panIslamic or panturanian tendencies or of reestablishing the Ottoman empire, even in disguised form, and was firmly looking to create 'an independent and sovereign Turkey for the Turks'. In place of the internally heterogeneous empire, he was going to found a state destined 'to follow an exclusively national, perfectly attuned policy based on internal organisation'. The implementation of this policy presupposed the preservation or the expansion only of the territory in which the Turkish (or at least the related Muslim) element was predominant. The achieving of this fundamental aim would be combined with the consolidation of the determining principles that would henceforth have to motivate Turkish diplomacy: the safeguarding of security, the territorial integrity and independence of the ethnic Turkish state, respect for international legitimacy, and the preservation of peace.[75]

The conclusion of the Lausanne Treaty also gave the go ahead to the new Greek domestic policy. The conditions that had determined Athens's basic options in the diplomatic field for almost a century had been totally overthrown. The partial satisfaction of the free kingdom's territorial demands – particularly in the sensitive area of the southern Balkans and the Aegean – combined with the dramatic exodus of the Greek populations from their ancestral homelands in Asia Minor, on the Black Sea, and in eastern Thrace, had essentially removed the main support for Greece's irredentist policy aimed at Turkey. In contrast, the concentration of the major part of the Greek ethnic family on the territory of the Greek state and the latter's consequent elevation to the status, to quote Venizelos, of 'possibly the most ethnically coherent state in eastern Europe' made it all the more important to secure the conditions for completing and safeguarding its independence. Under these changed circumstances, the fulfil-ment of its as yet unsatisfied irredentist demands (particularly with regard to northern Epirus, the Dodecanese, and Cyprus – all areas that were thickly populated by Greeks) ceased to be the main strategic aim of Greek foreign policy. Its basic goal was now to safeguard the country's defensive security and territorial integrity. In consequence, its unwavering parameters were henceforth to be respect for the terms of the treaties and for the principles of international legitimacy.

Quite clearly, the Greek–Turkish agreement for the compulsory exchange of populations was of decisive importance for the develop-ment of the two nations' new strategic orientation. The implement-ation of the terms of this bilateral treaty confirmed in practice the removal of the motives that had fed the two peoples' long antagonism, whose principal objective had been to extend the range of their own national sovereignty. Relieved now of the presence of foreign elements over a broader expanse of their territory, the national states of Greece and Turkey no longer had any justification for expansionist designs in each other's direction.

Under these circumstances, it was not only possible but necessary to restore stable relations of mutual friendship and trust between Greece and Turkey. Furthermore, the realisation that the two countries no longer had any serious justification for hostile confront-ation was matched by the confirmation that they had shared interests on both a regional and an international level. This shared conviction encouraged them to take fruitful mutual initiatives that resulted in the development of a bilateral Athens–Ankara axis, which was to be a factor for stability and peace for decades to come.

The Implementation of the Convention for the Exchange of Population Between Greece and Turkey

If one looks in the sphere of practical policy for the first expression of the need to consolidate friendly relations and cooperation between Greece and Turkey, one's attention is caught by the assertions of Eleftherios Venizelos, and also of Ismet Pasha, during the negotiations at Lausanne. However, it was not possible to implement this policy until the Greek statesman, with the support of a strong parliamentary majority, returned to power in July 1928.

In the meantime, the development of Greek–Turkish relations was influenced less by the desire for a general political settlement than by the impossibility of resolving the particular problems that had been left pending after the signing, or had cropped up during the implementation, of the Lausanne agreements. In particular, apart from the deliberate creation of difficulties and the pressures put on the ecumenical patriarchate and the Greek minorities of Istanbul, Imbros, and Tenedos, the most serious and long lasting unresolved bilateral problem lay in the implementation of the terms of the agreement concerning the 'established' and the 'exchangeable' populations. As explained above, according to the Greek–Turkish agreement of 30 January 1923, the 'established' residents were considered to be the Greek inhabitants of Istanbul who had settled there prior to 30 October 1918 and the Muslims living to the east of the 1913 frontier, that is in western Thrace. Despite the apparent clarity of these definitions, the implementation of the provision provoked fresh disagreement, particularly with regard to the Greeks of Istanbul. The difficulties should in part be attributed to their not being registered with the Ottoman authorities. Even the International Tribunal at the Hague, to which both sides appealed, failed to provide an unchallengeable definition. Those to be exchanged were considered to be the Orthodox inhabitants of the rest of Turkey and the Muslim inhabitants of the rest of Greece.

The assessment of the property of both groups was a source of serious disagreement from the start. According to the agreement of 30 January 1923, in exchange for the estates they had left behind, the exchanged populations would receive land of commensurate value, while the difference in the balance of payments would be made up by the debtor country. The property of the 'established' populations, however, would have to be restored to its previous owners.

The Mixed Commission's inability to deal effectively with the disagreements led Andreas Michalakopoulos, Prime Minister in 1924, to propose that all the unresolved problems be submitted to arbitration. The Turks, however, basically still clung to the idea of arbitrary overall assessments. The number of Greeks entitled to remain in Istanbul would be determined by a simple rough estimate, and the disagreements over property would be resolved by wiping out the mutual demands and giving the Turkish government the £500 000 sterling that the Athens International Finance Commission had awarded in December 1926 as compensation to the Muslims who were to remain. These views were utterly opposed by the Greek government, which not only questioned the accuracy of the assessment of what was owed to those people but also maintained that a responsible evaluation of the property of those who were exchanged would work out in favour of the Greek claimants.[76]

These problematic differences were surmounted and a general political agreement decisively boosted thanks to Venizelos's unwavering will and Ankara's positive response to his drastic initiatives. Directly upon his return to power, the Greek Prime Minister sent a letter to his Turkish counterpart on 30 August 1928 outlining the new aspects of Greek–Turkish relations. Both the new Turkey and Greece accepted the peace treaties frankly and unreservedly; neither state had territorial designs on the other; the signing of a bilateral friendship and non-aggression pact ought to confirm a decisive renunciation of past antagonism and a steady orientation towards peace and cooperation. Ismet's response was unequivocal: the disagreements over the interpretation of the Lausanne Treaties, which were bound up chiefly with private interests, ought not henceforth to hold back the definitive establishment of concord between their two neighbouring peoples.[77]

The agreement for the final settlement of the differences that had arisen out of the agreement for the exchange of populations was signed on 10 June 1930. It was based on the principle of property compensation not only for the property of the 'exchangeables' but also for that of the 'non-exchangeables' which had been given to the refugees. At the same time, the Greek side was charged with paying a debit balance of £425 000 sterling, as against the Turkish government's obligation to give the Greek claimants their appropriated estates in and around Istanbul. The agreement was clearly weighted in the Turks' favour, but it served as the basic precondition for the final settlement of the financial controversy and was a decisive factor in promoting political concord.

The spirit of concord was consolidated and cooperation was broadened on many fronts when the Greek Prime Minister visited Ankara and a series of bilateral agreements was concluded. On 30 October 1930, both sides signed the Agreement for Friendship, Neutrality, and Arbitration, which went so far as to prohibit either signatory from participating in any political or economic alliance that went against the other. The pact was accompanied by a trade agreement, which included a consular agreement and a residence agreement, as also by a special convention on naval armaments: the two governments engaged to inform each other in good time before ordering any naval vessel, in order to forestall antagonism 'by a friendly exchange of views'.[78]

Despite the objections and reservations it was bound to engender at first, in the course of time the Greek–Turkish concord proved to be an act in absolute accord with the dictates of political realism. Ismet's visit to Athens in October 1931 and the Security Agreement signed on 14 September 1933 promoted the concord between the two countries, in Venizelos's words, to the status of a 'purely defensive alliance against Bulgaria, in the event of the latter's attempting to violate our common frontier'.[79] Under these circumstances, although it had originally aroused the suspicion that it was accomplished under the protection or the guidance of non-Balkan powers (particularly Italy), in the course of time it became internationally apparent that the Greek–Turkish rapprochement was an expression of the two peoples' free and independent desire to overcome past hostility and together to tread the road of friendship and cooperation.

In conclusion, one might observe that the compulsory exchange of populations between Greece and Turkey became the basis both for the reorientation of their foreign policy and for the establishment of close relations of friendship and cooperation between the two countries. Carried out not long after the foundation of the League of Nations, far from conforming to the rules and principles governing the new international organisation and morality, this brutally realistic act decisively helped to keep the presence of foreign ethnic elements in the interior of the two countries to an insignificant, or at least less important, level. In consequence it encouraged the two governments to accept and to practise respect for international legitimacy and the territorial status quo created by the peace treaties and to reject any expansionist tendency, whether geopolitically or otherwise inspired, that entailed unlawful recourse to force. One might even say that in the long term the restoration of peace in the relations of these two neighbours who had been so violently opposed in the past, as also the restoration of security in their separate geographical areas, was destined to be conditioned by their firm attachment to these fundamental principles.

Notes

1. See, for example, Ténékidès (1924), pp.15–16; Séfériadès, pp.327 ff; and Streit, pp. 23 ff.
2. See, for example, Pallis (1933), pp.16 ff; Psomiades, p. 60, and Petropoulos, pp.143 ff.
3. For a stimulating discussion of the transfer of populations issue even during the

Second World War see, for example, Claude, pp.93 ff.; and see also the lecture by N. Politis, 'Le transfert des populations' and the ensuing discussion at the 'Centre d'études de politique étrangère' (7 March 1940, Paris) in Archive of N. Politis, Bibliothèque de la Société des Nations, Geneva.

4. See also Eddy, p. 51.
5. For the number of refugees who finally came to Greece, see Kitromilides and Alexandris, pp. 9–44. It is indicative that out of 1 547 952 Ottoman Greeks in Asia Minor in 1912, only 847 954 were found in Greece in 1928. As for the rest, some (mainly from Pontus) sought refuge in the Soviet Union, a smaller number in other European countries or the USA, some died of natural causes, while the greatest part was liquidated (by violence or in exile) between 1912 and 1922. A general picture of the installation of refugees in Greece is given in: League of Nations, L'établissement des Réfugiés en Grèce, Geneva, 1926.
6. See Ténékidès (1914–18).
7. Venizelos Papers, 30, N. Politis (Athens) to Venizelos, no. 3535, 8–21 October 1922. See also, similarly, League of Nations Archives, A. 48/24318/24318, 'Chiffres d'habitants d'origine turque des différentes provinces de la Grèce, fournis par le service de statistique du gt. Royal hellénique'. See Svolopoulos (1981) p. 15, and for the most recent research on the basis of the ecumenical patriarchate census data for the Greek population of Asia Minor, Kitromilides and Alexandris.
8. On these developments, from a general point of view, see Smith; Pallis; (1973); Davison, pp. 172–209.
9. On the conditions of this exodus, see Housepian; Smyrna 1922. The destruction of a city, London 1972; Η Έξοδος (The Exodus), Athens : Center for Asia Minor Studies, 1980–2. For a general bibliography: Hatzimoyssis.
10. League of Nations archives, A. 48/24318/24318, E. Venizelos (London) to F. Nansen (Constantinople), 13 October 1922. See Svolopoulos (1981), pp. 11–12.
11. Svolopoulos (1981), pp. 21–26. See also, Lausanne Conference on Near Eastern Affairs 1922–1923, Records of Proceedings and Draft Terms of Peace, p. 113.
12. Also in this sense, Streit, p. 10.
13. See, Conférence de Lausanne sur les Affaires du Proche–Orient, Actes signés à Lausanne le 30 janvier et le 24 juillet 1923 – Lettres et Accords en date du 24 juillet 1923 relatifs à diverses clauses de ces Actes, Paris, Imprimerie Nationale, 1923. More particularly, besides the main peace treaty which dealt with territorial questions, nationality, protection of minorities, public debt, financial and other economic issues, organisation of Mixed Arbitral Tribunals, communications, sanitary matters, prisoners of war, graves etc., other matters were dealt with by a series of protocols and conventions. The Final Act, of 24 July 1923, enumerated all these instruments. The cumulative effect of this peace settlement, hammered out at Lausanne, was the surrender by Turkey, in its new nationalist guise, of all claim to territories of the Ottoman empire occupied by non-Turks and the replacement of the regime of capitulations. The Bosphorus and Dardanelles were demilitarised. Greece was awarded western Thrace and abandoned Asia Minor, eastern Thrace and the Aegean islands Imbros and Tenedos, which were returned to Turkey. The annexations of the Dodecanese by Italy and of Cyprus by Great Britain were confirmed.
14. For the discussion respecting the Exchange convention, see Lausanne Conference on Near Eastern Affairs, pp. 113–24, 183–4, 188, 203–4, 207, 210, 212, 223–5, 227, 315–37, 407–13, 433–7.
15. Thus, for example, Streit, p. 6, Séfériadès, pp. 327 ff.; see, however, Redslob, p. 42. For a relevant account of historical instances of transfers of population since ancient times see Séfériadès, pp. 317 ff. and 332 ff. as well as Ladas, pp. 1–2.
16. See text in French in Ladas, pp. 18–19.

17. See text in French in Séfériadès, p. 351, note 2.
18. See Ladas, pp. 18–20, Séfériadès, pp. 352–4, Eddy, p. 49.
19. See Eddy, pp. 49–50, Ladas, pp. 20–3. Psomiades, pp. 61 ff., Séfériadès, pp. 354–62.
20. Séfériadès, p. 356 and Leontiades, p. 549.
21. See also Leontiades, p. 550.
22. See Streit, pp. 22–3, Eddy, pp. 219–25, Séfériadès, pp. 365 ff. and the outstanding study of Ladas, pp. 27 ff.
23. Eddy, p. 219, Ladas, p. 122.
24. See Ladas, pp. 721–2.
25. *Ibid.*, p. 122.
26. See Petropoulos, p. 148, and Ladas, pp. 107–8.
27. See also Leontiades, p. 552.
28. See above, p. 289.
29. See, for example, Streit, pp. 23–4 and 30, Séfériadès, pp. 327 ff., Redslob, pp. 43 and 45–6, Ténékidès, pp. 11 and 15 ff.; Eddy, p. 51.
30. Leontiades, pp. 552–3.
31. Compare, however, Psomiades, p. 66.
32. See *Conférence de Lausanne, Recueil des Actes, 1ère série*, I, pp. 577, 604.
33. Also in this sense Ladas, pp. 377–81.
34. See above, p. 288.
35. See also Séfériadès, p. 403 and Leontiades, p. 557.
36. In this sense, Ladas, p. 396, Séfériadès, p. 403, Leontiades, pp. 557–8.
37. Between the Allied powers and Turkey at the end of the First World War.
38. See above, p. 290.
39. In this respect Séfériadès, pp. 388–9, observes that the interpretation of this article would have been much easier if it had been inversely formulated, for example, that the Greeks of Istanbul should not be included in the exchange, with the exception of those Greeks who had come to Istanbul after 30 October 1918. See also Leontiades, p. 553 and footnote 33.
40. See also Ladas, at p. 402 and Devedji, pp. 102–3.
41. *Permanent Court of International Justice Publications, Series B, No. 10.*
42. *Ibid.*, p. 18.
43. *Ibid.*, p. 19.
44. *Ibid.*, p. 20.
45. See also Ladas, pp. 407–8, Psomiades, pp. 75–6, Devedji, p. 120.
46. See above, p. 297.
47. See Psomiades, pp. 76–7.
48. Namely, the convention of Angora, dated 21 June 1925, and the convention of Athens, dated 1 December 1926.
49. See, generally, Psomiades, pp. 81 ff.; Eddy, pp. 215 ff; and, very systematically, Ladas, pp. 567 ff.
50. See Leontiades, at p. 556 and footnote 45.
51. See p. 288, above.
52. See also Devedji, p. 73.
53. *Ibid.*, at p. 76; and Ténékidès, at p. 13.
54. Ladas, p. 380 and for a detailed account see pp. 384 ff.
55. See above, footnote 13.
56. See also Devedji, p. 75; Ladas, pp. 418–9.
57. See *Conférence de Lausanne . . . Actes signés à Lausanne le 30 janvier et le 24 juillet 1923*, p. 109.
58. These men, between 15 and 50 years of age, were detained and deported mostly in the interior of Asia Minor but also in Smyrna; they suffered many hardships

and were subjected to forced labour and road building, and were not released before 1924. See Ladas, pp. 434–5; and Devedji, pp. 78–9.
59. See Ladas, p. 398.
60. See the relevant discussions in Séfériadès, pp. 404–5; Leontiades, pp. 558–9; Devedji, pp. 79–80; Ladas, p. 398.
61. See pp. 289–90 above.
62. For a detailed account and discussion, see Ladas, pp. 443–56.
63. *Ibid.*, pp. 453–4 and see also Séfériadès, p. 405.
64. For a detailed account and discussion, see Ladas, pp. 417–18.
65. See also Devedji, pp. 81–2.
66. See also Eddy, pp. 211–12.
67. See pp. 291–3 above.
68. See Eddy, p. 210 and also Psomiades, pp. 76 ff; Ladas, pp. 467 ff; Devedji, pp. 139 ff.
69. See p. 293.
70. For details concerning the names and personalities of the original and subsequent members of the Mixed Commission, the organisation of its work, the rotation of the presidency, the creation of Sub-Commissions, the minutes of the Commission's meetings and so on, see the indispensable description and account of Ladas, pp. 353–76.
71. Compare Devedji, p. 78.
72. Compare Ladas, p. 369.
73. For interesting evaluation and criticism of the work of the Mixed Commission, see Eddy, pp. 211 ff. and Ladas, pp. 374 ff.
74. *Lausanne Conference on Near Eastern Affairs*, p. 412.
75. Davison, pp. 173–4.
76. See Alexandris, pp. 105–70. See also Ladas, pp. 467 ff. and Psomiades, pp. 79–81. On the Muslim minority in Greece, see Andreades.
77. Svolopoulos (1977), pp. 144–6.
78. Anastasiadou.
79. See Svolopoulos (1974), p. 49.

Select Bibliography

Alexandris, A. (1983), *The Greek Minority of Istanbul and Greek–Turkish Relations 1918–1974*, Athens.
Anastasiadou, I. (1980), 'Venizelos and the Greek-Turkish friendship pact of 1930' (in Greek), in *Studies on Venizelos and his period*, Athens.
Andreades, K.G. (1956), *The Moslem minority in Western Thrace*, Thessaloniki.
Claude, I.L., jr. (1955), *National minorities – an international problem*, Cambridge, Mass.
Conférence de Lausanne sur les Affaires du Proche-Orient (1922–3): Actes signés à Lausanne le 30 janvier et le 24 juillet 1923 – Lettres et Accords en date du 24 juillet 1923 relatifs à diverses clauses de ces Actes (1923), Imprimerie Nationale, Paris.
Davison, R.H. (1974), 'Turkish Diplomacy from Mudros to Lausanne', in Craig, G.A. and Gilbert, F. (eds), *The Diplomats 1919–39*, vol. I, New York.
Devedji, A. (1929), *L'échange obligatoire des minorités grecques et turques en vertu de la Convention de Lausanne du 30 janvier 1923*, Paris.
Documents Diplomatiques du Ministère des Affaires Etrangères, Conférence de Lausanne, vol. 1 (21 Nov. 1922–1 Feb. 1923) (1923), Paris.
Eddy, C.B. (1931), *Greece and the Greek Refugees*, London.
Gounaraki, P.N. (1927), *An Address on the Treaty of Lausanne and in particular on the Convention concerning the Exchange of Populations*, (in Greek), Athens.

Guggenheim, P. (1925), 'Das Gutachten des Weltgerichtshofes betreffend den griechisch–türkischen Bevölkerungsaustausch', *Die Friedenswarte*, vol. 25.
Hatzimoyssis, P. (1981), *Bibliography, 1919–1978. Asia Minor, campaign, defeat, refugees*, (in Greek), Athens.
Housepian, M. (1966), *The Smyrna Affair*, New York.
Kiosseoglou, T. (1926), *L'échange forcé des minorités d'après le Traité de Lausanne*, Nancy.
Kitromilides, P.M. and Alexandris, A. (1984–5), 'Ethnic Survival, Nationalism and Forced Migration. The Historical Demography of the Greek Community of Asia Minor at the close of the Ottoman era', *Δελτιον κεντρον Μικρασιατικών Σπονδών*, vol. 5.
Ladas, S. (1932), *The Exchange of Minorities – Bulgaria, Greece and Turkey*, New York.
Lausanne Conference on Near Eastern Affairs 1922–1923. Records of Proceedings and Draft terms of Peace (1923), London.
League of Nations (1925), *Treaty Series*, vol. 32.
Leontiades, L. (1935), 'Der griechisch–türkische Bevölkerungsaustausch', *Zeitschrift für ausländisches öffentliches Recht und Völkerrecht*, vol. 5.
Pallis, A.A. (1925) 'The Exchange of Populations in the Balkans', *The Nineteenth Century and After*, vol. 97.
Pallis, A.A. (1933), *The Exchange of Populations from a Legal and Historical Point of View and its Significance for the International Position of Greece* (in Greek), Athens.
Pallis, A.A. (1973), *Greece's Anatolian Venture and After*, London.
Pentzopoulos, D. (1962), *The Balkan Exchange of Minorities and its Impact upon Greece*, The Hague.
Petropoulos, J.A. (1976), 'The Compulsory Exchange of Populations: Greek–Turkish Peacemaking, 1922–1930', *Byzantine and Modern Greek Studies*, vol. 2.
Politis, N. (1940), 'Le transfert de populations', *L'ésprit international*, Paris.
Psomiades, H. (1968), *The Eastern Question: The Last Phase – A Study in Greek–Turkish Diplomacy*, Thessaloniki.
Redslob, R. (1931), 'Le principe des nationalités', in *Recueil des Cours*, vol. 37, Academy of International Law, The Hague.
Rustem Bey, A. (1925), 'The future of the Oecumenical Patriarchate', *Foreign Affairs*, vol. 3.
Séfériadès, S. (1928), 'L'échange des populations', *Recueil des Cours*, vol. 24, Academy of International Law, The Hague.
Smith, M. Llewellyn (1973), *Ionian Vision, Greece in Asia Minor 1919–1922*, London.
Streit, G. (1929), *Der Lausanner Vertrag und der griechisch–türkische Bevölkerungsaustausch*, Berlin.
Svoupoulos, C. (1974), *The Balkan Pact and Greece's Foreign Policy 1928–1934* (in Greek), Athens.
Svolopoulos, C. (1977), *Greek foreign policy after the Treaty of Lausanne; the crucial turning point, July–December 1928* (in Greek), Thessaloniki.
Svolopoulos, C. (1981), *The Decision for the Compulsory Exchange of Populations between Greece and Turkey* (in Greek), Thessaloniki.
Ténékidès, C.G. (1914–18), *Les persécutions de l'Hellenisme en Turquie*, Constantinople (Istanbul).
Ténékidès, C.G. (1924), 'Le statut des minorités et l'échange obligatoire des populations gréco–turques', *Revue Générale de Droit International public*, Paris.

13 Spanish Policy and the Sephardic Jews, 1918–1940

ANTONIO MARQUINA BARRIO

During the nineteenth century, the question of the Sephardic Jews began to arouse a certain interest in Spain. In 1812, for example, the *Cortes* (parliament) of Cadiz promulgated several liberalising measures and abolished the Holy Office, the institution that represented the intolerance inherent in the old regime. On 15 June 1834, the Inquisition was abolished once and for all. Subsequently, a series of political upheavals and convulsions, both conservative and liberal, took place, resulting in the question of religious tolerance and freedom becoming a central problem in political party relations. Without religious tolerance and freedom, it was not possible to address the question of the return of the Sephardic Jews to Spain. Moreover, it should be taken into account that the Jewish question was approached with a certain amount of hostility by public opinion, presupposing a considerable popular prejudice.

The debate on religious freedom in the *Cortes* in 1869 constituted an important landmark, centred as it was on several occasions on the Jewish question in Spain. Once the new constitution was approved, in this same year, allowing the public and private practice of any religious cult, many unfounded fears were aroused. Only 16 Jews obtained Spanish nationality and the majority of them were not Sephardim.

Six years later, the monarchy was restored and a new constitution was approved in 1876, under which religious cults distinct from the Roman Catholic church were merely 'tolerated'. Nevertheless, the outlook of the liberal party was clearly progressive in this matter, as was demonstrated by the policy of accepting Jews fleeing the anti-Semitic movements prevailing in Russia at the time. However, the number of Jews that entered Spain in this era was not very significant, totalling not more than 51. Toward the end of the nineteenth century, it was estimated that only 2000 Jews were living in Spain.

The policy of accepting Jewish peoples received a new impulse at the beginning of the twentieth century, due to the activities of liberal circles, and, more concretely, to the actions of the liberal senator and medical doctor Angel Pulido, who published many works on the Sephardic Jews. These books and articles were initially received with prejudice, both in Spain and abroad, even by Jews themselves, reflecting the existing difficulties in a country whose state religion was Catholicism and where an inherent intolerance was present in many sectors of the population. However, it was evident that the ideas of Angel Pulido and the importance of the Sephardic communities scattered throughout the Mediterranean and the Balkans, which had preserved Spanish traditions, encouraged various intellectuals to show a greater receptivity toward the Jews.

The Hispano–Hebrew Alliance was created in 1910, and two years later a new association was formed to which various politicians, writers and journalists belonged; personalities that were influential in the government of the day. In 1913 the Spanish government asked the Hebraist and orientalist Abraham Shalom Yahuda to give several lectures on the contributions of the Jews to Spanish culture and thought. In 1915 the government made plans to create a chair of Hebrew language and literature at the University of Madrid and named Yahuda as the head. This initiative was hailed by the Zionist leader Max Nordau as the 'Spanish surprise'.

During the First World War, pro-Jewish groups in Spain became interested in the fate of the Jewish exiles from Turkey who were living in France and Italy. The Spanish government actively lobbied the Turkish government in attempts to alleviate the plight of the Jews living in Palestine. The king of Spain, Alfonso XIII, intervened personally with the German Kaiser, appealing for his support against the obstacles presented by the Turks. Likewise, the Spanish administration concerned itself with the situation endured by the Sephardic Jews protected by Spain who were living in the Balkan region. The Greek case was the most significant, because, once the Treaty of Athens was signed, on 14 November 1913, Greece no longer recognised the rights of foreign powers to maintain protected citizens in Macedonia. Up to that point, Turkey had permitted the concept of protected citizens under the system of capitulations that she had maintained in that territory. Now, however, the question of the protection of the Sephardic community became, for the most part, a problem of nationality. In this sense, the Ministry of Foreign Affairs established, by means of a royal order on 17 April 1917, that, since the majority of the matters of protection were becoming questions of nationality, it was necessary to unify the resolution of these problems within the Ministry itself. This was the first step toward the new policies that would be formulated in the following years.[1]

Spanish Policy after the First World War

At the end of the First World War, Spain attempted to frame a policy that would protect the Sephardic Jews living in the Balkans. There were several reasons for this. The first was that the pro-Sephardic intellectual movement in Spain was at its height. In 1920, the Universal House of the Sephardim was created; in order to promote economic links with the Sephardic communities that existed in diverse countries, to maintain close contacts with the Jewish press, to carry out an international census of Sephardic communities throughout the world, and to spread Spanish language and literature. Second was the perception of the importance of public opinion in the field of international relations, and third was the necessity of taking into consideration public opinion in other nations. This made necessary the systematic cultivation and coordination of the diverse opinions with respect to cultural relations.

In order to achieve these goals, an Office of Cultural Relations was created in 1921 within the Ministry of Foreign Affairs. The purpose of this Office was to plan, organise and implement a cultural policy in foreign countries which would be similar to the policies of other countries. With this end in mind, the first programmes for cultural dissemination among Latin American countries, groups of Spanish emigrants and Sephardic communities throughout the world were established. Special attention was given to the Sephardic communities in the Balkans.

In January 1922 an order was sent to the Spanish legations and consulates in Romania, Yugoslavia, Bulgaria, Greece and Egypt explaining the creation of the Office and the new policy which paid special attention to the Spanish heritage and culture. At the end of the month a new circular ordered the implementation of a questionnaire. The replies to this questionnaire give us a useful guideline as regards the situation of the Sephardic population in places where there was Spanish diplomatic representation. According to this questionnaire, the population of Spanish speaking peoples was distributed as follows: 80 000 in Salonika; 24 000 in Yugoslavia; 30 000 in Romania; 10 000 in Cairo; 6000 in Alexandria; 250 in Port Said; and approximately 50 000 in Bulgaria.[2]

The number of native Spaniards in these places varied from country to country. In Salonika the Spanish community consisted of 350 families; in Belgrade there were only 200 Spanish nationals; in Bucharest very few had actually obtained Spanish nationality, and all the others who spoke Spanish were of Romanian nationality. In Cairo it was extremely difficult to determine nationality because it was one of the places where there were many people without a definite nationality. In Bulgaria only a few hundred people had Spanish documents that protected them. Many Spanish speaking people had received Italian, French or British protection.

In spite of these differences in nationality, all or almost all of the Spanish speaking people of these countries were of the Jewish faith and varying economic and cultural status. In all of these communities there existed a common element of sympathy and interest for Spain, mixed with pride in their origins and, in some cases, interest in obtaining protection and advantages from the Spanish government. As for Spanish cultural action, the panorama was bleak. There were no Spanish cultural institutions in most of the countries and the majority were educated in Jewish schools. A particular case was that of well-to-do Sephardim of Egypt, who were protected by either Italy or France. They received their primary and secondary instruction in private schools, primarily managed by religious orders. Also, it was noted that some Sephardim from Belgrade were educated in France or Switzerland.

Generally, the Sephardim maintained Spanish as the family language, but in Bucharest this custom was disappearing. It was noted that Spain's cultural initiatives would be well received, varying from country to country. It was said that there were 16 newspapers in old Spanish all told. With respect to emigration to Latin America and other countries, no cases were recorded, with the exception of Cairo and Bucharest. There were, however, no statistics with respect to these data, only purely personal observations. Nevertheless, it was emphasised that in three countries, Bulgaria, Romania and to a lesser extent Yugoslavia, the Sephardic communities were especially prosperous and the possibilities of diplomatic and cultural action were more promising, given also the liberal legislation.[3] These exploratory initiatives had some tangible effects, for instance, the creation of a *Casa de España* (Spanish house) in Turkey, founded by a group of notable Sephardim.

The Royal Decree of 1924

With these initiatives, Spain attempted to break out of its isolation and to restore its position in the international arena. In June 1924 it was suggested that an international university be set up in Madrid which would accept primarily Sephardic students. This idea was proposed with a view to the benefits that Spanish trade would derive from it; previous speculations had already come to this conclusion.

A special event was to enable the Spanish government to implement some of these ideas. The Treaty of Lausanne, signed on 24 July 1923, repealed the system of capitulations which permitted certain residents of Turkey to enjoy extra-territorial rights and benefits, as well as the protection of a foreign power. The repeal of the system of capitulations by the Turkish regime was later extended to other countries of the Balkans and the Middle East, which arose from the ruins of the Ottoman empire. Consequently, the protected Spanish residents found themselves in a new legal situation which was in many cases anomalous with respect to third countries. With the idea of correcting this legal situation, the dictatorship of Primo de Rivera approved the royal decree of 20 December 1924, which granted Spanish nationality to the Sephardim.

There is no doubt that the object of the royal decree was to take advantage of the opportunity that was presented to the government for the expansion of Spanish influence in these Sephardic communities, which still had a real, though weak, bond with Spain.[4] It was to remain in force for six years, until 31 December 1930. The immediate results of this official policy are not well known, but it is certain that until 1927, the Ministry of the Interior turned down many applications from protected Sephardim who wished to obtain Spanish nationality, because they did not meet the requirements stipulated by this royal decree. This resulted in the publication of a royal order explaining the implementation of the royal decree. Subsequently, various circulars were published to clarify this order; these were numbered 857, 862 and 1005, the latest being dated 30 March 1928.

One of the problems which emerged from the elimination of the system of capitulations, and, previously, when Greece included Salonika in its territory, was that the protected Sephardim were considered Spanish citizens by the countries concerned while for Spain they remained 'protected' Spaniards. This caused serious difficulties for the Sephardim in their relations with the authorities of other countries. In addition Spain had continued to issue passports to the protected Sephardim as Spanish nationals, even as late as 1926. For this reason, a large number of Sephardim with Spanish passports did not consider it necessary to have recourse to the royal decree of 1924, but, instead, continued applying for documentation as they had done in previous years.

Finally, the Spanish representative in Athens put an end to this type of ambiguity by explaining to the Spanish authorities in Madrid that 'by presenting this type of passport at any Spanish consulate it was always possible to obtain Spanish nationality if not yet acquired'. To clarify the question of nationality yet again, a new circular, approved on 7 May 1928, was sent to consulates in Tangiers, Istanbul, Alexandria, Athens, Jerusalem, Beirut and Salonika. This circular was to provide a provisional solution – until 31 December 1930 – to the situations created in countries where there were persons under Spanish protection and the system of capitulations was in force.[5]

The Initiative of The Council of Cultural Relations

In 1929 the Council of Cultural Relations took another step forward when they sent Ernesto Giménez Caballero to obtain first hand information about more efficient methods for the cultural expansion of Spain in these countries. Another purpose of Giménez Caballero's visit was to get in touch with people who might have relations with Spain, to give lectures, and to contact the diplomatic representatives of Spain in the different countries; Yugoslavia, Greece, Turkey, Bulgaria and Romania. Upon his return to Madrid, Giménez Caballero drafted a new plan of action for the progressive re-integration of the 'Spiritual province of more than one million souls'. He also indicated the need to repeal the edict of expulsion of 1492 and to facilitate acquisition of Spanish nationality. In his opinion, these measures would make it possible to collect half a million pesetas a year, which could be used for propaganda within the Sephardic communities.[6]

At the same time the Foreign Ministry tried once more to clarify the royal decree of 1924. The questions were the following: first, the question of nationality itself, which revealed the anomalous situation of many persons under Spanish protection who thought they were already nationalised. Secondly, there was the question of Sephardic immigration into Spain, as a direct consequence of the concession of nationality. Finally, new attempts were made by some Spanish diplomats – in particular by José María Doussinague – to link Spanish expansion in the Balkans and trade, using the Sephardic communities.

With regard to nationality, the problem continued and was made evident when some Sephardim had to travel abroad or had to have their lawsuits resolved in their country of residence. For these countries they were Spaniards, while Spain considered them only 'protected' Spaniards. This caused grave difficulties for the Sephardic Jews protected by Spain, because they did not know their real situation. It seems that from 1926 these difficulties were communicated to the Spanish government, as was the desirability of resolving with foreign governments the question of protected and naturalised Sephardim. An attempt was made by the Foreign Ministry to resolve these problems, but nevertheless, they continued.[7]

With respect to immigration, after 1929, when the initial Sephardic response to the royal decree was known, a wide cross section of opinion was stirred up in the Spanish government concerning the situation of the Jewish communities in the world, with particular reference to the Sephardim, who considered themselves eligible to return to Spain if they could obtain Spanish nationality. However, the Spanish government did not want the immigration of these people into Spain. The Jewish press in various countries and Jewish propaganda spread the news of the supposed return of the Sephardic Jews to Spain. News and proposals were received from countries such as France, the USA, Poland, Bulgaria, Palestine and from Jerusalem as well.[8] However, the mistaken interpretation of Spanish policy in favour of the Sephardic communities gave rise to internal problems and prejudice in Spain.[9]

In conclusion it can be said that until 1931, the year in which the Second Spanish Republic was established, Spanish foreign action and policy towards the Sephardic communities in the Balkans and the eastern Mediterranean tried to regularise the situation of these communities through the promotion of the naturalisation of the former protected persons, while at the same time it placed obstacles to immigration into Spain. The possible use of these communities for the benefit of Spain was also considered. Nevertheless the activities and suggestions of the Spanish diplomats abroad were aimed at preventing, by any means whatsoever, a massive immigration of Sephardic Jews into Spain, as well as at promoting an expansion, more economic than cultural, aimed at the enhancement of Spanish prestige in the Mediterranean and the Balkans, and Spanish industry. In practice none of this went beyond the project stage, given the lack of resources, the tardy character of the attempts at action, the competitiveness already established by other countries and the deep distrust towards the Sephardim felt by the majority of Spanish diplomats.

As regards the granting of nationality, while there are no statistics available, the number of grants could not have been very high, owing to the problems already explained; problems which were to continue during the Second Republic. Nor was the reaction of the Sephardic communities very enthusiastic toward these initiatives in the countries where they were being implemented. This was due to several factors: after the passing of more than four centuries, the protected Sephardim were not very attracted by the Spanish concessions, nor did Spain appear to them to be a country of significant material well-being. Neither did the various governments which had clear assimilation policies specially formulated after the First World War leave much room for manoeuvre for the former protected Spaniards. The most extreme cases were Greece, Turkey and Egypt. In other countries, such as Yugoslavia, Romania and Bulgaria, the room for manoeuvre was somewhat greater. In Bulgaria, for example, only eight families who had previously been protected by Spain were not received under the terms of the royal decree of 20 December 1924. This situation, together with the scant publicity given the new Spanish policy, explains the poor results obtained.

The Second Republic

From May 1931, diplomatic correspondence from Spanish representatives in Smyrna, Cairo, Sofia, Paris, Istanbul, Quito, Beirut, Santiago
de Chile, Jerusalem, Vienna, London, California and other countries
commented on the Spanish Jewish problem and the impact of the
coming of the Second Republic, heralded in the press and among the
Sephardic communities. In such reports, reference was made to the
intentions of the Republic concerning these people. Applications for
passports with a visa permitting immigration to Spain came in a
steady stream, and even increased in certain countries, a development which alarmed Spanish representatives, who immediately
asked for orders from the government in Madrid. Madrid answered
by taking the political line formulated by the dictatorship of Primo de
Rivera, that of not giving visas to settle in Spain.

The impact made on the Jewish communities all over the world had
been very noticeable, due to the fact that from the very beginning
freedom of religion and the secular nature of the state had been
declared. As a result, it had been said in the press and in the
Sephardic communities that the Sephardim could return to Spain.
Spanish diplomats abroad continued sending messages and news
relating to this attitude and asked for instructions. At the same time,
opinions on a possible return of the Sephardim to Spain were taking
shape within these communities. There was a group of Sephardim
who, apart from being in favour, proposed basic points to carry out
this integration in Spain. Another group was the one that was led by
the Sephardim most indifferent or distrustful about possible re-
integration into their 'homeland'. They had either settled in countries
where a fierce nationalism prevailed, or they simply did not believe in
the possibility of a mass return to Spain for fear that it would produce
a wave of anti-semitic sentiment in the country.[10]

The problems on which Spanish diplomats focussed their attention
remained the granting of nationality and possible immigration into
Spain. With regard to this latter issue, there was a constant increase
in the number of applications, which became particularly numerous
in 1933, as a result of the rise of Nazism in Germany. Consequently,
shortly after the establishment of the Second Republic, several
Spanish diplomats asked for instructions concerning the true status
of the decisions which the Republic had taken concerning the
Sephardic Jews. At the same time, the Foreign Ministry was notified
of the petitions of many people to immigrate to Spain. The answer
was that immigration to Spain was open to all foreigners, that there
was no discrimination on the grounds of race or religion and that
there were only personal and police conditions established by law.
The government did not take any particular measures to influence or

shape the opinions that were developing abroad. As a result, expectations grew unchecked.

At the same time, the Ministry of Foreign Affairs was made aware of the difficulties that some members of the Sephardic community in Paris, Havana, Jerusalem, Istanbul, Sofia and Antwerp were going through. Many Sephardim had allowed their passports to expire, and they were unable to renew them in the Spanish consulates in these countries. As a result, they were stateless, with the aggravating circumstance that many of them were in transit in the countries with which they had business. This would continue to be a problem without a clear solution.

A circular, no. 1208, authorised Spanish consuls to issue provisional passports to the Sephardim protected by Spain who had applied for Spanish nationality before the first of January of that year (1931) and had neither obtained their nationality nor been refused. It was established that the validity of these provisional passports would expire on 1 May 1932, without the possibility of their being renewed or exchanged for new ones.

It might be thought, once this extension had been given, that the problem was solved, but unfortunately this was not the case. From March 1932 on, reports from Spanish diplomats abroad again began to reach the Ministry of Foreign Affairs. The issue was once more the renewal and extension of passports for Sephardim protected by Spain whose applications for naturalisation were awaiting a decision by the Ministry of the Interior.[11] On 1 April 1932 the Ministry of the Interior communicated to the Undersecretary's office at the Ministry of Foreign Affairs by telex that there was no objection to extending the deadline for three months longer so as to enable the issue of provisional passports to Spanish protected persons who had applied for nationality. The answer to the Spanish representatives abroad was swiftly dispatched. On 5 April they were sent a circular, no. 1240, from the Ministry of Foreign Affairs, in which it was recognised that the circumstances which had motivated the earlier order still remained, because many of the applications for naturalisation were unresolved. By agreement with the Ministry of the Interior, the consuls were authorised once again, from 1 May, to continue to issue Spanish passports or renew those already issued, to anyone who, having applied for recognition of nationality, was still awaiting an official decision. This new extension was to expire on 1 August of the same year.

In subsequent communications, new requests for extension were received. On 11 August 1932, the Undersecretary's office at the Foreign Ministry made known the situation to the Ministry of the Interior. On 1 November a new circular, no. 1285, was issued. This informed the Spanish representatives abroad of the new extension granted and warned them that it would expire on 1 February 1933, adding: 'the passport must be taken back as soon as you receive information that the application of the Spanish protected person to whom the passport was issued has been refused'. Emphasis was placed on the zeal that had to be put into the renewal of these passports. The documents presented to justify the issue of passports had to be closely examined so as to prove without doubt the existence of protection and that the application for nationality was awaiting a decision.[12]

The Circular Order of 1933

The first real official attempt to carry out a Sephardic policy during the Second Republic was contained in the circular order of 27 February 1933. It was a declaration of intentions more than a preparation of policies to follow, and its main objective was to put into force article 23 of the constitution. The circular contained two important but distinct questions. The first was the implementation of article 23 of the constitution which stipulated that a law would establish the procedure to facilitate the acquisition of Spanish citizenship. The second, following on from earlier regulations, was the draft of a legal provision whereby the protected Sephardic Jews could acquire Spanish citizenship.

There were some precedents. On the one hand, the numerous requests for further extensions of the royal decree of December 1924 and, on the other hand, the reports and studies promoted by the Council of Cultural Relations from 1929, in order to carry out a policy towards the Sephardic Jews. Various notes and commentaries had been sent by various Spanish representatives in connection with this. Nevertheless, the most important immediate precedent was the report of José María Doussinague, of the Department of Foreign Affairs, which brought the question to the Minister on 15 February 1933. It contained a summary of his 1930 report entitled *Sephardic Economics*, and once again insisted on the need to make use of the Sephardic Jews in the expansion of the Spanish economy, for which it was essential to increase the number of Sephardic Jews who had Spanish citizenship. It was also urged that the government study an earlier bill that, together with article 23 of the constitution, would make it easier for those persons of Sephardic background who desired Spanish citizenship to acquire it. The circular took into account this suggestion, and, at the same time, information was requested from the Spanish representatives in the Balkans and eastern Mediterranean countries.

The Sephardic policy was considered to be oriented around three objectives:

- Juridical: the granting of citizenship.
- Economic: the expansion of Spanish trade and the creation of Chambers of Commerce.
- Cultural: the teaching of the Spanish language.

The most interesting part of the information sent by the Spanish representatives was the assessment of what had been done to date. They submitted a series of well informed criticisms concerning the way in which some actions had been carried out, so as to prevent the government from making more mistakes of the kind that had already been committed, but should have been avoided. They considered as counterproductive the guidelines set out in the report *Sephardic Economics* of José María Doussinague.

Another issue that arose from the communications was the fact that many of the Spanish representatives, having taken an interest in this issue of Hispano–Sephardic relations, had not obtained an answer to their requests for information. It was also reiterated that policy towards the Sephardim had always been approached from a prejudiced standpoint, one that tried to take advantage of the Sephardic communities, but never encouraged these communities to appreciate Spain. Yet this could later work in Spain's favour, since these communities were attracted by a nation which was prestigious in the eyes of others. It was considered that the creation of official agencies should have been the result of a need rather than something implanted hurriedly without prior study.[13]

In Madrid, after the information of the Spanish representatives had been analysed, a naturalisation project was drafted, according to article 23 of the constitution. The requisites were very stringent, demanding documents proving that the applicant was, or had been, registered at a Spanish consulate. However, the project was not at all effective, since everything concerning naturalisation in article 23 of the constitution was suspended on 2 March 1934 by orders of the Undersecretary of the Ministry of Foreign Affairs.[14]

From Hope to Disillusionment

It was obvious that Spanish foreign policy towards the Sephardic communities left much to be desired and that the new Republican initiatives were no more than a continuation of past policies. It appeared that in this field, Spain could not, or would not, succeed in carrying out an effective policy.

It is true that the socio-economic situation and political instability continued to prevent the implementation of any important foreign policy line. However, the Republican authorities made several declarations showing sympathy towards the Sephardic Jews. Such well known leaders as the President, Niceto Alcalá Zamora and Alejandro Lerroux continued to attract the interest of the world press and the Jewish press by their declarations. It was claimed that Alcalá Zamora was the first to come out openly in favour of the Jews and also that Lerroux had declared that he was preparing a law to allow for the return of the Jews to Spain. As a consequence of those declarations, it was said that the Republic wanted to change the old Spanish attitude towards the Jews, putting special emphasis on the fact that 'the political leaders with socialist ideas' wanted the return of the Jews and the improvement of the economic situation facilitated by their return.[15]

Also, during the Azaña government (1931–3) there were expressions of sympathy for the Jewish communities in the League of Nations, supporting the demands of the Jews of Upper Silesia and the laws in favour of minorities in general. It was Luis Zulueta who came out in support of these communities and the Sephardic Jews in particular, pointing out that Spain 'today' looked with profound sympathy and a certain material interest upon the thousands of families that in centuries past had been forced to leave Spanish territory and yet had conserved the country's language and traditions.

Moreover, the historian Salvador de Madariaga, nominated as *rapporteur* of minorities in the League of Nations, intervened in the affair of the Jews in Upper Silesia and said that 'the attitude of Spain in this matter had been dictated solely by its respect for the German nation'. In the great debate held in the League of Nations in the autumn of 1933, he spoke up for the persecuted Jews:

At a time when we are endeavouring, in the international field, to ensure the peace of the world, by respect for the liberty of each people and by free discussion, it is, to say the least, disturbing, and gives the impression that anarchy within men's minds is increasing, to observe the rise of movements in which the authoritarian element predominates too strongly over the liberal element: such systems can only be regarded as in decreasing harmony with the Geneva system which believes and has always believed in freedom of discussion and liberty . . . . Today when the Jewish question is in the forefront, the Spanish Republic turns its eyes towards that great race to which it is indebted for illustrious men of letters, lawyers, mystics, doctors and statesmen. Spain believes that the attempt to be made in the twentieth century should cover the entire world and – to use the words of a famous French writer – nothing but the world, that it should embrace all men, all races, all religions, all nations.[16]

As the Spanish ambassador in Paris, Madariaga had intervened many times in favour of the Sephardic community, which had numerous problems as a consequence of not having recognised the royal decree of 1924 in time. He also explained the position of the Spanish government to a German Jewish reporter, George Bernhard, as regards the attitude of the republican government to a possible immigration of German Jews into Spain. Madariaga informed Madrid that he did not know the official position and that he had expressed some general ideas that in fact were not different from the statements of other personalities in the government:

In Spain there is no anti-Semitic prejudice. It does not exist in the constitution and there are no laws limiting the rights of Jews.

- There is some trace of economic protectionism, which is very natural under the present circumstances, on behalf of organised labour and the professional classes which is not necessarily directed against Jews as such. It is aimed in general at all types of large scale foreign invasion of manual workers and intellectuals who, by acquiring importance, could transform these traces into a vigorous protectionist tendency which could eventually take shape in laws and decrees.
- An ostentatious large scale entry of Jews into Spain could eventually create an anti-semitic tendency in Spain. Fortunately today that tendency is non-existent, but there is already a nucleus of opinion prepared to take up any banner of that type, a nucleus of ex-monarchists defeated by the present regime. Because of this it would not be very expedient to give them a weapon such as an official and ostentatious admission of German Jews.

In conclusion, he considered it appropriate to indicate to the reporter Bernhard that the admission of individual Jews into Spain would be accepted by the government and public opinion as long as a pace of easy absorption, from the economic and political standpoint, was created.[17]

The definition of the Spanish position took place in the League of Nations. In October 1933, the League invited the Spanish government to occupy a seat in the Administrative Council that would assist the High Commissioner in charge of finding a solution to the problem of refugee German Jews and other German expatriates who had settled in neighbouring nations. The response of the Spanish government was not made known until 23 November 1933. In a short preamble it was affirmed that there were various reasons for Spain's not being interested in this matter.

In the first place, it was said that the problem of the refugee Jews had been set out in terms that were both obscure and indefinite. It was known with certainty neither how many refugees there were, nor what their present social and financial situation was, and although it had been said that these refugees were devoid of all means of subsistence, this was a source of serious doubts to the Spanish government, which believed that if an investigation had been carried out beforehand, it would have proved that the setting up of this High Commission was not necessary.

Secondly, at that time the number of refugees was 50 000, and the fact that the High Commission was interested in placing them in different countries would enable the numbers to be increased as time went on. After a year's work, the League of Nations would find out that after placing many of the refugees, instead of 50 000 candidates, there were perhaps 100 000 or more. This would result in the enlargement of the original conflict.

It was recalled that there was a tendency – according to what had been agreed to in the fourteenth General Assembly of the League of Nations – to distribute the Jews expelled from Germany among different countries and that the Spanish government did not believe that this redistribution, made indiscriminately, would turn out to be advantageous for those expelled. Therefore, the distribution of the German refugees should be made to German speaking countries, or countries with Germanic languages, but not to countries that in terms of race, language and such were quite different from Germany. This would create new and troublesome problems as a result of the lack of integration in or adaptation to society.

Finally it was made clear that if these were the objective reasons put forward by the Spanish government, there remained others of a more subjective nature. If for any reason the High Commission and the Administrative Council concluded that it was necessary to begin distributing German refugees in various countries, Spain would have to be excluded from the list of nations considered appropriate to receive them. This was to be viewed in the light of the special circumstances involving Spain as a normal country of immigration for many years.[18]

This was in fact the first time that the Spanish government had defined its position on this matter and did not imply a new orientation. The statistics available of German Jewish residents in Spain in 1933 are very relevant in this respect. The Spanish Director General of Security, according to data and information provided by the provincial Civil Governors, from 15 February to May 1933, cited only four Jews in Alicante; seven in Gerona; one in Malaga; one in Pontevedra; seven in Valencia; and 225 in Madrid. In the rest of the provinces, according to this information, there were no Jews of German nationality; they did not take note if they belonged to the Jewish religion, because it was not marked in their passports. The absence of German Jews in Barcelona is striking precisely because it was the city which, from the early months of 1933 until 1936, received a large number of German refugees. Likewise, the scant number of German immigrants in other Spanish provinces who declared themselves as Jewish suggests the possibility of a feeling of fear or lack of confidence in Spanish society, possibly because of the conflicting attitudes to their arrival.[19]

Nevertheless, the arrival in Spain of German Jews was noticed. The newspapers of various countries dealt with the event in different ways. The reports in favour of, and against, the reception that the government and the Spanish people had given to the German Jews did nothing to continue to awaken the interest of the Jews who had escaped to various European countries and were searching for a safer place to live.

An event which favoured a climate of sympathy on the part of the intellectuals and the Republican government was the celebration of the eight hundredth anniversary of Maimonides in March 1935. Amongst the personalities invited was Rabbi Dr Armand Kaminta. In the official speeches of the mayor and the representatives of the Academy of Science, Literature and the Arts of the city of Cordoba, the theme of the expulsion of Jews from Spanish territories was recalled; with the warning that any European country which expelled them would regret it just as Spain had done. In his speech the Civil Governor of Cordoba invited the Jews to return to Spain. This would have further enormous consequences for those Jewish communities that were searching for a refuge in order to flee from Nazi persecution, and the newspapers spread the news. Even some Spanish representatives abroad asked for clarification of these government initiatives that were in clear contradiction with the last circular.

Many requests for visas came to the Spanish government from different countries.[20] For instance, Arthur von Rosthorn, the former Austrian Minister to China and Imperial Adviser, delivered a memorandum to the Spanish Chancery regarding the use of Jewish immigration to Spain. This initiative was a consequence, like so many others, of recent international press information on the Spanish government's invitation to Jews to establish themselves in Spain. On 31 December 1935, the Ministry of Foreign Affairs replied to the Spanish representative in Vienna that such an initiative could not be considered without knowing how the departments concerned would receive it. The first question to be resolved was whether a large contingent of workers should be permitted to enter a country that already had 800 000 unemployed.[21]

As has been indicated, one subject that had no definite solution was the naturalisation of Sephardic Jews who did not have recourse within the stipulated period to the 1924 royal decree. Indeed, until 1936 the Foreign Ministry continued to receive requests that the decree be extended, or that article 23 of the constitution, regarding naturalisation, be activated.

The situation continued to be dramatic for those Sephardim previously protected, who now found themselves stateless. The reports of the Spanish representatives in Paris, Berne, Geneva, Sofia, Naples and Trieste highlighted this situation. Naples was the only community that received an encouraging response in the sense that Spanish documentation papers continued to be provided for its members, although great care was of course taken to grant documentation only to those individuals of irreproachable background and behaviour. Other petitions received no response, or at least there is no proof of any response.

The Civil War

The beginning of the Spanish Civil War on 17 July 1936 signified the breaking up of the Spanish nation. The stand adopted by the diverse Sephardic communities in Spain and in the rest of the world with respect to the opposing groups in the war was quite similar. The great majority was in favour of the Republic or sympathised with its cause. The communities that remained in the Nationalist zone had, however, to support the Nationalist cause, in spite of the fact that in this zone, due to the tremendous religious persecution, freedom of religion disappeared as the war developed into a Catholic religious crusade, serving to unite the diverse forces that participated in the struggle.

Nevertheless, the existence of money loans from some wealthy Sephardim from the Moroccan protectorate to the Nationalists is known. On the other side of the coin, were incidents involving fines and 'voluntary' contributions' levied from the various Jewish communities.[22] The Nazi and Fascist influence on the Falange and its organizations, especially in the press and propaganda, made possible the publication of speeches of Nazi leaders that were clearly anti-semitic, and the diffusion of the idea that communists, Jews and freemasons were Spain's main enemies. Moreover, anti-Jewish pamphlets were even distributed in the Spanish protectorate of Morocco, although the Falange did not yet have its own propaganda campaign there. When the National Propaganda service was created, its anti-communist branch continued the anti-Jewish campaign carried out by its brother organisations in Italy and Germany.[23]

The sympathy shown by the different Jewish communities throughout the world toward the Republican cause that encouraged many Jews to join the International Brigades should also be stressed.[24] General Franco tried, however, to avoid further international conflicts. The news that appeared in the international media on the anti-semitism of the National Movement led Franco publicly to deny strongly these accusations, while General Queipo de Llano's radio broadcasts, being considered anti-Jewish, were suppressed.[25]

In terms of Franco's foreign policy with respect to the Sephardic communities in Europe and the Mediterranean, from the very beginning he tried by all means to prevent the entrance of Jews into the national zone, even those Spanish Sephardim with legal documents. The diplomatic correspondence coming from Romania, Greece, Turkey, Bulgaria and Yugoslavia throughout the period 1937–1938 shows the concern that existed about the situation of the Sephardic communities. A great majority opposed the nationalist cause or were indifferent to it.[26]

In July 1938 circular order 35 was sent to all the diplomatic representatives of the Nationalist government aiming to coordinate and unify their actions. It was stated that any Spaniard who had supported the enemy did not have the right to be assisted by the Spanish representatives abroad. Consequently they should abstain from issuing documents in their favour, such as notary documents, certificates of origin, legalisations or visas. Spaniards who had been at any time 'hostile' were denied the renewal of their certificates of nationality until new legal orders were issued.

Concerning passports, these could be given to those who were considered enemies, as long as the following requirements were respected:

- The passport should be used only to come to Spain.
- It should be pointed out to those who were thus permitted to enter Spain that the passport would be valid for only one month after the date of issue.
- The point of entry into Spain should be made known.
- Information on the likely date of arrival in Spain as well as the personal record should be supplied.

Those who were not considered 'hostile' were treated in a different way as it was considered necessary to attract the neutral mass toward the Nationalist cause, even though individually they merited sanction.[27]

Concerning the sanctions to be adopted, the opinion of the diplomatic representatives was requested, and the matter was resolved with circular orders numbers 70 and 85, of 8 August and 2 September respectively, which established an extra charge in the fee for the national identity card to those Sephardic Spaniards who had stayed aloof from the diplomatic representation; and the refusal of documents, except passports, to enter Spain, to those who were indifferent or opposed to the Nationalist cause. Border police were to be informed beforehand so they could take the necessary measures. A new circular Order, 143, of 7 September 1938, established that Jews who were openly against the Nationalist cause would not be considered Spanish.[28]

However, it was soon realised that allowing the entrance into Spain of any Spanish Sephardim could constitute a serious problem. Following a suggestion made by the consulate in Geneva, the issue was analysed and debated by the Nationalist cabinet. Even so, the cabinet did not adopt measures that would imply the loss of nationality for those who did not enroll in the national army, who had not paid the fee to be excluded from military service, or who had not paid an extra charge for not supporting the National Movement. General Franco preferred to defer any such decisions until the end of the Civil War. With respect to the Sephardic Spaniards who were indifferent to the Nationalist cause, it was also decided that no sanctions would be imposed so as to avoid adverse reactions.[29]

The problem posed by the hostility and indifference shown by the greater part of the Sephardic communities outside Spain was thus initially postponed until the end of the Civil War. Later on, the measures taken in this respect were quite meticulous in the granting of passports, giving rise to a very detailed study of personal records. This, together with the fact that the constitution and the laws of the Republic were suppressed, which in turn saw the disappearance of religious freedom, made the situation of the Jews in Spain very difficult. At the end of the Civil War, no more than 100 Jewish families remained in Madrid and Barcelona. The synagogues of these cities were closed, circumcision, marriage and Jewish cemeteries were forbidden and Jewish children were compelled to learn the Catholic religion in school.

A further important point to be stressed, given that it has been left aside by researchers and writers on this subject, is the fact that the edict of expulsion issued by the Catholic kings recovered its previous legal force with Franco's victory.[30] All these factors, together with the ambiguous policy carried out by the Second Republic with respect to the Sephardim, had extremely negative consequences for these communities during the Second World War.

Notes

1. For the historical precedents, see Marquina Barrio and Ospina pp. 15–40 and Aronsfeld (1988).
2. The facts obtained from this investigation can be found in the archives of the

Spanish Foreign Office (AMAE), R 752/80 Circular Order no. 716, December 1921. The document cites 24 000 in Belgrade and 30 000 in Bucharest. It is safe to apply these figures to Yugoslavia and Romania, not just to the capitals of those states. The facts vary according to the reports of the period. Thus, in Yugoslavia, according to a report drawn up by the diplomat José María Doussinague in 1930, the existence of 7000 Sephardim in Belgrade was revealed, whereas, two years later, Agustín de Foxá indicated in his report, entitled 'The Sephardim in the Balkans', that a total of 25 000 Sephardic Jews were living in Yugoslavia. Concerning Romania, the approximate number that the diplomat Gimenez Caballero gave in 1929 was 20 000 for the whole of Romania, while in the previously mentioned report, Agustín de Foxá indicated the number of 30 000, also corresponding to the whole of Romania. With respect to Bulgaria, the statistics also remain unreconciled. According to the 1912 official census, the number of Sephardim was 38 553, of which 37 000 lived in cities and the remaining 1553 in rural areas. In the report produced by the diplomat Gimenez Caballero in 1929, following his visit to several countries, the number given is 48 000 for all of Bulgaria. Agustín de Foxá, in his report, provides two statistics; 44 000 and 48 000. Two years earlier, the report by José María Doussinague indicated a number of 25 000 Sephardim in Sofia alone. As can be readily seen, major discrepancies exist among the data of certain countries.

3. AMAE, R 752/80, reports drawn up by the legations of Spain in the various Balkan nations and Egypt in 1922.
4. In 1925, a book written by the diplomat Sangroniz indicated that the most important problems concerning Spain's cultural expansion still prevailed and stressed the need of a cultural programme which would rely on the Sephardim. In his opinion, Spain was 'totally unknown' in the Balkans, and it was therefore necessary to rely on the Sephardim, 'a true aristocracy within its own race'. The programme proposed by Sangroniz consisted in the creation of schools in the centres with a major Sephardic population, such as Salonika and Smyrna, the assignment of Spanish professors to high schools and universities in the principal Balkan cities, the utilization of the Franciscan Spanish influence, the support of the Sephardic press and the creation of a Spanish Institute of Biology to be established in Jerusalem.
5. On this subject, see AMAE, R, 1526/1.
6. As to the report by Giménez Caballero, see Marquina Barrio, 'Spain's external action'.
7. AMAE, R 1526/2.
8. See AMAE, R 1075/43 and R 516/4, R 1526/3 E1, E2, E3.
9. AMAE, R 1526/3 E1.
10. AMAE, R 516/4 numerous references.
11. AMAE, R 1526/2, E1.
12. Ibid.
13. Various references in AMAE, R 515/5 and 7.
14. AMAE, R 515/7 Ministry of State, Europe, 9 June 1933, and the supplementary decree.
15. See the periodical Doar Hayon, 15 April, 16 May 1934 and 29 March 1935.
16. Quoted by Aronsfeld (1979), p. 42.
17. AMAE, R 516/4, Paris, 26 April 1933.
18. AMAE, R 515/7, conveyed to the General Secretary of the League of Nations, Geneva.
19. AMAE, R 515/7 Dirección General de Seguridad, Madrid, 25 May 1933.
20. See Doar Hayon, 13 February 1934; Wiener Sonn- und Montag-Zeitung, Berne, 20 May 1935; Die Stimme, Prague, 15 March 1935.

21. AMAE, R 516/4 Memorandum of Arthur von Rosthorn: 'Modo de Utilizar la Inmigración Separdita en España'.
22. Aronsfeld (1979), p. 45.
23. See Marquina Barrio and Ospina, Chapter 3. The policy followed by the Republican zone was different to that of Franco's zone. In the first instance, 1000 Jews who had arrived in Barcelona in previous years decided to return to their countries of origin. The development of the war prohibited the consolidation of the Jewish communities in this area. The Republican authorities showed their sympathy for the Jewish people, and they studied some plans of cultural action in the Sephardic communities in the Balkans to bring together those communities. Furthermore, the Republican authorities sent a delegation to the International Sephardic Congress that was held in Amsterdam in May 1938. According to the inquiries made by the delegate Conat, 'the diverse, influential Sephardim promised to support the Republican cause differently'.
24. An Italian investigation at the end of the Spanish civil war cited 6000 Jews, quoting the Jewish publications of that time. Hugh Thomas, in his work *The Spanish Civil War*, cites 3000 and David Diamant gives a number of 5000. See *Ministero Degli Affari Esteri*. B–52, Spain 1939 and Avni, p. 226.
25. Avni, p. 47; Aronsfeld (1979), p. 45.
26. Spanish Office of Diplomatic Information (OID), Folder on Sephardic Jews; AMAE, R 1716/2.
27. OID, Folder on Sephardic Jews. Circular no. 35, Burgos, 19 July 1938.
28. OID, Burgos, 24 September 1938.
29. OID, Burgos, 13 October 1933; Burgos, 25 October 1938; Berlin, 23 November 1938.
30. See Marquina Barrio and Ospina, Chapters 3, 4 and 5.

Bibliography

Amador de los Ríos, J. (1984), *Historia de los judíos en España y Portugal*, Madrid, 1984.
American Jewish Year Book, 1920–40, New York.
Aronsfeld, C. C. (1979), *The Ghost of 1492*, New York.
Aronsfeld, C. C. (1988), 'Los espectros de 1492', *Historia 16*.
Avni, H. (1974), *España, Franco y los judíos*, Madrid.
Caro Baroja, J. (1978) *Los judíos en la España Moderna y Contemporánea*, Madrid.
González Garcia, I. (1984), *La cuestión judía y los orígenes del sionismo (1881–1905)*, Madrid.
Marquina Barrio, A., Ospina G.I. (1987), *España y los judíos en el siglo XX, La acción exterior*, Madrid.
Marquina Barrio, A. (1987), 'Spains' external action with regard to the Sephardim in the Balkans,' at the International Congress on 'The Jewish people in the History of Spain', 28–30 March 1985, in Beinart, H. et al, *Encuentros en Sefarad*, Instituto de Estudios Manchegos, Ciudad Real.
Pulido Fernández, A. (1920), *Reconciliación hispano-hebrea*, Madrid.
Pulido Fernández, A. (1905), *Españoles sin patria y la raza sefardí*, Madrid.
Pulido Fernández, A. (1904), *Los israelitas españoles y el idioma castellano*, Madrid.
Sangróniz, J. A. (1925), *La expansión cultural de España*, Madrid.
Ysart, F. (1973), *España y los judíos*, Barcelona.

Unpublished Sources

Archivo General del Ministerio de Asuntos Exteriores (AMAE), **Madrid**.
Serie R. Folder: 515, 516, 698, 725, 728, 752, 895, 1075, 1102, 1112, 1114, 1117, 1190, 1192, 1260, 1261, 1271, 1307, 1343, 1344, 1366, 1372, 1526.
Serie Política. Folder: 2334.
Oficina de Información Diplomática (OID), **Madrid**.
Folder: Judíos I and II (1936–1940).

14 Conclusion
ARNOLD SUPPAN

This concluding chapter briefly aims to classify the preceding twelve case studies according to the kinds of significance and the forms of involvement of non-dominant ethnic groups in international relations which they best represent, and then summarily to consider the impact of the role of such groups in international relations on their domestic relationships with the states of which they form a part.

The Significance of Non-dominant Ethnic Groups in International Relations

The case studies presented in this volume have sought to illustrate:

1 the significance of non-dominant ethnic groups in relations between states;
2 the significance of non-dominant ethnic groups in trans-state relations;
3 the protection of non-dominant ethnic groups by the peace treaties which concluded the First World War and through the institution of the League of Nations;
4 other forms of international regulation of the status of non-dominant ethnic groups.

The Significance of Non-dominant Ethnic Groups in Relations Between States

The significance which non-dominant ethnic groups assume in relations between states is linked to the kinds of external relationship in which they may find themselves (see Introduction, pp. 8–9). Three cases emerge in these studies as possessing particular interest and importance: that where non-dominant ethnic groups form *Grenzland-minderheiten* (borderland minorities) having a 'motherland' or 'mother' nation just across the border; that where such minorities exist on both sides of the same border and involve their respective states in a reciprocal problem; and that where non-dominant ethnic groups are the objects of patronage by outside states with which they do not necessarily share an ethnic identity or national consciousness.

Non-dominant Ethnic Groups as 'Borderland' Minorities Having a 'Mother-land' Across the Border   One of the best examples in European history is provided by the Alsatians after the annexation of their province to the German empire in 1871 (see chapter 4). The claims upon them of the French and German states, their symbolic importance for French and German nationalism, and the continuing attachment of some of them to France up to the First World War and to Germany after the return of the territory to France in 1919, made the question of Alsace (and of Lorraine) a standing bone of contention between France and Germany and a focus of attention, especially in the pre–1914 era, from those who saw it as a classic case both of the problem of minority rights in European politics and of the sort of threat which a 'minority' problem could pose to European peace. But the issue of Alsace–Lorraine was never the prime determinant of relations between France and Germany, and can hardly be considered a cause of either of the two world wars which brought about successive transfers of the provinces between the two powers. It illustrated not the centrality but the marginality of a non-dominant ethnic group problem to the vital interests and national policies of the two states, both of which used for their own ends and conceptualised according to their own needs an Alsatian population which strove tenaciously to preserve within both what it considered to be its special identity and role.

Non-dominant Ethnic Groups as Constituting a Reciprocal 'Borderland Minorities' Problem Between their States   Three important examples are contained in this volume. One which extends across the whole of our period concerns the German and Danish minorities existing at various times respectively to the north and to the south of the disputed Danish–German border in Schleswig (see chapter 5). The other two (see chapters 8 and 11), are concerned with the situation after the First World War of, first, the German minorities (mostly in the borderlands) in Czechoslovakia and Poland, as contrasted with the Sorb and Polish minorities in Germany, and, second, the German speaking minority in the southern Styria region inside Yugoslavia and the Slovene minority in the southern Carinthia region of Austria. In all these instances, the fortunes of the groups depended not only on their intrinsic strength but on a process of negotiation between their respective states in which the degree of support they could expect to receive from their 'mother' country depended partly on the significance of the reciprocal concessions which the prosecution of their claims might require it to offer to their opposite numbers. The interwar German governments, with large German minorities just across their borders, championed their cause in a way to which neighbours like Denmark, Czechoslovakia, or Poland could hardly reply in kind, because the advantages they might hope to obtain for their own minorities in Germany were unimportant compared with the dangers inherent in reciprocal concessions which might undermine the cohesion of their own states and pave the way for frontier revisions adverse to their interests – all the more so when, after 1933, National Socialist policy began to use Germany's eastern minorities as a lever in an expansionist policy.

The governments of Austria and Yugoslavia came up hard against the difficulty of finding a bilateral minorities' policy that would work equally in the interests of both: for instance, the adoption of the much discussed model of a 'Slovene cultural autonomy in Carinthia' – following the example of the cultural autonomy of the ethnic minorities in Estonia in 1925 – would have brought much greater advantages to the relatively well to do Germans of southern Styria than to the economically less developed Slovene population in southern Carinthia. The principle of reciprocity which the two governments actually followed meant the subordination of the claims of their minorities to the requirements of good Austro–Yugoslav relations. The fear of a German irredentism in southern Styria and of a Slovene irredentism in southern Carinthia – with possible border revision – determined minority policy up to 1938. All these examples reveal the potential of non-dominant ethnic groups as instruments and bargaining counters in the external policies of some states and as points of weakness for the external relations and internal security of others, and show how their claims might be promoted or stifled accordingly by their 'mother' nations across the border.

Non-dominant Ethnic Groups as Recipients of Extranational Patronage   Where a group received the patronage of an outside state with which it shared neither ethnic nor national identity, the fact was likely to be due to its instrumental value for that state. Such is the conclusion suggested by studying the way in which the German, Czech, and Soviet governments of the interwar years exploited the position of the Ukrainians in Poland in their manoeuvrings against the Polish state (see chapter 9). The opportunity for outside interference created by the national aspirations of some five million Ukrainians was not the least of the reasons for the repression directed against them by the Polish authorities. Even when the group and its patron state have a closer kinship, the relationship may be largely instrumental. Despite the Spanish affinities of the Sephardic Jews of the Balkans and the existence of an important pro-Sephardic intellectual movement in Spain, the Spanish state's protection of the Balkan Sephardic communities between the wars and the granting of Spanish citizenship to their members represented in the main the attempt of Spanish policy to break out of its isolation and to restore its position in the international arena, as well as to expand Spanish economic influence (see chapter 13).

The Significance of Non-dominant Ethnic Groups in Trans-state Relations

In addition to the Ukrainians, two examples of groups functioning as such across state boundaries, and even conducting a kind of diplomacy as groups, are supplied in this volume by the Jews and the Frisians (see chapters 3 and 6). Virtually unique as a group traversing all European borders, the Jews developed both transnational political organisation and 'diplomatic' action based on the growing prosperity and self confidence of the upper and middle ranks of their society in western and central Europe, and a modern national tendency embodied in Zionism, each of which posed complex problems for their relations with the states in which they lived and with which the protection of their interests and the furtherance of their aspirations had to be negotiated. On a much smaller scale, the Frisians are another case of a group which sought to affirm its identity and promote its concerns across the state boundaries which divided it, setting questions for the governments of Denmark, the Netherlands, and Germany, and presenting a critical instance of the problem of what constituted a 'national minority' to the body which, between the wars, acted as an international forum for the collective interest of non-dominant ethnic groups, the European Congress of Nationalities. The tendency of trans-state groups was thus to emerge on to the international scene as something like independent actors, even when the achievement of independent national statehood was not a necessary or universally accepted goal.

The Protection of Non-dominant Ethnic Groups by the Peace Treaties Following the First World War and Through the League of Nations

The formal international recognition of groups and their claims was powerfully stimulated by the First World War, and the attempts subsequently made to provide for collective international protection of their rights are the subject of chapter 2. The highly imperfect application of the principle of self-determination by the treaties which concluded the First World War meant that the peace settlement increased rather than diminished the need to supply the means of minority protection. A model was furnished by the so-called 'minor treaty' of Versailles of 28 June 1919, in which the principal allied and associated powers imposed minority protection provisions on the new Polish state, and the task of supervising the fulfilment of the obligations towards minorities which were written into the series of peace treaties was entrusted to the League of Nations. The system was from the beginning seen as discriminatory by states compelled by the great powers to accept limitations on their sovereignty which the latter did not adopt for themselves, and it could not easily be enforced by the League against governments which resented it. While the League gave considerable attention to complaints and disputes arising out of the operation of minority provisions, the self interest of states remained a barrier. The withdrawal of Germany from the League in 1933 and the Polish government's decision a year later to repudiate international intervention in Polish minority questions until a uniform system of international protection of minority rights was introduced spelt the effective end of the League system.

Other Forms of International Regulation of the Status of Non-dominant Ethnic Groups

Between the exercise of force by states against each other on the one hand and the intervention of a supra-national institution like the League of Nations on the other, there was a variety of forms of international action and agreement whereby the problems posed by non-dominant ethnic groups could be regulated. Three in particular have been illustrated in this volume: bilateral agreement under international auspices (the Åland Islands case, in chapter 7); plebiscite and partition under international auspices (Upper Silesia, in chapter 10); and bilateral agreement for exchange of populations (the Lausanne Convention between Greece and Turkey, in chapter 12). The Åland Islands agreement of 1921, whereby, under the aegis of the council of the League of Nations, Finland and Sweden agreed on the granting by the former state of a large measure of autonomy to its ethnic Swedish subjects in the islands, was a rare instance of successful reconciliation between the interests of a group, those of the state which it inhabited, and those of the state to which it was ethnically affiliated. Much more difficult was finding a solution to the violent antagonisms between Germans and Poles in Upper Silesia after the First World War. The question of the future status of the territory divided not only the states which claimed it, Germany and Poland, but also Britain and France, both taking opposite views as to the settlement most conducive to European stability and their own interests. The plebiscite decreed in the treaty of Versailles and supervised by an inter-allied commission in 1920–1 was accomplished against a background of open conflict. The partition subsequently decided upon by the council of the League of Nations was accompanied, in 1922, by provisions to secure the rights of national minorities on either side of the new border and by the setting up of a mixed commission under a neutral chairman to deal with the problems certain to arise; but the attitude of both sides conveyed the impression that this was a temporary solution which could not be maintained in the long run. Liquidation of a reciprocal minorities' problem by compulsory exchange of the populations concerned was the more drastic recipe adopted by Greece and Turkey in 1923: an approach which paid no attention to the human rights of their uprooted subjects, but contributed effectively to their national consolidation and to the long term improvement of their relations.

The Impact on the Relationship of Non-dominant Ethnic Groups with their States

As suggested in the Introduction (pp. 9–10), the relationship between groups and the states which they inhabited could be influenced in a variety of ways by the actual or potential significance of the former for the international relations of the latter. The forms of state policy and of ethnic group response, and their results, were governed especially by the extent to which the international dimension sharpened the problems posed by groups for national cohesion and security or enlarged the resources on which groups could call in asserting their claims.

Forms of State Policy towards Non-dominant Ethnic Groups

The Policy of Assimilation   Through the administrative authorities, in the courts, in school, in the army and in the workplace, the minority was consistently confronted with and thus acquired command of the language of the majority. Being gradually integrated into the culture of the majority (acculturation), it was deprived of its cultural *identity*. Even an appeal for patriotism could have an assimilating effect. A tendency towards such a policy was to be observed both before and after 1918 in Alsace–Lorraine – at first on the part of the Germans, and later on the part of the French. Between the two world wars the Polish government pursued a similar policy with regard to the Ukrainians, Byelorussians and Jews, and so did the Carinthian government with regard to the Carinthian Slovenes, and the Slovene government towards the Germans of South Styria. The German government discriminated against the Polish minority, and the Polish government and the Polish administration of Upper Silesia adopted a similar policy towards the German minority. The German, Dutch and Danish governments pursued a policy of assimilation towards the Frisians.

The Policy of Segregation   Isolation of the minority from the majority was intended to provide the basis for discrimination against the minority in all social aspects. This policy was adopted by many states before and after 1918, especially with regard to Jews and gypsies (by limiting admission to the university for example), and in Yugoslavia towards the Albanians.

The Policy of Integration   Government policies were aimed at integrating the non-dominant ethnic groups into the overall society, but the special cultural characteristics of such groups were taken into account and a co-existence between various cultures was promoted. Such a policy was partly applied before 1918 in Cisleithania but between the two world wars it was pursued further only in Finland (with regard to the Swedes) and in Estonia (towards Germans, Russians and Swedes).

As there was a number of states with several minorities in Europe before and after the borderlines were fixed in 1919–23, no uniform policy was adopted towards the various minorities. Among other things the location of the settlements of the minorities either along the border or in the centre of the country was decisive. Thus Bucharest showed a more friendly attitude towards the Saxons of Transylvania and the Swabians of the Banat than towards the Magyars and Szeklers of Transylvania, who were accused of latent irredentism. The same distinction was made by the Serbs with regard to their policy towards the Magyars and Germans in the Voivodina; while Slovene policy towards the German minorities of South Styria was characterised by pronounced distrust. In Poland and in Czechoslovakia most minorities, with the exception of the Jews, were accused of irredentism. But to some extent Poland, and after 1933 also Czechoslovakia, had obvious reasons for their distrust, as some of their neighbouring countries openly made revisionist claims, in particular Germany on Poland and Hungary on Czechoslovakia.

The Motivation and Mechanisms of State and Regional Policy

Ideological Factors   Policies of assimilation were spurred on either by consciousness of superiority or by reaction against previous inferiority. Before 1914 the French, Germans, Russians, British, Italians, Austrians, Hungarians and Osmanlis generally regarded their policies of assimilation as a 'cultural mission' which was intended to convey a 'higher' stage of civilisation. On the other hand, from 1919 onwards, the new *Staatsnationen* (nations constituting states) in north east, east central and south east Europe considered themselves the new 'lords' and tried to impose their political will on the new minorities, who in many instances had been their former 'lords'.

Security Factors   Especially in territories with national minorities near state boundaries these factors were of major importance. Such territories existed already before 1918 – although relatively small in number – but after 1918 there were more than two dozen: the Memel region; West Prussia; Posen; Upper Silesia; Sudetenland; south Slovakia; south Styria; south Carinthia; Istria; south Tyrol; and north Schleswig, to name a few. Nearly all states were suspicious of potential irredentism and suspected revisionist claims on the part of their neighbouring countries, a suspicion which was successfully nourished by clearly chauvinistic publications.

Socio-economic Factors   Even before 1918 a special kind of 'land policy' was pursued in some ethnically disputed regions of east central Europe. Thus, Prussian credit organisations financed the acquisition of land and the resettlement of German peasants in Posen and north Schleswig, and German–Austrian peasants were resettled in south Styria by German–Austrian organisations. After 1918 the new states of east central Europe 'nationalised' large estates and big enterprises on the basis of a land reform which made it possible to expropriate large estates against payment of compensation. As a result, millions of hectares of land were distributed among a similarly large number of peasant families belonging to the new *Staatsnationen*.

In Poland this policy especially affected the big German landowners. In Bohemia, Moravia and Slovenia Austrian *fideicommissum* estates were expropriated. In Slovakia, Transylvania, the Banat and in Batchka this policy particularly affected estates belonging to Hungarian noblemen; and in Bessarabia and in the Baltic region former Russian estates. In the same way, the Danish majority of north Schleswig took possession of the estates of the German minority. Shares of the major enterprises of Upper Silesia and Bohemia as well as in the banks of Prague, Posen (Poznań) and Pressburg (Bratislava) were acquired by Polish and Czech capital in an attempt to secure a controlling influence. All these 'measures of nationalisation' were taken to destroy the socio-economic power of the former upper class and to support the new political power of the new *Staatsvölker* (peoples constituting the state). Naturally the impact was most detrimental to the new minorities, who as individuals were probably more affected by the loss of property than by the loss of power. It led to determined resistance. A considerable number of these cases of 'nationalisation' therefore had to be dealt with bilaterally or even directly by the League of Nations (such as the expropriation of the *Deutsches Haus* (German House) in Cilli (Celje).

The Reactions of Non-dominant Ethnic Groups to State Policies

These varied considerably according to the groups' demographic strengths, including the compactness of settlement; to the stage of their socio-economic development; and to the extent of their political and cultural activity. They ranged from acceptance and passivity to latent and open resistance.

Acceptance   was exhibited basically only by small groups who were already in the process of assimilation, like the Sorbs, Batchka-Rusini, Frisians.

Passivity   was usually the attitude of groups without any support, as with a large number of Jews, Armenians, and gypsies.

Latent Resistance   Minorities with effective political, economic and cultural organisations made continuous efforts to strengthen their position, which since the 1880s had developed in many regions into a latent fight between the nationalities, involving each club, each school and each farm. These forms of latent resistance were continued also after 1918, but partly in different regions.

Open Conflict   Latent resistance of the minorities against state policies resulted again and again in violent actions, which started with demonstrations and strikes and ended with the declaration oɪ a state of emergency and with military intervention. Posen, East Galicia, Upper Silesia, north Bohemia, Transylvania, Bosnia–Herzegovina and Trieste are well known examples.

The Results of State Policies towards the Non-dominant Ethnic Groups

These were frequently negative as state policy could neither bring about a reasonable form of integration of the non-dominant ethnic groups into the state nor maintain law and order in the regions concerned. This was particularly evident in Posen, east Galicia, Bosnia and in the Küstenland before 1914, and in Transylvania after 1918. Of course there were various tendencies towards assimilation –most accurately displayed by the Hungarian statistics of 1880–1910 –but the shifts in political power of 1919–23 and 1938–9 reversed this trend to a large extent, and only the Second World War brought about 'final' decisions for many minorities in the form of resettlement, genocide, flight and expulsion. But it is not only the most negative and drastic results but also the linguistic, social, legal and psychological consequences that are of interest.

Linguistic   In many multiethnic regions of Europe a number of social groups – intellectuals, big landowners, tradesmen, industrialists, merchants, officers, skilled workers – had developed a far reaching bilingualism and biculturalism, in some cases even a trilingualism, by the mid-nineteenth century. The linguistic nationalisation of state officials, teachers and clergymen, which had started in the 1880s, led to a marked decline in multilingualism and as a consequence to serious language conflicts. The best known example is the conflict caused by the introduction of Badeni's language ordinance in Bohemia in 1897. Typically, the *Egerer Zeitung* of 25 May 1912 contained the following polemical statement: 'Bilingualism leads to an ambiguous command of languages, depriving the speakers of their character.' This negative trend towards monolingualism in multilingual regions increased after 1918.

Social   The development of national societies gave rise to disputes about *Besitzstände* (proprietorship). As a consequence, the communities in multiethnic regions were systematically split up despite their manifold common traditions. It was an expression of the spirit of the time to attach more importance to separating than to uniting elements. Accordingly, people had to make a decision in favour of one and against another nation, even if they had been born into a bilingual family (see the partition of the University of Prague in 1882).

Legal Protection   This as enacted since 1860, tried to afford the minority groups the right to use their language, but completely neglected political participation and social integration. Moreover, the effect of many nationality laws and minority treaties was to deepen rather than bridge the gap between the majority and the minority. Only when individual cases were tried in court could minority laws be applied in support of the minorities.

The Psychological Results   These were most serious. Between 1850 and 1940 – as had been envisaged by Austria's poet Franz Grillparzer ('*Der Weg der neuern Bildung geht von Humanität durch Nationalität zur Bestialität*') – in many parts of Europe nationalism turned into chauvinism, intolerance and atrocity. The major cause for this development was a feeling of superiority retained by the former ruling nations, which provoked resistance on the part of the new nations. Favourable concepts of their own national image as well as negative images of other nations were exaggerated, cliches and stereotypes replaced a historical view, above all of the neighbouring nations. Numerous mutual social relations, as for instance marriages, made only small difference. The exchange of roles after 1918 was considered an act of discrimination by the new non-dominant ethnic groups, whereas there was on the part of the dominant groups a permanent feeling of distrust. The formation of negative images of aliens culminated in racialism, which was to become the characteristic element of the many totalitarian movements.

Index